Knowledge Management

Knowledge Management: Systems and Processes in the AI Era, Third Edition, is aimed at students and managers who seek detailed insights into contemporary knowledge management (KM). It explains the concepts, theories, and technologies that provide the foundation for knowledge management; the systems and structures that constitute KM solutions; and the processes for developing, deploying, and evaluating these KM solutions. This book serves as a complete introduction to the subject of knowledge management, incorporating technical and social aspects, as well as concepts, practical examples, traditional KM approaches, and emerging topics. This third edition has been revised and expanded to include more coverage of emergent trends such as cloud computing, online communities, crowdsourcing, and artificial intelligence. Aimed at advanced undergraduate, postgraduate, and MBA students who are seeking a comprehensive perspective on knowledge management, *Knowledge Management* is also complemented by online support for lecturers including suggested solutions to the many review questions and application exercises contained within the book.

Irma Becerra-Fernandez is President of Marymount University, USA.

Rajiv Sabherwal is Distinguished Professor and Edwin and Karlee Bradberry Chair in information systems at the University of Arkansas, USA.

Richard Kumi is an Associate Professor at the University of Arkansas, Little Rock, USA.

Knowledge Management

Systems and Processes in the AI Era

Third Edition

Irma Becerra-Fernandez, Rajiv Sabherwal, and Richard Kumi

Routledge
Taylor & Francis Group

LONDON AND NEW YORK

Designed cover image: Getty © Prostock-Studio

Third edition published 2024
by Routledge
4 Park Square, Milton Park, Abingdon, Oxon OX14 4RN

and by Routledge
605 Third Avenue, New York, NY 10158

Routledge is an imprint of the Taylor & Francis Group, an informa business

First edition published by Routledge 2010
Second edition published by Routledge 2015

British Library Cataloguing-in-Publication Data
A catalogue record for this book is available from the British Library

Library of Congress Cataloging-in-Publication Data
Names: Becerra-Fernandez, Irma, 1960- author. | Sabherwal, Rajiv, author. |
Kumi, Richard, author.
Title: Knowledge management : systems and processes in the AI era / Irma Becerra-Fernandez, Rajiv Sabherwal and Richard Kumi.
Description: Third edition. | Abingdon, Oxon ; New York, NY : Routledge, 2024. |
Includes bibliographical references and index.
Identifiers: LCCN 2023042960 | ISBN 9781032417394 (hardback) |
ISBN 9781032428024 (paperback) | ISBN 9781003364375 (ebook)
Subjects: LCSH: Knowledge management. | Information technology.
Classification: LCC HD30.2 .B438 2024 | DDC 658.4/038--dc23/eng/20230914
LC record available at https://lccn.loc.gov/2023042960

ISBN: 978-1-032-41739-4 (hbk)
ISBN: 978-1-032-42802-4 (pbk)
ISBN: 978-1-003-36437-5 (ebk)

DOI: 10.4324/9781003364375

Typeset in Times New Roman
by Taylor & Francis Books

Contents

Preface

Knowledge Management: Systems and Processes in the AI Era is for students and managers who seek detailed insights into contemporary knowledge management (KM). It explains the concepts, theories, and technologies that provide the foundation for KM; the systems and structures that constitute KM solutions; and the processes for developing, deploying, and evaluating these KM solutions. We hope this book will help readers acquire the relevant suite of managerial, technical, and theoretical skills for managing knowledge in the modern business environment.

The purpose of this book is to provide a thorough and informative perspective on the emergent practices in knowledge management. Information technology has been, and will continue to be, an important catalyst of this innovative field. Web-based technologies including Web 3.0, artificial intelligence, expert systems, cloud computing, analytics, and social media continue to support and transform the field of KM. However, these technologies would not be effective without the day-to-day social aspects of organizations such as "water-cooler conversations," brainstorming retreats, and communities of practice. To further complicate matters, the current business environment renders new skills obsolete in years or even months.

Knowledge management is defined in this book as *doing what is needed to get the most out of knowledge resources.* KM is an increasingly important discipline that promotes the discovery, capture, sharing, and application of the firm's knowledge. Indeed, we are witnessing a new era with advanced industrial economies being revolutionized with the advent of the knowledge age and highly skilled knowledge-based workers replacing industrial workers as the dominant labor group. Although the benefits of KM may be obvious, it may not necessarily be so obvious to know how to effectively manage this valuable resource. In this book, the discussion of KM reflects the intimacy the authors have with this topic from a theoretical as well as a practical standpoint and through their substantial and diverse experiences.

The book is divided into four parts:

Part I Principles of Knowledge Management—This section provides a more detailed discussion of the concepts of knowledge and knowledge management and describes the key constituents of KM solutions including infrastructure, processes, systems, tools, and technologies. Four types of KM processes are described and illustrated: knowledge application, knowledge capture, knowledge sharing, and knowledge discovery systems. The section also examines and provides examples of the ways in which KM impacts contemporary organizations.

Part II Knowledge Management Technologies and Systems—This section is devoted to a discussion of the underlying technologies that enable KM systems associated with the above four types of KM processes. Accordingly, four types of KM systems are discussed in this section: knowledge application systems, knowledge capture systems, knowledge sharing systems, and knowledge discovery systems. The mechanisms and technologies to support these KM systems are discussed, and case studies related to their implementation are presented.

Part III Influencers of Knowledge Management—Effective KM systems and processes depend on several factors. Hence, this section examines the factors that affect KM and identifies the specific effects of these factors. Some of the issues related to management practices and direction of knowledge management are presented in this section. Furthermore, this section evaluates KM processes and describes leadership and assessment of KM.

Part IV Emergent Trends in KM—Advances in technology are driving the innovative application of emerging technologies. This section describes how emerging technologies support and facilitate KM systems and processes. It explains how KM can benefit from emergent practices and technologies, including social networks, virtual community platforms, crowdsourcing, business intelligence, and cloud computing. Additionally, this section reviews the role of KM in the management of crises. This section and the book conclude by examining aspects that are likely to be important in the future of KM, including crowd sourcing and collective intelligence and concerns related to privacy and confidentiality.

This book may be adopted in several different ways, depending on the course and the students. It can be used as a one-semester course on KM for graduate students in management information systems by covering selected topics from Parts I, II, III, and IV. A professor teaching a course for engineering or computer science students may opt to concentrate on KM technologies and systems by covering Chapters 1, 6, 7, 8, 9, and 10, and chapters in Part IV. Alternatively, if the course is being taught to students in a master's in business administration (MBA) program, a number of case studies could be assigned to complement the discussions presented in the book, and the discussion of Chapters 6, 7, 8, and 9 could be emphasized less. Additionally, the illustrative examples and case studies from the text should be useful to MBA students.

Instructors adopting the book are encouraged to share with the authors any relevant material that could be included on the Web site to reinforce and enhance the students' experience.

Acknowledgments

We have so many people to acknowledge! First, we want to recognize our families who were so supportive during the time we spent with our heads buried in our laptops.

Writing a book, much like joining the professoriate, is a labor of love. When the first two authors set out to publish the first edition of this book, we had in mind capturing our research insights, as well as those of others, in the then nascent field of knowledge management. Our goal was to use this book to capture and help us to better share this knowledge with our students, who were mostly pursuing graduate studies, and who would then use this newly acquired knowledge to inspire their research and their work. The first edition was accompanied by a CD full of demos created with the collaboration of students working at the Florida International University (FIU) Knowledge Management Lab.

What the authors never expected is that 20 years later, the book would still find relevance among researchers and students around the world, and that excitement is what motivated the authors to write the third edition of our original book, now published by Routledge, and we welcome our new co-author Dr. Richard Kumi.

It has been a wonderful experience to have had the opportunity to meet collaborators in the field of KM from around the world, whom we may have met at global KM conferences. Over the twenty years since our first edition was published, this book has been cited thousands of times in every language imaginable. To have had the opportunity to make this kind of impact continues to make us smile. After all, our labor of love provides us the reward of reading how others have also applied this knowledge.

We further thank those organizations that provided us with the fertile ground to develop many of our ideas about KM: NASA-Kennedy Space Center, Goddard Space Flight Center, Ames Research Center, NAVY Center for Advanced Research in Artificial Intelligence, and the Institute for Human and Machine Cognition, among others. We especially thank the individuals at these organizations who made it possible for us to formalize some of the concepts and techniques presented in this book. We also thank all the authors that individually contributed to the many vignettes and case studies presented throughout.

We also thank our colleagues and administrators, who throughout our careers have supported our scholarly pursuits. Our sincere thanks are also directed to Dr. Avelino Gonzalez, who coauthored the first edition of this book. Dr. Sabherwal is also grateful for the support he has received over the years through the Edwin and Karlee Bradberry Chair. We also gratefully acknowledge the contributions of all the students who previously studied and worked at the respective institutions with the authors. Finally, we are deeply indebted to many individuals at Routledge who enabled us to publish this book, especially our editor, Andrew Harrison.

We look forward to reading how this work will continue to inspire students and researchers around the globe.

1 Introducing Knowledge Management

The scientific endeavor that culminated on July 20, 1969, with the first American walking on the Moon is considered one of the most significant accomplishments in the history of humankind. What is especially noteworthy about this undertaking is that when President John F. Kennedy issued the promise in 1961 that the United States would land a man on the Moon and return him safely to Earth before the end of that decade, most of the scientific and technological knowledge required to take this "one small step for man, one giant leap for mankind" did not exist.

The necessary science and technology knowledge had to be discovered and developed to accomplish this extraordinary task. However, many of those technological advances now have permanent presence in the landscape of our lives, from cordless tools to cellular phones. These first missions to space carried less computer power on board than what some of us typically lug around airports on our phones and portable computers. The computers on board Apollo 11, considered "state-of-the-art" in the 1960s, had four KB of RAM, no disk drive, and a total of 74 KB of auxiliary memory! From the knowledge management (KM) perspective, how did they manage the extraordinary quantities of knowledge that had to be developed to accomplish the task? The required knowledge about space travel, rocketry, aerodynamics, systems, communications, biology, and many other disciplines had to be developed and validated prior to being used in the space mission. From the knowledge creation perspective, this was an extraordinarily successful endeavor. On the other hand, a closer look reveals that attempts to elicit and capture the knowledge resulting from these efforts may have been largely unsuccessful, and some studies even suggest that NASA may have actually lost that knowledge. In fact, in the words of Sylvia Fries, who was NASA's chief historian between 1983 and 1990 and who interviewed 51 NASA engineers who had worked on the Apollo program:

> The 20th anniversary of the landing of an American on the surface of the Moon occasioned many bittersweet reflections. Sweet was the celebration of the historic event itself … Bitter, for those same enthusiasts, was the knowledge that during the twenty intervening years much of the national consensus that launched this country on its first lunar adventure had evaporated … a generation of men and women who had defined their lives to a large extent in terms of this nation's epochal departure from Earth's surface was taking its leave of the program they had built.
>
> (Fries 1992, p. vii)

In this book, we hope to impart what we know about the important field of knowledge management—what it is and how to implement it successfully with the tools provided

DOI: 10.4324/9781003364375-1

by the technological advances of our times. The book presents a balanced discussion between theory and application of knowledge management to organizations. The reader will find an overview of knowledge management theory and implementation, with a special emphasis on the technologies that underpin knowledge management and how to successfully integrate those technologies. The book includes implementation details about both knowledge management mechanisms and technologies.

In this chapter, we first discuss what knowledge management is and what the forces are that drive it. We also discuss organizational issues related to knowledge management. Specifically, we introduce knowledge management systems and their roles in the organization. Finally, we discuss how the rest of the book is organized.

What Is Knowledge Management?

Knowledge management (KM) may simply be defined as *doing what is needed to get the most out of knowledge resources*. Although KM can be applied to individuals, it has attracted the attention of organizations over the last two decades. KM is viewed as an increasingly important discipline that promotes the creation, sharing, and leveraging of the corporation's knowledge. Peter Drucker (1994, pp. 66–69), whom many consider the father of KM, best defines the need for it:

> Knowledge has become the key resource, for a nation's military strength as well as for its economic strength ... is fundamentally different from the traditional key resources of the economist—land, labor, and even capital ... we need systematic work on the quality of knowledge and the productivity of knowledge ... the performance capacity, if not the survival, of any organization in the knowledge society will come increasingly to depend on those two factors.

Thus, it can be argued that the most vital resource of today's enterprise is the collective knowledge residing in the minds of an organization's employees, customers, and vendors. Learning how to manage organizational knowledge has many benefits, some of which are readily apparent, others not. These benefits may include leveraging core business competencies, accelerating innovation and time-to-market, empowering employees, innovating and delivering high-quality products, improving cycle times and decision-making, strengthening organizational commitment, and building sustainable competitive advantage (Davenport and Prusak 1998). In short, they make the organization better suited to compete successfully in a much more demanding environment.

Organizations are increasingly valued for their intellectual capital. An example of this fact is the widening gap between corporate balance sheets and investors' estimation of corporate worth. It is said that knowledge-intensive companies around the world are valued at three to eight times their financial capital. Consider for example Apple Inc., the highest-valued company in the world, with a market capitalization that was estimated at around US$2.98 trillion as of June 2023. Clearly, this figure represents more than Apple's net worth in buildings, computers, and other physical assets. Apple's valuation also represents an estimation of its intellectual assets. This includes structural capital in the form of copyrights, customer databases, and business-process software. Added to that is human capital in the form of the knowledge that resides in the minds of all of Apple's software developers, researchers, academic collaborators, and business managers.

In general, KM focuses on organizing and making available important knowledge, wherever and whenever it is needed. The traditional emphasis in KM has been on knowledge that is recognized and already articulated in some form. This includes knowledge about processes, procedures, intellectual property, documented best practices, forecasts, lessons learned, and solutions to recurring problems. Increasingly, KM has also focused on managing important knowledge that may reside solely in the minds of organizations' experts.

Consider, for example, the knowledge of commercial pilots. Not only they are expected to ensure the safety of passengers, but also keep their flights on time under various weather conditions. They need to discover and establish the relevance of all available information related to problems during flight, diagnose problems, identify alternative actions, and estimate the risk associated with each alternative within the available time. The number of flight hours and years of flying experience have been considered as indicators of a pilot's level of expertise. This level of knowledge has been obtained through many years of experience in flight and successful decisions. With the large number of pilots' retirements looming, how can an airline organization elicit and catalog this knowledge so that new generations may benefit?

KM is also related to the concept of **intellectual capital**, which is considered by many as the most valuable enterprise resource. An organization's intellectual capital refers to the sum of all its knowledge resources, which exist in aspects within or outside the organization (Nahapiet and Ghoshal 1998). There are three types of intellectual capital: human capital, or the knowledge, skills, and capabilities possessed by individual employees; organizational capital, or the institutionalized knowledge and codified experience residing in databases, manuals, culture, systems, structures, and processes; and social capital, or the knowledge embedded in relationships and interactions among individuals (Gogan et al. 2016). Recent research shows that utilizing intellectual capital and knowledge management capabilities would lead to innovation and firms' performance improvement (Hsu and Sabherwal 2011).

Forces Driving Knowledge Management

Contemporary organizations rely on their decisionmakers to make "mission critical" decisions based on inputs from multiple domains. The ideal decisionmaker possesses a profound understanding of specific domains that influence the decision-making process, coupled with the experience that allows her to act quickly and decisively on the information. This profile of the ideal decisionmaker usually corresponds to someone who has lengthy experience and insights gained from years of observation. This profile does not mark a significant departure from the past, but the following four trends are increasing the stakes in decision-making.

1. Increasing Domain Complexity

The complexity of the underlying knowledge domains is increasing. As a direct consequence, the complexity of the knowledge required to complete a specific business process task has increased as well. Intricacy of internal and external processes, increased competition, and the rapid advancement of technology all contribute to increasing domain complexity. For example, new product development no longer requires only brainstorming sessions by the freethinking product designers of the organization, but instead it requires the partnership of interorganizational teams representing various functional subunits—from finance to marketing to engineering. Thus, we see an increased emphasis from professional recruiters around the world seeking new job applicants who not only possess excellent educational and professional qualifications, but who also have outstanding communication and team-collaboration skills. These skills will enable them to share their knowledge for the benefit of the organization.

2. Accelerating Market Volatility

The pace of change, or volatility, within each market domain has increased rapidly in the past decade. For example, market and environmental influences can result in overnight changes in an organization. Corporate announcements of a missed financial quarterly target could send a company's capitalization, and perhaps that of a whole industry, in a downward spiral. Stock prices on Wall Street have become increasingly volatile in the past few years resulting in the phenomenon of day trading, where many nonfinancial professionals make a living from taking advantage of the steep market fluctuations.

3. Intensified Speed of Responsiveness

The time required to take action based upon subtle changes within and across domains is decreasing. The rapid advance in technology continually changes the decision-making landscape, making it imperative that decisions be made and implemented quickly, lest the window of opportunity closes. For example, in the past, the sales process incorporated ample processing time, thus allowing the stakeholders a "comfort zone" in the decision-making process. Typically, in response to a customer request, the sales representative would return to the office, discuss the opportunity with his manager, draft a proposal, and mail the proposal to the client, who would then accept or reject the offer. The time required by the process would essentially provide the stakeholders sufficient time to ponder the most adequate solution at each of the decision points. Contrast yesterday's sale process with today's, for example the process required by many online bidding marketplaces thriving on the Web. Consider the dilemma faced by a hotel manager that participates in an Internet auctioning market of hotel rooms: "Should I book a US$200 room for the bid offer of US$80 and fill the room or risk not accepting the bid hoping to get a walk-in customer that will pay the US$200?" Confronted with a decision to fill a room at a lower rate than what the hotel typically advertises poses an important decision that the hotel manager must make within minutes of a bid offer.

4. Employee Turnover

Organizations continue to face employee turnover, both voluntary (i.e., decided by the employee, for example, due to opportunities for career advancement) and involuntary (i.e., for reasons beyond the employee's control, such as health-related problems and termination of employment by the employer). Employee turnover is especially important in tough economic conditions and during crisis events, such as the 2008 to 2009 recession or the COVID-19 pandemic, when several companies laid off large numbers of employees. Such employee turnover inevitably leads to the organization losing some of the knowledge possessed by the departing individuals. Moreover, in some cases these individuals might have knowledge that would be valuable to competitors. When employees leave, it affects company resources because of the loss of productivity, cost of hiring replacement personnel, and training of new employees. This strains company resources and hinders growth. In addition to the cost of training, there is considerable time required for a new employee to be effectively productive (Skelton et al. 2020).

Artificial intelligence, machine-learning, cloud computing, and other enabling technologies play an important role in the processes of knowledge discovery, capture, sharing, and application, enabling the development of KM systems. We provide a short introduction to these technologies in each of these chapters. Because KM systems provide access to explicit corporate knowledge, it is easy to learn from previous experiences. **Experience management** is another term related to knowledge management. Basically, experience develops over time to coalesce into more general experience, which then combines into general knowledge. Experiences captured over time can be managed using technology. Chapters 12 through 14, examine how emerging technologies are used to manage experiences as well as create new knowledge.

Box 1.1 Is Knowledge Management for Everybody?

John Smith owns an independent auto repair shop in Stillwater, Oklahoma, which he established in 1985. Prior to opening his own shop, he had been repairing foreign cars as a mechanic for the local Toyota dealership. In these days of increasing complexity in automobiles, he had to learn about such new technologies as fuel injection, computer-controlled ignition, and multi-valve and turbocharged engines. This has not been easy, but he managed to do it, and at the same time created a successful business, one with an outstanding reputation. As his business grew, he had to hire mechanics to help him with the workload. At first, training them was easy since cars were simple. That has radically changed in the last ten years. He now finds himself spending more time training and correcting the work of his mechanics instead of working on cars himself, which is what he truly enjoys. To further complicate matters, his mechanics are so well-trained that the local Toyota dealership is hiring them away from him for significant salary increases. Being a small business, he cannot afford to compete with them, so he finds himself doing more and more training and correcting all the time. The turnover has now begun to affect the quality of the work he turns over to his customers, increasing complaints and damaging his hard-earned reputation. Basically, he has a knowledge problem. He has the knowledge and needs to capture it in a way that is easy to disseminate to his mechanics. He must find a way to manage this knowledge to survive. How successful he is will dictate his future survival in this business.

Issues in Knowledge Management

In practice, given the uncertainty in today's business environments and the reality of continuing layoffs, what could make employees feel compelled to participate in knowledge management initiatives? Although many attempts have been made to launch KM initiatives, including the design and implementation of KM systems, not all KM implementations have been successful. In fact, many KM systems implementations, for example of lessons learned systems (discussed in Chapter 8), have fallen short of their promise. Many KM systems implemented at organizations have failed to enable knowledge workers to share their knowledge for the benefit of the organization. Effective KM uses all the options available to motivated employees to put knowledge to work. Effective KM depends on recognizing that all these options basically need each other.

One of the primary differences between traditional information systems and KM systems is the active role that users of KM systems play on building the content of such systems. Users of traditional information systems are typically not required to actively contribute to building the content of such systems, an effort typically delegated to the MIS department or to information systems consultants. Therefore, traditional IS research has concentrated much of its efforts in understanding the factors leading users to accepting, and thereby using, IT. As we will see later in Chapter 8, users of lessons learned systems will not only utilize the system to find a lesson applicable to a problem at hand but will typically also contribute lessons to the system database. As a result, the successful implementation of KM systems requires that its users not only effectively "use" such systems as in traditional information systems but that in fact they also "contribute" to the knowledge base of such systems. Therefore, seeking to understand the factors that lead to the successful implementation of KM systems is an important area of research that is still growing.

Whereas technology has provided the impetus for managing knowledge, we now know that effective KM initiatives are not only limited to a technological solution. An adage states that effective KM is 80 percent related to organizational culture and human factors and 20 percent related to technology. This means that there is an important human component in KM. This finding addresses the fact that knowledge is first created in the people's minds. KM practices must first identify ways to encourage and stimulate the ability of employees to develop new knowledge. Second, KM methodologies and technologies must enable effective ways to elicit, represent, organize, reuse, and renew this knowledge. Third, KM should not distance itself from the knowledge owners but instead celebrate and recognize their position as experts in the organization. This, in effect, is the essence of knowledge management. More about the controversies surrounding KM will be presented in Chapters 3, 5, and 16.

Text Overview

Part I Principles of Knowledge Management

This section of the book includes the overview of knowledge management that we have presented in this chapter, including the role that IT plays in KM and the relevance of KM to modern organizations. Chapter 2 discusses the concept of knowledge in greater detail and distinguishes it from data and information, summarizes the perspectives commonly used to view knowledge, describes the ways of classifying knowledge, and identifies some key characteristics of knowledge. Chapter 3 explains in greater detail the concept of knowledge management. It also describes knowledge management foundations, which are the broad organizational aspects that support KM in the long-term and includes KM infrastructure, KM mechanisms, and KM technologies. KM foundations support KM solutions. Chapter 4 describes and illustrates KM solutions, which include two components: KM processes and KM systems. Chapter 5 describes the variety of ways in which KM can affect individuals and various aspects of organizations.

Part II Knowledge Management Technologies and Systems

This section of the book is devoted to a discussion of the underlying technologies that enable the creation of knowledge management systems. Chapter 6 introduces the reader to **knowledge application** systems, which refer to systems that utilize knowledge and summarize the most relevant intelligent technologies that underpin them, specifically rule-based expert systems and case-based reasoning. Case studies of knowledge application systems are also discussed in this chapter. In Chapter 7 we introduce the reader to **knowledge capture** systems, which refer to systems that elicit and preserve the knowledge of experts so that it can be shared with others. Issues related to how to design the knowledge capture system, including the use of intelligent technologies, are discussed. The role of RFID technologies in knowledge capture is also presented in this chapter and specific examples of knowledge capture systems are discussed. The chapter also includes a discussion on mechanisms for knowledge capture and the use of storytelling in organizations, and it concludes with a short discussion on research trends on knowledge capture systems. In Chapter 8 we describe **knowledge sharing** systems, which refer to systems that organize and distribute knowledge and comprise most of the KM systems currently in place. This chapter also discusses how the Internet, the World Wide Web, is used to facilitate communications. Search techniques used in Web-based searches are also discussed. Design considerations and special types of knowledge sharing systems are covered: lessons learned systems and expertise locator systems. Case studies of knowledge sharing systems are discussed based on the experience gained from their development. Finally, in Chapter 9 we introduce **knowledge discovery** systems, systems and technologies that create knowledge. The chapter presents a description of knowledge discovery in databases and data mining (DM), including both mechanisms and technologies to support the discovery of knowledge. The material covers design considerations and the CRISPDM process. Two very relevant topics, DM and its relationship to discovering knowledge on the Web and customer resource management (CRM), are also presented including the importance of "knowing" about your customer. Barriers to the use of knowledge discovery are also discussed and case studies of the use of knowledge discovery systems are also presented. The chapter includes a discussion on mechanisms for knowledge discovery and the use of socialization to catalyze innovation in organizations.

Part III Management of Knowledge Management

This section of the book presents some of the issues related to management practices and the future of knowledge management. Chapter 10 presents emergent KM practices including a discussion of social networks and communities of practice, how they facilitate knowledge sharing, and how they benefit from communication technologies. This chapter also incorporates a discussion of such emergent technologies as wikis, blogs, and open-source development and examines how they enable KM. Chapter 11 describes some of the factors influencing KM, including a discussion of the impact of the type of knowledge, the business strategy, and the industry environment on KM. It also describes a methodology to prioritize implementation of KM solutions based on knowledge, organizational, and industry characteristics.

Part IV Emergent Trends in Knowledge Management

Chapter 12 explains how cloud computing technologies support and enable KM systems and processes. Information technologies are critical to KM systems and processes and cloud computing makes technology easily accessible. Through cloud computing technologies, organizations can deploy cutting edge technologies that improve the methods and practices of capturing, storing, organizing, and applying knowledge. Chapter 13 describes crowdsourcing and online communities as virtual platforms for organizing and coordinating knowledge and expertise embedded in the experience, skills, and expertise of individuals and groups in an organization or a domain. Chapter 14 describes how artificial intelligence, business intelligence, and analytics are developing new ways of discovering, capturing, organizing, and applying knowledge. The capacity to capture and store large amounts of data has created new opportunities for the discovery, extraction, and combination of knowledge. Chapter 14 describes how emerging technologies are making it possible to exploit new ways of knowledge discovery and capture. Chapter 15 describes some of the challenges of capturing, sharing, and applying knowledge during a crisis. Crisis events present unique challenges to organizations, and Chapter 15 explains how KM processes can be useful in managing crisis events. Chapter 16 presents some issues in organizational leadership and the future of KM. As KM becomes widely accepted in corporate organizations, it will increasingly become critical for corporate managers to supply adequate leadership for it as well as important safeguards for ensuring the security and adequate use of this knowledge. Also in this chapter, we present a discussion on the future of KM. In the future, knowledge management systems are expected to help decisionmakers make more humane decisions and enable them to deal with "wicked," one-of-a-kind problems. We anticipate a future where people and advanced technology will continue to work together, enabling knowledge integration across diverse domains and with considerably higher payoffs.

Summary

In this chapter, you have learned about the following knowledge management issues as they relate to the learning objectives:

1   A description of KM ranging from the system perspective to the organizational perspective.
2   A discussion of the relevance of KM in today's dynamic environments that are augmented with increasing technological complexity.
3   Benefits and considerations about KM are presented, including an overview of the nature of the KM projects currently in progress at public and private organizations around the world.
4   Finally, IT plays an important role in KM. The enabling role of IT is discussed, but the adage of "KM is 80 percent organizational, and 20 percent about IT" still holds today.

Review

1   Describe knowledge management.
2   Discuss the forces driving knowledge management.

3   What are knowledge management systems? Enumerate the four types of KM systems.
4   Describe some of the issues facing knowledge management.

Application Exercises

1   Identify an example of a knowledge management initiative that has been undertaken in your organization. Has the initiative been successful? What are some of the issues, both technical and nontechnical, that were faced during its implementation?
2   Design a knowledge management initiative to support your business needs.
3   Describe the non-technical issues that you will face during its implementation.
4   Consider the four forces driving KM described in this chapter. Think of another example that illustrates each of these forces.

References

Davenport, T.H., and Prusak, L. 1998. *Working knowledge: How organizations manage what they know.* Boston: Harvard Business School Press.

Drucker, P. 1994. The age of social transformation. *The Atlantic Monthly*, 274(5), 53–70.

Fries, S. 1992. *NASA engineers and the age of Apollo.* Washington, DC (NASA SP-4104). https://history.nasa.gov/SP-4104.pdf.

Gogan, L.M., Artene, A., Sarca, I., and Draghici, A. 2016. The impact of intellectual capital on organizational performance. *Procedia-Social and Behavioral Sciences*, 221, 194–202.

Hsu, I.-C., and Sabherwal, R. 2011. From intellectual capital to firm performance: The mediating role of knowledge management capabilities, *IEEE Transactions on Engineering Management*, 58 (4), 626–642.

Nahapiet, J., and Ghoshal, S. 1998. Social capital, intellectual capital, and the organizational advantage. *Academy of Management Review*, 23, 242–266.

Skelton, A.R., Nattress, D., and Dwyer, R.J. 2020. Predicting manufacturing employee turnover intentions. *Journal of Economics, Finance and Administrative Science*, 25(49), 101–117.

Part I

Principles of Knowledge Management

2 The Nature of Knowledge

In the previous chapter, we provided an introduction to the basic concepts of knowledge management. This chapter takes the next step by explaining in detail what we mean by **knowledge**. It also distinguishes knowledge from **data** and from **information** and illustrates these three concepts using some examples. This chapter also summarizes some of the perspectives commonly used to view knowledge, including both subjective and objective viewpoints. Moreover, it describes some of the ways to classify knowledge and identifies some attributes that may be used to characterize different types of knowledge. It also relates knowledge to the concept of **intellectual capital** and its various dimensions. Finally, the chapter also explains the various reservoirs, or locations, in which knowledge might reside.

What Is Knowledge?

"Knowledge" is quite distinct from "data" and "information," although the three terms are sometimes used interchangeably. In this section, we define and illustrate these concepts and differentiate among them. This discussion also leads to our definition of knowledge.

Data comprise facts, observations, or perceptions (which may or may not be correct). Data represent raw numbers or assertions and may therefore be devoid of context, meaning, or intent. Let us consider three examples of what is considered to be data. We will then build upon these examples to examine the meaning of information and knowledge.

> *Example 1*: That a sales order at a restaurant included two large burgers and two medium-sized vanilla milkshakes is an example of data.
> *Example 2*: The observation that upon tossing a coin it landed heads also illustrates data.
> *Example 3*: The wind component (u and v) coordinates for a particular hurricane's trajectory, at specific instances of time, are likewise considered data.

Although data are devoid of context, meaning, or intent it can be easily captured, stored, and communicated using electronic or other media.

Information is a subset of data, only including those data that possess context, relevance, and purpose. Information typically involves the manipulation of raw data to obtain a more meaningful indication of trends or patterns in the data. Let us continue with the three aforementioned examples:

DOI: 10.4324/9781003364375-3

Example 1: For the manager of the restaurant, the numbers indicating the daily sales (in dollars, quantity, or percentage of daily sales) of burgers, vanilla milk-shakes, and other products are information. The manager can use such information to make decisions regarding pricing and raw material purchases.

Example 2: Let us assume that the context of the coin toss is a betting situation where John is offering to pay anyone US$10 if the coin lands heads but take US$8 if the coin lands tails. Susan is considering whether to take up John's bet, and she benefits from knowing that the last 100 times the coin was tossed, it landed heads 40 times and tails on 60 occasions. The result of each individual toss (head or tail) is data but is not directly useful. It is therefore data but not information. By contrast, that 40 heads and 60 tails that resulted from the last 100 tosses are also data, but they can be directly used to compute probabilities of heads and tails and hence to make the decision. Therefore, they are also information for Susan.

Example 3: Based on the *u* and *v* components, hurricane software models may be used to create a forecast of the hurricane trajectory. The hurricane forecast is information.

As can be seen from these examples, whether certain facts are information or only data depends on the individual who is using those facts. The facts about the daily sales of burgers represent information for the store manager but only data for a customer. If the restaurant is one out of a chain of 250 restaurants, these facts about daily sales are also data for the CEO of the chain. Similarly, the facts about the coin toss are simply data for an individual who is not interested in betting.

Knowledge has been distinguished from data and information in two different ways. A more simplistic view considers knowledge as being at the highest level in a hierarchy with information at the middle level and data at the lowest level. According to this view, knowledge refers to information that enables action and decisions or information with direction. Hence, knowledge is intrinsically similar to information and data, although it is the richest and deepest of the three, and is consequently also the most valuable. Based on this view, data refer to bare facts void of context, for example a telephone number. Information is data in context, for example a phone book. Knowledge is information that facilitates action, for example, individuals who are the domain experts within an organization. An example of knowledge includes recognizing that a phone number belongs to a good client who needs to be called once per week to get his orders.

Although this simplistic view of knowledge may not be completely inaccurate, we feel it doesn't fully explain the characteristics of knowledge. Instead, we use a more complete perspective, according to which knowledge is intrinsically different from information. Instead of considering knowledge as a richer or more detailed set of facts, we define knowledge in an area as *justified beliefs about relationships among concepts relevant to that particular area*. This definition has support in the literature (Nonaka 1994). Let us now consider how this definition works for the above examples.

Example 1: The daily sales of burgers can be used, along with other information (e.g., information on the quantity of bread in the inventory), to compute the amount of bread to buy. The relationship between the quantity of bread that should be ordered, the quantity of bread currently in the inventory, and the daily sales of burgers (and other products that use bread) is an example of knowledge. Understanding of this relationship (which could conceivably be stated as a mathematical formula) helps to use the information (on quantity of bread in the inventory and daily sales of burgers, etc.) to compute the quantity of bread to be purchased. However, the quantity of bread to be ordered should itself be considered information and not knowledge. It is simply more valuable information.

Example 2: The information about 40 heads and 60 tails (out of 100 tosses) can be used to compute the probability of heads (0.40) and tails (0.60). The probabilities can then be used, along with information about the returns associated with heads (US$10 from Susan's perspective) and tails (–US$8, again from Susan's perspective) to compute the expected value to Susan from participating in the bet. Both probabilities and expected values are information, although more valuable information than the facts that 40 tosses produced heads and 60 produced tails. Moreover, expected value is more useful information than the probabilities; the former can directly be used to make the decision, whereas the latter requires computation of expected value.

The relationship between the **probability** of heads, the number of times the coin lands heads, and the total number of tosses (i.e., the probability of heads, or $p_H = n_H/(n_H + n_T)$, assuming that the coin can only land heads or tails) is an example of knowledge. It helps compute the probability from the data on outcomes of tosses. The similar formula for probability of tails is knowledge as well. In addition, the relationship between expected value (EV) and the probabilities (p_H, p_T) and returns (R_H, R_T) for heads and tails (i.e., $EV = p_H*R_H + p_T*R_T$) is also knowledge. Using these components of knowledge, probability of heads and tails can be computed as 0.40 and 0.60, respectively. Then, the expected value for Susan can be computed as $0.40*(+\$10) + 0.60*(-\$8) = -\$0.80$.

Example 3: The knowledge of a hurricane researcher is used to analyze the *u* and *v* wind components as well as the hurricane forecast produced by the different software models, to determine the probability that the hurricane will follow a specific trajectory.

Thus, knowledge helps produce information from data or more valuable information from less valuable information. In that sense, this information facilitates action such as the decision of whether to bet or not. Based on the new generated information of the expected value of the outcome as well as the relationship with other concepts, such as Susan's anticipation that the coin may be fair or not, knowledge enables Susan to decide whether she can expect to win at the game. This aspect of the relationship between data and information is depicted in Figure 2.1, which shows the relationship between data (which has zero or low value in making the decision), and information (which has greater value than data, although different types of information might have differing values).

The above relationships between data, information, and knowledge are illustrated using Example 2 in Figure 2.2. As may be seen from the figure, knowledge of how to count helps convert data on coin tosses (each toss producing a head or tail, with the set of 100 tosses producing 100 such observations, shown as H and T, respectively) into information (number of heads and number of tosses). This information is more useful than the raw data, but it does not directly help the decisionmaker (Susan) to decide on whether to participate in the bet. Using knowledge of how to compute probabilities, this information can be converted into more useful information—that is, the probabilities of heads and tails. Moreover, combining the information about probabilities with information about returns associated with heads and tails, it is possible to produce even more information—that is, the expected value associated with participation in the

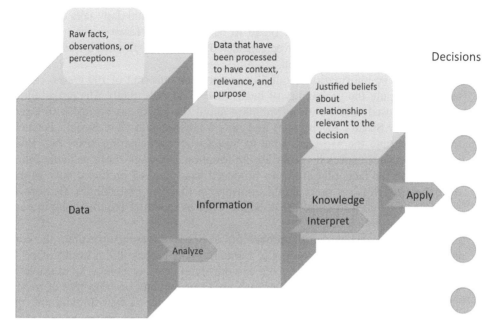

Figure 2.1 Data, Information, and Knowledge

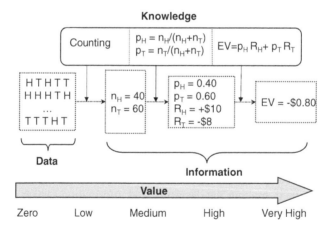

Figure 2.2 An Illustration of Data, Information, and Knowledge

bet. In making this transition, knowledge of the formula for computing expected value from probabilities and returns is utilized. Figure 2.2 illustrates how knowledge helps produce information from data (e.g., probabilities based on outcomes of tosses of 60 heads and 40 tails) or more valuable information (expected value) from less valuable information (e.g., probabilities and payoffs associated with heads and tails).

The above distinctions among data, information, and knowledge are consistent with Nonaka and Takeuchi's (1995) definition of knowledge as "a justified true belief." It is also consistent with Wiig's (1999, p.46) view of knowledge as being fundamentally different from data and information:

> Knowledge consists of truths and beliefs, perspectives and concepts, judgments and expectations, methodologies, and know-how. It is possessed by humans, agents, or other active entities and is used to receive information and to recognize and identify; analyze, interpret, and evaluate; synthesize and decide; plan, implement, monitor, and adapt—that is, to act more or less intelligently. In other words, knowledge is used to determine what a specific situation means and how to handle it.

Figure 2.3 depicts how knowledge, data, and information relate to information systems, decisions, and events. As discussed, knowledge helps convert data into information. The knowledge could be stored in a manual or computer-based information system, which receives data as input and produces information as output. Moreover, the use of information to make the decision requires knowledge as well (e.g., in the context of the second example above, the knowledge that expected value above zero generally suggests that the decision is a good one). The decisions, as well as certain unrelated factors, lead to events, which cause generation of further data. The events, the use of information, and the information system might cause modifications in the knowledge itself. For example, in the context of example 1 on ordering raw materials based on sales, information about changes in suppliers (e.g., a merger of two suppliers) might cause changes in the perceived relationship (i.e., knowledge) between the quantity on hand, the daily sales, and the quantity to be ordered. Similarly, in example 2 on betting on the outcome of a coin toss, the individual's risk aversion, individual wealth, and so forth, might cause changes in beliefs related to whether expected value above zero justifies the decision to participate in the bet.

Alternative Views of Knowledge

Knowledge can be viewed from a subjective or objective stance. The subjective view represents knowledge using two possible perspectives: as a state of mind or as a

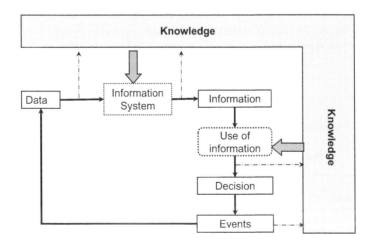

Figure 2.3 Relating Data, Information, and Knowledge to Events

practice. On the other hand, the objective view represents knowledge in three possible perspectives: as an object, as access to information, or as a capability. The perspectives on knowledge are shown in Figure 2.4.

Subjective View of Knowledge

According to the subjective view, reality is socially constructed through interactions with individuals (Schultze 1999). Knowledge is viewed as an ongoing accomplishment that continuously affects and is influenced by social practices (Boland and Tenkasi 1995). Consequently, knowledge cannot be placed at a single location, as it has no existence independent of social practices and human experiences. According to the subjective view, knowledge could be considered from two perspectives, either as a state of mind or as practice.

Knowledge as State of Mind

This perspective considers knowledge as being a state of an individual's mind. Organizational knowledge is viewed here as the beliefs of the individuals within the organization. Moreover, to the extent the various individuals have differing experiences and backgrounds, their beliefs, and hence knowledge, could differ from each other. Consequently, the focus here is on enabling individuals to enhance their personal areas of knowledge so that they can apply them to best pursue organizational goals (Alavi and Leidner 2001).

Knowledge as Practice

According to this perspective, knowledge is also considered as subjective but it is viewed as being held by a group and not as being decomposable into elements possessed by individuals. Thus, from this perspective, knowledge is "neither possessed by any one agent, nor contained in any one repository" (Schultze 1999, p. 10). Moreover, knowledge resides not in anyone's head but in practice. Knowledge is comprised of beliefs, consistent with our definition earlier, but the beliefs themselves are collective rather than individual, and therefore, are better reflected in organizational activities rather than in the minds of the organization's individuals. Viewed from this perspective, knowledge is "inherently indeterminate and continually emerging" (Tsoukas 1996, p. 22).

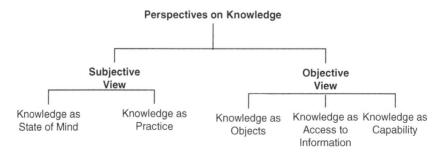

Figure 2.4 Various Perspectives on Knowledge

Objective View of Knowledge

The objective view is the diametrical opposite of the subjective stance. According to the objective view, reality is independent of human perceptions and can be structured in terms of *a priori* categories and concepts (Schultze 1999). Consequently, knowledge can be located in the form of an object or a capability that can be discovered or improved by human agents. The objective view considers knowledge from three possible perspectives.

Knowledge as Objects

This perspective considers knowledge as something that can be stored, transferred, and manipulated. Consistent with the definition of knowledge as a set of justified beliefs, these knowledge objects (i.e., beliefs) can exist in a variety of locations. Moreover, they can be of several different types, as discussed in the next section.

Knowledge as Access to Information

This perspective considers knowledge as the condition of access to information (Alavi and Leidner 2001). Thus, knowledge is viewed here as something that enables access and utilization of information. This perspective extends the above view of knowledge as objects, emphasizing the accessibility of the knowledge objects.

Knowledge as Capability

This perspective is consistent with the last two perspectives of knowledge as objects or as access to information. However, this perspective differs in that the focus here is on the way in which knowledge can be applied to influence action. This perspective places emphasis on knowledge as a strategic capability that can potentially be applied to seek a competitive advantage.

Thus, the five perspectives discussed above differ in their focus in viewing knowledge, but they are all consistent in viewing knowledge as a set of beliefs about relationships. The first perspective, knowledge as a state of mind, focuses on beliefs within human minds; while the second perspective, knowledge as a practice, focuses on beliefs implicit to actions or practice. In either case, the beliefs, and the knowledge they comprise, are considered subjective. In contrast, the last three perspectives (knowledge as objects, knowledge as access to information, and knowledge as a capability) view knowledge as objective, focusing on beliefs as objects to be stored and managed, as the condition of access to information, and as a capability that affects action. We recognize all five perspectives as important, and consider them as simply providing different ways of examining knowledge. However, in the remainder of the book, we adopt a position that is more objective than subjective. This is due to the desire to make this textbook useful for students and managers responsible for managing knowledge in their organizations; an objective view facilitates making practical recommendations about how organizations should manage knowledge, whereas a subjective view helps with understanding knowledge management but may be less valuable in recommending actions for knowledge management.

We next examine the different forms of knowledge, which are clearly consistent with the objective perspective of knowledge. However, an argument could also be made that at least some types of knowledge discussed below (e.g., tacit) are not inconsistent with a subjective view.

Different Types of Knowledge

Knowledge has been classified and characterized in several different ways. For example, knowledge has been categorized as individual, social, causal, conditional, relational, and pragmatic (Alavi and Leidner 2001) and also as embodied, encoded, and procedural (Venzin et al. 1998). In this section, we examine some of the more important classifications of knowledge. It is important to understand the nature of these various types of knowledge because different types of knowledge should be managed differently, as discussed in detail in some of the later chapters.

Procedural or Declarative Knowledge

The first distinction we examine is that between **declarative knowledge** (facts) and **procedural knowledge** (how to ride a bicycle) (Kogut and Zander 1992; Singley and Anderson 1989). Declarative knowledge (or substantive knowledge, as it is also called) focuses on beliefs about relationships among variables. For example, all other things being equal, a greater price charged for a product would cause some reduction in its number of sales. Declarative knowledge can be stated in the form of propositions, expected correlations, or formulas relating concepts represented as variables. For example, stating that the sum of the square of the sine of an angle and the square of the cosine of the same angle would equal one is an example of declarative knowledge. Similarly, identifying the specific product features a specific customer likes is also an example of declarative knowledge.

Procedural knowledge, in contrast, focuses on beliefs relating sequences of steps or actions to desired (or undesired) outcomes. An example of such procedural knowledge is the set of justified beliefs about the procedure that should be followed in a government organization in deciding on whom to award the contract for a particular area (e. g., information system development).

Declarative knowledge may be characterized as "know what," whereas procedural knowledge may be viewed as "know-how." To further understand the difference between these two types of knowledge, let us consider the example of a hypothetical automobile manufacturing firm. An instance of declarative knowledge in this context is the set of justified beliefs about the effect that the quality of each component would have on the final product. This could include the effect of quality on such features as reliability, fuel consumption, deterioration over time, and quality of the ride of a particular model. Such declarative knowledge, combined with information about the set of components needed for each model and the prices of various alternatives for each component, would help determine the specific components that should be used in each model. An example of procedural knowledge in the same context would be the set of beliefs about the process used to assemble a particular model of the car. This could include such things as the steps in the engine assembly process, which tasks can be performed in parallel, the amount of time that each step should take, the amount of waiting time between successive steps, and so on.

Tacit or Explicit Knowledge

Another important classification of knowledge views it as tacit or explicit (Nonaka 1994; Polanyi 1966). **Explicit knowledge** typically refers to knowledge that has been expressed into words and numbers. Such knowledge can be shared formally and systematically in the form of data, specifications, manuals, drawings, audio- and videotapes, computer programs, patents, and the like. For example, the basic principles for stock market analysis contained in a book or manual are considered explicit knowledge. This knowledge can be used by investors to make decisions about buying or selling stocks. It should also be noted that although explicit knowledge might resemble data or information in form, the distinction mentioned earlier in this chapter is preserved; although explicated, the principles of stock market analysis are justified beliefs about relationships rather than simple facts or observations. Also, the rules about how to process a travel reimbursement, which becomes embedded in an enterprise resource planning system, is considered explicit knowledge.

In contrast, **tacit knowledge** includes insights, intuitions, and hunches. It is difficult to express and formalize, and therefore difficult to share. Tacit knowledge is more likely to be personal and based on individual experiences and activities. For example, through years of observing a particular industry, a stock market analyst might gain knowledge that helps him make recommendations to investors in the stock market regarding the likely short-term and long-term market trends for the stocks of firms within that industry. Such knowledge would be considered tacit, unless the analyst can verbalize it in the form of a document that others can use and learn from. Tacit knowledge may also include **expertise** that is so specific that it may be too expensive to make explicit; therefore, the organization chooses to let it reside with the expert.

As discussed above, explicit and tacit forms of knowledge are quite distinct. However, it is possible to convert explicit knowledge into tacit, as occurs, for example, when an individual reads a book and learns from it, thereby converting the explicit knowledge contained in the book into tacit knowledge in the individual's mind. Similarly, tacit knowledge can sometimes be converted into explicit knowledge, as happens when an individual with considerable tacit knowledge about a topic writes a book or manual formalizing that knowledge. These possibilities are discussed in greater detail in the next chapter on knowledge management solutions.

General or Specific Knowledge

The third classification of knowledge focuses on whether the knowledge is possessed widely or narrowly (Sabherwal and Becerra-Fernandez 2005). **General knowledge** is possessed by a large number of individuals and can be transferred easily across individuals. For example, knowledge about the rules of baseball can be considered general, especially among the spectators at a baseball park. One example of general knowledge in this context is recognizing that when a baseball player takes the fourth "ball," he gets a walk; when he takes the third "strike," he is out. It is general because everyone with a basic understanding of baseball would possess this knowledge.

Unlike general knowledge, **specific knowledge**, or "idiosyncratic knowledge," is possessed by a very limited number of individuals, and is expensive to transfer (Hayek 1945; Jensen and Meckling 1996; Sabherwal and Becerra-Fernandez 2005; Sabherwal et al. 2023). Consider the distinction between a professional coach and a typical fan watching a baseball game. The coach has the knowledge needed to filter, from the chaos of the game, the information required to evaluate and help players through advice such as when to try to hit the ball, when to steal a base, and so on. For example, if Albert Pujols is at bat, a slow man is on first, his team has two outs and is behind by one run against a left-handed pitcher, Pujols should be allowed to swing away. Few fans may have this knowledge, and so it is considered specific.

Specific knowledge can be of three types: technology-specific knowledge, context-specific knowledge, and context-and-technology-specific knowledge. **Technology-specific knowledge** is deep knowledge about a specific area. It includes knowledge about the tools and techniques that may be used to address problems in that area. This kind of knowledge is often acquired as a part of some formal training and is then augmented through experience in the field. Examples include the scientific knowledge possessed by a physicist and the knowledge about computer hardware possessed by a computer engineer. Within the engineering directorate at NASA-Kennedy Space Center, the knowledge of project management techniques (such as PERT charts and critical path analysis) is technology specific, as it pertains to project management in general without being specific to NASA or Kennedy Space Center.

On the other hand, **context-specific knowledge** refers to the knowledge of particular circumstances of time and place in which work is to be performed (Hayek 1945; O'Reilly and Pondy 1979; Sabherwal and Becerra-Fernandez 2005). Contextually specific knowledge pertains to the organization and the organizational subunit within which tasks are performed. For example, the detailed knowledge a design engineer possesses about the idiosyncrasies of the particular design group in which she is working is contextually specific. Another example is a baseball catcher's knowledge of the team's pitching staff. Contextually specific knowledge cannot be acquired through formal training but instead must be obtained from within the specific context (such as membership in the same design group or baseball team). Within the engineering directorate at NASA-Kennedy Space Center, the knowledge of the mechanisms used to patent and license NASA-developed technology for public use is context-specific, because it depends primarily on the Kennedy Space Center's context with minimal effect of the particular technical discipline.

A third kind of specific knowledge, which may be called **context-and-technology-specific knowledge**, is specific in terms of both the context and the technical aspects. Context-and-technology-specific knowledge simultaneously involves both rich scientific knowledge and an understanding of the particular context (Machlup 1980; Sabherwal and Becerra-Fernandez 2005). For example, knowledge of how to decide on the stocks to acquire within an industry is context-and-technology-specific; it blends an understanding of that industry's dynamics as well as the tools used to analyze stock performance. Similarly, in the engineering directorate at NASA-Kennedy Space Center, the knowledge of how to plan and develop ground and flight support systems is context-and-technology-specific because it depends on both the design context of flight systems at Kennedy Space Center and principles of engineering.

Combining the Classifications of Knowledge

The above classifications of knowledge are independent. In other words, procedural knowledge could be either tacit or explicit and either general or specific. Similarly, declarative knowledge could be either tacit or explicit and either general or specific.

Combining the above three classifications and considering technically specific and contextually specific knowledge as distinct, 12 ($2 \times 2 \times 3$) types of knowledge can be identified as indicated and illustrated in Table 2.1.

Knowledge and Expertise

We define **expertise** to be knowledge of higher quality. It addresses the degree of knowledge. That is, one who possesses expertise is able to perform a task much better that those who do not. This is specific knowledge at its best. The word "expert" can be used to describe people possessing many different levels of skills or knowledge. A person can be an expert at a particular task irrespective of how sophisticated that area of expertise is. For example, there are expert bus drivers just as there are expert brain surgeons. Each of them excels in the performance of tasks in their respective field.

Thus, the concept of expertise must be further classified for different types of domains. The skill levels of experts from different domains should not be compared to each other. All experts require roughly the same cognitive skills. The difference

Table 2.1 Illustrations of the Different Types of Knowledge

	General	*Contextually Specific*	*Technically Specific*
Declarative			
Explicit	A book describing factors to consider when deciding whether to buy a company's stock. This may include information on price to earnings ratio and dividends.	A company document identifying the circumstances under which a consultant team's manager should consider replacing a team member who is having problems with the project.	A manual describing the factors to consider in configuring a computer so as to achieve performance specifications.
Tacit	Knowledge of the major factors to consider when deciding whether to buy a company's stock.	A human relations manager's knowledge of factors to consider in motivating an employee in a particular company.	A technician's knowledge of symptoms to look for in trying to repair a faulty television set.
Procedural			
Explicit	A book describing steps to take in deciding whether to buy a company's stock.	A company document identifying the sequence of actions a consultant team's manager should take when requesting senior management to replace a team member having problems with the project.	A manual describing how to change the operating system setting on a computer so as to achieve desired performance changes.
Tacit	Basic knowledge of the steps to take in deciding whether to buy a company's stock.	A human relations manager's knowledge of steps to take in motivating an employee in a particular company.	A technician's knowledge of the sequence of steps to perform in repairing a television set.

lies in the depth of their expertise when compared to others from their own domains. For example, a highly skilled bus driver has greater abilities than a novice driver, just as an expert brain surgeon has greater skills than a surgical intern. Prior empirical research on expertise indicates the importance of knowledge management: "It takes time to become an expert. Even the most gifted performers need a minimum of ten years of intense training before they win international competitions" (Ericsson et al. 2007, p. 18).

Expertise can be classified into three distinct categories. Expert systems have had varying degrees of success when representing expertise from each of these categories. These categories, discussed in the following subsections, are (1) associational (black box), (2) motor skills, and (3) theoretical (deep) expertise.

Associational Expertise

In most fields, it is usually desirable that experts have a detailed understanding of the underlying theory within that field. But is this absolutely necessary? What about the television repair technician considered an expert repairman but who does not understand all of the complex internal workings of a transistor or a picture tube? He can associate the observations of the performance of the device to specific causes purely based on his experience. This individual may have expert-level **associational understandings** of these devices and may be able to fix almost any problem encountered. However, if he encounters a new, previously unseen problem, he may not know how to proceed because he does not understand the inner workings of the device.

Motor Skills Expertise

Motor skill expertise is predominantly physical rather than cognitive; therefore, knowledge-based systems cannot easily emulate this type of expertise. Humans improve these skills by repeated and coached practice. While some people have greater abilities for these types of skills than others, real learning and expertise result from persistent guided practice. For example, consider the tasks of riding a bicycle, hitting a baseball, and downhill snow skiing. When you observe experts performing these activities, you notice that their reactions seem spontaneous and automatic. These reactions result from the experts' continual and persistent and coached practice. For example, when a skilled baseball player bats, he instinctively reacts to a curveball, adjusting his swing to connect with the ball. This appropriate reaction results from encountering thousands of curveballs over many years and the coaches' recommendations on how to hit the ball in a particular situation. A novice batter might recognize a curveball being thrown, but due to a lack of practice reacts more slowly and consequently may strike out.

These processes do not involve conscious thinking per se. The batter merely reacts instinctively and almost instantaneously to the inputs. In fact, many coaches maintain that thinking in such situations degrades performance. Of course, some cognitive activity is necessary—the batter must follow the track of the ball, recognize its motion (curve, changeup, etc.), and make a decision on what to do (swing, let it go, etc.). The issue, however, is that the result of the decision-making is manifested in very quick physical actions and not in carefully pondered statements.

Theoretical (Deep) Expertise

Finding a solution to a technical problem often requires going beyond a superficial understanding of the domain. We must apply creative ingenuity—ingenuity that is based on our theoretical knowledge of the domain. This type of knowledge allows experts to solve problems that have not been seen before and, therefore, cannot be solved via associational expertise.

Such deeper, more theoretical knowledge is acquired through formal training and hands-on problem-solving. Typically, engineers and scientists who have many years of formal training possess this type of knowledge. Box 2.1 illustrates **deep theoretical knowledge**.

Box 2.1 Deep Theoretical Knowledge Enables Competitive Advantage

During the 1980s, two firms were involved in competition for a long-term (multiple decades) and large (multibillion dollar) government contract for tactical missiles. Neither company had a significant performance advantage over the other.

A scientist at one of the firms, who was not a member of the project team, broke the stalemate. He had deep expertise in developing missiles due to over 20 years of experience in this area. He was well regarded as a technical expert, and when he called a meeting of the major participants in the project they all came. For several hours, he enchanted them with a comprehensive description of design changes that he had identified within a single week of committed effort. Making no use of any kind of notes, he guided them through the reconfiguration of the entire missile. To implement the extensive changes he suggested in hardware, wiring, and software, 400 individuals would need to work full-time for a year and a half. However, the expert's audience was convinced that the redesign would produce tremendous competitive advantage. His proposal led to a frenzy of activity and enabled his firm to win the contract. More than 20 years later, in 2004, the redesign that this individual with deep expertise had created was still producing benefits.

Source: Compiled from Leonard and Swap (2004)

Some Concluding Remarks on the Types of Knowledge

In addition to the above types of knowledge, some other classifications also deserve mention. One of these classifications views knowledge as either simple or complex. Whereas **simple knowledge** focuses on one basic area, **complex knowledge** draws upon multiple distinct areas of expertise. Another classification focuses on the role of knowledge within organizations. It divides knowledge into: **support knowledge**, which relates to organizational infrastructure and facilitates day-to-day operations; **tactical knowledge**, which pertains to the short-term positioning of the organization relative to its markets, competitors, and suppliers; and **strategic knowledge**, which pertains to the long-term positioning of the organization in terms of its corporate vision and strategies for achieving that vision.

Based in part on the above types of knowledge, a number of characteristics of knowledge can be identified. One such characteristic is explicitness of knowledge, which reflects the extent to which knowledge exists in an explicit form so that it can be stored and transferred to others. As a characteristic of knowledge, explicitness indicates that rather than simply classifying knowledge as either explicit or tacit, it may be more appropriate to view explicitness as a continuous scale. Explicit and tacit kinds of knowledge are at the two ends of the continuum, with explicit knowledge being high in explicitness and tacit knowledge being low in this regard. Any specific knowledge would then be somewhere along this continuum of explicitness.

Specific knowledge is directly related to the concept of knowledge specificity (Choudhury and Sampler 1997). A high level of knowledge specificity implies that the knowledge can be acquired and/or effectively used only by individuals possessing certain prior knowledge (Jensen and Meckling 1996). Knowledge specificity implies that the knowledge is possessed by a very limited number of individuals and is expensive to transfer (Choudhury and Sampler 1997). Taking a step further, technically specific and contextually specific knowledge lead us to break down knowledge specificity into **contextual knowledge specificity** and **technical knowledge specificity**. Of course, contextually specific knowledge and technically specific knowledge are high in contextual knowledge specificity and technical knowledge specificity, respectively (Sabherwal et al. 2023).

In addition, the distinction between simple and complex knowledge may be represented using complexity as a knowledge attribute. Similarly, the organizational role of knowledge reflects the distinction among support, tactical, and strategic knowledge.

An organization does not have only one of the above types of knowledge. Instead, in any given organization, multiple different types of knowledge exist together. In Box 2.2, we provide an example of how different types of knowledge exist together within an organization.

Box 2.2 Different Types of Knowledge at Hill and Knowlton

Founded in 1927, Hill and Knowlton is a leading international communications consultancy headquartered in New York, with 74 offices in 41 countries and an extensive associate network. It is part of WPP Group Plc, which is one of the world's largest communications services groups and provides services to local, multinational, and global clients. Among other things, the company is hired by organizations to manage their product launches, media relations, and communication during crises.

In the late 1990s, turnover rates in certain practices in public relations, such as those related to technology, increased from 15 percent to over 30 percent. The loss of talented individuals led to a leakage of important knowledge as well as information about specific projects. In 1988, in response to concerns by several key clients of the company, the Worldwide Advisory Group (a summit of the company's 200 managers) considered ways of addressing this issue of knowledge leakage. This group identified three broad types of knowledge that were important to the company. One of these was the company's internal knowledge about its own products and services. The second was external knowledge, such as economic forecasts and other related research by outside experts. The third type of knowledge related to clients including budgets, templates, and account activity.

Subsequently, Ted Graham was appointed as Hill and Knowlton's worldwide director of knowledge management. He concluded that while the company was performing well in terms of capturing the structured knowledge such as case studies, proposals, and staff bios, it was not doing so well in capturing unstructured knowledge such as knowledge embedded in speeches, e-mail messages, and other information that had not been classified in any fashion. To deal with this problematic situation, the advisory group decided to replace the current global Intranet with "hK.net," a "Web-based virtual workspace" serving the company's offices across the world. Based on Intraspect Software Inc.'s Salsa application and a password-protected website, hK.net was designed to enable both the employees and clients to access internal and external repositories of information and knowledge such as news about the company and the industry, client-related budget information and e-mail archives, staff biographies, presentations, spreadsheets, case studies, pictures, video clips, conference notes, research reports, and so on. Clients as well as Hill and Knowlton executives appreciated hK.net because it reduced the time spent in educating new members of project teams as well as training new employees.

Sources: Compiled from Hill and Knowlton Strategies (n.d.); Meister and Mark (2004)

Locations of Knowledge

Knowledge resides in several different locations or reservoirs, which are summarized in Figure 2.5. They include people, including individuals and groups; artifacts, including practices, technologies, and repositories; and organizational entities, including organizational units, organizations, and interorganizational networks. These locations of knowledge are discussed in the rest of this section.

Knowledge in People

A considerable component of knowledge is stored in people. This relates to the arguments some scholars make about all learning being inherently inside human minds. For example, Simon (1991, p. 125) remarks:

> All learning takes place inside individual human heads; an organization learns in only two ways: (a) by the learning of its members, or (b) by ingesting new members who have knowledge the organization didn't previously have.

Knowledge could reside among people, either at the individual level or within a group or a collection of people (Felin and Hesterly 2007; Sabherwal et al. 2023). Some knowledge is stored in *individuals* within organizations. For instance, in professional service firms, such as consulting or law firms, considerable knowledge resides within the

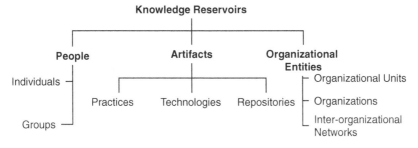

Figure 2.5 The Reservoirs of Knowledge

minds of individual members of the firm (Argote and Ingram 2000; Felin and Hesterly 2007). The knowledge stored in individuals is the reason several companies continually seek ways to retain knowledge that might be lost because of individuals retiring or otherwise leaving the organization.

In addition, considerable knowledge resides within *groups* because of the relationships among the members of the group (Felin and Hesterly 2007). When three individuals have worked together for a long time, they instinctively know each other's strengths and weaknesses, understand the other's approach, and recognize aspects that need to be communicated and those that could be taken for granted (Skyrme 2000). Consequently, groups form beliefs about what works well and what does not, and this knowledge is over and above the knowledge residing in each individual member. In other words, the collective knowledge is synergistic—greater than the sum of their individual knowledge. Communities of practice that first develop as individuals interact frequently with each other (physically or virtually) to discuss topics of mutual interest, and they illustrate such embedding of knowledge within groups.

Knowledge in Artifacts

Over time, a significant amount of knowledge is stored in organizational artifacts as well. Some knowledge is stored in *practices*, organizational routines, or sequential patterns of interaction. In this case, knowledge is embedded in procedures, rules, and norms that are developed through experience over time and guide future behavior (Levitt and March 1988). For example, fast-food franchises often store knowledge about how to produce high-quality products in routines (Argote and Ingram 2000).

Considerable knowledge is also often stored in *technologies* and systems. As discussed earlier in this chapter, in addition to storing data, information technologies and computer-based information systems can store knowledge about relationships. For example, a computerized materials requirement planning system contains considerable knowledge about relationships among demand patterns, lead times for orders, and reorder quantities.

Knowledge repositories represent a third way of storing knowledge in artifacts. Knowledge repositories could either be paper-based, such as books, papers, and other documents, or electronic. An example of a paper-based repository is a consultant's set of notes to herself about the kind of things the client might focus on more, when examining the proposals submitted by the consultant firm and its competitors. On the other hand, a website containing answers to frequently asked questions (FAQs) about a product represents an electronic knowledge repository.

Knowledge in Organizational Entities

Knowledge is also stored within organizational entities. These entities can be considered at three levels: organizational units (parts of the organization), an entire organization, and in interorganizational relationships (such as the relationship between an organization and its customers).

Within an *organizational unit*, such as a department or an office, knowledge is stored partly in the relationships among the members of the units. In other words, the organizational unit represents a formal grouping of individuals, who come together not because of common interests but rather because of organizational structuring. Over time, as individuals occupying certain roles in an organizational unit depart and are replaced by others, the incumbents inherit some, but not all, of the knowledge developed by their predecessors. This knowledge may have been acquired through the systems, practices, and relationships within that unit. Moreover, contextually specific knowledge is more likely to be related to the specific organizational unit.

An *organization* such as a business unit or a corporation, also stores certain knowledge, especially contextually specific knowledge. The norms, values, practices, and culture within the organization, and across its organizational units, contain knowledge that is not stored within the mind of any one individual. The way in which the organization responds to environmental events is dependent, therefore, not only upon the knowledge stored in individuals and organizational units but also in the overall organizational knowledge that has developed through positive and negative experiences over time.

Finally, knowledge is also stored in *interorganizational relationships.* As organizations establish and consolidate relationships with customers and suppliers, they draw upon knowledge embedded in those relationships. Customers who use the focal organization's products, and suppliers who provide the basic components from which the products are made, often have considerable knowledge about the strengths and weaknesses of those products. Consequently, organizations often learn from their customers' experience with products about how these can be improved. They can also learn about new products that might be appealing to customers.

Knowledge in Communities of Practice

A community of practice is an organic and self-organized group of individuals who are dispersed geographically or organizationally but communicate regularly to discuss issues of mutual interest (Lave and Wenger 1991). Lave and Wegner argue that learning is not a process solely within an individual's mind but is instead a process that occurs through social interactions. This process of learning is facilitated by discussions with colleagues and mentors or by observing how others apply the knowledge and then trying it themselves (Kimble et al. 2008). There are many examples of communities of practice in real life, such as the community of researchers at a scientific conference and investors at forums related to the stock market. The members of a community of practice do not need to be co-located but they necessarily interact to learn, share, and communicate their tacit and explicit knowledge about shared interests.

Communities of practice have become associated with finding, sharing, transferring, and archiving knowledge, as well as making explicit or tacit knowledge. Therefore, communities of practice have significant value because they contain rare sources of tacit knowledge.

Knowledge Locations and Forms of Intellectual Capital

An organization's intellectual capital refers to the sum of all its knowledge resources, which may be within or outside the organization (Stewart 1997; Subramaniam and Youndt 2005; Youndt et al. 2004). **Intellectual capital** has been viewed as being of different types in terms of where the knowledge resides. Intellectual capital has recently been classified into three types (Hsu and Sabherwal 2011; Subramaniam and Youndt 2005; Youndt et al. 2004): *human capital*, or the knowledge, skills, and capabilities possessed by individual employees; *organizational capital*, or the institutionalized knowledge and codified experience residing in databases, manuals, culture, systems, structures, and processes; and *social capital*, or the knowledge embedded in relationships and interactions among individuals. These three types of intellectual capital relate directly to the locations discussed above: human capital relates to knowledge in people, structural capital relates to knowledge in artifacts, and organizational capital relates to knowledge in organizational entities.

Summary

In this chapter, we have explained the nature of knowledge in considerable detail. Knowledge is distinguished from data and information; highlighting that knowledge should best be considered as fundamentally different from data and information rather than considering data, information, and knowledge as being part of a hierarchy. We defined knowledge in an area as *justified beliefs about relationships among concepts relevant to that particular area*. Furthermore, we examined subjective and objective perspectives for viewing knowledge, including perspectives that consider knowledge as a state of mind, as practice, as an object, as access to information, and as a capability. We then distinguished between procedural and declarative knowledge, between tacit and explicit knowledge, and between general and specific knowledge. Some other ways of classifying knowledge were also described. Based on the various classifications of knowledge, we introduced knowledge characteristics such as tacitness, specificity, and so on. This chapter also described the possible locations of knowledge including people, artifacts, and organizational entities, and related these locations to different types of intellectual capital. The next chapter builds on this one by explaining knowledge management and describing the various aspects of KM infrastructure.

Review

1 How do the terms data and knowledge differ? Describe each term with the help of a similar example, elucidating the difference between the two.
2 Information contains data but not all data are information. Justify this statement.
3 Explain why the same set of data can be considered as useful information by some and useless by others. Further, could this useful information be termed as knowledge? Why?
4 Describe the ways in which knowledge differs from data and information. Justify your answer with a relevant diagram.
5 Explain the importance of knowledge in creation and utilization of information.
6 How does the subjective view of knowledge differ from the objective view? Explain how knowledge can be viewed as a state of mind, as a practice, as objects, as access to information, and as capability.
7 What is the difference between knowledge characterized as know what and know-how? In the above situations, how would you classify the knowledge a computer programmer has?
8 Does a player in a card game use tacit or explicit knowledge? Why? Define and explain the difference between the two.
9 What is general knowledge? How does it differ from specific knowledge? Describe the types of specific knowledge with suitable examples.

10 What is expertise? Distinguish among the three types of expertise.

11 What is a community of practice? What role does it play in knowledge management?

12 Contrast the differences between knowledge in people and knowledge in artifacts. Describe the various repositories of knowledge within organizational entities.

13 What is intellectual capital? What are the three types of intellectual capital, and how do they relate to different knowledge locations?

Application Exercises

1 Consider five decisions you have made today. (They could be simple things like taking a turn while driving or even choosing a soda at a convenience store.) In each case determine the data, information, and/or knowledge that were involved in the decision. Now consider how those decisions would have been influenced by the lack of pre-existing data, information, or knowledge.

2 You have recently invented a new product. Collect demographic data from a sample population and determine how you would use this data and convert it into information for marketing the product. Give an example about knowledge that may be useful in converting the data into information.

3 Interview a manager in a manufacturing organization and one in a services-based organization. Determine the contrasting views of knowledge between the two due to the nature of their businesses.

4 Determine the various locations of knowledge within your organization (or that of a friend/family member). Classify them appropriately. Now speculate on the negative effects of not having one or more of those knowledge repositories and accordingly determine which repository is the most critical to the organization. Which is the least?

5 Determine the various types of knowledge you used to read this chapter. You should be able to state at least one of each type.

6 Interview organizations in your area to determine the explicit and tacit knowledge within the organization. Rank the explicit knowledge on the basis of its codifiability and teachability. Further, suggest ways in which the tacit knowledge could be made explicit.

7 You are considering buying a new 2023 Ford Mustang. Gather tacit knowledge and explicit knowledge on buying cars from various resources: for example, Ford's website (www.ford.com). List your findings and explain what source of knowledge is important for your choice.

8 Suppose you desperately need technical advice on an Apple Inc. product. You have several options. Four of them are: (a) call Apple's technical support; (b) use Apple's online customer support; (c) use Apple's online discussion groups; and (d) visit the genius bar at the nearest Apple store. Define your preferred option and briefly explain your choice with the concepts of accessibility to knowledge reservoir.

9 Wal-Mart Stores, Inc. (www.walmart.com) is said to be one of the leading employers of older workers and consider seniors vital to its unique corporate culture. Store managers are encouraged to recruit from senior citizen groups, local AARP chapters, and churches. Analyze Wal-Mart's above strategy in terms of knowledge management.

10 Use any organization with which you are familiar to answer this question. This organization could be one where you currently work or one where you have

previously worked. For this organization, describe one example of knowledge that would be classified as structural capital, one example of knowledge that would be classified as organizational capital, and one example of knowledge that would be classified as social capital.

References

Alavi, M., and Leidner, D. 2001. Knowledge management and knowledge management systems: Conceptual foundations and research issues. *MIS Quarterly*, 25(1), 107.

Argote, L., and Ingram, P. 2000. Knowledge transfer: Basis for competitive advantage in firms. *Organizational Behavior and Human Decision Processes*, 82(1) (May), 150–169.

Boland, R.J., and Tenkasi, R.V. 1995. Perspective making and perspective taking in communities of knowing. *Organization Science*, 6(4), 350–372.

Choudhury, V., and Sampler, J. 1997. Information specificity and environmental scanning: An economic perspective. *MIS Quarterly*, 21(1), 25–53.

Ericsson, K.A., Prietula, M.J., and Cokely, E.T. 2007. The making of an expert. *Harvard Business Review* (July–August), 114–121.

Felin, T., and Hesterly, W.S. 2007. The knowledge-based view, nested heterogeneity, and new value creation: Philosophical considerations on the locus of knowledge. *Academy of Management Review*, 32(1), 195–218.

Hayek, F.A. 1945. The use of knowledge in society. *American Economic Review*, XXXV(4) (September), 519–530.

Hill and Knowlton Strategies. n.d. https://www.hkstrategies.com.

Hsu, I.-C., and Sabherwal, R. 2011. From intellectual capital to firm performance: The mediating role of knowledge management capabilities, *IEEE Transactions on Engineering Management*, 58 (4) (November), 626–642.

Jensen, M.C., and Meckling, W.H. 1996. Specific and general knowledge, and organizational structure. In *Knowledge management & organizational design*, ed. P.S. Myers, 17–38. Newton, MA: Butterworth-Heinemann.

Kimble, C., Hildreth, P., and Bourdon, I. 2008. *Communities of practice: Creating learning environments for educators*. Information Age Publishing.

Kogut, B., and Zander, U. 1992. Knowledge of the firm, combinative capabilities and the replication of technology. *Organization Science*, 3(3), 383–397.

Lave, J., and Wenger, E. 1991. *Situated learning: Legitimate peripheral participation*. Cambridge, England & New York: Cambridge University Press.

Leonard, D., and Swap, W. 2004. Deep smarts. *Harvard Business Review*, 82(9) (September), 88–97.

Levitt, B., and March, J.G. 1988. Organizational learning. *Annual Review of Sociology*, 14, 319–340.

Machlup, F. 1980. *Knowledge: Its creation, distribution and economic significance*, vol. 1. Princeton, NJ: Princeton University Press.

Meister, D., and Mark, K. 2004. *Hill & Knowlton: Knowledge management*. Case #9B04E003. London, ONT: Ivey Publishing.

Nonaka, I. 1994. A dynamic theory of organizational knowledge creation. *Organization Science*, 5(1), 14–37.

Nonaka, I., and Takeuchi, H. 1995. *The knowledge creating company*. New York: Oxford University Press.

O'Reilly, C.A., and Pondy, L. 1979. Organizational communication. In *Organizational behavior*, ed. S. Kerr, 119–150. Columbus, OH: John Wiley & Sons.

Polanyi, M. 1966. *The tacit dimension*. London: Routledge and Keoan.

Sabherwal, R., and Becerra-Fernandez, I. 2005. Integrating specific knowledge: Insights from Kennedy Space Center. *IEEE Transactions on Engineering Management*, 52(3).

Sabherwal, R., Steelman, Z., and Becerra-Fernandez, I. 2023. Knowledge management mechanisms and common knowledge impacts on the value of knowledge at individual and organizational levels. *International Journal of Information Management*, 72 (October) (102660).

Schultze, U. 1999. Investigating the contradictions in knowledge management. In *Information systems: Current issues and future changes*, ed. T.J. Larsen, L. Levine, and J.I. De Gross, 155–174. Laxenberg: International Federation for Information Processing.

Simon, H.A. 1991. Bounded rationality and organizational learning. *Organization Science*, 2(1), 125–134.

Singley, M., and Anderson, J. 1989. *The transfer of cognitive skill*. Cambridge, MA: Harvard University Press.

Skyrme, D.J. 2000. Developing a knowledge strategy: From management to leadership. In *Knowledge management: Classic and contemporary works*, ed. D. Morey, M. Maybury, and B. Thuraisingham, 61–84. Cambridge, MA: The MIT Press.

Stewart, T.A. 1997. *Intellectual capital*. New York: Doubleday-Currency.

Subramaniam, M., and Youndt, M.A. 2005. The influence of intellectual capital on the types of innovative capabilities. *Academy of Management Journal*, 48(3), 450–463.

Tsoukas, H. 1996. The firm as a distributed knowledge system: A constructionist approach. *Strategic Management Journal*, 17 (Winter), 11–25.

Venzin, M., von Krogh, G., and Roos, J. 1998. Future research into knowledge management. In *Knowing in firms: Understanding, managing and measuring knowledge*, ed. G. von Krogh, J. Roos, and D. Kleine. Thousand Oaks, CA: Sage Publications.

Wiig, K. 1999. Introducing knowledge management into the enterprise. In *Knowledge management handbook*, ed. J. Liebowitz, 31–41. Boca Raton, FL: CRC Press.

Youndt, M.A., Subramaniam, M., and Snell, S.A. 2004. Intellectual capital profiles: An examination of investments and returns. *Journal of Management Studies*, 41(2), 335–361.

3 Knowledge Management Foundations

Infrastructure, Mechanisms, and Technologies

In Chapter 2, we examined the nature of knowledge as well as its various forms and locations. This chapter explains in greater detail the concept of knowledge management. It also describes knowledge management solutions, which refer to the variety of ways in which knowledge management can be facilitated. **KM solutions** include two components: KM processes and KM systems. KM solutions depend on three foundations: KM mechanisms, KM technologies, and KM infrastructure. This chapter describes these three **KM foundations**. It is followed by a discussion of KM solutions— that is, KM processes and KM systems—in Chapter 4.

In this chapter we first discuss knowledge management, and then we describe the five components of KM solutions. We subsequently describe and illustrate KM mechanisms, KM technologies, and KM infrastructure, followed by a brief discussion of the management of these KM foundations and some concluding remarks.

Knowledge Management

Managing any resource may be defined as doing what is necessary to get the most out of that resource. Therefore, at a very simple level, knowledge management may be defined as *doing what is needed to get the most out of knowledge resources*. Let us now consider this simple definition in some detail by providing a few elaborations.

First, it is important to stress that this definition can be applied at the individual as well as organizational levels. Depending on the level, knowledge resources might be those resources that are relevant to the decisions, goals, and strategies of an individual or an organization. The "organization" may be a corporation, a firm, a field office of a firm, a department within a corporation or firm, and so forth. Moreover, the term knowledge resources refers not only to the knowledge currently possessed by the individual or the organization but also to the knowledge that can potentially be obtained (at some cost, if necessary) from other individuals or organizations.

Second, "get the most" reflects the impacts of knowledge management on the goal achievement of the individual or the organization. Considering the impact knowledge can have on individuals and organizations (as summarized in Chapter 1 and to be discussed in greater detail in Chapter 4), the objective of knowledge management is to enhance the extent to which knowledge facilitates the achievement of individual or organizational goals. Furthermore, a cost/benefit assumption is implicit here. In other words, the objective is to enhance the impact of knowledge in a cost-effective fashion, such that the benefits of knowledge management exceed the costs of doing so.

DOI: 10.4324/9781003364375-4

Finally, "the things needed" refers to a variety of possible activities involved in knowledge management. These activities are broadly intended to: (a) discover new knowledge, (b) capture existing knowledge, (c) share knowledge with others, or (d) apply knowledge.

Based on these elaborations, a more detailed definition of knowledge management can now be offered.

> Knowledge management can be defined as performing the activities involved in discovering, capturing, sharing, and applying knowledge so as to enhance, in a cost-effective fashion, the impact of knowledge on the unit's goal achievement.

Another important emergent technology related to knowledge management—**business intelligence (BI)**—is sometimes used interchangeably with KM. Although KM and BI are somewhat interrelated, they are quite distinct. BI focuses on providing decision makers with valuable information and knowledge by utilizing a variety of sources of data and structured and unstructured information (Sabherwal 2007, 2008), via the discovery of the relationships that may exist between these sources of data and information.

Unlike KM, which starts with information and knowledge as inputs, BI begins with data and information as inputs. KM directly results in the discovery of new knowledge, the conversion of knowledge from one form to another (i.e., from tacit to explicit or vice versa), the sharing of knowledge, or the application of knowledge while making a decision. In contrast, BI directly results in information (which is presented in a friendly fashion, such as through dashboards) and newly created knowledge or insights obtained by revealing previously unknown connections, relationships, or patterns within data and information. Thus, KM is by and large not directly concerned with data (with the exception of knowledge discovery from data and information using techniques such as data mining, which represents an area of overlap between KM and BI). In contrast, data are critical to BI, which often depends on activities like data warehousing and data mining. However, the results of BI can be, and often are, useful inputs to KM.

KM incorporates **knowledge capture**, **sharing**, and **application** in addition to **discovery**. On the other hand, BI focuses on data access, analysis, and presentation. The connection between BI and knowledge is limited to **knowledge creation** (by discovering patterns based on existing explicit data and information). Even in this respect, BI focuses directly on discovery of explicit knowledge whereas KM concerns discovery of both tacit and explicit knowledge. In other words, only explicit knowledge can directly result from BI, whereas KM is concerned with activities that produce both explicit and tacit knowledge.

Finally, KM involves using both social aspects as well as information technology, and is sometimes viewed as being more social than technical. On the other hand, BI is primarily technical in nature, and does not incorporate social mechanisms related to knowledge discovery, such as meetings and **brainstorming retreats**.

The above distinctions between knowledge management and business intelligence are summarized in Table 3.1.

Knowledge Management Solutions and Foundations

Knowledge management depends on two broad aspects: KM solutions, which are specific in nature; and KM foundations, which are broader and more long-term. **KM solutions** refer to the ways in which specific aspects of KM (discovery, capture, sharing,

Table 3.1 A Comparison of Knowledge Management and Business Intelligence

	Knowledge Management	Business Intelligence
Intellectual Components	Primary: Knowledge (Explicit and Tacit)	Primary: Data
	Secondary: Information, Data	Secondary: Information, Explicit Knowledge
Processes	Knowledge Capture, Sharing, Application, and Discovery	Data Access, Analysis, and Presentation
Key components	Social Mechanisms and Information Technology	Mainly Information Technologies

and application of knowledge) can be accomplished. KM solutions include KM processes and KM systems. **KM foundations** are the broad organizational aspects that support KM in the short and long term. They include KM infrastructure, KM mechanisms, and KM technologies. Thus, KM solutions depend on KM foundations, as shown in Figure 3.1. Next, we briefly explain the three components of KM foundations and the two components of KM solutions.

KM infrastructure reflects the long-term foundation for knowledge management. In an organizational context, KM infrastructure includes five major components (e.g., organization culture and the organization's information technology infrastructure).

KM mechanisms are organizational or structural means used to promote knowledge management. They may (or may not) involve the use of information technology, but they do involve some kind of organizational arrangement or social or structural means of facilitating KM. They depend on KM infrastructure and facilitate KM systems.

KM technologies are information technologies that can be used to facilitate knowledge management. Thus, KM technologies are intrinsically no different from information technologies, but they focus on knowledge management rather than information

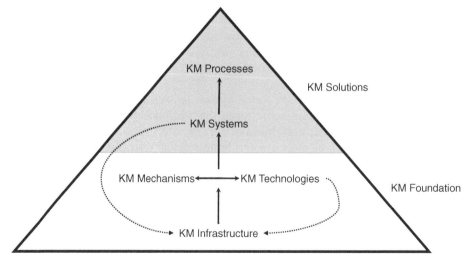

Figure 3.1 An Overview of Knowledge Management Solutions and Foundation

processing. KM technologies also support KM systems and benefit from the KM infrastructure, especially the information technology infrastructure.

KM processes are the broad processes that help in discovering, capturing, sharing, and applying knowledge. Box 3.1 illustrates the use of one of these processes—knowledge sharing—at a health-care company. These four KM processes are supported by KM systems and seven important types of KM subprocesses (e.g., exchange).

Box 3.1 Performance Improvement in Healthcare through Knowledge Sharing

To improve their development and submission of a capital plan to their budget holders, the operations administration department of a non-profit health care company used facilitated and peer-assisted work-sessions. In these work-sessions, peers shared and transferred relevant knowledge and experience with members of another team who were facing challenging issues. This approach helped the team to draw upon the experience of a diverse group of peers from across their regional parent organization.

The team consequently revised its plan such that it effectively addressed the latest shifts in patients' long-term care needs, while incorporating the key concerns of the company's decision makers. The end result was a revised capital plan that met the needs of the customers, providers, and budget holders. Moreover, participation in the process not only benefitted the team that needed assistance, but also the "visiting peers" that helped them.

Source: Compiled from Greenes Consulting (n.d.-a, n.d.-b)

KM systems are the integration of technologies and mechanisms that are developed to support the above four KM processes. KM processes and systems are described further in Chapter 4, and each of the four kinds of KM systems is then discussed in considerable detail in Part II of the book.

Thus, KM infrastructure, which is at the organizational level, supports KM mechanisms and technologies. KM mechanisms and technologies are used in KM systems, with each KM system utilizing a combination of multiple mechanisms and multiple technologies. Moreover, the same KM mechanism or technology could support multiple KM systems. KM systems enable KM processes, with a KM system focusing on one specific KM process. Therefore, KM processes and KM systems are specific solutions for KM needs whereas KM infrastructure, mechanisms, and technologies are broader: KM mechanisms and technologies support multiple KM solutions, and the KM infrastructure supports (through KM mechanisms and technologies) all KM solutions. However, over time, KM infrastructure itself benefits from KM mechanisms and technologies as well as KM processes, as shown by the curved arrows in Figure 3.1.

The remainder of this chapter describes the three components of the KM foundation—that is, KM infrastructure, mechanisms, and technologies—in further detail. The two aspects of KM solutions—KM processes and systems—are described in Chapter 4.

Knowledge Management Infrastructure

KM mechanisms and technologies rely on the KM infrastructure, which reflects the long-term foundation for knowledge management. In an organizational context, **KM**

infrastructure includes five major components: organization culture, organization structure, information technology infrastructure, common knowledge, and physical environment. These components are discussed in greater detail the next five sections.

Organization Culture

Organization culture reflects the norms and beliefs that guide the behavior of the organization's members. It is an important enabler of knowledge management in organizations. Indeed, a survey of KM practices in U.S. companies (Dyer and McDonough 2001) indicated that the four most important challenges in knowledge management are nontechnical in nature and include, in order of importance: (1) the organization's employees have no time for knowledge management; (2) the current organization culture does not encourage knowledge sharing; (3) inadequate understanding of knowledge management and its benefits to the company; and (4) inability to measure the financial benefits from knowledge management.

Though the second of the above challenges specifically mentions organization culture, the first and third challenges are also directly dependent on organization culture—a supporting organization culture helps motivate employees to understand the benefits of knowledge management and also to find time for knowledge management. Indeed, getting people to participate in knowledge sharing is considered the hardest part of KM. For example, individuals are usually reluctant to contribute knowledge to knowledge repositories, as illustrated by the following comment by one knowledge worker "If I share my knowledge, others may take advantage of that. Will they do the same for me?" (Standing and Benson 2000, p. 343). It is often believed that of the organizations trying to implement KM, less than 10 percent have succeeded in making it part of their culture (Koudsi 2000).

Attributes of an enabling organizational culture include understanding the value of KM practices, management support for KM at all levels, incentives that reward knowledge sharing, and encouragement of interaction for the creation and sharing of knowledge (Armbrecht et al. 2001). In contrast, cultures that stress individual performance and hoarding of information within units encourage limited employee interaction, and lack of an involved top management creates inhibited knowledge sharing and retention. Moreover, people are often afraid of asking others if they know the answer to a certain question, and especially if posting a question for the entire company to see, fear it might reveal their ignorance (Koudsi 2000).

A case study of a baby food manufacturer revealed that built-in competition within the corporate structure inhibited knowledge sharing practices that could have significantly increased revenues. The performance of front-line salespeople was evaluated comparing it to that of other salespeople. Because of this, a group of front-line salespeople found a market niche in selling baby food to aging adults who could no longer eat hard food, but they kept knowledge of their customer base to themselves and let only their successful sales figures reveal their find. Because the company's culture bred competition among employees and offered incentives based on a curve, the firm missed out not only on increased revenues across the organization but also through additional sales in that niche market and also on potential product development to better address the needs of this niche market (DeTienne and Jackson 2001).

In another case study, the CEO of a Web consulting company instituted several measures to enhance the use of the company's KM system (Koudsi 2000). He started publicly recognizing people who stood out as strong knowledge contributors. He also made usage of the KM system a part of everyone's job description. He even started paying employees to use this system. Each task on the KM system was assigned points. If a consultant placed his résumé in the system, he would receive one point. If a consultant created a project record, she would receive five points. The company's knowledge manager acted as judge, deciding if entries deserved points. The totals were tallied every three months, and the resulting score accounted for 10 percent of a consultant's quarterly bonus. Before these metrics were introduced in January 1999, only a third of the company's employees were rated as good or better in the usage of the KM system, but two months later, that usage had almost doubled (Koudsi 2000).

Providing appropriate incentives is one way of building a culture that supports knowledge sharing. Some companies (e.g., Shell Oil Company and Giant Eagle, Inc.) provide informal recognition for individuals sharing knowledge by mentioning their accomplishments in a newsletter, an e-mail, or during a meeting. Halliburton Company uses a "most valuable player" program, acknowledging each month the person who provides the best idea. The prestigious consulting firm Bain & Company provides its employees with only two annual awards, and one of them is for the employee that best pursued the goals of knowledge management and innovation. Companies often incorporate knowledge sharing within employees' formal job reviews; some companies make employees' promotions and bonuses subject to their sharing knowledge, while some other companies use it as one factor in the overall evaluation process (Paul 2003). Box 3.2 illustrates the use of incentives for knowledge sharing at Hill & Knowlton, Inc.

Box 3.2 Incentives for Knowledge Sharing at Hill and Knowlton

Hill and Knowlton, which was founded in 1927, is a leading international communications consultancy headquartered in New York with 74 offices in 41 countries and an extensive associate network. It is part of one of the world's largest communications services groups (WPP), and provides services to local, multinational, and global clients. The company is hired by organizations to manage their product launches, media relations, and communication during crises.

Hill and Knowlton offered "Beenz," which was a system of micropayments, each worth US$0.001, to encourage employees to contribute case studies and bios. Employees could redeem Beenz online for books and other items. For example, an employee could win a weekend for two in a Caribbean villa for 110,000 Beenz. After the company offering Beenz shut down on August 17, 2001, some offices started rewarding employees through gift certificates and pizza parties.

Hill and Knowlton also offered bonuses to individuals managing departments that were active in knowledge sharing. This was based on two criteria: whether the department made knowledge contributions and whether the department extracted and used knowledge from another department. Bonuses varied from one year to the next.

Hill and Knowlton also established a "best-seller" list to publicize the contributions that were most frequently accessed. Users were encouraged to discuss their rank on the best-seller list during conversations about advancement opportunities.

Sources: Compiled from Hill and Knowlton Strategies (n.d.); Meister and Mark (2004)

Organization Structure

Knowledge management also depends to a considerable extent on the **organization structure**. Several aspects of organization structure are relevant. First, the **hierarchical structure** of the organization affects the people with whom each individual frequently interacts, and to or from whom he is consequently likely to transfer knowledge. Traditional reporting relationships influence the flow of data and information as well as the nature of groups who make decisions together, and consequently affect the sharing and creation of knowledge. By decentralizing or flattening their organization structures, companies often seek to eliminate organizational layers, thereby placing more responsibility with each individual and increasing the size of groups reporting to each individual. Consequently, knowledge sharing is likely to occur with a larger group of individuals in more decentralized organizations. In addition, matrix structures and an emphasis on "leadership" rather than on "management" also facilitates greater knowledge sharing primarily by cutting across traditional departmental boundaries.

Second, organization structures can facilitate knowledge management through **communities of practice** (see Chapter 2). For example, a tech-club at DaimlerChrysler included a group of engineers who didn't work in the same unit but met regularly, on their own initiative, to discuss problems related to their area of expertise. Similarly, at Xerox Corporation, a strategic community of IT professionals, involving frequent informal interactions among them, promotes knowledge sharing (Storck and Hill 2000). Box 3.3 further illustrates communities of practice, using the example of Montgomery Watson Harza.

Box 3.3 Communities of Practice at Montgomery Watson Harza

Montgomery Watson Harza (MWH) is a global engineering firm with over 3,600 specialists spread across about 200 offices in 38 countries. From 1995 to 1999, its KM efforts had focused primarily on information technologies and had encountered problems.

In 1999, it adopted a new KM approach characterized as "People First, Technology as Support." This approach led to a new name being given to the KM strategy: "KnowledgeNet." KnowledgeNet relied on formal and informal communities of practice, which would be supported by establishing a global Intranet, called KNet. Each formal community—called a Knowledge Center and partially funded by management—also established its theme as well as specific business objectives. Each informal community, called a Knowledge Base, was locally driven and easier to set up. Whereas Knowledge Centers were created from the top down to facilitate strategic initiatives, Knowledge Bases were organic and started by practitioners themselves. Knowledge Bases could also be networked together to represent a larger theme. Moreover, if a Knowledge Base became strategic to the entire company, it could be converted into a Knowledge Center.

The implementation of this new strategy began in 2000. By early 2004, MWH had three Knowledge Centers (a fourth center was being established) and 120 Knowledge Bases. MWH had about 6,000 employees at that time, and about 1,600 of them belonged to one of these formal or informal communities. The new KM strategy based on communities of practice received positive responses from top management, other employees, and clients. Top management perceived KnowledgeNet as having provided the company with a competitive advantage in terms of obtaining client accounts.

Sources: Compiled from MWH (n.d.); Parise et al. (2004)

Communities of practice provide access to a larger group of individuals than possible within traditional departmental boundaries. Consequently, there are more numerous potential helpers, and this increases the probability that at least one of them will provide useful knowledge. Communities of practice also provide access to external knowledge sources. An organization's external stakeholders—for example, customers, suppliers, and partners—provide a far greater knowledge reservoir than the organization itself (Choo 1998). For instance, relationships with university researchers can help new biotechnology firms to maintain their innovativeness.

Although communities of practice are usually not part of a company's formal organization structure, company executives can facilitate them in several ways. For example, they can legitimize them through support for participation in them. Moreover, they can enhance the perceived value of participation in communities of practice by seeking advice from them. They can also help communities of practice by providing them with resources, such as money or connections to external experts and access to information technology that supports their virtual meetings and knowledge sharing activities. Communities of practice benefit considerably from other emergent information technologies, including blogs and social networking technologies.

Third, organization structures can facilitate knowledge management through *specialized structures and roles* that specifically support knowledge management. Three possibilities deserve special mention. First, some organizations appoint an individual to the position of Chief Knowledge Officer and make this individual responsible for the organization's KM efforts. Second, some organizations establish a separate department for knowledge management, which is often headed by the Chief Knowledge Officer. Finally, two traditional KM units—the R&D department and the corporate library—also facilitate knowledge management, although they differ in focus. Whereas the R&D department supports management of knowledge about the latest, or future, developments, the corporate library supports business units by facilitating knowledge sharing activities and serving as a repository of historical information about the organization, its industry, and competitive environment. The leadership of the KM function is further examined in Chapter 12.

Information Technology Infrastructure

Knowledge management is also facilitated by the organization's **information technology (IT) infrastructure**. Although certain information technologies and systems are directly developed to pursue knowledge management, the organization's overall information technology infrastructure, developed to support the organization's information systems needs, also facilitates knowledge management. The information technology infrastructure includes data processing, storage, and communication technologies and systems. It comprises the entire spectrum of the organization's information systems, including transaction processing systems and management information systems. It consists of **databases (DB)** and **data warehouses**, as well as enterprise resource planning systems. One possible way of systematically viewing the IT infrastructure is to consider the capabilities it provides in four important aspects: *reach, depth, richness*, and *aggregation* (Daft and Lengel 1986; Evans and Wurster 1999).

Reach pertains to access and connection and the efficiency of such access. Within the context of a network, reach reflects the number and geographical locations of the nodes that can be efficiently accessed. Keen (1991) also uses the term reach to refer to the locations an IT platform is capable of linking, with the ideal being able to connect to "anyone, anywhere." Much of the power of the **Internet** is attributed to its reach and the fact that most people can access it quite inexpensively. Reach is enhanced not just by advances in hardware but also by progress in software. For instance, standardization of cross-firm communication standards, and languages such as XML, make it easier for firms to communicate with a wider array of trading partners, including those with whom they do not have long-term relationships.

Depth, in contrast, focuses on the detail and amount of information that can be effectively communicated over a medium. This dimension closely corresponds to the aspects of bandwidth and customization included by Evans and Wurster (1999) in their definition of richness. Communicating deep and detailed information requires high bandwidth. At the same time, it is the availability of deep and detailed information about customers that enables customization. Recent technological progress—for instance, in channel bandwidth—has enabled considerable improvement in depth.

Communication channels can be arranged along a continuum representing their "relative richness" (Carlson and Zmud 1999). The *richness* of a medium is based on its ability to: (a) provide multiple cues (e.g., body language, facial expression, tone of voice) simultaneously; (b) provide quick feedback; (c) personalize messages; and (d) use natural language to convey subtleties (Daft and Lengel 1986). Information technology has traditionally been viewed as a lean communication medium. However, given the progress in information technology, we are witnessing a significant increase in its ability to support rich communication.

Finally, rapid advances in IT have significantly enhanced the ability to store and quickly process information. This enables the *aggregation* of large volumes of information drawn from multiple sources. For instance, data mining and data warehousing together enable the synthesis of diverse information from multiple sources, potentially to produce new insights. **Enterprise resource planning systems (ERPs)** also present a natural platform for aggregating knowledge across different parts of an organization. A senior IS executive at PricewaterhouseCoopers LLP, for example, remarks:

> We're moving quite quickly on to an Intranet platform, and that's giving us a greater chance to integrate everything instead of saying to people, "use this database and that database and another database." Now it all looks—and is—much more coordinated.
>
> (Thomson 2000, p. 24)

To summarize, the above four IT capabilities enable knowledge management by enhancing common knowledge or by facilitating the four KM processes. For example, an **expertise locator system** (also called knowledge yellow pages or a people-finder system) is a special type of knowledge repository that pinpoints individuals having specific knowledge within the organization. These systems rely on the reach and depth capabilities of IT by enabling individuals to contact remotely located experts and seek detailed solutions to complicated problems. Another IS solution attempts to capture as much of the knowledge in an individual's head as possible and archive it in a searchable database. This is primarily the aim of projects in artificial intelligence, which capture the expert's knowledge in systems based on various technologies, including rule-based system and case-based reasoning, among others (Wong and Radcliffe 2000). But the most sophisticated systems for eliciting and cataloging experts' knowledge in models that can easily be understood and applied by others in the organization (see for example Ford et al. 1996) require strong knowledge engineering processes to develop. Such sophisticated KM systems have typically not been advocated as frequently for use in mainstream business environments, primarily because of the high cost involved in the knowledge engineering effort.

Common Knowledge

Common knowledge (Grant 1996) represents another important component of the infrastructure that enables knowledge management. It refers to the organization's cumulative experiences in comprehending a category of knowledge and activities and the organizing principles that support communication and coordination (Zander and Kogut 1995). Common knowledge provides unity to the organization. It includes: a common language and vocabulary, recognition of individual knowledge domains, common cognitive schema, shared norms, and elements of specialized knowledge that are common across individuals sharing knowledge (Grant 1996; Nahapiet and Ghoshal 1998; Sabherwal et al. 2023). The following comment by a senior executive at NASA-Kennedy Space Center illustrates problems that might arise due to a lack of common knowledge (Sabherwal and Becerra-Fernandez 2005, p. 302):

> I used to consider myself a systems engineer. When I was in the shuttle program a systems engineer was somebody who was an expert on a particular shuttle system. In the outside world a systems engineer has a completely different definition. I was a technical expert on the shuttle toilet. I called myself a systems engineer, my position description said I was a systems engineer, but I could go over to the Payloads' IT department and ask them what their competency was, what their key effort was, and they would say "systems engineering." And I would say, "what system?" Because from my frame of reference, I was doing systems engineering, from theirs, they were doing something called systems engineering.

Common knowledge helps enhance the value of an individual expert's knowledge by integrating it with the knowledge of others. However, because the common knowledge is based on the above definition common only to an organization, this increase in value is also specific to that particular organization and does not transfer to its competitors. Thus, common knowledge supports knowledge transfer within the organization but impedes the transfer (or leakage) of knowledge outside the organization (Argote and Ingram 2000).

Absorptive capacity is also important and related to the concept of common knowledge. Absorptive capacity is the ability of a firm to recognize the value of new and external information, assimilate it, and apply it to commercial ends. It is also very critical to a firm's innovativeness (Cohen and Levinthal 1990). Cohen and Levinthal also argue that development of absorptive capacity is highly dependent on previously acquired knowledge and expertise.

Another important concept related to common knowledge is **shared domain knowledge**. Shared domain knowledge is defined as the ability of IT and business executives, at a deep level, to understand and be able to participate in others' key processes and to respect each other's unique contribution and challenges (Reich and Benbasat, 2000). Reich and Benbasat found that shared domain knowledge is one of the most important influential factors on long-run congruence of IT vision between IT and business executives.

Physical Environment

The **physical environment** within the organization is often taken for granted, but it is another important foundation upon which knowledge management rests. Key aspects of the physical environment include the design of buildings and the separation between them; the location, size, and type of offices; the type, number, and nature of meeting rooms; and so on. Physical environment can foster knowledge management by providing opportunities for employees to meet and share ideas. Even though knowledge sharing there is often not by design, coffee rooms, cafeterias, water coolers, and hallways do provide venues where employees learn from and share insights with each other. A 1998 study found that most employees thought they gained most of their knowledge related to work from informal conversations around watercoolers or over meals rather than from formal training or manuals (Wensley 1998).

A number of organizations are creating spaces specifically designed to facilitate this informal knowledge sharing. For example, the London Business School created an attractive space between two major departments, which were earlier isolated, to enhance knowledge sharing between them. Reuters News Service installed kitchens on each floor to foster discussions. Moreover, a medium-sized firm in the United States focused on careful management of office locations to facilitate knowledge sharing (Stewart 2000). This company developed open-plan offices with subtle arrangements to encourage what one senior executive calls *knowledge accidents*. Locations are arranged in this company so as to maximize the chances of face-to-face interactions among people who might be able to help each other. For example, an employee might walk down the hall so that she might meet someone who knows the answer to her question, and she will meet such an individual not due to chance but because a snack area is positioned where four project teams' work areas intersect.

Table 3.2 summarizes the five dimensions of KM infrastructure, indicating the key attributes related to each dimension.

Knowledge Management Mechanisms

Knowledge management mechanisms are organizational or structural means used to promote knowledge management. They enable KM systems, and they are themselves supported by the KM infrastructure. KM mechanisms may (or may not) utilize technology, but they do involve some kind of organizational arrangement or social or structural means of facilitating KM.

Examples of KM mechanisms include learning by doing, on-the-job training, learning by observation, and face-to-face meetings. More long-term KM mechanisms include the hiring of a Chief Knowledge Officer, cooperative projects across departments, traditional hierarchical relationships, organizational policies, standards, initiation process for new employees, and employee rotation across departments. Box 3.3 provides some examples of the use of KM mechanisms to facilitate knowledge management.

Knowledge Management Technologies

As mentioned earlier, KM technologies are information technologies that can be used to facilitate knowledge management. Thus, KM technologies are intrinsically no different from information technologies, but they focus on knowledge management rather

Table 3.2 A Summary of Knowledge Management Infrastructure

Dimensions of KM Infrastructure	Related Attributes
Organization Culture	Understanding of the value of KM practices
	Management support for KM at all levels
	Incentives that reward knowledge sharing
	Encouragement of interaction for the creation and sharing of knowledge
Organization Structure	Hierarchical structure of the organization (decentralization, matrix structures, emphasis on "leadership" rather than "management")
	Communities of practice
	Specialized structures and roles (Chief Knowledge Officer, KM department, traditional KM units)
Information Technology Infrastructure	Reach
	Depth
	Richness
	Aggregation
Common Knowledge	Common language and vocabulary
	Recognition of individual knowledge domains
	Common cognitive schema
	Shared norms
	Elements of specialized knowledge that are common across individuals
Physical Infrastructure	Design of buildings (offices, meeting rooms, hallways)
	Spaces specifically designed to facilitate informal knowledge sharing (coffee rooms, cafeterias, water coolers)

than information processing. KM technologies also support KM systems and benefit from the KM infrastructure, especially the information technology infrastructure.

KM technologies constitute a key component of KM systems. Technologies that support KM include **artificial intelligence (AI)** technologies, including those used for knowledge acquisition and case-based reasoning systems, electronic discussion groups, computer-based simulations, databases, decision support systems, enterprise resource planning systems, expert systems, management information systems, expertise locator systems, videoconferencing, and information repositories including best practices databases and lessons learned systems. KM technologies also include **Web technologies**, such as wikis and blogs, which are discussed in Chapter 13.

Examples of the use of KM technologies include the World Bank's use of a combination of video interviews and hyperlinks to documents and reports to systematically record the knowledge of employees that are close to retirement (Lesser and Prusak 2001). Similarly, at BP plc, desktop videoconferencing has improved communication and enabled many problems at offshore oil fields to be solved without extensive traveling (Skyrme 2000).

Box 3.4 provides examples of the use of technologies to facilitate knowledge management at three organizations. Box 3.5 provides a more detailed example of how Industrial Manufacturing Company used information and communication technologies to enable knowledge workers during the COVID pandemic, and how that experience has had lasting effects after the pandemic (Wasko and Dickey 2023). Box 3.6 describes how Instituto Boliviano de Comercio Exterior (Bolivian Institute of Foreign Commerce) implemented knowledge management to address knowledge loss due to "brain drain."

Box 3.4 Knowledge Management Mechanisms from Three Organizations

At Phonak, Inc., a worldwide leader in digital hearing instruments, a series of events occur throughout the year (every six weeks or so) enabling employees to get to know each other through informal interactions including barbecues, company days out, and bicycle tours.

BP Amoco Chemical Company has benefitted from retrospect meetings at the conclusion of projects. Each retrospect meeting is facilitated by someone outside that project team and focuses on the following questions: What was the goal of the project? What did we accomplish? What were the major successes? Why? How can we repeat the successes? What were the significant disappointments? Why? How can we avoid them in the future?

Katzenbach Partners uses light-hearted contests and events to facilitate knowledge management. One example is "Stump Niko," in which the managing director, who had the reputation that he knew everything that was going on, would be asked a question about knowledge management and the knowledge management system would then be asked the same question. The objective was to demonstrate the potential of the knowledge management system.

Sources: Compiled from Burgelman and Blumenstein (2007) and Hoegl and Schulze (2005)

Box 3.5 Knowledge Management at Industrial Manufacturing Company during the COVID Pandemic and Beyond

Industrial Manufacturing Company (IMC)—the fictitious name used by Wasko and Dickey (2023)—is a century-old private global manufacturer and distributor of specialized heavy-duty vehicles, which Wasko and Dickey call "industrial trucks." Catering to various sectors, including construction, energy, utilities, and telecoms, IMC operates from its southern U.S. headquarters with three manufacturing plants, 12 operations facilities, and 45 service centers in the U.S. and Canada. With a significant international presence, IMC serves over 100 countries through 65 distributors. Boasting 60+ patents, IMC's innovative designs enhance operational efficiency, safety, and working conditions, with customer feedback driving technology developments. IMC excels in crisis response, mobilizing trucks during natural disasters, rooted in a crisis-ready organizational culture.

Working Arrangements and Operations at IMC before the COVID-19 Pandemic

Industrial Manufacturing Company (IMC) operates with a hierarchical structure and has five primary business operations directly connected to customers: Manufacturing & Operations, Engineering & Design, Sales & Marketing, Technical Sales Support, and Financial Services. Support activities include Administrative Support and Information Services. Pre-pandemic, most IMC associates worked on-site, with exceptions for salespeople and traveling technicians. The company values customer needs and associates' dedication, leading to a highly motivated workforce and industry leadership. ICT investments primarily focused on manufacturing and design capabilities, while internal systems were considered sufficient. Information Services served as a support function, maintaining the ERP platform, enabling internal communications, and enhancing customer service. The Office 365 migration was a significant pre-pandemic project, initially met with some skepticism.

How IMC's Working Arrangements Changed during the Pandemic

During the COVID-19 pandemic, IMC faced unique challenges as it had to continue on-site work while its customers, mainly working outdoors, experienced fewer disruptions. IMC's indoor business operations, relying on heavy equipment and machinery, were significantly disrupted, making it difficult to meet customer demand. To maintain operations and prevent virus spread, IMC minimized co-location and implemented safety protocols. The company's crisis-readiness mindset and commitment to associates played a crucial role in adapting and ensuring business continuity. Work arrangements varied across functional units, with support activities going virtual, Engineering & Design adopting a hybrid schedule, and Manufacturing & Operations continuing on-site. Jobs requiring physical intensity remained on-site, while information-intense support roles shifted to remote work. This change affected associates differently, with Sales & Marketing seeing positive impacts from information technologies investments, while Manufacturing & Operations faced challenges in increasing production. The use of information technologies created tensions between information-intense work and high physical intensity tasks, and affected each of the three groups of associates during the pandemic, as discussed below, which created tensions with the organization's values.

Impact of ICT on Virtual Associates: IMC asked its associates in support functions like HR, Information Services, and Accounting to work virtually throughout the pandemic. However, it distinguished between virtual and remote worker categories. While "remote" referred to "off-site" associates who had worked at non-IMC locations/facilities before the pandemic, "virtual" referred to associates who worked on IMC facilities before the pandemic but were now expected to work online using information and communication technologies. IMC faced challenges when transitioning these associates to virtual work. Even high information-intensity work activities required access to physical resources like computers, monitors, and reliable Internet. IMC allowed associates to take equipment home and made additional purchases to support virtual work. The shift to virtual work also required changes in information management, with Office 365 playing a crucial role in replacing face-to-face interactions. However, using the Oracle ERP platform from home proved frustrating due to VPN and security restrictions. Office 365 facilitated anytime, anywhere access to essential information and software, improving connectivity with partners and suppliers. Despite a learning curve, virtual associates eventually adapted to the new systems, with HR staff taking on additional responsibilities. IMC focused on supporting virtual associates and emphasized the importance of maintaining synchronous human connections. Social events and engagement activities were implemented to enhance virtual worker integration and satisfaction with the off-site, online work arrangement. Virtual workers were fairly satisfied with the new work arrangement, following the initial learning.

Impact of ICT on Hybrid Associates: IMC asked Engineering & Design associates to adopt a hybrid work schedule during the pandemic, alternating between working from home and working in the office. Hybrid associates at IMC adapted to using Office 365 for communication and information processing, but faced challenges with their physical work activities in Engineering & Design. They developed new processes, like using Facetime, to address issues when relevant expertise was off-site. IoT technologies became essential for monitoring trucks and gaining insights remotely. Initially frustrated, hybrid associates eventually found satisfaction in their work arrangement, appreciating the flexibility of working from home while still being able to collaborate with colleagues on-site. They felt they had the best of both worlds, combining the benefits of remote work and in-person interactions.

Impact of ICT on On-Site Associates: During the pandemic, on-site workers at IMC faced safety measures such as mask-wearing, social distancing, and limited facility usage. The visual cues of these safety measures constantly reminded them of the virus threat, leading to fear and concern. On-site associates primarily relied on face-to-face interactions for information exchange, but with safety protocols in place, these channels were reduced. They felt hindered in accessing necessary information and were left feeling isolated at work. IMC installed computer terminals to expand communication channels for on-site associates. Moreover, supply chain disruptions caused frustration among Manufacturing & Operations associates, who had previously felt prioritized by the company. The sense of isolation and lack of equitable treatment during the pandemic affected their work-life balance and employee satisfaction. Despite being grateful for still having jobs, on-site workers experienced challenges and stresses related to working in a changed environment alongside others, including feeling being "left at work," finding it difficult to reach their virtual colleagues, and the risk associated with having to work in person and on-site with others during the pandemic.

New Blended Workforce after the Pandemic

By spring 2022, IMC decided to continue with a "blended" workforce, including virtual, hybrid, and on-site workers, to balance flexibility and support physical operations. Virtual workers have the most flexibility, working from home with self-set on-site schedules. Hybrid workers can work from home part-time, and on-site workers continue their regular in-person work. IMC is concerned about the long-term impact on the company's culture and values due to the blend. New associates' ability to work completely virtually from day one may affect emotional bonds and commitment to the organization's values. The pandemic has made IMC more open to adopting new ICT, leading to greater digital transformation. Virtual and hybrid workers desire more ICT systems for internal virtual work and expanded social media engagement with customers. On-site workers also embrace new technologies, such as communication and automated/robotic processing in manufacturing.

The company's Information Services played a crucial role in developing online systems and supporting dispersed associates. Going forward, ICT investments will vary depending on job roles. The tension between the blended workforce and attitudes toward co-located work persists, especially with on-site workers feeling they lost priority status. Virtual associates adjusted well to the new work model, experiencing increased productivity and benefiting from reduced commuting costs and more personal time. On the other hand, on-site workers feel like they have lost out. Although they have not faced changes in their work conditions, seeing others benefit from flexibility has left them feeling discontented. While an across-the-board return-to-the-office mandate may make on-site workers feel prioritized, it could demoralize other groups. IMC faces the challenge of finding a balanced approach to accommodate various worker preferences and maintain a positive work environment.

Source: Wasko and Dickey (2023)

Box 3.6 Knowledge Management Helps Address Knowledge Loss at Instituto Boliviano de Comercio Exterior

Knowledge loss due to "brain drain" is a major challenge for most organizations. Recognizing the value of its in-house knowledge, the Instituto Boliviano de Comercio Exterior (IBCE) documented its critical work procedures and processes. This enabled consistent delivery of its core services to the Bolivian business community, despite employee rotation or turnover. More specifically, IBCE took the following steps.

1   IBCE developed a large collection of video footage, screen recordings, and slideshows describing the organization's work processes. This repository helps retain most of IBCE's critical knowledge in-house.
2   IBCE started actively using an online collaboration tool that facilitates the sharing of training materials, process descriptions, and other documents among its employees.
3   IBCE reduced traditional departmental boundaries, beginning with strategic and interactive sessions on knowledge management, followed by with an operational phase, adopting the new tools and way-of-working. As a result, the mentality in the organization is gradually changing from "isolated thinking" into synergies and collaborative approaches.

Since the teams observed the benefits of the above changes from the beginning, the changes were received well and helped improve knowledge management across the organization.

Source: Compiled from IBCE (n.d.)

Management of Knowledge Management Foundations (Infrastructure, Mechanisms, and Technologies)

Knowledge management infrastructure, mechanisms, and technologies are the underlying foundations for any organization's KM solutions. KM infrastructure is of fundamental importance with long-term implications and needs to be managed carefully, with close involvement from top executives. In any case, all components of KM infrastructure (i.e., organization structure, organization culture, IT infrastructure, common knowledge, and physical environment) affect not only KM but also all other aspects of the organizational operations. Therefore, KM infrastructure does receive attention from top management, although it is important that KM be explicitly considered in making decisions regarding these infrastructural aspects. In this regard, a strong relationship between the leaders of the KM function (discussed in Chapter 11) and the top executives of the organization plays an important role.

KM mechanisms and technologies work together and affect each other. KM mechanisms depend on technology, although some mechanisms do so to a greater extent than others. Moreover, improvement in KM technologies could, over time, lead to changes in KM mechanisms (either improvements, or in some cases a reduced emphasis). In managing KM mechanisms and technologies, it is important to recognize such interrelationships between mechanisms and technologies. Moreover, it is important to achieve an appropriate balance between the use of technology and social or structural mechanisms. Technological progress could lead to people focusing too much on technology while ignoring structural and social aspects. On the other hand, an organization with weak IT infrastructure may rely on social and structural mechanisms while ignoring potentially valuable KM technologies.

Consequently, some organizations focus more on KM technologies, some focus more on KM mechanisms, and some make a somewhat balanced use of KM technologies and mechanisms. For example, senior executives at Groupe Danone (Groupe Danone 2009), which is a leading consumer-goods company with headquarters in Paris and is known as Dannon in the United States (it is discussed in greater detail later in Chapter 10, Box 10.1), believe that using IT to share knowledge would not work as well for the company, and therefore rely primarily on social and structural mechanisms (Edmondson et al. 2008).

Several other organizations switch from a focus on mechanisms to a focus on technology, or vice versa. For example, Katzenbach Partners, LLC, relied almost entirely on social and structural mechanisms to manage knowledge until 2005, but then, in the light of its organizational growth, started focusing much more on KM technologies, first using an Intranet and then using Web technologies (which we discuss in greater detail in Chapter 13). This is in contrast to Montgomery Watson Harza (MWH Global, Inc.), as discussed in Box 3.2, which focused primarily on information technologies from 1995 to 1999, and then switched to a KM strategy based on "People First, Technology as Support" (Parise et al. 2004).

Summary

Building on the discussion of knowledge in Chapter 2, we have described the key aspects of knowledge management in this chapter. We have provided a working definition of knowledge management and discussed KM solutions as involving five components: KM processes, KM systems, KM mechanisms, KM technologies, and KM infrastructure. We have also discussed and illustrated three foundational components—KM mechanisms, KM technologies, and KM infrastructure—and briefly talked about how they could be managed. The next chapter examines the other key aspects of KM solutions including KM systems, KM mechanisms and technologies, and KM infrastructure.

Review

1   What is knowledge management? What are its objectives?
2   What is business intelligence? How does knowledge management differ from business intelligence?
3   Describe the ways to facilitate knowledge management and give suitable examples.
4   Distinguish between KM foundation and KM solutions. What are the components of KM foundation and KM solutions?
5   What is common knowledge? What does it include, and how does it support knowledge management?
6   State the role of organizational culture in the development of a good knowledge management infrastructure.
7   State the role of organizational structure in the development of a good knowledge management infrastructure.
8   In what way does information technology infrastructure contribute to knowledge management within an organization?

Application Exercises

1   Interview a manager of an organization where knowledge management practices have recently been implemented. Use the interview to study the nature of the KM infrastructure and the ways in which its components are helping or inhibiting those KM practices.
2   Consider an organization where you currently work, or are familiar with (either through your own prior experience or through interactions with someone who works there). What kind of mechanisms does this organization use to manage knowledge? What are their effects?
3   Determine ways in which a local hospital would benefit from communities of practice. Conduct interviews if necessary.
4   Consider a high school with which you are familiar. How can knowledge management at this high school benefit from information technologies? What kinds of technologies does it currently use, and how could they be improved?
5   Interview at least three managers from local organizations that have recently implemented knowledge management. Contrast the differences in organization culture, structure, IT infrastructure, common knowledge, and physical environment within the organizations.

References

Argote, L., and Ingram, P. 2000. Knowledge transfer: Basis for competitive advantage in firms. *Organizational Behavior and Human Decision Processes*, 82(1) (May), 150–169.
Armbrecht, F.M.R., Chapas, R.B., Chappelow, C.C., Farris, G.F., Friga, P.N., Hartz, C.A., McIlvaine, M.E., Postle S.R., and Whitwell, G.E. 2001. Knowledge management in research and development. *Research Technology Management*, 44(4), 28–48.
Burgelman, R.A., and Blumenstein, B. 2007. Knowledge management at Katzenbach Partners LLC. Stanford Graduate School of Business, Case SM162.
Carlson, J.R., and Zmud, R.W. 1999. Channel expansion theory and the experiential nature of media richness perceptions. *Academy of Management Journal*, 42(2), 153–170.

Choo, C.W. 1998. *The knowing organization: How organizations use information to construct meaning, create knowledge, and make decisions.* New York: Oxford University Press.

Cohen, W.M., and Levinthal, D.A. 1990. Absorptive capacity: A new perspective on learning and innovation. *Administrative Science Quarterly*, 35(1), 128–152.

Daft, R.L., and Lengel, R.H. 1986. Organization information requirements, media richness, and structural design. *Management Science*, 32(5), 554–571.

DeTienne, K.B., and Jackson, L.A. 2001. Knowledge management: Understanding theory and developing strategy. *Competitiveness Review*, 11(1), 1–11.

Dyer, G., and McDonough, B. 2001. The state of KM. *Knowledge Management* (May), 31–36.

Edmondson, A., Moingeon, B., Dessain, V., and Jensen, D. 2008. Global knowledge management at Danone. Harvard Business School Publishing, Case 9–608–107, April 16.

Evans, P., and Wurster, T.S. 1999. Getting real about virtual commerce. *Harvard Business Review*, 77(6) (November–December), 85–94.

Ford, K.M., Coffey, J.W., Cañas, A.J., Andrews, E.J., and Turner, C.W. 1996. Diagnosis and explanation by a nuclear cardiology expert system. *International Journal of Expert Systems*, 9, 499–506.

Grant, R.M. 1996. Toward a knowledge-based theory of the firm. *Strategic Management Journal*, 17, 109–122.

Greenes Consulting. n.d.-a. Health care. http://www.greenesconsulting.com/success-stories/health-care.

Greenes Consulting. n.d.-b. Team learning & performing. http://www.greenesconsulting.com/services/list-services/team-learning-performing.

Groupe Danone. 2009. http://www.danone.com/?lang=en.

Hill and Knowlton Strategies. n.d. https://www.hkstrategies.com.

Hoegl, M., and Schulze, A., 2005. How to support knowledge creation in new product development: An investigation of knowledge management methods. *European Management Journal*, 23(3), 263–273.

Instituto Boliviano de Comercio Exterior (IBCE). n.d. Brochure. https://ibce.org.bo/documentos/brochure/Brochure-International-(ver-English).pdf.

Keen, P. 1991. *Shaping the future: Business design through information technology.* Boston: Harvard Business School Press.

Koudsi, S. 2000. Actually, it is like brain surgery. *Fortune*, March 20.

Lesser, E., and Prusak, L. 2001. Preserving knowledge in an uncertain world. *Sloan Management Review* (Fall), 101–102.

Meister, D., and Mark, K. 2004. *Hill & Knowlton: Knowledge management.* Case #9B04E003. London, ONT: Ivey Publishing.

MWH. n.d. MWH is a leading global project delivery company with a focus on our world's most precious resource: Water. https://mwhconstructors.com/.

Nahapiet, J., and Ghoshal, S. 1998. Social capital, intellectual capital, and the organizational advantage. *Academy of Management Review*, 23(2), 242–266.

Parise, S., Rolag, K., and Gulas, V. 2004. Montgomery Watson Harza and knowledge management. Harvard Business School Publishing, Case BAB102, November 15.

Paul, L.G. 2003. Why three heads are better than one (How to create a know-it-all company). *CIO Magazine* (December).

Reich, B.H., and Benbasat, I. 2000. Factors that influence the social dimension of alignment between business and information technology objectives. *MIS Quarterly*, 24(1), 81–113.

Sabherwal, R. 2007. Succeeding with business intelligence: Some insights and recommendations. *Cutter Benchmark Review*, 7(9), 5–15.

Sabherwal, R. 2008. KM and BI: From mutual isolation to complementarity and synergy. *Cutter Consortium Executive Report*, 8(8), 1–18.

Sabherwal, R., and Becerra-Fernandez, I. 2005. Integrating specific knowledge: Insights from the Kennedy Space Center. *IEEE Transactions on Engineering Management*, 52(3), 301–315.

Sabherwal, R., Steelman, Z., and Becerra-Fernandez, I. 2023. Knowledge management mechanisms and common knowledge impacts on the value of knowledge at individual and organizational levels. *International Journal of Information Management*, 72 (October) (102660).

Skyrme, D.J. 2000. Developing a knowledge strategy: From management to leadership. In *Knowledge management: Classic and contemporary works*, ed. D. Morey, M. Maybury, and B. Thuraisingham, 61–84. Cambridge, MA: The MIT Press.

Standing, C., and Benson, S. 2000. Knowledge management in a competitive environment. In *Decision support through knowledge management*, ed. S.A. Carlsson, P. Brezillon, P. Humphreys, B.G. Lundberg, A.M. McCosh, and V. Rajkovic, 336–348. Stockholm, Sweden: Department of Computing Systems Sciences, University of Stockholm and Royal Institute of Technology.

Stewart, T.A. 2000. The house that knowledge built. *Fortune*, October 2.

Storck, J., and Hill, P. 2000. Knowledge diffusion through "strategic communities". *Sloan Management Review*, 41(2), 63–74.

Thomson, S. 2000. Focus: Keeping pace with knowledge. *Information World Review*, Issue 155 (February) 23–24.

Wasko, M., and Dickey, A. 2023. Managing where employees work in a post-pandemic world, *MIS Quarterly Executive*, 22(2), Article 5.

Wensley, A. 1998. The value of story telling. *Knowledge and Process Management*, 5(1), 1–2.

Wong W., and Radcliffe D. 2000. The tacit nature of design knowledge. *Technology Analysis and Strategic Management*, 12(4), 493–512.

Zander, U., and Kogut, B. 1995. Knowledge and the speed of the transfer and imitation of organizational capabilities: An empirical test. *Organization Science*, 6, 76–92.

4 Knowledge Management Solutions

Processes and Systems

In Chapter 3, we provided an introductory discussion of **knowledge management solutions**, which refer to the variety of ways in which knowledge management can be facilitated. We indicated that KM solutions include KM processes and KM systems and that KM solutions depend on **KM foundations** that include KM mechanisms, technologies, and infrastructure. We discussed KM foundations in detail in Chapter 3. This chapter provides a detailed discussion of KM solutions, including KM processes and systems.

The next section describes and illustrates the various processes used to manage knowledge including processes for applying knowledge, processes for capturing knowledge, processes for sharing knowledge, and processes for creating knowledge. In discussing these KM processes, we also examine the seven subprocesses that facilitate them. The discussion of KM processes is followed by a discussion of KM systems, followed by a discussion of the processes for managing KM processes and systems, and then some concluding remarks.

Knowledge Management Processes

We earlier defined knowledge management as *performing the activities involved in discovering, capturing, sharing, and applying knowledge so as to enhance, in a cost-effective fashion, the impact of knowledge on the unit's goal achievement.* Thus, knowledge management relies on four main kinds of KM processes. As shown in Figure 4.1, these include the processes through which knowledge is discovered or captured. It also includes the processes through which this knowledge is shared and applied. These four KM processes are supported by a set of seven KM subprocesses, as shown in Figure 4.1, with one subprocess—socialization—supporting two KM processes (discovery and sharing). Of the seven KM subprocesses, four are based on Nonaka (1994). Focusing on the ways in which knowledge is converted through the interaction between tacit and explicit knowledge, Nonaka identified four ways of managing knowledge: socialization, externalization, internalization, and combination. The other three KM subprocesses—exchange, direction, and routines—are largely based on Grant (1996) and Nahapiet and Ghoshal (1998).

Knowledge Discovery

Knowledge discovery may be defined as *the development of new tacit or explicit knowledge from data and information or from the synthesis of prior knowledge.* The discovery of new

DOI: 10.4324/9781003364375-5

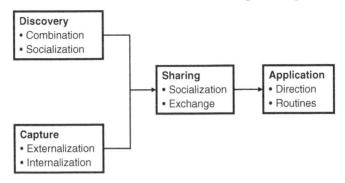

Figure 4.1 Knowledge Management Processes

explicit knowledge relies most directly on combination, whereas the discovery of new tacit knowledge relies most directly on socialization. In either case, new knowledge is discovered by synthesizing knowledge from two or more distinct areas with explicit knowledge from two areas being synthesized through combination, and tacit knowledge from two areas being synthesized through socialization. Combination and socialization are discussed now.

Combination

New explicit knowledge is discovered through **combination**, wherein the multiple bodies of explicit knowledge (and/or data and/or information) are synthesized to create new, more complex sets of explicit knowledge (Nonaka 1994). Through communication, integration, and systemization of multiple streams of explicit knowledge, new explicit knowledge is created—either incrementally or radically (Nahapiet and Ghoshal 1998). Existing explicit knowledge, data, and information are reconfigured, recategorized, and recontextualized to produce new explicit knowledge. For example, when creating a new proposal to a client, explicit data, information, and knowledge embedded in prior proposals may be combined into the new proposal. Also, data mining techniques may be used to uncover new relationships among explicit data that may lead to predictive or categorization models that create new knowledge.

Socialization

In the case of tacit knowledge, the integration of multiple streams for the creation of new knowledge occurs through the mechanism of socialization (Nonaka 1994). **Socialization** is the synthesis of tacit knowledge across individuals, usually through joint activities rather than written or verbal instructions. For example, by transferring ideas and images, apprenticeships help newcomers to see how others think. Daven-port and Prusak (1998) described how conversations at the watercooler helped knowledge sharing among groups at IBM.

In Box 4.1, we illustrate the knowledge discovery process using the example of Xerox.

Box 4.1 Knowledge Discovery at Xerox

Julian Orr, who was earlier an anthropologist at Xerox's Palo Alto Research Center (PARC), studied the actions of customer service representatives who fix Xerox machines. One day, he observed a representative working with an especially troublesome machine, which had been recently installed but had never worked properly. Each time the machine failed, it generated a different error message. Following the prescribed process for each particular message, such as adjusting or replacing parts, failed to correct the overall problem. Moreover, the messages did not make sense when considered together.

Frustrated with his inability to fix the troublesome machine, the representative called a specialist, but the specialist also failed to understand why the machine was behaving in this fashion. Subsequently the representative and the specialist spent the afternoon cycling the machine repeatedly, waiting for its crashes and recording its state when it crashed. While doing this, they discussed other incidents of apparently similar problems.

> The afternoon resembled a series of alternating improvisational jazz solos, as each man took the lead, ran with it for a little while, then handed it off to the other, this all against the bass-line continuo of the rumbling machine.
>
> (Brown and Duguid 2000, p. 78)

During this process, the representative and the specialist gradually brought their different ideas closer together toward a shared understanding of the machine. Finally, late in the day, everything clicked. The erratic behavior of the machine, the experiences of the representative and the specialist, and the stories they both shared eventually formed a single, coherent account. They were able to make sense of the machine and figure out how to fix it. Thus, by bringing very different perspectives and experiences and then sharing them during their conversation—with the problems encountered with the machine providing a common context—they were able to create new knowledge and thereby solve the problem. Very soon, this new solution was passed around for other technicians to use if they faced the same problem.

Source: Compiled from Brown and Duguid (2000)

Knowledge Capture

As we discussed in Chapter 2, knowledge can exist within people (individuals or groups), artifacts (practices, technologies, or repositories) and organizational entities (organizational units, organizations, interorganizational networks). Moreover, knowledge could be either explicit or tacit. It might sometimes reside within an individual's mind without that individual being able to recognize it and share it with others. Similarly, knowledge might reside in an explicit form in a manual but few people might be aware of it. It is important to obtain the tacit knowledge from individuals' minds as well as the explicit knowledge from the manual, such that the knowledge can then be shared with others. This is the focus of **knowledge capture**, which may be defined as *the process of retrieving either explicit or tacit knowledge that resides within people, artifacts, or organizational entities*. Also, the knowledge being captured might reside outside the organizational boundaries, including consultants, competitors, customers, suppliers, and prior employers of the organization's new employees.

The knowledge capture process benefits most directly from two KM subprocesses—externalization and internalization. Based on work by Nonaka (1994), externalization and internalization help capture the tacit knowledge and explicit knowledge, respectively.

Externalization involves converting tacit knowledge into explicit forms such as words, concepts, visuals, or figurative language (e.g., metaphors, analogies, and narratives; Nonaka and Takeuchi 1995). It helps translate individuals' tacit knowledge into explicit forms that can be more easily understood by the rest of their group. This is a difficult process because tacit knowledge is often difficult to articulate. Nonaka (1994) suggested that externalization may be accomplished through the use of metaphor—that is, understanding and experiencing one kind of thing in terms of another. An example of externalization is a consultant team writing a document that describes the lessons the team has learned about the client organization, client executives, and approaches that work in such an assignment. This captures the tacit knowledge acquired by the team members.

Internalization is the conversion of explicit knowledge into tacit knowledge. It represents the traditional notion of **learning**. The explicit knowledge may be embodied in action and practice so that the individual acquiring the knowledge can re-experience what others have gone through. Alternatively, individuals could acquire tacit knowledge in virtual situations, either vicariously by reading manuals or others' stories or experientially through simulations or experiments (Nonaka and Takeuchi 1995). An example of internalization is a new software consultant reading a book on innovative software development and learning from it. This learning helps the consultant, and her organization, capture the knowledge contained in the book.

Box 4.2 provides an illustration of knowledge capture.

Box 4.2 Knowledge Capture at Viant

The Boston-based company Viant uses a variety of means to capture knowledge. It employs a number of simple but unavoidable forms. Before every project, consultants are required to complete a *quicksheet* describing the knowledge they will need, what aspects of knowledge can be leveraged from prior projects, and what they will need to create along with the lessons they hope to learn that they can share with others later. A longer report, a sunset review, is produced at a team meeting to document what worked and what did not work well. Forgetting these reports is hard due to several reasons (Stewart 2000, p. 278):

> First, almost every document ends up on Viant's internal Web site, hot-linked every which way. Second, sunset reviews are done with a facilitator who wasn't on the team, which helps keep them honest. Third, every six weeks Newell's knowledge management group prepares, posts, and pushes a summary of what's been learned.

Knowledge Sharing

Knowledge sharing is the process through which explicit or tacit knowledge is communicated to other individuals. Three important clarifications are in order. First, knowledge sharing means effective transfer, so that the recipient of knowledge can understand it well enough to act on it (Jensen and Meckling 1996). Second, what is shared is knowledge rather than recommendations based on the knowledge; the former involves the recipient acquiring the shared knowledge as well as being able to take action based on it, whereas the latter (which is direction, discussed in the next section) simply involves utilization of knowledge without the recipient internalizing the shared knowledge. Third, knowledge sharing may take place across individuals as well as across groups, departments, or organizations (Alavi and Leidner 2001).

If knowledge exists at a location that is different from where it is needed, either knowledge sharing or knowledge utilization without sharing (discussed in the next section) is necessary. Sharing knowledge is clearly an important process in enhancing organizational innovativeness and performance. This is reflected in the fact it was one of the three business processes for which General Electric Company CEO Jack Welch took personal responsibility (the others were allocation of resources and development of people) (Stewart 2000).

Depending on whether explicit or tacit knowledge is being shared, exchange or socialization processes are used. Socialization, which we have discussed above, facilitates the sharing of tacit knowledge in cases in which new tacit knowledge is being created as well as when new tacit knowledge is not being created. There is no intrinsic difference between the socialization process when used for knowledge discovery or knowledge sharing, although the way in which the process may be used could be different. For example, when used to share knowledge a face-to-face meeting (a mechanism that facilitates socialization) could involve a question-and-answer session between the sender and recipient of knowledge, whereas when used to create knowledge a face-to-face meeting could take more the form of a debate or joint problem-solving, as seen in Box 4.1.

Exchange, in contrast to socialization, focuses on the sharing of explicit knowledge. It is used to communicate or transfer explicit knowledge among individuals, groups, and organizations (Grant 1996). In its basic nature, the process of exchange of explicit knowledge does not differ from the process through which information is communicated. An example of exchange is a product design manual being transferred by one employee to another, who can then use the explicit knowledge contained in the manual. Exchanging a document could also be used to transfer information.

Box 4.3 provides an illustration of knowledge sharing.

Box 4.3 Knowledge Sharing at the Veteran's Health Administration

Until 1997, the Veteran's Health Administration (VHA) did not have any systematic mechanism to enable its 219,000 employees to share their informal knowledge, innovations, and best practices. To address this need and also to serve as a place where any VHA employee can access knowledge capital of colleagues, the VHA Lessons Learned Project and its website, the Virtual Learning Center (VLC), were initiated in 1997. The VHA indicates that a major reason for initiating this project was a recognized need to transform the organization into a learning organization. In 1999, the VLC became available on the Internet. The site now has international participation from Korea, Canada, Spain, Pakistan, and elsewhere. By reducing red tape, cutting across organizational silos, partnering and benchmarking with others, and establishing best processing, the VHA is saving countless hours of staff time by not having to reinvent the wheel at its 173 medical centers, more than 600 clinics, 31 nursing home care units, 206 counseling centers, and other federal and private healthcare institutions, Veterans Benefits and National Cemetery offices.

Source: Compiled from U.S. Department of Veterans Affairs (n.d.)

Knowledge Application

Knowledge contributes most directly to organizational performance when it is used to make decisions and perform tasks. Of course, the process of **knowledge application** depends on the available knowledge, and knowledge itself depends on the processes of knowledge discovery, capture, and sharing, as shown in Figure 4.1. The better the processes of knowledge discovery, capture, and sharing, the greater the likelihood that the knowledge needed is available for effective application in decision-making and task performance.

In applying knowledge, the party that makes use of it does not necessarily need to comprehend it. All that is needed is that somehow the knowledge be used to guide decisions and actions. Therefore, knowledge utilization benefits from two processes—routines and direction—that do not involve the actual transfer or exchange of knowledge between the concerned individuals but only the transfer of the recommendations that are applicable in a specific context (Grant 1996).

Direction refers to the process through which the individual possessing the knowledge directs the action of another individual without transferring to that individual the knowledge underlying the direction. Direction involves the transfer of instructions or decisions and not the transfer of the knowledge required to make those decisions, and hence it has been labeled as *knowledge substitution* (Conner and Prahalad 1996). This preserves the advantages of specialization and avoids the difficulties inherent in the transfer of tacit knowledge. Direction is the process used when a production worker calls an expert to ask her how to solve a particular problem with a machine and then proceeds to solve the problem based on the instructions given by the expert. He does this without himself acquiring the knowledge so that if a similar problem reoccurs in the future, he would be unable to identify it as such and would therefore be unable to solve it himself without calling an expert. Similarly, a student taking a test who asks his fellow classmate for the answer to a question gets a direction (which of course could be wrong), and no knowledge is effectively shared between the two, which means the next time the student faces that question, posed perhaps in a slightly different form, he will not be able to discern the right answer. Note the difference between direction and socialization or exchange, where the knowledge is actually transferred to the other person in either tacit form (socialization) or explicit form (exchange).

Routines involve the utilization of knowledge embedded in procedures, rules, and norms that guide future behavior. Routines economize on communication more than directions as they are embedded in procedures or technologies. However, they take time to develop, relying on "constant repetition" (Grant 1996). Routines could be automated through the use of IT, such as in systems that provide help desk agents, field engineers, consultants, and customer end users with specific and automated answers from a knowledge base (Sabherwal and Sabherwal 2007). Similarly, an inventory management system utilizes considerable knowledge about the relationship between demand and supply, but neither the knowledge nor the directions are communicated through individuals. Also, enterprise systems are coded with routines that describe business process within industry segments.

Next, we examine KM systems that utilize KM mechanisms and technologies to support the KM processes. In this discussion, we also identify the roles of several specific KM technologies in enabling KM systems.

Knowledge Management Systems

Knowledge management systems are the integration of technologies and mechanisms that are developed to support the four KM processes. Knowledge management systems utilize a variety of KM mechanisms and technologies, discussed before, to support the KM processes discussed in Chapter 3. Each KM system utilizes a combination of multiple mechanisms and multiple technologies. Moreover, the same KM mechanism or technology could, under differing circumstances, support multiple KM systems.

Depending on the KM process most directly supported, KM systems can be classified into four kinds, which are discussed in detail in Part II: knowledge application systems (Chapter 6), knowledge capture systems (Chapter 7), knowledge sharing systems (Chapter 8), and knowledge discovery systems (Chapter 9). Here we provide a brief overview of these four kinds of systems and examine how they benefit from KM mechanisms and technologies.

Knowledge Discovery Systems

As discussed in Chapter 3, **knowledge discovery systems** support the process of developing new tacit or explicit knowledge from data and information or from the synthesis of prior knowledge. These systems support two KM subprocesses associated with knowledge discovery: combination, enabling the discovery of new explicit knowledge; and socialization, enabling the discovery of new tacit knowledge.

Thus, mechanisms and technologies can support knowledge discovery systems by facilitating combination and/or socialization. Mechanisms that facilitate combination include collaborative problem solving, joint decision-making, and collaborative creation of documents. For example, at the senior-management level, new explicit knowledge is created by sharing documents and information related to midrange concepts (e.g., product concepts) augmented with grand concepts (e.g., corporate vision) to produce new knowledge about both areas. This newly created knowledge could be, for example, a better understanding of products and a corporate vision (Nonaka and Takeuchi 1995). Mechanisms that facilitate socialization include apprenticeships, employee rotation across areas, conferences, brainstorming retreats, cooperative projects across departments, and initiation process for new employees. For example, Honda Motor Company, Ltd., "set up 'brainstorming camps' (*tama dashi kai*)—informal meetings for detailed discussions to solve difficult problems in development projects" (Nonaka and Takeuchi 1995, p. 63).

Technologies facilitating combination include knowledge discovery systems (see Chapter 9), databases, and Web-based access to data. According to Nonaka and Takeuchi (1995, p. 67), "reconfiguration of existing information through sorting, adding, combining, and categorizing of explicit knowledge (as conducted in computer databases) can lead to new knowledge." Repositories of information, **best practice** databases, and lessons learned systems (see Chapter 8) also facilitate combination. Technologies can also facilitate socialization, albeit to a lesser extent than they can facilitate combination. Some of the technologies for facilitating socialization include videoconferencing and electronic support for communities of practice (see Chapter 10).

Knowledge Capture Systems

Knowledge capture systems support the process of retrieving either explicit or tacit knowledge that resides within people, artifacts, or organizational entities. These systems can help capture knowledge that resides within or outside organizational boundaries, including within consultants, competitors, customers, suppliers, and prior employers of the organization's new employees. Knowledge capture systems rely on mechanisms and technologies that support externalization and internalization.

KM mechanisms can enable knowledge capture by facilitating externalization—that is, the conversion of tacit knowledge into explicit form; or internalization—that is, the conversion of explicit knowledge into tacit form. The development of models or prototypes and the articulation of best practices or lessons learned are some examples of mechanisms that enable externalization. Box 4.2, presented earlier, illustrates the use of externalization to capture knowledge about projects in one organization.

Learning by doing, on-the-job training, learning by observation, and face-to-face meetings are some of the mechanisms that facilitate internalization. For example, at one firm, "the product divisions also frequently send their new-product development people to the Answer Center to chat with the telephone operators or the 12 specialists, thereby 're-experiencing' their experiences" (Nonaka and Takeuchi 1995, p. 69).

Technologies can also support knowledge capture systems by facilitating externalization and internalization. Externalization through **knowledge engineering**, which involves integrating knowledge into information systems to solve complex problems that normally require considerable human expertise (Feigenbaum and McCorduck 1983), is necessary for the implementation of intelligent technologies such as artificial intelligence/machine learning systems, neural networks, and case-based reasoning systems (see Chapter 6), and knowledge capture systems (see Chapter 7). Technologies that facilitate internalization include social media, computer-based training, and communication technologies. Using such communication facilities, an individual can internalize knowledge from a message or attachment thereof sent by another expert, an AI-based knowledge capture system, or computer-based simulation.

Knowledge Sharing Systems

Knowledge sharing systems support the process through which explicit or tacit knowledge is communicated to other individuals. They do so by supporting exchange (i.e., sharing of explicit knowledge) and socialization (which promotes sharing of tacit knowledge).

Mechanisms and technologies that were discussed as supporting socialization also play an important role in knowledge sharing systems. Discussion groups or chat groups facilitate knowledge sharing by enabling an individual to explain her knowledge to the rest of the group. In addition, knowledge sharing systems also utilize mechanisms and technologies that facilitate exchange. Some of the mechanisms that facilitate exchange are memos, manuals, progress reports, letters, and presentations. Technologies facilitating exchange include groupware and other team-collaboration mechanisms; Web-based access to data and databases; and repositories of information, including best practice databases, lessons learned systems, and expertise locator systems. Box 4.3 on the Veteran's Health Administration (VHA), which was presented earlier, provides one illustration of the importance of knowledge sharing.

Knowledge Application Systems

Knowledge application systems support the process through which some individuals utilize knowledge possessed by other individuals without actually acquiring, or learning, that knowledge. Mechanisms and technologies support knowledge application systems by facilitating routines and direction.

Mechanisms facilitating direction include traditional hierarchical relationships in organizations, help desks, and support centers. On the other hand, mechanisms supporting routines include organizational policies, work practices, organizational procedures, and standards. In the case of both direction and routines, these mechanisms may be either within an organization (e.g., organizational procedures) or across organizations (e.g., industry best practices).

Technologies supporting direction include experts' knowledge embedded in expert systems (see Chapter 8) and decision-support systems, as well as troubleshooting systems based on the use of technologies like case-based reasoning. On the other hand, some of the technologies that facilitate routines are expert systems (see Chapter 6), enterprise resource planning systems, and traditional management information systems. As mentioned for KM mechanisms, these technologies can also facilitate directions and routines within or across organizations. These are discussed in detail in Chapter 6.

Box 4.4 illustrates KM technologies using Cisco as an example. Moreover, Box 4.5 examines the adverse effect artificial intelligence can have on on-the-job learning, how individuals respond to it through *shadow learning*, and what organizations can do about it (Beane 2019).

Box 4.4 KM Technologies at Cisco

Cisco Systems Inc. utilizes Directory 3.0, which is its internal Facebook, in which the employee listings are designed to identify the employee's expertise area and promote collaboration. To further promote knowledge sharing, it utilizes a variety of technologies, including: Ciscopedia, which is an internal document site; C-Vision, which is Cisco's version of YouTube; and the Idea Zone, which is a wiki for employees to post and discuss business ideas. Cisco has also been developing a companywide social computing platform to enable knowledge creation and sharing through strengthening of existing networks and facilitation of new connections (Fitzgerald 2008). According to Cisco's VP, Communication and Collaboration IT:

> Blogs and wikis are popping up all over the Cisco website at an exciting pace. But we're finding that actual adoption of wikis is outpacing that of blogs at an exponentially higher rate. This is most likely because wikis are part of the natural workflow—they are where work gets done. People are more driven to wikis because it is a primary form of communication and collaboration within a group.
>
> (Fitzgerald 2008)

Cisco's CIO remarked in 2008 (Fitzgerald 2008): "CIOs need to consider issues of privacy, data security, and the ability to scale across a global organization. It's no good, if 15 different business units develop 15 different online communities that can't talk to each other."

In April of 2015, Cisco launched Cisco Collaborative Knowledge, a knowledge sharing platform, which Cisco believes can help build a smarter and more agile workforce. The Cisco team provided a concise product overview, highlighting five key features:

1 **Mobile Knowledge:** The platform offers employees portable knowledge accessible from any device, even offline.
2 **Expert Discovery:** Collaborative Knowledge enables users to access their personal LinkedIn network, connecting and identifying experts through voice, video, and chat.
3 **Learning Management System:** Offering both prescribed and personalized learning, this component utilizes collaboration technology to enhance accessibility.
4 **Knowledge Center:** An institutionalized digital depository housing various learning assets such as documents, files, and videos.
5 **Social Community:** Catering to learners who prefer informal peer or mentor learning over formal classes, this feature incorporates gamification elements for continuous feedback on content, participation, and individuals.

Kathy Bries, Senior Director and General Manager for Learning@Cisco, remarked in April 2015: "The workforce is becoming more fluid, mobile, distributed and multi-generational. In order to foster a culture of learning, you need to make all knowledge accessible to everyone."

Sources: Alcala (2015); Jordan (2008)

Box 4.5 How Artificial Intelligence Can Hurt On-the-Job Learning

It's 6:30 in the morning, and Kristen is wheeling her prostate patient into the operating room. She's a senior resident, a surgeon in training. Today she's hoping to do some of the procedure's delicate, nerve-sparing dissection herself. The attending physician is by her side, and their four hands are mostly in the patient, with Kristen leading the way under his watchful guidance. The work goes smoothly, the attending backs away, and Kristen closes the patient by 8:15, with a junior resident looking over her shoulder. She lets him do the final line of sutures. She feels great: The patient's going to be fine, and she's a better surgeon than she was at 6:30.

Fast-forward six months. It's 6:30 AM again, and Kristen is wheeling another patient into the OR, but this time for robotic prostate surgery. The attending leads the setup of a thousand-pound robot, attaching each of its four arms to the patient. Then he and Kristen take their places at a control console 15 feet away. Their backs are to the patient, and Kristen just watches as the attending remotely manipulates the robot's arms, delicately retracting and dissecting tissue. Using the robot, he can do the entire procedure himself, and he largely does. He knows Kristen needs practice, but he also knows she'd be slower and would make more mistakes. So she'll be lucky if she operates more than 15 minutes during the four-hour surgery. And she knows that if she slips up, he'll tap a touch screen and resume control, very publicly banishing her to watch from the sidelines.

(Beane 2019, p. 5)

The first scenario illustrates on-the-job learning (OJL), while the later scenario shows how the use of robots and other artificial intelligence (AI) tools could adversely affect OJL, an important way for novices to learn from experts. Beane (2019) identifies four specific obstacles to OJL:

1   **Trainees are being relocated from their zone of optimal learning:** Training people in any work incurs costs and can compromise quality due to the slower progress and mistakes of novices. As organizations adopt intelligent machines, they address this by limiting trainees' involvement in risky and complex tasks, hindering their growth at the boundaries of their capabilities. Similar trends were observed in investment banking, where junior analysts were separated from senior partners due to algorithm-assisted valuations. While this division improved short-term efficiency, it hindered junior analysts' learning and the firm's future potential for handling intricate tasks.

2   **The work is kept away from experts:** AI can create a gap between trainees and their job, while also limiting experts' engagement in critical hands-on work. Robotic surgery serves as an example, where surgeons lack direct visibility of the patient's body and robot during procedures, challenging effective management. This has two learning implications: surgeons can't practice skills for a holistic understanding, and they must develop new abilities through others' feedback. A case study by Benjamin Shestakofsky on a pre-IPO start-up using machine learning (ML) mirrors this scenario. To improve matches in the ML application, managers hired people in the Philippines to manually create matches, and out-sourced customer support to a call center team in Las Vegas that addressed users experiencing platform difficulties. Delegation allowed focus on business and ML coding, but deprived them of vital learning from direct customer input, hindering their understanding of customer needs and challenges.

3   **Learners are required to excel in both traditional and innovative approaches:** Robotic surgery presents a new array of techniques and technologies aiming for the same outcomes as traditional surgery. Despite the potential for greater precision and ergonomics, it was simply integrated into the curriculum without sufficient time allocated for thorough learning, leading to a troubling result: residents mastered neither approach, a problem termed "methodological overload." A similar challenge is faced by professors utilizing technology platforms to develop massive open online courses (MOOCs), which provide course-design tools and instructional advice based on algorithmic analysis of student interactions. Professors had to acquire new skills while maintaining their traditional teaching abilities, creating tension for the professors. Constantly changing tools, metrics, and expectations further complicated matters, making it difficult for everyone. Those who navigated this dual demand well were already technically proficient and had substantial organizational support.

4   **Traditional learning methods are commonly assumed to be effective:** For decades, the medical field has adhered to the "See one, do one, teach one"

method, but it proves inadequate for robotic surgery. Despite the need for an update, the pressure to stick to approved learning methods remains strong, and deviations are rare. Similarly, in policing, traditional approaches clash with the demands of using algorithm-generated beat assignments. The reliance on "old-fashioned learning on the beat" hinders officers' ability to incorporate crime forecasts effectively. Chiefs hesitate to micromanage and reduce officers' autonomy, inadvertently undermining learning and creating confusion, resistance, and decreased trust in the predictive policing tool.

Confronted with these obstacles, employees will learn to work alongside intelligent machines through a widespread and informal process known as shadow learning, i.e., norm-challenging practices that are pursued discreetly and tolerated due to the positive results they yield. Shadow learning allows individuals to adapt to the new challenges posed by intelligent machines and acquire the necessary skills outside of traditional and formal training settings.

Shadow learners resort to bending or breaking the rules covertly to acquire the necessary instruction and experience. This behavior shouldn't come as a surprise, because when legitimate means fail to achieve valued goals, deviance emerges. Expertise, being a coveted occupational objective, is no exception. Due to the barriers discussed, it is natural for individuals to seek unconventional ways to acquire vital skills. Although their approaches can be inventive and effective, they may carry personal and organizational consequences: shadow learners could face punishment, lose opportunities, status, and even lead to waste or harm. Despite the risks, individuals persist with these practices because they may prove effective. While it is unwise to blindly adopt such practices, organizations can learn from them to address the shortcomings of traditional learning approaches.

As these learners find innovative ways to work effectively with the technology, organizations can learn from these practices to better integrate and support the collaboration between employees and intelligent machines. Beane suggests three specific organizational strategies that may facilitate using lessons from shadow learning:

1   **Continuously explore it:** Shadow learning is a rapidly evolving process, adapting to the increasing capabilities of intelligent technologies. New forms of shadow learning will emerge over time, presenting valuable insights and lessons. However, caution is crucial. Shadow learners often recognize the nature of their practices and the potential for penalties if exposed. Middle managers may turn a blind eye to these practices due to the positive results they yield, as long as they remain discreet. Consequently, learners and managers may be hesitant to share information when an observer, especially a senior manager, expresses interest in studying these practices for skill development. To address this, employing a neutral third party can ensure strict anonymity while comparing diverse cases. Building trust with early technology-adopters and safeguarding their identities is essential for them to open up and share their experiences.

2   **Adapt and use shadow learning practices to shape the organizations, work, and technology:** Organizations have often embraced AI in a way that allows a single expert to take more control over tasks, reducing reliance on trainees' assistance. For instance, in robotic surgery, senior surgeons can now operate with less help from trainees due to advanced robotic surgical systems. Similarly,

investment banking systems empower senior partners to exclude junior analysts from complex valuations. To drive progress, all stakeholders must advocate for organizational, technological, and work designs that not only enhance productivity but also foster on-the-job learning. By adapting and applying shadow learning practices, organizations can ensure continuous improvement and successful integration of intelligent technologies in the workforce.

3   **Harness AI as part of the solution:** AI can coach learners as they face challenges, support experts in their mentorship roles, and facilitate smart connections between the two groups. For instance, technology can be used to enable crowd-sourced annotation of instructional videos, providing clarification and practice opportunities based on previous users' interactions. Augmented reality systems, such as smart glasses or tablets, integrate expert instructions into real-time work scenarios. More sophisticated systems are on the horizon, allowing for super-imposing expert demonstrations onto apprentices' visual fields, recording their attempts, and facilitating real-time connections with mentors. While formal training has been the primary focus, the deeper crisis lies in enhancing on-the-job learning, necessitating a redirection of efforts in that direction.

Source: Beane (2019)

Table 4.1 summarizes the discussion of KM processes and KM systems, and also indicates some of the mechanisms and technologies that might facilitate them. As may be seen from this table, the same tool or technology can be used to support more than one KM process.

Managing Knowledge Management Solutions

The management of KM systems will be discussed in Chapters 6 through 9, which will examine each of the four types of KM systems in greater detail. Moreover, the selection of KM processes and KM systems that would be most appropriate for the circumstances will be discussed in Chapter 11. Finally, the overall leadership of the KM function will be discussed in Chapter 12. Therefore, in this section, we focus on some overall recommendations regarding the management of KM processes and systems.

First, organizations should use a combination of the four types of **KM processes and systems**. Although different KM processes may be most appropriate in the light of the organization's business strategy, focusing exclusively on one type of KM processes (and the corresponding type of KM systems) would be inappropriate because they serve complementary objectives. More specifically, it is important to note the following:

- Knowledge application enables efficiency. However, too much emphasis on knowledge application could reduce knowledge creation, which often benefits from individuals viewing the same problem from multiple different perspectives and thereby leads to reduced effectiveness and innovation.
- Knowledge capture enables knowledge to be converted from tacit form to explicit, or from explicit form to tacit, and thereby facilitates knowledge sharing. However, it might lead to reduced attention to knowledge creation. Moreover, knowledge

Table 4.1 KM Processes and Systems, and Associated Mechanisms and Technologies

KM Processes	KM Systems	KM Subprocesses	Illustrative KM Mechanisms	Illustrative KM Technologies
Knowledge Discovery	Knowledge Discovery Systems	Combination	Meetings, telephone conversations, documents, and collaborative creation of documents	Databases, Web-based access to data, data mining, repositories of information, Web portals, best practices, and lessons learned
		Socialization	Employee rotation across departments, conferences, brainstorming retreats, cooperative projects, and initiation	Videoconferencing, electronic discussion groups, and e-mail
Knowledge Capture	Knowledge Capture Systems	Externalization	Models, prototypes, best practices, and lessons learned	Social media, best practices, neural networks, and lessons learned databases
		Internalization	Learning by doing, on-the-job training, learning by observation, and face-to-face meetings	Artificial intelligence systems, computer-based simulations, and chat groups
Knowledge Sharing	Knowledge Sharing Systems	Socialization	See above	See above
		Exchange	Memos, manuals, letters, and presentations	Team collaboration tools, Web-based access to data, databases, repositories of information, best practices databases, lessons learned systems, and expertise locator systems
Knowledge Application	Knowledge Application Systems	Direction	Traditional hierarchical relationships in organizations, help desks, and support centers	Capture and transfer of experts' knowledge, troubleshooting systems, and case-based reasoning systems; decision support systems
		Routines	Organizational policies, work practices, and standards	Expert systems, enterprise resource planning systems, and management information systems

capture could lead to some knowledge being lost in the conversion process; not all tacit knowledge is converted into explicit form during externalization, and not all explicit knowledge is converted into tacit form during internalization.

- Knowledge sharing enables efficiency by reducing redundancy. However, too much knowledge sharing could lead to knowledge leaking from the organization and becoming available to competitors, and consequently reduce the benefits to the focal organization.

- Knowledge discovery enables innovation. However, too much emphasis on knowledge discovery could lead to reduced efficiency. It is not always suitable to create new knowledge, just as it may not always be appropriate to reuse existing knowledge.

Second, each KM process could benefit from two different subprocesses, as depicted in Figure 4.1. The subprocesses are mutually complementary, and should be used depending on the circumstances as discussed in Chapter 11. For example, knowledge sharing could occur through socialization or exchange. If knowledge being shared is tacit in nature, socialization would be appropriate, whereas if knowledge being shared is explicit in nature, exchange would be suitable. However, when individuals need to share both tacit and explicit knowledge, the two subprocesses (socialization and exchange) could be integrated together, such as in a face-to-face meeting (i.e., using socialization to transfer tacit knowledge) where the participants are also sharing printed reports containing explicit knowledge (i.e., using exchange to transfer explicit knowledge). Overall, the seven KM subprocesses should be developed within a group such that they can complement each other in an efficient fashion.

Third, each of the seven KM subprocesses of the KM processes depends on the KM mechanisms and technologies, as discussed before. Moreover, the same mechanism could be used to support multiple different subprocesses. Development and acquisition of these mechanisms and technologies, respectively, should be done in the light of the KM processes that would be most appropriate for the organizational circumstances.

Finally, the KM processes and systems should be considered in the light of each other, so that the organization builds a portfolio of mutually complementary KM processes and systems over time. This requires involvement from senior executives, a long-term KM strategy for the organization, and an understanding of the synergies as well as common foundations (i.e., mechanisms and technologies that might support multiple KM systems and processes) across the various KM systems and processes.

Alignment between Knowledge Management and Business Strategy

Alignment between business strategy and knowledge management helps enhance organizational performance (Kaplan and Norton 2004). Greater alignment between a firm's business strategy and its KM efforts indicates that these efforts are targeted on areas that are critical to the firm's success. For knowledge to become a source of competitive advantage, firms need to match their learning and knowledge strategy with their business strategy.

When a firm's learning and knowledge strategy matches its business strategy, the impact of knowledge and learning is positive. If this match is not achieved, knowledge and learning may have no impact or even have a negative impact on performance (Vera and Crossan 2003).

Summary

Building on the discussion of knowledge management foundations in Chapter 3, we have examined KM solutions, including KM processes and systems, in this chapter. Figure 4.2 provides a summary of the various aspects of knowledge management, indicating the

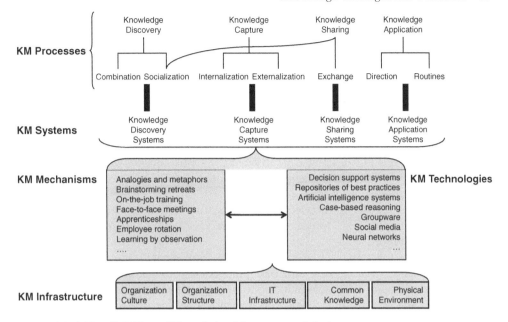

Figure 4.2 A Detailed View of Knowledge Management Solutions

various aspects of KM processes (including the four overall processes as well as the seven specific processes that support them), KM systems, KM mechanisms and technologies, and KM infrastructure. The next chapter examines the value of knowledge and KM solutions, highlighting their importance for organizational performance.

Review

1 Give an example of one knowledge management mechanism that could be used to facilitate each of the four knowledge management processes.

2 Give an example of one knowledge management technology that could be used to facilitate each of the four knowledge management processes.

3 Briefly explain the four kinds of classifications for knowledge management systems based on the process supported.

4 Distinguish between direction and routines. How do they relate to knowledge substitution?

5 Socialization could be used for knowledge discovery as well as knowledge sharing. Would the underlying process be any different depending on whether it is being used for knowledge discovery or knowledge sharing?

6 How does knowledge management relate to business strategy?

7 What effect does alignment between knowledge management and business strategy have on organizational performance?

8 Tacit knowledge could be transferred from one person to another in two distinct ways. One possibility is to transfer it directly through socialization. The other possibility is to convert it into explicit form (through externalization), then transfer it in explicit form to the recipient (through exchange), who then converts it into tacit form (through internalization). What are the pros and cons of each approach?

If the purpose is to transfer knowledge from one person to one other person, which approach would you recommend? If the purpose is to transfer knowledge from one person to 100 other individuals in different parts of the world, which approach would you recommend? Why?

Application Exercises

1   How would you, as a CEO of a manufacturing firm, facilitate the growth of knowledge management practices within your organization?
2   How would you utilize knowledge discovery systems and knowledge capture systems in an organization that is spread across the globe? Does geographic distance hamper the utilization of these systems?
3   Suggest reasons why a knowledge sharing system could be established between rival organizations (e.g., Mastercard Inc. and Visa Inc.) for the mutual benefit of both organizations.
4   Critique the following statement: "We have implemented several IT solutions: expert systems, chat groups, and best practices/lessons learned databases. These powerful solutions will surely induce our employees to internalize knowledge."
5   Consider the organization where you currently work or one with which you are familiar (either through your own prior experience or through interactions with someone who works there). What kind of knowledge management systems and processes does this organization use to manage knowledge? What are their effects on this organization's performance? In what order did the organization develop these KM systems and processes, and why?
6   Interview at least three managers from local organizations that have recently implemented a knowledge management system. How do these organizations differ in terms of the KM systems they have developed? What reasons led these organizations to develop these systems?

References

Alavi, M., and D. Leidner. 2001. Knowledge management and knowledge management systems: Conceptual foundations and research issues. *MIS Quarterly*, 25(1), 107–136.

Alcala, L. 2015. Cisco launches knowledge sharing and learning platform. *CMSWIRE*, https://www.cmswire.com/cms/social-business/cisco-launches-knowledge-sharing-and-learning-platform-028894.php, April 21.

Beane, M. 2019. Learning to work with intelligent machines. *Harvard Business Review* (September–October), 4–10.

Brown, J.S., and Duguid, P. 2000. Balancing act: How to capture knowledge without killing it. *Harvard Business Review* (May–June), 73–80.

Conner, K.R., and Prahalad, C.K. 1996. A resource-based theory of the firm: Knowledge versus opportunism. *Organization Science*, 7(5), 477–501.

Davenport, T., and Prusak, L. 1998. *Working knowledge.* Boston, MA: Harvard Business School Press.

Feigenbaum, E., and McCorduck, P. 1983. *The fifth generation.* Reading, MA: Addison-Wesley.

Fitzerald, M. 2008. Why social computing aids knowledge management. *CIO*, June 13. https://www.cio.com/article/276582/enterprise-software-why-social-computing-aids-knowledge-management.html.

Grant, R.M. 1996. Toward a knowledge-based theory of the firm. *Strategic Management Journal*, 17, 109–122.

Jensen, M.C., and Meckling, W.H. 1996. Specific and general knowledge, and organizational structure. In *Knowledge management & organizational design*, ed. P.S. Myers, 17–18. Newton, MA: Butterworth-Heinemann.

Jordan, S. 2008. VP, communication and collaboration IT. Interview. "Cisco—making the most of technology now!" *Strategic Path*, April 16. http://www.strategicpath.com.au/page/Sponsor_Articles/CISCO/Cisco_-_Making_the_most_of_Technology_Now_Ciscos_Sheila_Jordan_reveals_how_Cisco_is_Embracing_Web_20/.

Kaplan, R.S., and Norton, D.P. 2004. The strategy map: guide to aligning intangible assets. *Strategy & Leadership*, 32(5), 10–17.

Nahapiet, J., and Ghoshal, S. 1998. Social capital, intellectual capital, and the organizational advantage. *Academy of Management Review*, 23(2), 242–266.

Nonaka, I. 1994. A dynamic theory of organizational knowledge creation. *Organization Science*, 5(1) (February), 14–37.

Nonaka, I., and Takeuchi, H. 1995. *The knowledge creating company: How Japanese companies create the dynamics of innovation*. New York: Oxford University Press.

Sabherwal, R., and Sabherwal, S. 2007. How do knowledge management announcements affect firm value? A study of firms pursuing different business strategies. *IEEE Transactions on Engineering Management*, 54(3) (August), 409–422.

Stewart, T.A. 2000. The house that knowledge built. *Fortune*, 142(7) October 2, 278.

U.S. Department of Veterans Affairs. n.d. https://www.va.gov/.

Vera, D., and Crossan, M. 2003. Organizational learning and knowledge management: Toward an integrative framework. In *The Blackwell handbook of organizational learning and knowledge management*, ed. M. Easterby-Smith and M.A. Lyles, 122–142. Malden, MA: Blackwell.

5 Organizational Impacts of Knowledge Management

In the previous two chapters, we examined what we mean by knowledge management and discussed KM foundations including KM infrastructure, mechanisms, and technologies; and KM solutions including KM processes and solutions. In this chapter, we examine the impacts of knowledge management. Consistent with our emphasis on the use of KM in organizations, we focus our discussion on the impact of KM on companies and other private or public organizations.

The importance of knowledge (and KM processes) is well recognized. According to Benjamin Franklin, "an investment in knowledge pays the best interest" (NASA 2007). KM can impact organizations and organizational performance at several levels: people, processes, products, and the overall organizational performance (Becerra-Fernandez and Sabherwal 2008). KM processes can impact organizations at these four levels in two main ways. First, KM processes can help create knowledge, which can then contribute to improved performance of organizations along the above four dimensions. Second, KM processes can directly cause improvements along these four dimensions. These two ways in which KM processes can impact organizations is summarized in Figure 5.1.

Figure 5.2 depicts the impacts of KM on the four dimensions mentioned above and shows how the effect on one dimension can have an impact on another. The impact at three of these dimensions—individuals, products, and the organization—was clearly indicated in a joint survey by IDC[1] and *Knowledge Management Magazine* in May 2001 (Dyer and McDonough 2001). This survey examined the status of knowledge management practices in U.S. companies, and found three top reasons why U.S. firms adopt knowledge management: (1) retaining expertise of employees, (2) enhancing customers' satisfaction with the company's products, and (3) increasing profits or revenues. We will examine these issues closely in the next four sections.

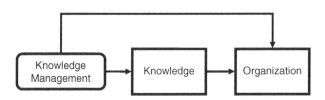

Figure 5.1 How Knowledge Management Impacts Organizations

DOI: 10.4324/9781003364375-6

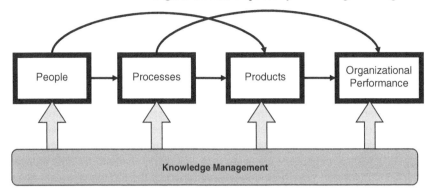

Figure 5.2 Dimensions of Organizational Impacts of Knowledge Management

Impact on People

Knowledge management can affect the organization's employees in several ways. First of all, it can facilitate their learning (from each other as well as from external sources). This learning by individual employees allows the organization to be constantly growing and changing in response to the market and the technology (Sabherwal 2008). Knowledge management also causes the employees to become more flexible and enhances their job satisfaction. This is largely because of their enhanced ability to learn about solutions to business problems that worked in the past, as well as those solutions that did not work. These effects are now discussed.

Impact on Employee Learning

Knowledge management can help enhance the employee's learning and exposure to the latest knowledge in their fields. This can be accomplished in a variety of ways including externalization and internalization, socialization, and communities of practice, which were all discussed in Chapter 3.

We earlier described **externalization** as the process of converting tacit knowledge into explicit forms, and **internalization** as the conversion of explicit knowledge into tacit knowledge (Nonaka and Takeuchi 1995). Externalization and internalization work together in helping individuals learn. One possible example of externalization is preparing a report on lessons learned from a project. In preparing the report, the team members document, or externalize, the tacit knowledge they have acquired during the project. Individuals embarking on later projects can then use this report to acquire the knowledge gained by the earlier team. These individuals acquire tacit knowledge through internalization—that is, by reading the explicit report and thereby re-experiencing what others have gone through. Thus, an expert writing a book is externalizing her knowledge in that area, and a student reading the book is acquiring tacit knowledge from the knowledge explicated in the book.

Socialization also helps individuals acquire knowledge but usually through joint activities such as meetings, informal conversations, and so on. One specific, but important, way in which learning through socialization can be facilitated involves the use of a **community of practice**, which we defined in Chapter 3 as an organic and self-organized group of individuals who may be dispersed geographically or organizationally but communicate regularly to discuss issues of mutual interest. In Box 5.1, we describe how one organization was able to enable individual learning via the implementation of communities of practice.

Box 5.1 Strategic Communities of Practice at Xerox

Xerox Corporation enabled individual learning through a strategic community of practice. Consistent with our definition of a community of practice, the groups at Xerox included geographically distributed individuals from the headquarters as well as business units. However, these groups were somewhat different from a traditional community of practice because they were not voluntarily formed by the individuals themselves but instead were deliberately established by the top management at Xerox with the goal of providing strategic benefits through knowledge sharing. This is the reason Storck and Hill (2000) characterized them as "strategic" communities. One of these strategic communities, which had been tasked to help in the management of technology infrastructure, consisted of a large group of information technology professionals who provided leading-edge solutions, addressed unstructured problems, and stayed in touch with the latest developments in hardware and software.

According to the group members surveyed by Storck and Hill, about two-thirds of the group's value resulted from face-to-face networking at the group's meetings. This attention to knowledge management, by focusing on informal groups of employees, has helped Xerox in its recent push in global services. Jim Joyce, a senior executive at Xerox remarked: "It is about understanding where knowledge is and how it is found. By working with human elements of this, there are real things you can do to help people embrace the technology and incorporate it into the workflow" (Moore 2001). Similarly, Tom Dolan, president, Xerox Global Services, recognized:

> At the core of Xerox's heritage of innovation is a deep understanding of how people, processes and technology interact with each other in the creation of great work. As a result, our practical, results-oriented, knowledge management solutions can help businesses streamline work processes, enable better customer service, and grow revenue.
>
> (Business Wire 2002)

Xerox has continued the use of communities of practice, with about 15 learning communities, including more than 1,000 employees, being launched in 2007 and 2008. According to Kent Purvis, a managing principal with Xerox's global services division: "We know there is a groundswell of knowledge among our managing principals, along all the lines of business. Now there is a structure in place for sharing it" (Kranz 2008).

Sources: Compiled from Business Wire (2002); Kranz (2008)

The experience of Xerox illustrates the way in which knowledge management can enable the organization's employees to learn from each other as well as from prior experiences of former employees. It is also indicative of how such processes for individual learning can lead to continued organizational success.

Impact on Employee Adaptability

When the knowledge management process at an organization encourages its employees to continually learn from each other, the employees are likely to possess the information and knowledge needed to adapt whenever organizational circumstances so require. Moreover, when they are aware of ongoing and potential future changes, they are less likely to be caught by surprise. Awareness of new ideas and involvement in free-flowing discussions not only prepare them to respond to changes, but they also make them more likely to accept change. Thus, knowledge management is likely to engender greater adaptability among employees.

When Buckman Laboratories International, Inc., a privately owned U.S. specialty chemicals firm with about 1,300 employees, was named "the 2000 Most Admired Knowledge Enterprise," its Chairman, Bob Buckman, remarked that the company's knowledge management efforts were intended to continually expose its employees to new ideas and enable them to learn from them (Business Wire 2000). He also emphasized that the employees were prepared for change as a result of being in touch with the latest ideas and developments, and they consequently embraced change rather than being afraid of it. The increased employee adaptability due to knowledge management enabled the company to become a very fast-changing organization around the needs of its customers. Buckman Laboratories has subsequently won the Most Admired Knowledge Enterprise award in 2001, 2003, 2004, 2005, and 2006, and been nominated Best Practice Partner by American Productivity and Quality Center (APQC) for their contributions to Leveraging Knowledge Across the Value Chain in 2006 (Buckman Laboratories International 2007).

Impact on Employee Job Satisfaction

Two benefits of knowledge management that accrue directly to individual employees have been discussed above: (a) they are able to learn better than employees in firms that are lacking in KM, and (b) they are better prepared for change. These impacts cause the employees to feel better, because of the knowledge acquisition and skill enhancement, and the impacts also enhance their market value relative to other organizations' employees. A recent study found that in organizations having more employees sharing knowledge with one another, turnover rates were reduced thereby positively affecting revenue and profit (Bontis 2003). Indeed, exit interview data in this study indicated that one of the major reasons many of the brightest knowledge workers changed jobs was because, "they felt their talent was not fully leveraged." Of course, it is possible to argue for the reverse causal direction; that is, more satisfied employees are likely to be more willing to share knowledge. The causal direction of the relationship between employee job satisfaction and knowledge sharing needs to be researched further.

In addition, knowledge management also provides employees with solutions to problems they face in case those same problems have been encountered earlier and effectively addressed. This provision of tried-and-tested solutions (for example, through the direction mechanism discussed in Chapter 3) amplifies employee's effectiveness in performing their jobs. This helps keep those employees motivated, for a successful employee would be highly motivated while an employee facing problems in performing his job would likely be demotivated.

Thus, as a result of their increased knowledge, improved market value, and greater on-the-job performance, knowledge management facilitates employees' job satisfaction. In addition, some approaches for knowledge management, such as mentoring and training, are also directly useful in motivating employees and therefore increasing employee job satisfaction. Similarly, communities of practice provide the involved employees intimate and socially validated control over their own work practices (Brown and Duguid 1991).

Figure 5.3 summarizes the above impacts knowledge management and knowledge can have on employees of organizations.

Impact on Processes

Knowledge management also enables improvements in organizational processes such as marketing, manufacturing, accounting, engineering, public relations, and so forth. These impacts can be seen along three major dimensions: effectiveness, efficiency, and degree of innovation of the processes. These three dimensions can be characterized as follows:

- **Effectiveness:** Performing the most suitable processes and making the best possible decisions.
- **Efficiency:** Performing the processes quickly and in a low-cost fashion.
- **Innovation:** Performing the processes in a creative and novel fashion that improves effectiveness and efficiency—or at least marketability.

Knowledge management can improve the above interrelated aspects of organizational processes through several means, including better knowledge being imparted to individuals (through exchange, socialization, and so on) and the provision of workable solutions (through directions and routines), for employees to solve the problems faced in their tasks. The effects of KM on effectiveness, efficiency, and innovation are discussed in more detail below.

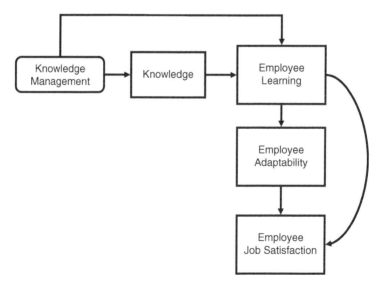

Figure 5.3 How Knowledge Management Impacts People

Impact on Process Effectiveness

Knowledge management can enable organizations to become more effective by helping them to select and perform the most appropriate processes. Effective knowledge management enables the organization's members to collect information needed to monitor external events. This results in fewer surprises for the leaders of the organization and consequently reduces the need to modify plans and settle for less effective approaches. In contrast, poor knowledge management can result in mistakes by the organization because they risk repeating past mistakes or not foreseeing otherwise obvious problems. For example, Ford Motor Company and Firestone (now part of Bridgestone Corporation) incurred numerous problems which could have been reduced through greater knowledge sharing, either by exchanging explicit knowledge and information or by using meetings (and other means of socialization) to share tacit knowledge. These firms did possess the necessary information to warn them about the mismatch of Ford Explorers and Firestone tires. However, the information was not integrated across the two companies, which might have inhibited either company from having the "full picture." It is interesting to note that although Ford had a good knowledge management process (the Best Practices Replication Process, discussed later in this chapter), it was not used to manage the information and knowledge relating to the Ford Explorer and the Firestone tires, or identify the potential risk of the tire's tread peeling off, leading to tire disintegration with the likelihood of accident in case the vehicle was then traveling at a high speed (Stewart 2000). The result was significant loss in lives for their customers and unprecedented legal liability.

Knowledge management enables organizations to quickly adapt their processes according to the current circumstances, thereby maintaining process effectiveness in changing times. On the other hand, organizations lacking in knowledge management find it difficult to maintain process effectiveness when faced with turnover of experienced and new employees. An illustrative example is from a large firm that reorganized its engineering department in 1996. This reorganization achieved a 75 percent reduction of the department's workforce. An external vendor subsequently absorbed many of the displaced engineers. However, like many organizations undergoing significant downsizing, this company failed to institutionalize any mechanisms to capture the knowledge of the employees that were leaving the department. A two-month review of the results following the reorganization effort showed that several key quality indicators were not met. This was a direct result of the loss of human knowledge with the displacement of the workforce. One important reason for the lack of attention to retaining knowledge is that the alternative approaches for capturing individual knowledge (which were discussed in Chapter 3) are not well understood. We will discuss some of these methods and technologies to capture knowledge in Chapter 7. Box 5.2 illustrates how one particular organization was able to significantly improve its processes in disaster management response through effective KM.

Box 5.2 Knowledge Management at Tearfund

Tearfund is a large relief and development agency, based in the United Kingdom. It regularly responds to natural and humanitarian disasters such as floods, hurricanes, typhoons, famine, and displacement. Tearfund was introduced to knowledge management by Paul Whiffen, who was earlier a knowledge management champion at British

Petroleum (Milton 2004). Its knowledge management efforts were founded on the recognition that learning from successes and failures during responses to disasters, both natural and man-made, should improve responses to later ones. It has proved this by identifying, consolidating, and then utilizing lessons learned in response to floods in Bangladesh, the Orissa Cyclone in India, the Balkan crisis, and other disasters. Its knowledge management efforts comprise of two main components. First, they utilize the learning opportunities that arise during and after any major activity by involving key participants in the activity to perform after-action reviews that describe lessons learned from the activity. In each project, the key project members participate in a structured, facilitated process to identify the key lessons learned and retrieve them again when they are next required. Second, Tearfund creates communities of practice to connect people with similar roles, issues, challenges, and knowledge needs. This enables Tearfund's employees to share their knowledge with its 350 United Kingdom and overseas partner organizations. Both these steps rely on cultural change and use of technology.

Through these KM efforts, Tearfund has been consciously learning different disaster responses, in each case identifying specific and actionable recommendations for future application. The explicit and conscious sharing of these recommendations provides Tearfund with the confidence and shared understanding needed to implement some of the lessons its many individuals have learned. The outcome has been a more proactive and integrated response to disasters that provides help to the beneficiaries more effectively. For example, Tearfund has modified its processes so that someone would be in the field no later than 48 hours after a disaster. It has also identified 300 specific and actionable recommendations.

> During the summer of 2000 and into the early autumn, we had done lots of Retrospects on various disasters responses, but we had never had the time to take these lessons and consolidate and disseminate them to find out what was going on. There was a person in the disaster response area called Tony who was frustrated with this, because he had never had time to assimilate the lessons, and I remember saying to him that eventually these disasters will stop, and we will find a quiet period and then we will do it. And sure enough, a quiet period came, by which time we had held eight Retrospects in various different forms, and he went home with lots of lessons and lots of yellow Post-it notes, and wrote them all up, and discovered that there were lots of lessons that had been learned and relearned over the year. It was a case of focusing on the ones we had learned many times. He focused on the 25 lessons that had come up three times out of the eight Retrospects. One of the lessons had come out every single time! Tony focused on embedding those lessons in the processes, procedures, guidelines, etc. for future disaster responses.
>
> (Milton 2004, p. 152)Sources: Compiled from Milton (2004); Tearfund (n.d.);
> Whiffen (2001); Wilson (2002)

Impact on Process Efficiency

Managing knowledge effectively can also enable organizations to be more productive and efficient. Upon exploring the "black box" of knowledge sharing within Toyota Motor Corporation's network, Dyer and Nobeoka (2000, p. 364) found that "Toyota's ability to effectively create and manage network-level knowledge sharing processes, at least partially, explains the relative productivity advantages enjoyed by Toyota and its suppliers." Knowledge diffusion was found to occur more quickly within Toyota's production network than in competing automaker networks. This was because Toyota's network had solved three fundamental dilemmas with regard to knowledge sharing by devising methods to: (1) motivate members to participate and openly share valuable knowledge (while preventing undesirable spillovers to competitors); (2) prevent free riders—that is, individuals who learn from others without helping others learn; and (3) reduce the costs associated with finding and accessing different types of valuable knowledge.

Another example of improved efficiency through knowledge management comes from British Petroleum (Echikson 2001). A BP exploration geologist located off the coast of Norway discovered a more efficient way of locating oil on the Atlantic seabed in 1999. This improved method involved a change in the position of the drill heads to better aim the equipment and thereby decrease the number of misses. The employee posted a description of the new process on BP's Intranet for everyone's benefit in the company. Within 24 hours, another engineer working on a BP well near Trinidad found the posting and e-mailed the Norwegian employee requesting necessary additional details. After a quick exchange of e-mail messages, the Caribbean team successfully saved five days of drilling and US$600,000. Of course, in utilizing this knowledge, the employees of the Caribbean unit needed to either trust their Norwegian colleagues or be able to somehow assess the reliability of that knowledge. Issues of trust, knowledge ownership, and knowledge hoarding are important and need to be examined in future research. This case study points to a real instance where knowledge sharing and taking advantage of information technology to quickly disseminate it resulted in a major cost saving to a company. Overall, the use of knowledge management and Internet technologies enabled BP to save US$300 million during the year 2001 while also enhancing innovation at every step of its value chain.

Impact on Process Innovation

Organizations can increasingly rely on knowledge shared across individuals to produce innovative solutions to problems as well as to develop more innovative organizational processes. Knowledge management has been found to enable riskier brainstorming (Storck and Hill 2000) and thereby enhance process innovation. In this context, Nonaka's (1998) concept of "ba"—which is equivalent to "place" in English and refers to a shared space (physical, virtual, or mental) for emerging relationships—is relevant. Unlike information, knowledge cannot be separated from the context. In other words, knowledge is embedded in ba, and therefore a foundation in ba is required to support the process of knowledge creation. J.P. Morgan Chase & Co. recognized the impact knowledge can have on process innovation when the following statement appeared in bold in their debut annual report: "The power of intellectual capital is the ability to breed ideas that ignite value" (Stewart 2001, p. 192).

Buckman Laboratories, discussed earlier in this chapter, linked their research and development personnel and technical specialists to their field-based marketing, sales, and technical support staffs to ensure that new products were developed with the customers' needs in mind and that customer needs were quickly and accurately communicated to the product development group (Zack 1999). As a result, new knowledge and insights were effectively exploited in the marketplace, leading to better products. In addition, the regular interactions with customers generated knowledge to guide future developments.

Another example of the impact of KM on process innovation (and efficiency), may be seen in the case of the Office of Special Projects, Veteran's Health Administration (VHA), which was discussed in Box 4.3 in Chapter 4. VHA significantly enhanced innovation by reducing bureaucracy, breaking down organizational barriers, benchmarking and partnering with others, and institutionalizing best processes.

Through these process improvements, knowledge management also contributes to the organization's **dynamic capabilities**, which are viewed as identifiable and specific organizational processes such as strategic decision-making and product development that create value for organizations in dynamic environments (Eisenhardt and Martin 2000; Prieto and Easterby-Smith 2006). In one leading chemical company, knowledge management, especially technical training, word-of-mouth transfer of market knowledge, and informal exchanges between sales managers, seemed to facilitate dynamic capabilities (Prieto and Easterby-Smith 2006).

Figure 5.4 summarizes the above impacts of knowledge management and knowledge on organizational processes.

Impact on Products

Knowledge management also impacts the organization's products. These impacts can be seen in two respects: **value-added products** and **knowledge-based products**. Whereas the impacts on the above dimensions come either through knowledge or directly from KM, the impacts below arise primarily from knowledge created through KM. This is depicted in Figure 5.5.

Impact on Value-Added Products

Knowledge management processes can help organizations offer new products or improved products that provide a significant additional value as compared to earlier products. One such example is Ford's Best Practices Replication Process in

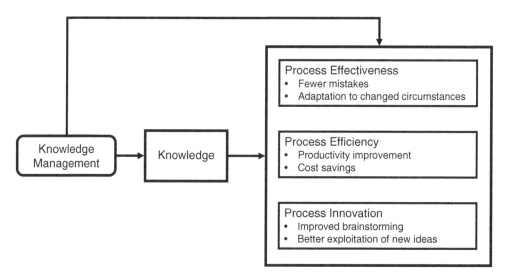

Figure 5.4 How Knowledge Management Impacts Organizational Processes

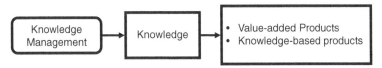

Figure 5.5 How Knowledge Management Impacts Products

manufacturing. Every year Ford headquarters provides a "task" to managers, requiring them to come up with a 5 percent, 6 percent, or 7 percent improvement in key measures—for example, improvements in throughput or energy use. Upon receiving their task, the managers turn to the **best-practices** database to seek knowledge about prior successful efforts. Ford claims that its "best-practice replication" system, whose use Ford tracks in meticulous detail, saved the company US$245 million from 1996 to 1997 (Anthes 1998). Over a four-and-a-half-year period from 1996 to 2000, more than 2,800 proven superior practices were shared across Ford's manufacturing operations. The documented value of the shared knowledge in 2000 was US $850 million, with another US$400 million of value anticipated from work in progress, for a total of US$1.25 billion (Stewart 2000; Swarup 2005).

Value-added products also benefit from knowledge management due to the effect the latter has on organizational process innovation. For example, innovative processes resulting from knowledge management at Buckman Laboratories enables sales and support staff to feed customer problems into their computer network in order to access relevant expertise throughout the company and be able to develop innovative solutions for the customers. Similarly, Steelcase Inc., uses information obtained through video ethnography from its customers, the end-users of office furniture, to understand how its products are used and then to redesign the products to make them more attractive to customers (Skyrme 2000).

Impact on Knowledge-Based Products

Knowledge management can also have a major impact on products that are inherently knowledge based—for example, in consulting and software development industries. For instance, consultants at ICL[2] can quickly access and combine the best available knowledge and bid on proposals that would otherwise be too costly or too time-consuming to put together. Indeed, in such industries, knowledge management is necessary for mere survival.

Knowledge-based products can also sometimes play an important role in traditional manufacturing firms. A classic example is Matsushita's (now Panasonic Corporation) development of an automatic breadmaking machine. In order to design the machine, Matsushita sought a master baker, observed the master baker's techniques, and then incorporated them into the machine's functionality (Nonaka and Takeuchi 1995). Similarly, companies such as Sun Microsystems have enhanced the level of customer service by placing solutions to customer problems in a shareable knowledge base. Moreover, customers can download software patches from the Internet based on their answers to an automated system that prompts customers with a series of questions aimed at diagnosing the customer needs.

Impact on Organizational Performance

In addition to potentially impacting people, products, and processes, knowledge management may also affect the overall performance of the organization. Knowledge management enhances the employees' learning from each other and from external sources, and helps to facilitate innovativeness, effectiveness, and efficiency of organizational processes. KM can also contribute to a firm by facilitating new knowledge-based products or enabling improved products that provide significant additional value. However, it would take time for a KM effort to produce these organizational benefits (Sabherwal and Sabherwal, 2007).

Deutsche Bank put it all in a nutshell when it took out a big advertisement in the *Wall Street Journal* (Stewart 2001, p. 192) that said: "Ideas are capital. The rest is just money." This advertisement reflects the belief that investments in knowledge management should be viewed as capital investments. This investment may be capable of producing long-term benefits to the entire organization rather than as assets that provide value only at the present time.

Knowledge management can impact overall organizational performance either directly or indirectly as discussed below.

Direct Impacts on Organizational Performance

Direct impact of knowledge management on organizational performance occurs when knowledge is used to create innovative products that generate revenue and profit or when the knowledge management strategy is aligned with business strategy. Such a direct impact concerns revenues and/or costs and can be explicitly linked to the organization's vision or strategy. Consequently, measuring direct impact is relatively straightforward. It can be observed in terms of improvements in return on investment (ROI). For example, one account director at British Telecom (BT Groups plc) indicated that his sales team generated about US$1.5 million in new business based on briefings from a new knowledge management system (Compton 2001). Similarly, speaking to the Knowledge Management World Summit in San Francisco, California, on January 11, 1999, Kenneth T. Derr, the Chairman and CEO of Chevron Corporation stated:

> Of all the initiatives we've undertaken at Chevron during the 1990s, few have been as important or as rewarding as our efforts to build a learning organization by sharing and managing knowledge throughout our company. In fact, I believe this priority was one of the keys to reducing our operating costs by more than $2 billion per year—from about $9.4 billion to $7.4 billion—over the last seven years.
>
> (Derr, 1999)

Indirect Impacts on Organizational Performance

Indirect impact of knowledge management on organizational performance comes about through activities that are not directly linked to the organization's vision, strategy, revenues, or costs. Such effects occur, for example, through the use of knowledge management to demonstrate intellectual leadership within the industry, which, in turn, might enhance customer loyalty. Alternatively, it could occur through the use of knowledge to gain an advantageous negotiating position with respect to competitors or partner organizations. Unlike direct impact, however, indirect impact cannot be associated with transactions and, therefore, cannot be easily measured.

One example of indirect benefits is the use of knowledge management to achieve economies of scale and scope. Before examining these effects, we briefly examine what we mean by economies of scale and scope.

A company's output is said to exhibit **economy of scale** if the average cost of production per unit decreases with increase in output. Due to economy of scale, a smaller firm has higher costs than larger firms, which makes it difficult to compete with the larger firms in terms of price. Some of the reasons that result in economies of scale include large setup cost makes low-scale production uneconomic, possibilities for specialization increase as production increases, and greater discounts from suppliers are likely when production is large scale.

A company's output is said to exhibit **economy of scope** when the total cost of that same company producing two or more different products is less than the sum of the costs that would be incurred if each product was produced separately by a different company. Due to economy of scope, a firm producing multiple products has lower costs than those of its competitors focusing on fewer products. Some of the reasons that result in economies of scope include: incorporating new innovations into multiple products, joint use of production facilities, and joint marketing or administration. Economy of scope can also arise if the production of one good provides the other as a byproduct.

Knowledge management can contribute to economies of scale and scope by improving the organization's ability to create and leverage knowledge related to products, customers, and managerial resources across businesses. Product designs, components, manufacturing processes, and expertise can be shared across businesses thereby reducing development and manufacturing costs, accelerating new product development, and supporting quick response to new market opportunities. Similarly, shared knowledge of customer preferences, needs, and buying behaviors can enable cross-selling of existing products or development of new products. Finally, economies of scope also result from the deployment of general marketing skills and sales forces across businesses. Although economies of scale and scope could, and usually do, lead to improvements in return on investments, the effect of knowledge management on scale and scope economies and their subsequent effect on return on investments cannot be directly linked to specific transactions and this is therefore considered as an "indirect" impact.

Another indirect impact of knowledge management is to provide a sustainable **competitive advantage**. Knowledge can enable the organization to develop and exploit other tangible and intangible resources better than the competitors can, even though the resources themselves might not be unique. Knowledge, especially context-specific tacit knowledge, tends to be unique and therefore difficult to imitate. Moreover, unlike most traditional resources, it cannot easily be purchased in a ready-to-use form. To obtain similar knowledge, the company's competitors have to engage in similar experiences, but obtaining knowledge through experience takes time. Therefore, competitors are limited in the extent to which they can accelerate their learning through greater investment.

LeaseCo, an industrial garment and small equipment leasing company described by Zack (1999), illustrates the use of knowledge management to gain a sustainable competitive advantage. LeaseCo's strategy involved occasionally bidding aggressively on complex, novel, or unpredictable lease opportunities. These bidding, and subsequent negotiation, experiences provided the company with unique and leverageable knowledge while reducing the opportunity for competitors to gain that same knowledge. LeaseCo realized two significant benefits over its competitors: first by investing in its strategic knowledge platform and second by learning enough about the particular client to competitively and profitably price leases for future opportunities with the same client. Sufficient mutual learning occurred between LeaseCo and their client for the client to contracted LeaseCo for future leases without even going out for competitive bids. In essence, LeaseCo created a sustainable (or renewable), knowledge-based barrier to competition.

Thus, sustainable competitive advantage may be generated through knowledge management by allowing the organization to know more than its competitors about certain things. Competitors, on the other hand, would need considerable time to acquire that same knowledge. Figure 5.6 summarizes the direct and indirect impacts KM and knowledge can potentially have on organizational performance.

This chapter has focused on objective aspects of performance. However, perceptions matter as well, and could subsequently affect objective performance measures. Box 5.3 examines this aspect, especially the effect of KM on perceived value of knowledge at the individual level.

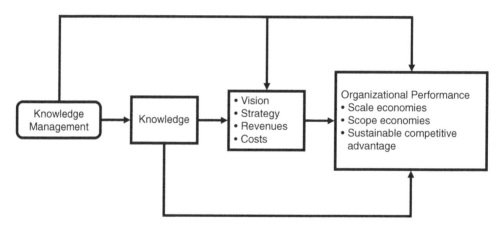

Figure 5.6 How Knowledge Management Impacts Organizational Performance

Box 5.3 Perceived Value of Knowledge

Sabherwal et al. (2023) examine how KM practices affect perceived value of knowledge, both at individual and organization levels. They empirically examine these effects using survey data (186 employees) and qualitative data (300+ employees) from the National Aeronautics and Space Administration.

To examine the potential differences in individual perceptions of value, the researchers use commodity theory, which defines commodities as resources that are: (a) useful; (b) potentially possessed by individuals; and (c) shareable between individuals. Knowledge meets all three criteria. Commodity theory focuses on the psychological effects of scarcity, arguing that a scarce commodity is valued more. A commodity's scarcity has four aspects: (a) limited supply or suppliers; (b) costly to obtain, retain, or provide; (c) restrictions on its possession; and (d) delays in provision. Scarcity may increase the commodity's distinctiveness and individuals' desire to possess it. Similarly, the perceived lack of information increases the desire for a commodity. Thus, a commodity's scarcity increases its perceived value to individuals. For example, individuals prefer scarce paintings or luxury handbags. Similarly, "classified" knowledge is considered more valuable than "accessible" knowledge, and tacit knowledge is more valuable than explicit knowledge.

Based on commodity theory, the research findings in the aforementioned study expect that utilizing KM mechanisms that enhance knowledge availability across the organization would reduce its potential value at the individual level, since having wide access to the knowledge reduces its scarcity (Sabherwal et al. 2023). More specifically, the scarcity of certain knowledge would lead one to conclude that those individuals who have access to the knowledge would: (a) have greater motivation to process it; (b) feel distinctive due to them possessing it; and (c) attach greater value to it. This finding explains the old adage that "knowledge is power," specifically if that knowledge is scarce. Prior literature also finds that individuals perceive greater uniqueness from possessing tacit knowledge than from explicit knowledge (Feldman and March 1981). The wide availability of certain knowledge may increase its perceived value at the organizational level whereas its scarcity might increase its perceived value to the individual.

The empirical study supports the arguments based on commodity theory. More specifically, let us consider knowledge substitution, which refers to novices applying an expert's knowledge without undergoing the learning process themselves. This is considered more efficient than traditional learning methods. Information technology (IT) plays a vital role in supporting knowledge substitution by providing direction, sequencing, and routines. IT-based knowledge substitution involves using IT tools to apply explicit knowledge without requiring individuals to learn the underlying knowledge. Various IT systems, such as trouble-shooting systems, advisor systems, and fault-diagnosis systems, facilitate knowledge substitution by enabling the direct application of expertise without extensive learning. By making knowledge more easily available for use, without even having to learn it, IT-based knowledge substitution—according to commodity theory—would reduce its perceived value to individuals. The research presented in Sabherwal et al. (2023) finds this to be indeed the case: IT-based knowledge substitution has a negative effect on the perceived value of knowledge at the individual level.

Sources: Compiled from Feldman and March (1981); Sabherwal et al. (2023)

Summary

In Table 5.1, we summarize the various impacts of knowledge management examined in this chapter. The impact KM has on one level might lead to synergistic impacts on another level as well. For example, employee learning facilitates impacts on processes as well as on products. Thus, KM has the potential to produce several interrelated impacts on people, products, processes, and organizations as we have described in this chapter.

Table 5.1 A Summary of Organizational Impacts of Knowledge Management

Levels of Impact	Impacted Aspects
People	• Employee learning
	• Employee adaptability
	• Employee job satisfaction
Processes	• Process effectiveness
	• Process efficiency
	• Process innovativeness
Products	• Value-added products
	• Knowledge-based products
Organizational Performance	• Direct Impacts
	• Return on investment
	• Indirect impacts
	• Economies of scale and scope
	• Sustainable competitive advantage

Review

1 Briefly enumerate the ways in which knowledge can impact an organization.
2 State the importance of knowledge management with specific reference to its impact on employee adaptability and job satisfaction.
3 Explain why poor knowledge management reduces the effectiveness of organizational processes.
4 What three dimensions are relevant for examining the impact of knowledge management on business processes?
5 Identify ways in which knowledge management helps improve process effectiveness, efficiency, and innovation.
6 Describe how knowledge management can contribute to an organization's products. Illustrate using the example of Xerox.
7 How can we assess: (a) the direct impacts and (b) the indirect impacts of knowledge management on organizational performance?
8 Knowledge management is an invaluable tool for the oil industry. Justify this statement with suitable examples.

Application Exercises

1 Identify the possible ways in which knowledge management (or the lack thereof) in your organization (it could be your academic institution or your workplace) affects your learning and job satisfaction.
2 Identify the biggest positive impact on your organization (it could be your academic institution or your workplace) due to the implementation of knowledge management. Speculate on the possibilities if there were no knowledge management practices in place.

3   Now identify the biggest negative impact on your organization (it could be your academic institution or your workplace) due to improper/insufficient knowledge management practices and suggest ways of improvement.

4   Interview a friend or a family member who works at a different organization than you, and examine the overall effects of knowledge management on that organization.

5   You are a CEO who considers implementing a knowledge management system in your company. You have to decide one option out of two: (a) Our knowledge management system can be accessed by customers, or (b) Our knowledge management system cannot be accessed by customers. Describe your decision and provide the reason in terms of organizational performance.

6   Critique the following analysis: Our investment in knowledge management seems to be unsuccessful. The ROI decreased from 10 percent to 5 percent at the year of system implementation. Since direct measure of organizational performance decreased, we need to uninstall the knowledge management system right away.

Notes

1   IDC is one of the world's leading providers of technology intelligence, industry analysis, market data, and strategic and tactical guidance to builders, providers, and users of information technology. More information on it can be obtained from www.idc.com.

2   Formed in 1968, ICL was bought by STC in 1984. Fujitsu bought an 80 percent stake in ICL-UK from STC in 1990. In 2002, the consulting arm of ICL-UK was merged with DMR Consulting, and its service division became Fujitsu Services.

References

Anthes, G. 1998. Defending knowledge. *ComputerWorld*, 32(7), February 16, 41–42.

Becerra-Fernandez, I., and Sabherwal, R. 2008. Individual, group, and organizational learning. In *Knowledge management: An evolutionary view*, ed. I. Becerra-Fernandez and D. Leidner, 13–39. Armonk, NY: M.E. Sharpe.

Bontis, N. 2003. HR's role in knowledge management. *Canadian HR Reporter*, 16(5), March 10, G8.

Brown, J.S., and Duguid, P. 1991. Organizational learning and communities-of-practice: Toward a unified view of working, learning, and innovation. *Organization Science*, 2(1), 40–57.

Buckman Laboratories International. 2007. Awards and recognitions for Buckman Laboratories. *Knowledge nurture*. http://www.knowledge-nurture.com/recognitions.html (accessed February 12, 2009).

Business Wire. 2000. 2000 most admired knowledge enterprises announced. *Business Wire*, June 5.

Business Wire. 2002. Xerox ranked as one of North America's most admired knowledge enterprises: Winning practices available to customers through Xerox Global Services. *Business Wire*, May 6.

Compton, J. 2001. Dial K for knowledge. *CIO*, June 15.

Derr, K.T. 1999. *Managing knowledge the Chevron way*. Knowledge Management World Summit. San Francisco, California, January 11, 1999. http://www.fordbrett.com/documents/website/Derr.pdf.

Dyer, G., and McDonough, B. 2001. The state of KM. *Knowledge Management* (May), 21–36.

Dyer, J.H., and Nobeoka, K. 2000. Creating and managing a high-performance knowledge-sharing network: The Toyota case. *Strategic Management Journal*, 23(3), 345–367.

Echikson, W. 2001. When oil gets connected. *Business Week*, December 3.

Eisenhardt, K.M., and Martin, J.K. 2000. Dynamic capabilities: What are they? *Strategic Management Journal*, 21, 1005–1121.

Feldman, M.S., and March, J.G. 1981. Information in organizations as signal and symbol. *Administrative Science Quarterly*, 26(2), 171–186.

Kranz, G. 2008. At Xerox, learning is a community activity. *Workforce Management Online* (December). http://www.workforce.com/section/11/feature/26/05/23/index.html (accessed February 12, 2009).

Milton, N. 2004. Knowledge management in the aid and development sector: A case study in implementation at Tearfund. In *Performance through learning: Knowledge management in practice*, ed. C. Gorelick, N. Milton, and K. April, 143–161. Boston: Elsevier Butterworth-Heinemann.

Moore, C. 2001. Xerox makes global services push. *InfoWorld*, November 19. *itWorldCanada*, https://www.itworldcanada.com/article/xerox-makes-global-services-push-2/38996.

National Aeronautics and Space Administration (NASA). 2007. Quotes related to knowledge management or collaboration. http://km.nasa.gov/whatis/KM_Quotes.html (accessed February 12, 2009).

Nonaka, I. 1998. The concept of ba: Building a foundation for knowledge creation. *California Management Review*, 40(3) (Spring), 40–54.

Nonaka, I., and Takeuchi, H. 1995. *The knowledge creating company: How Japanese companies create the dynamics of innovation.* New York: Oxford University Press.

Prieto, I.M., and Easterby-Smith, M. 2006. Dynamic capabilities and the role of organizational knowledge: An exploration. *European Journal of Information Systems*, 15, 500–510.

Sabherwal, R. 2008. KM and BI: From mutual isolation to complementarity and synergy. *Cutter Consortium Executive Report*, 8(8), 1–18.

Sabherwal, R., and Sabherwal, S. 2007. How do knowledge management announcements affect firm value? A study of firms pursuing different business strategies. *IEEE Transactions on Engineering Management*, 54(3) (August), 409–422.

Sabherwal, R., Steelman, Z., and Becerra-Fernandez, I. 2023. Knowledge management mechanisms and common knowledge impacts on the value of knowledge at individual and organizational levels. *International Journal of Information Management*, 72 (October) (102660).

Skyrme, D.J. 2000. Developing a knowledge strategy: From management to leadership. In *Knowledge management: Classic and contemporary works*, ed. D. Morey, M. Maybury, and B. Thuraisingham, 61–84. Cambridge, MA: The MIT Press.

Stewart, T.A. 2000. Knowledge worth $1.25 billion. *Fortune*, November 27, 302–303.

Stewart, T.A. 2001. Intellectual capital: Ten years later, how far we've come. *Fortune*, May 28, 192–193.

Storck, J., and Hill, P. 2000. Knowledge diffusion through strategic communities. *Sloan Management Review*, 41(2), 63–74.

Swarup, S. 2005. Applying KM to improve quality. *InsideKnowledge*, October 10.

Tearfund. n.d. http://www.tearfund.org.

Whiffen, P. 2001. Seizing learning opportunities at Tearfund. *Knowledge Management Review* (November/December).

Wilson, J. (Ed.). 2002. *Knowledge management review: The practitioner's guide to knowledge management*, Chicago: Melcrum Publishing Limited.

Zack, M.H. 1999. Developing a knowledge strategy. *California Management Review*, 41(3) (Spring), 125–145.

Part II
Knowledge Management Technologies and Systems

6 Knowledge Application Systems
Systems that Utilize Knowledge

In this chapter, we describe knowledge application systems, how they are developed, and review some practical applications of these systems. As we discussed in Chapter 4, knowledge application systems support the process through which individuals utilize the knowledge possessed by other individuals without acquiring or learning that knowledge. There are mechanisms and technologies that support knowledge application systems by facilitating the knowledge management processes of routines and direction. Knowledge application systems are typically enabled by intelligent technologies. We also summarize in this chapter some of the relevant intelligent technologies that underlie KM systems, including rule-based expert systems, case-based reasoning (CBR), and traditional management information systems. Additionally, we explore the practical applications of these knowledge systems in customer support, fault diagnosis, fraud detection, and healthcare. The case studies in this chapter review the application of knowledge systems and explore several types of intelligent technologies and applications in a variety of domains. Finally, this chapter discusses the limitations of knowledge application systems.

Knowledge Application

You may recall, from Chapter 4, that knowledge application depends on direction and routines. Hierarchical relationships and structures facilitate routines in the applications of knowledge. These relationships and structures are supported by standard procedures and structured processes that facilitate routines in knowledge application. On the other hand, lack of standard procedures and stable processes facilitates direction in knowledge application.

Technologies supporting direction and routines include expert systems, decision support, advisor systems, fault diagnosis (or troubleshooting) systems, and help desk systems. These technologies may support direction, as in the case of a field service technician seeking to troubleshoot a particular product; or may support routines, as in the case of a customer service representative who may need to identify alternative product delivery mechanisms while preparing the shipment of an order. Moreover, mechanisms and technologies can facilitate knowledge application through direction and routines either within or across organizations.

For a quick overview of what knowledge application systems are and how they are used, let us look at a brief case study in Box 6.1 of how Casio Computer Company implemented a call center using a knowledge application system. This case demonstrates how knowledge applications enable organizations to use the knowledge created

DOI: 10.4324/9781003364375-8

through customer interactions. Intelligent technologies within the eCustomerService and eKnowledgeManager solutions enabled the management, development team, and support staff to make decisions using knowledge accumulated through interactions with customers.

Box 6.1 Performance Improvement in Healthcare through Knowledge Sharing

Casio Computer Company has been manufacturing and selling business and consumer electronics since 1946. The company is headquartered in Japan, with worldwide branches across several countries and a significant presence in Canada and the U.S. Some of the company's products include timepieces, calculators, musical equipment, and medical devices. Casio is committed to earning and maintaining customer confidence and trust in the Casio brand, thus after sales technical support is critical to the operations of Casio.

Casio receives thousands of phone calls and e-mail inquiries per month from customers in the U.S. and Canada. These support calls generate a significant amount of documentation and information as technicians and support representatives respond to inquiries and document their interactions with customers. Furthermore, consumer feedback on products through e-mail also reflects attitudes of consumers toward the brand and products.

Casio lacked a call center solution with capabilities to integrate a knowledge base, leverage FAQs, or generate reports that could inform management, product design, and development. The inability to leverage the knowledge generated from interacting with thousands of customers was impeding the company's goal of providing high quality after-service to customers. To address these challenges the company wanted a call center solution with an integrated knowledge base and efficient reporting options that generated insightful reports and metrics for management. Furthermore, the company wanted to provide 24/7 customer support through the Web and use customer feedback to improve product development and design. To address these challenges the company implemented Giva's eCustomerService and eKnowledgeManager as the single solution for its USA and Canada customer service call center operation.

The call center solution enabled Casio to leverage knowledge across their interactions with customers. Since the call center solution keeps historical records of customer interactions, including the type of call, root cause of the problem, and solutions, technicians can review past interactions and solve customer issues in a timely manner. Support technicians can use past solutions in the knowledge base to better serve customers and enhance their technical skills. Using the integrated knowledge base, Casio also implemented a Frequently Asked Questions (FAQ) website for customers and support staff. In addition to deploying a Web-based 24/7 support center, product development teams can use customer feedback from the call center to improve product development and design.

The real-time reporting features of the eCustomerService and eKnowledgeManager provide management and support staff with meaningful call center metrics, including service level agreements, customer satisfaction ratings, and performance of support staff. These metrics assist the management in developing strategies to sustain their commitment to providing high quality after sales customer services.

Sources: Compiled from Casio Computer Company (n.d.); Giva Inc. (2006)

Rule-Based Systems

A *rule-based system* is an expert system for a specific domain that relies on *rules, heuristics,* or *rules-of-thumb* to make deductions or inferences (Frye et al. 1995; Hayes-Roth 1985). Traditionally, the development of knowledge-based application systems has relied on *rules* or *models* to represent domain knowledge. Rule-based system (RBS) knowledge applications combine tacit and explicit knowledge and encode that knowledge into rules so others can easily use that knowledge without necessarily acquiring the expertise. Thus, these systems facilitate the automation of decision-making tasks. This chapter reviews domain specific applications of rule-based expert systems, and the case study on the SBIR/STTR Online Advisor demonstrates how these systems are used in organizations and businesses.

RBS are the most used knowledge representation paradigms, perhaps due to their intuitive implementation and imitation of human intelligence by using human-made rules garnered from facts and experience. Usually, people make decisions by evaluating facts and making inferences and deductions based on how they perceive the facts.

The development of rule-based knowledge application systems requires the collaboration of a subject matter expert and a knowledge engineer. The subject matter experts develop heuristics and rules-of-thumb over years of practical experience at solving problems. Some of these rules are tacit, and others are explicit. Through the process of knowledge engineering, the knowledge engineer elicits knowledge from the expert. Typically, this is done through intensive and extensive interview of the **domain expert** to document the knowledge of the expert. The knowledge is then transformed into heuristics or rules-of-thumb that are encoded into production rules that a computer system can process. Figure 6.1 is an architecture of RBS showing the processes of eliciting rules from a domain expert. The knowledge engineer codifies theses heuristics and rules-of-thumb into production rules. The inference engine processes the facts using the production rules and recommends appropriate actions.

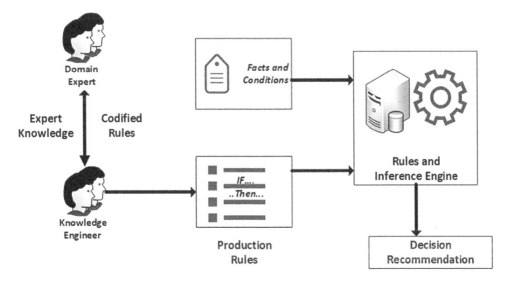

Figure 6.1 Rule-Based Reasoning Architecture

These *production rules* are encoded into *IF-THEN* statements that embody domain specific expertise, often in the form of condition-action. The *IF* part of the rule specifies the conditions and the *THEN* part defines one or more actions. The *IF* portion is the **rule antecedent** or **precondition** which is evaluated using pre-set criteria. The *THEN* part of the rule is the *action, conclusion*, or *consequence* that is dependent on the outcome of the evaluation in the *IF* part. For example: "IF the number of employees is less than 500, THEN the firm is a small business," is one of the rules that the SOS Advisor checks to ensure the firm is eligible for the SBIR/STTR program.

Rule-based knowledge systems automate decision-making and enable novices to make decisions like experts. Using these production rules, a rule-based expert system can help a technician diagnose a problem and make decisions on the appropriate solution. In addition to rules, other paradigms used to represent knowledge include *frames, predicates, associative networks*, and *objects*.

Rule-based systems have some shortcomings, including the limitation on the number of rules and exceptions to the rules. Expert systems with considerable numbers of rules offer many disadvantages, namely (1) difficulty in coding, verifying, validating, and maintaining the rules; and (2) reduction in the efficiency of the inference engine executing the rules. To address some of those shortcomings, knowledge application systems may combine RBS with *case-based reasoning* to drive knowledge applications (Abu-Nasser and Abu Naser 2018). For more details on rule-based systems refer to Chapter 8 of the book *Knowledge Management: Challenges, Solutions, and Technologies* (Becerra-Fernandez et al. 2004).

Case-Based Reasoning Systems

The RBS approach to knowledge representation has applications in many areas of business; however, many of these applications are increasingly integrating *case-based reasoning* (CBR), *artificial intelligence*, and *machine learning analytics*. CBR is an artificial intelligence technique designed to mimic human problem solving (Allen 1994). CBR is based on Schank's (1982) model of dynamic memory. When faced with a new problem, humans search their memories for past problems resembling the current problem and adapt the prior solution to "fit" the current problem. CBR is a method of analogical reasoning that utilizes old cases or experiences to solve problems, critique solutions, explain anomalous situations, or interpret situations (Aamodt and Plaza 1994; Tocimáková et al. 2020). A typical case-based knowledge application system will consist of four cycles: *retrieve, reuse, revise*, and *retain*, as depicted in the CBR Cycle in Figure 6.2.

1   **Retrieve:** In this first phase of the cycle, the system searches the case library database using attributes and values of the new problem as search parameters. A search engine algorithm compares each examined case to the current problem, quantifies their similarity, and ranks them in decreasing order of similarity.
2   **Reuse:** In this step of the cycle, the system uses retrieved cases that are similar in every way to the new problem, so the solutions for the past problem would address the current problem. However, in most situations, even when the cases are similar, the solution may require some adaptations as the context of the new problem may be different. As solutions are adapted to unfamiliar problems, the case library database is updated. If the current problem and the most similar case are not similar enough, then the solution may have to be adapted to fit the needs of the

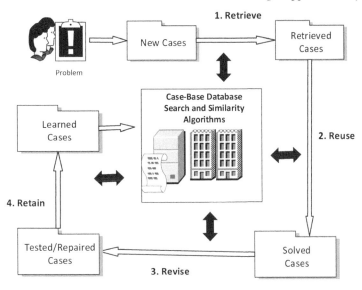

Figure 6.2 CBR Cycle

current problem. The new problem will be solved with the aid of an old solution that has been adapted to the new problem.

3   **Revision:** This step manages the updated problem descriptions and solutions when solutions are adapted to unfamiliar problems or new solutions are recommended for new problems. These new solutions or adapted solutions are evaluated by experts and, if deemed appropriate, then the problem and solution will be retained and added to the case-library database. Once a solution is retrieved and applied to a problem, its effect on the problem is fed back to the CBR system for capture and classification of its solution (as success or failure) in the subsequent step of the cycle.

4   **Retention:** In this last step of the cycle, the current solution for the problem or case is stored in the case database. A case information may include added information of the solution. This cycle enables the CBR system to 'learn' from the experiences of past problems and solutions. The new experience is likely to be useful in future problem solving. This step determines if the new case is worth adding to the library and placing it in the appropriate location in the case library.

These CBR cycles are depicted in Figure 6.2, where the cases are stored in a case library and search and similarity algorithms will search the case library for similar cases and return corresponding solutions (Perner 2019). The CBR is a self-learning system that grows and adapts as more cases are added to the case-library.

There are several variants of CBR, such as *exemplar-based reasoning, instance-based reasoning*, and *analogy-based reasoning*. These different variations of CBR are described below (Aamodt and Plaza 1994; Voskoglou and Salem 2014):

1   **Exemplar-based reasoning**—These systems seek to solve problems through classification, that is, finding the right class for the unclassified exemplar. Essentially the

class of the most similar past case then becomes the solution to the classification problem, and the set of classes are the possible solutions to the problem.

2   **Instance-based reasoning**—These systems require many instances (or cases) that are typically simple and are defined by a small set of attribute vectors. The major focus of study of these systems is automated learning, requiring no user involvement.

3   **Analogy-based reasoning**—These systems are typically used to solve new problems based on past cases from a different domain (Aamodt and Plaza 1994). Analogy-based reasoning focuses on case reuse, also called the mapping problem, which is finding a way to map the solution of the analogue case to the present problem.

Some other works use statistical frameworks to formalize CBR as a specific type of probabilistic inference, thereby enabling case-based predictions equipped with a certain level of statistical confidence (Eyke 2007).

There are several advantages to using CBR over rule-based models for developing knowledge application systems. These advantages are apparent when the relationship between the case attributes and the solution or outcome is not understood well enough to represent in rules. Alternatively, CBR systems are advantageous when the ratio of cases that are "exceptions to the rule" is high, as rule-based systems become impractical to implement in such applications. CBR is especially useful in such situations because it incorporates the solution of a newly entered case. In situations where there are many exceptions to the rules, CBR systems are more suitable because the system can adapt by combining solutions from multiple retrieved cases.

In summary, rule-based systems and case-based reasoning are all intelligent technologies used to develop knowledge application systems. The applicability of each technology is dictated primarily by the characteristics of the domain. Table 6.1 provides a list of the technologies and a description of the domain characteristics. The rule-based systems are suitable for domains where expert decisions are guided by a reasonable set of rules; however, as noted in Table 6.1, constraint-based reasoning is suitable for problems that are represented by constraints.

Constraint-based reasoning is a deductive problem-solving approach that specifies constraints and finds solutions that meet those constraints. Problems can be complex with interdependent variables, and constraints define the conditions and relationships between

Table 6.1 Technologies for Knowledge Application Systems

Technology	*Domain Characteristics*
Rule-Based Systems	Applicable when the domain knowledge can be defined by a manageable set of rules or heuristics.
Case-Based Reasoning	Applicable in weak-theory domains, that is, where an expert either doesn't exist or does not fully understand the domain. Also applicable if the experience base spans an entire organization, rather than a single individual.
Constraint-Based Reasoning	Applicable in domains that are defined by constraints, or what cannot be done.
Model-Based Reasoning	Applicable when designing a system based on the description of the internal workings of an engineered system. This knowledge is typically available from design specifications, drawings, and books, and can be used to recognize and diagnose its abnormal operation.

those variables. In constraint-based reasoning, problems are framed in terms of hypotheses and resolved through deductive reasoning to satisfy constraints. Constraint-based reasoning is suitable for complex problems with multiple constraints and dependencies, such as scheduling, planning, configuration, and decision support system.

On the other hand, model-based reasoning is suitable for problems or situations where direct observation is not possible. Model-based reasoning is a structured approach to solving problems using mental models. In model-based reasoning we use our cognitive experience to construct and evaluate models that specify the relationships, structures, and dynamics of a situation or problem. Model representation of a problem or situation enables reflection, reasoning, and deductions that inform decisions.

As we previously mentioned, it has become increasingly clear that one of the most popular techniques for the implementation of knowledge application systems in businesses today is case-based reasoning. The reasons why CBR is more commonly used in the development of such systems include the fact that CBR implementations are more intuitive and have the capabilities to "**adapt**" and "**learn**". In addition, CBR systems also rely on explicit knowledge that already exists in the organization, for example in problem reports, documents, and e-mails. We will see two examples of CBR systems applications in help desk and customer support, and in healthcare. In the next section we will discuss a methodology for the development and implementation of a knowledge application system, based on CBR technology, although the methodology also applies to the development of other intelligent systems and technologies.

Developing Knowledge Application Systems

Case-based reasoning knowledge applications require an information system to store cases, catalogue cases, structure cases, and establish similarities among cases using some form of attributes and values. Furthermore, the system should provide users with the ability to search cases and update the case information. The focus of mainstream information system development methodologies is not necessarily knowledge creation, capture, or application. In contrast, CBR systems are developed specifically to leverage and re-use existing knowledge to support decision-making. Since a case-based reasoning system has unique features and requirements, a methodology for implementing CBR system should account for how these features should be developed and implemented.

Effective implementation of a knowledge application system requires a carefully thought-out methodology that integrates the design and implementation of the unique features of a CBR system (Orenga-Roglá and Chalmeta 2019). To integrate a CBR system into the enterprise-wide information systems and supporting technologies, it should be supported by a methodology that incorporates traditional software development methodologies, such as waterfall or agile development. Furthermore, the development methodology should include the unique features of CBR systems, such as classifying and structuring cases.

The Case-Method Cycle methodology is an iterative approach to guide the development processes and implementation a CBR system (Kitano 1993; Elisabet et al. 2019). The Case-Method Cycle integrates traditional software development and addresses the unique features of a CBR system, such as knowledge transfer and case-base development. The Case-Method Cycle involves the processes outlined below:

1   **System development process**—This process is based on standard software development approaches. These approaches normally involve several iterative processes encompassing feasibility, analysis, design, implementation, and maintenance. The goal is to develop a knowledge application system that can store new cases and retrieve relevant cases. These processes will ensure that an information system is developed with the capability to store, retrieve, and update cases of problems and solutions to support a CBR system.

2   **Case library development process**—The goal of this process is to develop and maintain a large-scale case library that will adequately support the domain in question. The process should start with seed cases that will define the structure and format of cases, and as additional cases are collected, they are structured and stored using the predefined format. The cases are then indexed using all possible case elements to extract attributes and values. Creating a case library is an important initial step in developing a CBR system. Usually, the case library starts with the collection of seed cases, which provide an initial view of the application. The number of seed cases may vary according to the application and may even be generated artificially by creating permutations of the cases available. Seed cases typically do not follow a predefined structure; however, they are used in defining structures for the subsequent collection of cases. Thus, the collection of future cases will use the format defined by the seed cases. The case library development process documents keywords, attributes, and values in cases and establishes a hierarchy and a relationship between the attribute-value and keywords that can be mapped to a table in a relational database. A feedback mechanism for case documentation improves how cases are documented and reported to enhance the quality of cases in the database.

Case-based reasoning relies on a database of problem solutions to solve new problems. It stores the cases of problems and solutions in a structured format using attributes and values, as well as keywords. When a new case is identified, the system will first check if an identical problem case exists. If one is found, then the accompanying solution to that case is returned. If no identical case is found, then the CBR will search for cases with attributes and values like those of the new case. Conceptually, these cases may be considered similar, using similarity analysis. The CBR tries to combine solutions of similar cases to propose a solution for the new case. The CBR may rely on background information and problem-solving strategies to propose a feasible solution to the new case if an identical case is not located in the database.

The attribute-value extraction and hierarchy formation processes are essential for indexing and organizing the case library. The goal of this phase is to extract and index the attributes that define the case representation. This phase creates a list of attributes that define each case, a list of values for each attribute, and a possible grouping of such attributes. In addition, the process defines a relationship among the attributes, and the relative importance of each attribute. This phase creates a concept hierarchy for each attribute using similarity values and the hierarchies are mapped to a relational database or flat case library.

1   **System operation process**—This process is based on the standard software development life cycle and the relational database management procedures. The system operation process defines how the system will be installed and deployed to a user

environment. The system operation process specifies the software and hardware requirements for an installation. Furthermore, once the system is operational, the on-going maintenance and user support is essential for the viability of the system. Thus, the goals of the system operation process are to define the installation, deployment, and user support of a knowledge application system.

2   **Database mining process**—To efficiently retrieve cases and solutions, the data mining processes may rely on traditional SQL statements, inference rules, statistical analysis, ontology concepts, and semantics to evaluate cases in a library in response to search request by users. Over time, as users search the case library, new relationships can be drawn within the case library as patterns of search request emerge. Inferences from new relationships in the case library can improve the effectiveness of solutions recommended by a CBR system.

3   **Organizational management process**—This process describes how the project task force will be formed and what organizational support will be provided to the project. Organizational management support is a critical element in most information systems projects, especially when it comes to knowledge application systems. The organization's management support of processes that encourage the acceptance and use of these knowledge application systems is important for their successful implementation.

4   Effective processes that support knowledge discovery, capture, sharing, and application will depend on how well management articulates and communicates the importance of knowledge management strategies and provides adequate leadership for those strategies. Managerial incentives to encourage dedicated teams for the development of knowledge management processes and systems, as well as adequate rewards, can promote a culture that supports the sharing and applying of knowledge across the organization.

5   **Knowledge transfer process**—This process includes methods that share knowledge, which is the cases and extracted values, to relevant units of the organization that will apply this knowledge. In CBR systems, knowledge is represented by cases and associated solutions in a case library. The transfer process makes these cases available to those who can leverage the solutions to make timely and effective decisions. Management controls, incentive mechanisms, communicating the goals of the system to users, and training users on how to use the system can encourage users to share and capture their knowledge by updating the case library with new problems and validated solutions.

The Case Method Cycle has been shown to result in significant reduction in system development workload and costs. Case memories can provide humans with the experience base they may lack. Faced with a problem, experts may recall experiences from the case library, and perform the adaptation and evaluation of the solutions that is sometimes relegated to the knowledge application systems. Knowledge application systems have enabled the implementation of decision support systems to support diverse domains. A critical component in the development of these systems is the supporting indexing system used to perform the relevant case search. Finally, case libraries can serve to accumulate organizational experiences and can often be viewed as a corporate memory. For example, the case library for a help desk system could be considered a corporate memory of organizational experiences related to customer support. The same thing can be said of a rule-base driven expert system.

Domain Specific Implementations of Knowledge Application Systems

Knowledge application systems include advisor systems, fault diagnosis, troubleshooting systems, expert systems, help desk systems, and decision-support systems. In this section, we review knowledge application systems to demonstrate how these systems facilitate operational efficiency in specific domains, including fraud detection, fault diagnosis, and help desk operations.

Help Desk or Support Technologies

Most businesses interact with customers through several channels. Pre-sale and post-sale interactions are critical to the survival of most businesses and organizations. Hence, customer support, technical support, help desk, and customer services are critical functional units of most business operations. Although customer service and support operations are central to the success of most businesses, they are often unable to deliver effective and efficient customer services. Some of the challenges that many organizations face with customer services are the retention and turnover of personnel, and the lack of expertise and knowledgeable support staff. Help desk departments are particularly prone to these challenges. Knowledge application systems can address these help desk problems and challenges. For example, a case-base knowledge driven application system that keeps records of past problems and solutions can assist technicians, even if they lack the expertise, to resolve problems in a timely manner. The Web Help Desk solution in Box 6.2 by SolarWinds is a knowledge application system to support help desk operations that demonstrates how CBR can improve their performance and user-satisfaction.

Box 6.2 How SolarWinds Used Case-Based Reasoning to Improve Help Desk Operations

SolarWinds is a technology services company that provides services to business and government. SolarWinds' help desk solution, Web Help Desk, is designed to simplify IT help desk processes from the point of user problem request to problem resolution. The Web Help Desk has an intuitive Web interface to centrally manage service tickets and automate help desk task operations for technicians. The system relies on a comprehensive knowledge base management system that sorts and stores hundreds of images, documents, and videos addressing a vast array of topics. These data sources provide technicians with step-by-step answers to common and complicated questions.

The Web Help Desk system is a case-based knowledge system that assists technicians to solve problems by evaluating the solutions of similar past problems. Most often a service request refers to an issue that has happened before. Thus, it saves time when the support team has access to the most up-to-date knowledge base on historical problem cases and solutions. When there is a new problem, the knowledge base engine evaluates and finds other problems that are most similar to the current problem and the corresponding relevant information. Historical data on how complicated or time consuming a problem can be, and specifics of the problem, can help the technical staff manage customer expectations and satisfaction. For example, if a problem is submitted for a computer that shuts down unexpectedly, the knowledge base search engine—fueled by CBR intelligence technologies—can quickly find the most appropriate solution for the problem. When a service request refers to an issue that is new and with no known prior solution in the knowledge base, the support staff can quickly translate resolution notes into a new case problem-solution pair to help others resolve the same issue in the future. Furthermore, case-based reasoning systems are capable of "learning" and becoming "more intelligent" over time. As more cases and solutions are added and past cases are updated, the case-based reasoning engine becomes more intelligent. The capacity to learn and adapt makes case-based reasoning systems central to many of the knowledge application systems deployed by help desk departments.

Sources: Compiled from TechValidate (n.d.); SolarWinds (n.d.)

Fault Diagnosis

Fault diagnosis is critical to the maintenance of equipment and machinery, such as locomotive engines, manufacturing plants, airplanes, and automobiles. Most of these machinery and equipment consist of several interconnected components that may depend on each other to operate effectively. These complexities make fault diagnosis and decisions based on solutions time consuming and difficult, especially when the expertise and knowledge is dispersed or lacking. Because fault diagnosis is critical to operational efficiency, and in some cases the safety of systems, intelligent applications are increasingly used to monitor and diagnose faults (Eren et al. 2019; Xu et al. 2020). Some of these intelligent systems for fault diagnosis rely on CBR technologies. In Box 6.3 we present a review of the Car Fault Diagnosis System (CFDS) (De and Chakraborty 2018) which demonstrates the application of a CBR-based decision support system in fault diagnosis.

Box 6.3 Car Fault Diagnosis System (CFDS)

Accurately diagnosing a fault or problem is key to solving problems. If the fault diagnosis is inaccurate, then the recommended solution will be ineffective. For example, when automobiles develop mechanical faults, the first step in addressing the fault is diagnosing the fault to determine what is the cause of the fault and then recommend appropriate solutions. The CFDS uses CBR engine, decision tree, and the Jaccard similarity algorithm to classify cases and search the case library.

Figure 6.3 illustrates the architecture of the CFDS showing the interaction between the user interface and the case extractor module, CBR module, administrative module, and computational module. The CBR module handles the retrieve, reuse, revise, and retain processes which interact with the computational module and the knowledge case library. The case extractor module isolates the features of the new case, and the computational module computes the similarity percentage using the Jaccard Similarity Method to identify the most similar cases. Then the computational module relays identified case(s) to the CBR module, and the CBR module retrieves the exact solutions for the referred fault part of identified case(s) and displays the solutions to the technician. As shown in Figure 6.3, the CFDS has two types of interfaces: user interfaces and the knowledge worker interface. User interfaces include one for searching the case base library (as displayed in Figure 6.4), and one for the solution (as shown in Figure 6.5).

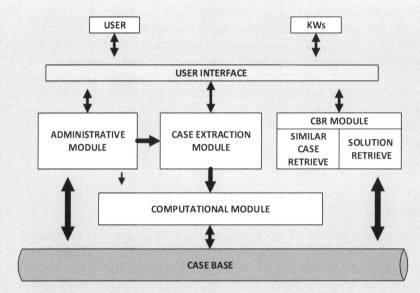

Figure 6.3 CBR CFDS Case Base Architecture
Source: adapted from De and Chakraborty (2018).

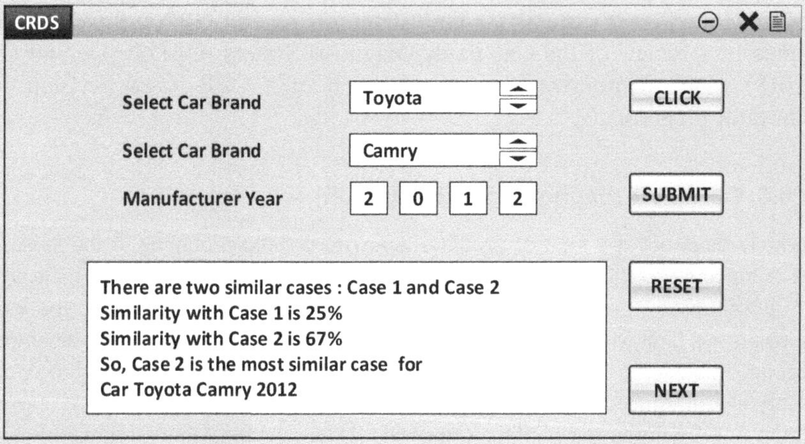

Figure 6.4 Search User Interface
Source: adapted from De and Chakraborty (2018).

Experts with in-depth knowledge of cars use the knowledge worker interface (as displayed in Figure 6.6) to populate the case library with structured cases. The interface for the knowledge worker uses a structured form to capture information on car description, fault description, and solution to create a case for the case library. This process ensures that all the solutions in the case have validated solutions.

A technician interacts with the user interface when making decisions on a new problem. The user interface in Figure 6.4 enables the technician to search for similar cases. The system prompts the user to select the car brand and model from a

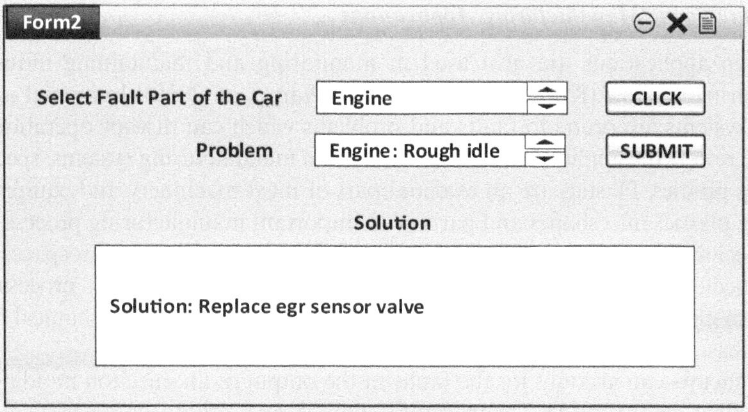

Figure 6.5 Solution User Interface
Source: adapted from De and Chakraborty (2018).

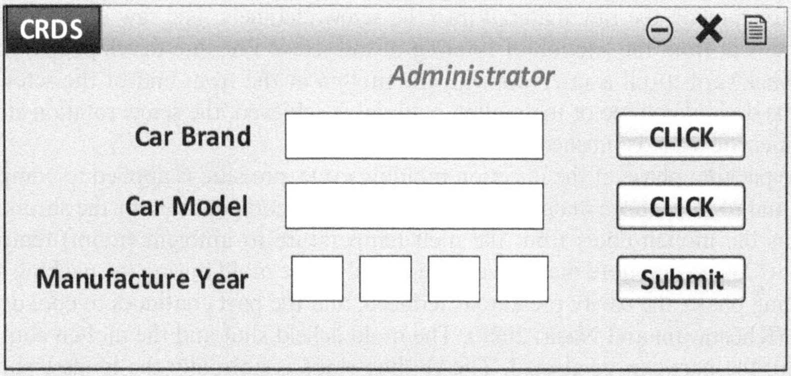

Figure 6.6 Knowledge Worker Interface
Source: adapted from De and Chakraborty (2018).

dropdown list, and then enter the year the car was manufactured. As shown in Figure 6.4, the search function returns all cases related to the new problem and their similarity values. The technician uses the solution of similar cases to address the problem. If similar cases are not found, then the problem is a new case, and a new solution is proposed for the problem. Experts will review the solution and the problem and once the solution is validated, it is added to the case-base library.

The CBR driven CFDS should help users and technicians make decision about faults quickly and accurately using previous cases and solutions. Inexperienced technicians can use the system and may also learn from the system. Additionally, since the system is updated with new cases, the capability of the system improves with time and the accuracy of solutions proffered by the system should also increase as more cases are added to the library. CBR systems rely on case representation; thus, how cases are stored, and what attributes and values are captured are important to the retrieval, reuse, revision, and retention processes in a CBR-driven system.

Source: Compiled from De and Chakraborty (2018)

CBR in Intelligent Manufacturing Applications

CBR-driven applications are also used in monitoring and maintaining industrial and manufacturing systems (Khosravani et al. 2019; Wan et al. 2019). Industrial and manufacturing systems are prone to faults and problems which can disrupt operations. In this section we review the application of CBR systems in manufacturing systems, specifically in fabricating plastics. Plastics are an essential part of most machinery and equipment, thus fabricating plastics into shapes and parts is an important manufacturing process. Injection molding technique is widely used to fabricate plastics for packaging, aerospace, construction, biomedical, automotive, and electronics devices. It is a complex process done by hydraulic or electric injection machines that are prone to numerous mechanical faults that could decrease the quality of the molded plastic end-product.

Several factors can account for the faults in the output of an injection molding process, including flow rate, pressure, temperature settings and mold characteristics. Injection molding is a cyclic four-phase process of filling, packing, cooling, and ejection. The quality of the product can be improved if all four phases are optimized. In the filling phase, the injection molding machine (IMM) fills the mold with polymer molten. The IMM controls the velocity and flow rate which can influence the quality of the product. A rotating screw is used for moving the raw material into the screw channels. The raw material is melted using the heat from the friction of rotating of the screw. Pressure develops and the screw moves backward to fill a reservoir with the molten at the front end of the screw barrel. When the desired volume of the molten material is achieved, the screw rotation stops, and the plasticizing stage is finished.

In the packing phase of the injection molding cycle, pressure is applied to compress the molten and to force more material into the mold. This compensates for the shrinkage that occurs as the molten cools from the melt temperature to ambient (room) temperature. From 5 to 25 percent more material can be added to the mold during the packing stage. In the cooling phase, the cavity pressure is reduced, and the part continues to cool down and solidify (Khosravani and Nasiri 2020). The mold is held shut and the molten continues to cool until the part can be ejected. The cooling stage is normally the longest part of the molding cycle and can account for up to 80 percent of the total cycle time.

Selecting the appropriate processing parameters plays a crucial role in determining the quality of the output. Different faults can occur on the output, such as warpage, bubbles, sink marks, brittles, cracks, and burn marks, which can compromise the quality and usability of the product. An intelligent CBR technology-based knowledge application system, can use a case base library to store all possible attributes and values that influence the output of injection molding.

The CBR system will store a molded part as a case, and the system will document and record all the parameters that were found to contribute to the molded part: mold injection process, appearance of defects, parameters on cooling, and compression. Previous cases are catalogued with structured attributes and values and new cases are catalogued and stored in the case-base library. Machine operators can use the case-base library to define the parameter of an injection mold based on previous mold and the quality level achieved. For example, if temperature settings at certain levels have caused bubbles on certain types of molten, then a technician can use that information to tweak the temperature settings when using certain types of molten. A CBR knowledge system can save a lot of time and reduce cost of injection molding by automating some of the decisions that a machine operator should make about the injection molding process to achieve desired quality standards.

CBR in Fraud Detection

Fraud detection and monitoring has increasingly relied on rule-based systems to detect anomalies and deviations from the norm and trigger warnings and alerts. Rule-based fraud detection systems use filters and rules to identify potential cases of fraud, using past experiences with fraud. For example, many financial institutions have rule-based systems to detect transactional fraud and these systems will trigger an alert or warning if a transaction is over a certain amount which is inconsistent with previous patterns of expenditure.

For example, SENTRY Detect (SQN Banking Systems n.d.) is a fraud detection solution by SQN Banking system that analyses online and in-person transactions to detect fraud. SENTRY Detect uses a rule-based system that relies on a 13-month customer history to offer a cross-channel view of transactions throughout the financial institution. Using knowledge, rules of thumb, and heuristics codified into business rules, SENTRY Detect can trigger warnings and alerts with specific reason codes when suspected transactions are detected. The software examines changes in transaction patterns to find inconsistencies, such as amounts that don't match customers' usual spending profiles, increases in activity, structured deposits, duplicate serial numbers, or other red flags, and triggers a warning for a potential problem. As the number of financial services and products for payments and transactions increases, fraudsters and criminals also look for new ways to compromise these services and products.

A static rule-based fraud detection system is unable to effectively deal with changes in tactics by criminals and thieves. Thieves can often find ways to initiate actions that are not flagged by static rule-based fraud detections systems. Furthermore, these static rules can also constrain customers making a legitimate transaction. Rule-based systems could face challenges when capturing all the unique and diverse ways that customers use in banking and financial services. Due to these shortcomings of rule-based fraud detection systems, artificial intelligence and machine learning analytics are increasingly used to complement rule-based systems for fraud detection. AI and machine learning analytics facilitate fraud detection in real time and can learn and adapt to detect new fraudulent activities.

Case Studies

In the next sections, we describe three knowledge application systems for three different purposes. The first case describes the development of SOS Advisor, a Web-based expert system built using a set of rules. The SOS Advisor system relied on a set of rules or heuristics, because a small number of rules can define the domain—that is, defining the eligibility potential for companies interested in applying for a specific federal program. Following that, we describe the development of the Advanced Bolus Calculator for Diabetes (ABC4D), a bolus calculator based on CBR technology, which offers patients recommendations on appropriate insulin levels. Finally, we review how Fidelity Life, an insurance company, uses a rule-based system to automate pricing of products and services.

The SBIR/STTR Online System (SOS) Advisor: A Web-Based Expert System to Profile Organizations

The SBIR/STTR Online System (SOS) Advisor, a Web-based expert system, was developed to assist potential applicants to the Small Business Innovation Research

(SBIR) and Small Business Technology Transfer Research (STTR) programs. Established by Congress in 1982, the SBIR and STTR programs help federal agencies develop innovative technologies by providing competitive research contracts to U.S.-owned small business companies with fewer than 500 employees. These programs also help by providing seed capital to increase private-sector commercialization of innovations resulting from federal research and development (NASA 2008). The goal of the SOS Advisor was to optimize the time required to examine the potential eligibility for companies seeking SBIR/STTR funding by prompting users through an interactive questionnaire that was used to evaluate the company's potential eligibility to be a grant recipient. The user only needed to click on *Yes* or *No* to answer the ten questions that frame the eligibility criteria.

Once the user submitted the registration information to the Web-based system, the SOS Advisor Questionnaire page was launched. The questionnaire consists of ten questions used to determine the eligibility of the company. The profile questions are listed in Table 6.2, to which users could respond by selecting the radio button next to the *Yes, No,* or *Not Sure*. Answering Not Sure will prompt users for more information, necessary in order to define the potential candidate's eligibility for funding. To match the SBIR winners' profile, users were expected to answer according to the responses specified in Table 6.2. Question 6 was for information purposes only since it does not constitute a necessary criterion for eligibility. Each question had a *Tip* icon that

Table 6.2 SBIR/STTR Profile Framing Questions

Question	SBIR winners' profile
1. I would like to know if your company is independently owned and operated.	Yes
2. Is this company located in the United States?	Yes
3. Is this company owned by at least 51 percent U.S. citizens or permanent U.S. residents?	Yes
4. Regarding your company size, does it have less than 500 employees?	Yes
5. What about your proposed innovation? Has it been patented, or does it have any patents pending?	No
6. Could it be patented, copyrighted, or otherwise protected?	Don't care
7. Are you planning on using SBIR/STTR funding to conduct any of the following: a Systems studies b Market research c Commercial development of existing products or proven concepts d Studies e Laboratory evaluations f Modifications of existing products without innovative changes	No
8. Does your technology area align with any of the following research areas of interest to NASA?	Yes
9. Is there a likelihood of your proposed technology having a commercial application?	Yes
10. Has your firm been paid or is currently being paid for equivalent work by any agency of the federal government?	No

allowed the user to obtain additional information related to the corresponding question using a pop-up window. In this manner, users could learn about SBIR/STTR requirements and the reasoning for each question. The one-page questionnaire format allowed users to spend minimum time when answering the profile questions. Furthermore, the user had the opportunity to see at once all the questions and answers to review and modify the answers before submission. The *Suggestions* field provided users with the option of providing feedback to the development team. Figure 6.7 describes the architecture of the SOS Advisor.

The user information provided and the corresponding answers to the questionnaire were stored in the SOS Advisor database and evaluated automatically by the system. Using a set of rules that evaluate the user responses, the system identified if the user profile matched the profile of an SBIR/STTR candidate. SOS Advisor then would automatically send an e-mail to the user with the results of the evaluation. At the same time, if the user profile match was positive the system automatically notified via e-mail the corresponding agency program personnel, with the user point-of-contact.

The rules used to evaluate the user profiles were developed using a scripting code. The scripts were used to evaluate the answers given and based on predefined rules to generate the user profiles. Based on the user's answers to the questionnaire, the SOS Advisor was able to determine whether the user profile indeed matched that of an SBIR/STTR recipient and provided sufficient information to educate potential applicants about related funding opportunities.

In summary, the SOS Advisor is a knowledge application system that was used to identify companies whose profiles matched that of an SBIR/STTR candidate and, therefore, helped focus the resources of federally funded assistance programs. The system prompted users to answer a set of questions that describe if the user's company met the stipulated criteria defined for companies interested in the SBIR/STTR program. The system then used a set of **heuristics** or rules to quickly examine each company's qualifications rather than attempting to transfer the knowledge about the program requirements to each of the companies interested in applying for the program

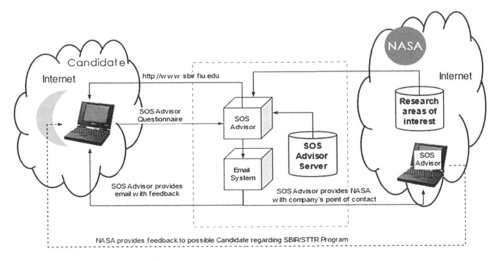

Figure 6.7 SOS Advisor Architecture

(although that option is available through launching the *Tip* section). For those companies with matching profiles, the SOS Advisor automatically sent the company's contact information to a federal agency employee who then identified appropriate assistance resources available for the benefit of the inquiring company. In this way, the SOS Advisor helped minimize distractions to the federal program representative caused by casual cyber surfers, since it would only forward the information for the companies that matched the qualification criteria. In addition, a by-product of this effort was the creation of a database with point-of-contact information for each company that completed the survey, which could be used to generate mailings and announcements of upcoming SBIR/STTR informative events.

The key importance of SOS Advisor is that it enabled federal agency personnel to apply the knowledge about qualification requirements for the SBIR/STTTR program without tying up the time of the program representative. Prior to the development of the SOS Advisor, a federal employee provided this information and performed the initial assessment of companies interested in the program. The federal agency representative repeatedly used her tacit knowledge base to perform the analysis. The SOS Advisor helped to apply this knowledge, freeing up the employee to use her time so she can provide more personalized advice to those companies that meet the program's stipulated criteria.

Advanced Bolus Calculator for Diabetes (ABC4D)

In healthcare, bolus is the administration of a discrete amount of medication within a specific time frame to raise its concentration in blood to an effective level. For people with diabetes, insulin bolus is necessary to maintain the appropriate level of insulin, thus an insulin bolus calculator is important to managing the daily dosage of insulin. Bolus calculators assist people with calculating the amount of insulin required during meals to achieve optimal glucose levels.

The ABC4D mobile application developed and proposed by Pesl et al. (2017) is an insulin bolus calculator that can be adjusted to suit specific situations and provides personalized insulin advice. ABC4D uses a CBR engine on a mobile application platform to store cases and solutions and uses those cases and appropriate solutions to offer personalized insulin advice to a user. The ABC4D system has mobile app interface for users and a personal-computer interface for clinicians. The mobile app interface runs the case-base modules and retrieves the most similar case compared to the current situation when a user requests insulin recommendation.

Typically, a case has three main parameters, problem description, solution to the problem, and the outcome. In the ABC4D application a case includes a set of parameters, attributes, and values that affect glucose levels, and the solution is the level of insulin required for the level of carbohydrates, i.e., insulin-to-carbohydrates ratio (ICR). Table 6.3 is a list of the attributes that can potentially influence required insulin levels.

These attributes include mealtime, alcohol consumption, and meal absorption; some of the values for these attributes are entered automatically with pre-set values while others are entered manually. As listed in Table 6.3, for example, the values for the mealtime attributes, breakfast/lunch/dinner, are entered automatically. The value for the alcohol attribute is entered manually, and the possible values are none or yes. Users use the mobile interface in Figure 6.8 to capture these case parameters. On the interface in Figure 6.8, the user can select values for all attributes listed in Table 6.3.

Table 6.3 Attributes that Can Influence Required Insulin Levels

Parameter	Discrete States	Automatic/Manual Input
Mealtime	Breakfast/Lunch/Dinner	Automatic
Exercise	None/Yes	Manual
Alcohol	None/Yes	Manual
Meal Absorption	Slow/Medium/Fast	Manual
Hyperglycaemia	No/Yes	Manual

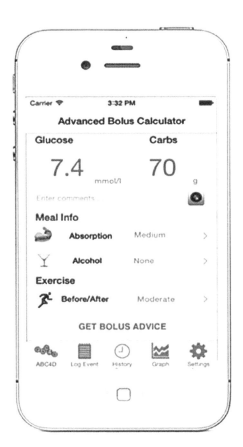

Figure 6.8 Input User Interface

The core engine of the ABC4D application is the CBR engine depicted in Figure 6.9. When an insulin recommendation is requested, it is considered a new problem that is compared to similar cases stored in the case library, then the most similar cases are retrieved. As shown in Figure 6.9, new case parameters, such as glucose level, time, and exercise are compared to similar cases in the case knowledge database.

When similar cases are retrieved the corresponding insulin level is recommended to the user. The image in Figure 6.10 is the interface that displayed the recommended insulin level. If the similarity between the new case and retrieved case is high, the

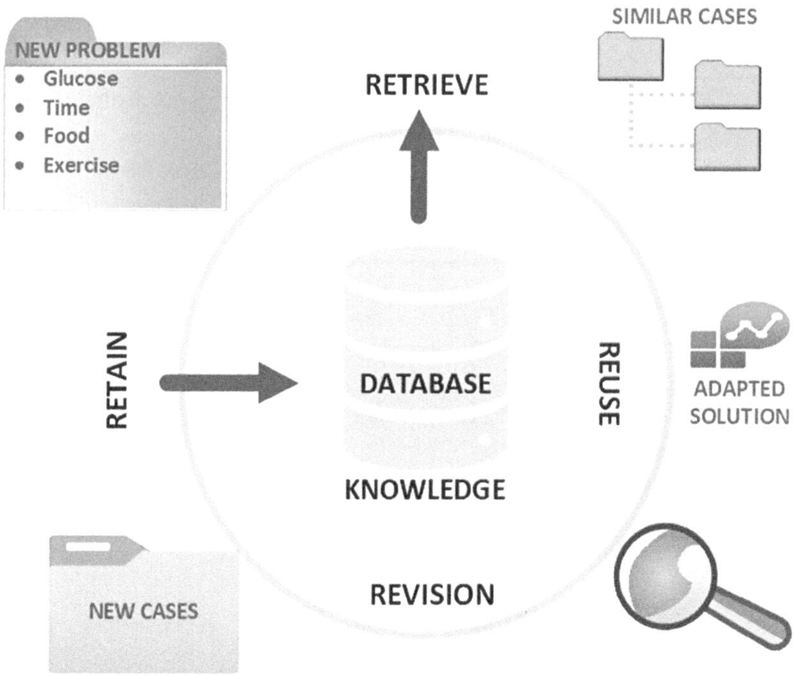

Figure 6.9 CBR Engine for ABC4D

recommended solution is adapted, if no similar cases are found a new case is created which is stored with a solution that is considered safe. The interface also has options for the user to accept or reject the recommendation.

If the recommended insulin bolus is accepted and administered, the outcome of the solution is evaluated through continuous glucose monitoring (CGM); if the outcome is unsatisfactory, the solution is revised. These processes are depicted in Figure 6.9, the ABC4D CBR knowledge database architecture. The personal-computer interface implements the revisions and the retentions steps of the CBR cycle and enables remote clinical supervision to manage changes in the patient's insulin therapy. The ABC4D CBR application utilizes cases' parameters, to enable individualization and adaptation of the insulin therapy for various meal scenarios.

Fidelity Life Insurance

In banking and finance, rule-based systems can automate decision-making on loan or credit application processes. A significant amount of personal information is collected and used in determining an applicant's qualifications for a loan or credit and the terms of the loan. Many banking and finance companies offer several products and services, and rule-based systems can help determine which products are suitable for a customer using some form of heuristics and the facts provided by an applicant.

Decisions[1] is a technology company that focuses on automating business decisions and processes using a rule-based decision support engine. Figure 6.11 shows the architecture of the Decision Rules Engine (DRE) solution by Decisions that can process billions of rules every hour.

Figure 6.10 Output User Interface

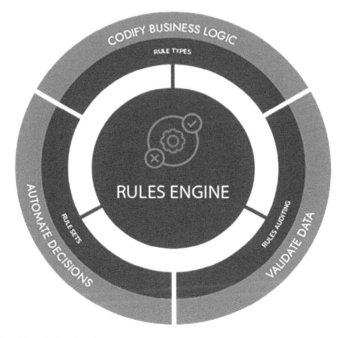

Figure 6.11 Decision Rules Engine

Businesses and organizations generate business artifacts in the form of data, documents, processes, guidelines, e-mails, and procedures. Many of these artifacts embody organizational knowledge and business rules. The DRE solution from Decisions can collate and validate data from various sources and codify the business logic and rules embodied in the data into a rule-based engine to drive knowledge application. The DRE can create custom and complex rules using a variety of rules' *styles* and *types* including *statement rules, truth tables, expression rules*, and *matrix rules*. These rules are stored in the rules engine and drive automated decision-making.

Fidelity Life Insurance is an insurance company in New Zealand. The company embarked on a strategy to digitize the value chain, maintain a versatile product suite, and meet the evolving needs of its customer base. The company wanted to leverage business rules to automate processes; however, business rules and logic at Fidelity Life were scattered across several legacy systems and this made it difficult for the company to use, maintain, and update these rules. To overcome these challenges and achieve those strategic goals, Fidelity implemented a process automation platform from Decisions to automate processes related to pricing and quotes. The implementation leveraged the DRE capabilities to integrate the rules and business logic from the legacy systems at Fidelity Life to create a rules engine for pricing and validation to automate the pricing and quote process.

Figure 6.12 shows the architecture of the price validation services engine demonstrating the relationship among the *pricing and validation engine, product rates*, and *product rules*. A request for policy pricing goes to the *pricing and validation* engine which interacts with *product rules* to determine which rules apply to the request.

The Decisions rules engine uses the request parameters and business rules to identify a policy based on the request parameters. The Decisions rules engine retrieves and decomposes a policy into available products. The *pricing and validation services* retrieves corresponding *product rates*, and the *pricing and validation engine* calculates a premium.

Business rules ensure that the pricing service provides a practical quote. Once the system determines and validates pricing for a policy, it is delivered to the front-end

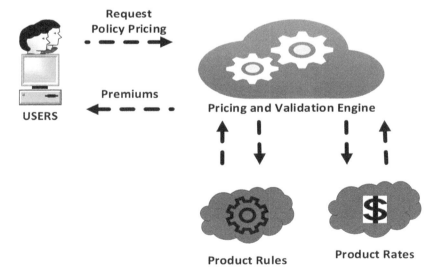

Figure 6.12 Pricing Validation Architecture

interface. The Decisions automation platform enables agents to update and add new rules, products, and pricing changes. The pricing and validation automation process demonstrates how a rule-based expert system can automate processes that enable insurance agents, who may not have the expertise of risk pricing, to provide customers with validated quotes. Additionally, the agents do not have to go through a lengthy process of training to use the system to make decisions like experts, and customers get their quotes in a timely manner.

Limitations of Knowledge Application Systems

There are some practical limitations to the development of knowledge application systems. These relate to the fact that most of these systems are developed to serve a task-specific domain problem and are typically not fully integrated with other enterprise systems. Other limitations may be specific to CBR technologies and other knowledge application systems. Some of the limitations of knowledge applications include the following:

1 *Security*: Cases may include sensitive information. Knowledge application systems must consider the incorporation of security measures, including role-based access controls, authentication, and authorization controls to manage access to the systems. If knowledge application systems do not incorporate security measures, systems may not realize their maximum value.
2 *Scalability*: Knowledge application systems must represent a large enough number of cases so that most of the new experiences are represented in the case-based system. This means the knowledge application system must reach saturation prior to its deployment. Reaching system saturation means that most typical cases would have already been reported in the system. The more complex the domain, the higher the importance of keeping the growth of the case base viable. Clearly, the continual growth of the case library will also require the use of complex indexing schemes, which may result in decreased system stability.
3 *Speed*: As the size of the case library grows to a more comprehensive representation of real environments, computing and searching costs will also increase. Therefore, developers of knowledge application systems must consider the use of complex indexing schemes that will guarantee acceptable case-retrieval times and performance levels.

In addition, knowledge application systems may not be able to solve all the problems that they encounter. Diagnosing problems can be increasingly difficult in complex environments. New intelligent technologies with diverse sets of capabilities are necessary to address these challenges. Furthermore, some rule-based systems could suffer from other limitations, namely the lack of scalability. Nevertheless, the benefits that the implementation of knowledge application systems brings to the organization outweigh their limitations, and they will continue to provide competitive advantages to those organizations that continue to implement them.

Summary

In this chapter, we discussed what knowledge application systems are, along with design considerations and specific types of intelligent technologies that enable such systems. This chapter introduced the Case-Method Cycle methodology for developing

CBR knowledge application systems. Also, the chapter discusses several types of knowledge application systems: expert systems, help desk systems, and fault diagnosis systems. Several domain specific knowledge application systems are reviewed to underline the different intelligent technologies and designs to accomplish different goals: provide advice, recognize fault detection, and spur creative reasoning. Finally, this chapter concludes with a discussion of the limitations of knowledge application systems.

Review

1 What are some of the intelligent technologies that provide the foundation for the creation of knowledge application systems?
2 Describe in your own words when you should use rules as opposed to CBR when developing a knowledge application system.
3 Describe the four steps in the CBR process.
4 Describe the steps and the importance of the Case-Method Cycle.
5 Explain the case library development process.
6 What are some of the limitations of knowledge application systems?

Application Exercises

1 Identify examples of knowledge application systems in use in your organization. What are some of the intelligent technologies that enable those systems?
2 Describe five knowledge application scenarios that could be supported via CBR systems and explain why. For example, one such scenario is a system that will identify the most likely resolution of a court case based on the outcome of prior legal cases.
3 Design a knowledge application system to support your business needs. Describe the type of system and the foundation technologies that you would use to develop such a system.
4 Design the system architecture for the system described in Question 2.
5 Identify three recent examples in the literature of knowledge application systems.

Note

1 Decisions is a technology company that offers Intelligent Process Automation platforms.

References

Aamodt, A., and Plaza, E. 1994. Case-based reasoning: Foundational issues, methodological variations, and system approaches. *AI Communications*, 7(1), 39–52.

Abu-Nasser, B.S., and Abu Naser, S.S., 2018. Rule-based system for watermelon diseases and treatment. *International Journal of Academic Information Systems Research (IJAISR)*, 2(7), 1–7.

Allen, B. 1994. Case-based reasoning: Business applications. *Communications of the ACM*, 37(3), 40–42.

Becerra-Fernandez, I., Gonzalez, A., and Sabherwal, R. 2004. *Knowledge management: Challenges, solutions, and technologies.* Upper Saddle River, NJ: Prentice Hall.

Casio Computer Company. n.d. https://world.casio.com.

De, S., and Chakraborty, B., 2018, Case based reasoning (CBR) methodology for car fault diagnosis system (CFDS) using decision tree and Jaccard similarity method. In *2018 3rd International Conference for Convergence in Technology (I2CT)*, 1–6. IEEE.

Elisabet, D., Sensuse, D.I., and Al Hakim, S., 2019. Implementation of case-method cycle for case-based reasoning in human medical health: A systematic review, *2019 3rd International Conference on Informatics and Computational Sciences (ICICoS)*. IEEE. 1–6.

Eren, L., Ince, T., and Kiranyaz, S., 2019. A generic intelligent bearing fault diagnosis system using compact adaptive 1D CNN classifier. *Journal of Sign Processing Systems*, 91(2), 179–189, https://doi.org/10.1007/s11265-018-1378-3.

Eyke, H. 2007. *Case-based approximate reasoning*. Berlin: Springer-Verlag.

Frye, D., Zelazo, P.D., and Palfai, T., 1995. Theory of mind and rule-based reasoning. *Cognitive Development*, 10(4), 483–527.

Giva Inc. 2006. Customer case study Casio. https://www.givainc.com/docs/Case%20Study%20-%20Giva%20&%20Casio.pdf (accessed December 12, 2022).

Hayes-Roth, F. 1985. Rule-based systems. *Communications of the ACM*, 28(9), 921–932.

Khosravani, M.R., and Nasiri, S., 2020. Injection moulding manufacturing process: review of case-based reasoning applications, *Journal of Intelligent Manufacturing*, 31, 847–864.

Khosravani, M.R., Nasiri, S., and Weinberg, K., 2019. Application of case-based reasoning in a fault detection system on production of drippers, *Applied Soft Computing Journal*, 75, 227–232.

Kitano, K. 1993. Challenges of massive parallelism. In *Proceeding of the 13th Annual Conference on Artificial Intelligence (IJCAI-93)*, Chabery, France, 813–834.

National Aeronautics and Space Administration (NASA). 2008. *SBIR and STTR solutions*. https://sbir.nasa.gov/content/nasa-sbirsttr-basics (accessed December 19, 2022).

Orenga-Roglá, S., and Chalmeta, R., 2019. Methodology for the implementation of knowledge management systems 2.0. *Business & Information Systems Engineering*, 61(2), 195–213.

Perner, P. 2019. Case-based reasoning—Methods, techniques, and applications. In *Iberoamerican Congress on Pattern Recognition*, 16–30. Cham: Springer.

Pesl, P., Herrero, P., Reddy, M., Oliver, N., Johnston, D.G., Toumazou, C., and Georgiou, P., 2017, Case-based reasoning for insulin bolus advice: evaluation of case parameters in a six-week pilot study. *Journal of Diabetes Science and Technology*, 11(1), 37–42.

Schank, R. 1982. *Dynamic memory: A theory of learning in computers and people*. New York: Cambridge University Press.

SolarWinds Inc. n.d. SolarWinds Web help desk features. https://www.solarwinds.com/web-help-desk/use-cases (accessed June 23, 2023).

SQN Banking Systems. n.d. Real-time fraud analysis SENTRY: Fraud alert. https://sqnbankingsystems.com/solutions/real-time-fraud-analysis/ (accessed December 20, 2022).

TechValidate. n.d. Research on SolarWinds help desk and IT support. https://www.techvalidate.com/product-research/solarwinds-help-desk-it-support/case-studies (accessed June 23, 2023).

Tocimáková, Z., Paralič, J., and Pella, D. 2020. Case-based reasoning for support of the diagnostics of cardiovascular diseases. In *Digital Personalized Health and Medicine*, 537–541). IOS Press.

Voskoglou, M.G., and Salem, A.B.M. 2014. Analogy-based and case-based reasoning: Two sides of the same coin. *International Journal of Applications of Fuzzy Sets and Artificial Intelligence*, 4, 5–51.

Wan, S., Li, D., Gao, J., and Li, J. 2019. A knowledge-based machine tool maintenance planning system using case-based reasoning techniques. *Robotics and Computer-Integrated Manufacturing*, 58, 80–96.

Xu, X., Cao, D., Zhou, Y., and Gao, J. 2020. Application of neural network algorithm in fault diagnosis of mechanical intelligence. *Mechanical Systems and Signal Processing*, 141.

7 Knowledge Capture Systems
Systems that Preserve and Formalize Knowledge

In the previous chapter, we discussed knowledge application systems. In this chapter, we discuss what knowledge capture systems are about and how they serve to elicit and store organizational and individual knowledge. Knowledge capture systems are designed to help elicit and store knowledge, both tacit and explicit. Knowledge can be captured using mechanisms or technologies so that the captured knowledge can then be shared and used by others. Perhaps the earliest mechanisms for knowledge capture date to the anthropological use of stories—the earliest form of art, education, and entertainment. **Storytelling** is the mechanism by which early civilizations passed on their values and their wisdom from one generation to the next.

In this chapter, we first discuss issues about organizational storytelling and how this mechanism can support knowledge capture. We then discuss how technology can enable the knowledge capture process. We also describe issues related to how to design the knowledge capture system, including the use of intelligent technologies in support of this process. In particular, the role of RFID technologies in knowledge capture is discussed. We discuss two types of knowledge capture systems: one that serves best to support educational settings; and a second system that serves best to capture tactical knowledge. Recall from Chapter 2 that tactical knowledge is defined as knowledge that pertains to the short-term positioning of the organization.

For a quick overview of how organizations can utilize strategic stories, let us look at a brief case study and how 3M Corporation uses stories to embody their innovative culture in Box 7.1.

Box 7.1 Using Stories to Build Effective Business Plans at 3M

Few companies rival 3M's 100 record years of innovation. From the invention of sandpaper in 1904 to the invention of masking tape in 1925 and Post-it Notes in 1980, 3M's culture is noted by its use of stories. Stories are part of 3M's sales representatives' training, award ceremonies, and in short a "habit-of-mind." At 3M, the power of stories is recognized as a means to "see ourselves and our business operations in complex, multidimensional forms—that we're able to discover opportunities for strategic change. Stories give us ways to form ideas about winning" (Shaw et al. 1998, p. 41).

Recently, recognition about the power of stories reached 3M's boardroom. Traditionally at 3M, business plans were presented through bulleted lists. Cognitive psychologists have proven that lists are ineffective learning artifacts since item recognition decreases with the length of the list (Sternberg 1975), and typically only items at the beginning or end of the list

---

DOI: 10.4324/9781003364375-9

are remembered (Tulving 1983). As a contrast, a good story can better represent a business plan, since it includes a definition of the relationships, a sequence of events, and a subsequent priority among the items which in turn causes the strategic plan to be remembered. Therefore, stories are currently used as the basic building blocks for business plans at 3M.

Shaw et al. (1998) define an effective business plan to be a lot like a good story, and appropriately illustrates this with a narrative example. The strategic business plan must first set the stage or define the current situation. For example:

> Global Fleet Graphics (a 3M division that makes durable graphic-marking systems for buildings, signs, and vehicles) was facing increasing demand from customers at the same time that they were experiencing eroding market share due to diminishing patent advantages and competitors' low-cost strategies.
>
> (Shaw et al. 1998, p. 48)

Next, the strategic story must introduce the dramatic conflict. Continuing with the same example:

> The 3M division had to effect a quantum change in the production system that enabled the quick and competitive delivery of products. The solution included the development of innovative technologies that enabled this group's product offerings to differentiate from its competitors. In addition, sales and marketing skills had to appropriately match the new strategy.
>
> (Shaw et al. 1998, p. 48)

Finally, the strategic narrative must reach a resolution. In other words, it must summarize how the organization will win through effectively drawing upon the diverse technological skills required to transform the business.

Studies at 3M show that the adequate use of a narrative business plan results in an improved understanding of the requirements for the plan to succeed. In addition, using a narrative strategy spurs excitement among 3M employees as well as generating commitment about the plan. As summarized by Shaw et al. (1998):

> When people can locate themselves in the story, their sense of commitment and involvement is enhanced. By conveying a powerful impression of the process of winning, narrative plans can motivate and mobilize an entire organization.
>
> Sources: Compiled from Shaw et al. (1998); Sternberg (1975); Tulving (1983).

What Are Knowledge Capture Systems?

As discussed in Chapter 4, **knowledge capture systems** support the process of eliciting either explicit or tacit knowledge that may reside in people, artifacts, or organizational entities. These systems can help capture knowledge existing either within or outside organizational boundaries, among employees, consultants, competitors, customers, suppliers, and even prior employers of the organization's new employees. Knowledge capture systems rely on mechanisms and technologies that support externalization and internalization. Both mechanisms and technologies can support knowledge capture systems by facilitating the knowledge management processes of externalization and internalization.

You may recall from Chapter 4 that **knowledge capture mechanisms** facilitate **externalization** (i.e., the conversion of tacit knowledge into explicit form) or **internalization** (i.e., the conversion of explicit knowledge into tacit form). The development of models or **prototypes**, and the articulation of stories are some examples of mechanisms that enable externalization. Learning by observation and face-to-face meetings are some of the mechanisms that facilitate internalization. Technologies can also support knowledge capture by facilitating externalization and internalization. Indeed, some companies have developed apps to capture knowledge, as illustrated in Box 7.2, which discusses a knowledge capture app by Zendesk.

Box 7.2 A Knowledge Capture App from Zendesk

Customer expectations can be demanding and challenging to meet, and sometimes hiring additional support staff may not be feasible. To address this, Zendesk has created Zendesk Guide, a self-service portal that empowers its customers with effective and manageable self-service options. This portal also allows both Zendesk's agents and customers to collaboratively build a helpful knowledge base. Customers can directly contribute through an online community, while Zendesk's agents can utilize their interactions in Zendesk Support to create informative help articles using Guide's Knowledge Capture app. This app is especially beneficial as it *captures valuable institutional knowledge in real-time*, helping agents respond to tickets more effectively and reducing ticket resolution times by 20 to 80 percent. With Zendesk Guide, Zendesk aims to provide a seamless and efficient self-service experience for both its customers and agents.

David Vauthrin, Co-Founder and CMO at FINALCAD (www.finalcad.com), a company that provides a collaborative platform for the management of construction projects, thus explained how self-service through Zendesk Guide has helped improve his company's support:

> Zendesk Guide has allowed us to triple the efficiency of our customer support organization. One year ago, we had a very small knowledge base of a dozen articles available for our customers. Now, a few months later, we have more than 100 articles in 10 languages, and all of our most frequently asked questions are answered there. By allowing customers to easily answer these common questions themselves, we have been able to maintain the same team of support agents while tripling our customer base.

David believes that this knowledge capture app empowers FINALCAD's agents. More specifically, he remarked:

> We use the Knowledge Capture app while replying within tickets. It allows us to ensure that every article we have is catalogued by keyword so that we can leverage the appropriate content when serving our customers. Previously, it fell to agents to search our existing articles to determine if there was one they could use or whether they needed to create a new one. Now that we have the Zendesk Knowledge Capture app installed, we have been able to increase productivity and improve article quality by automating a formerly manual process.

Finally, David believes that Zendesk prompts FINALCAD to tap into its team to create help center content more easily. More specifically, he said:

> It's all about process and ownership. First, we have dedicated a person to content creation and management within the team. This person developed strong collaboration with Product Team to ensure documentation is perfect, and also owns translation process, to deliver our Help Center in more than 10 languages.
>
> Sources: Compiled from FINALCAD (n.d.); Zendesk (n.d.)

Externalization through **knowledge engineering**, described earlier in Chapter 6, is necessary for the implementation of intelligent technologies such as expert systems and case-based reasoning systems, also described in Chapter 6. Technologies that facilitate internalization include computer-based communication and computer-based simulations. For example, an individual can use communication facilities to internalize knowledge from a message sent by another expert or an AI-based knowledge-acquisition system. Furthermore, computer-based simulations can also support individual learning. Both knowledge capture mechanisms and technologies can facilitate externalization and internalization within or across organizations.

Knowledge Management Mechanisms for Capturing Tacit Knowledge: Using Organizational Stories

The importance of using metaphors and stories as a mechanism for capturing and transferring tacit knowledge is increasingly drawing the attention of organizations. For example, as illustrated in Box 7.1, 3M currently uses stories as part of its business planning to set the stage, introduce dramatic conflict, reach a resolution to the challenges the company is facing, and generate excitement and commitment from all the members of the organization (Shaw et al. 1998). Storytelling at 3M has taken a center stage, as it seeks to develop a culture of problem preventers rather than "an eleventh-hour problem-solver." In order to reinforce this paradigm shift, 3M leaders turn to telling pet stories that describe "what not to do" (Clark 2004). Storytelling is now considered of strategic importance as organizations recognize the need to develop their company's next generation leaders and has been recognized as one of the most effective means to develop high-potential managers in a firm (Ready 2002).

Stories are considered to play a significant role in organizations characterized by a strong need for collaboration. **Organizational stories** are defined as

> a detailed narrative of past management actions, employee interactions, or other intra- or extra-organizational events that are communicated informally within organizations.
>
> (Swap et al. 2001)

Organizational stories typically include a plot, major characters, an outcome, and an implied moral. Stories originate within the organization and typically reflect organizational norms, values, and culture. Because stories make information more vivid, engaging, entertaining, and easily related to personal experience and because of the rich contextual details encoded in stories, they are the ideal mechanism to capture tacit knowledge (Swap et al. 2001). Stories have been observed to be useful to capture and communicate organizational managerial systems (how things are done), norms, and values.

Dave Snowden (1999), an early proponent of storytelling while he worked at IBM and now the Director of the Cynefin Centre, identifies the following set of guidelines for organizational storytelling:

1   Stimulate the natural telling and writing of stories.
2   Stories must be rooted in anecdotal material reflective of the community in question.
3   Stories should not represent idealized behavior.
4   An organizational program to support storytelling should not depend on external experts for its sustenance.
5   Organizational stories are about achieving a purpose, not entertainment.
6   Be cautious of overgeneralizing and forgetting the particulars. What has worked in one organization may not necessarily work in others.
7   Adhere to the highest ethical standards and rules.

According to Phoel (2006), the following eight steps to successful storytelling will help work magic in the organization:

1   Have a clear purpose.
2   Identify an example of successful change.
3   Tell the truth.
4   Say who, what, when.
5   Trim detail.
6   Underscore the cost of failure.
7   End on a positive note.
8   Invite your audience to dream.

But Phoel also emphasizes that to tell the story right, it is not just what you say but how you say it that will determine its success. In this regard, stories should speak as one person to another, they should present the truth as one sees it, should seem spontaneous but must be rehearsed, and one should relive the story as one tells it. Perhaps the one theme that all storytelling experts agree on is the "crucial importance of truth as an attribute of both the powerful story and the effective storyteller" (Guber 2007). In fact, according to Guber, there are four kinds of truth in each effective story:

1   Truth to the teller—the storyteller must be congruent to her story.
2   Truth to the audience—the story must fulfill the listeners' expectations by understanding what the listeners know about, meeting their emotional needs, and telling the story in an interactive fashion.
3   Truth to the moment—since great storytellers prepare obsessively and never tell a story the same way twice.
4   Truth to the mission—since great storytellers are devoted to the cause, which is embodied in the story, capturing and expressing the values that she believes in and wants others to adopt as their own.

Other important considerations in the design of an effective organizational storytelling program include (Post 2002):

1   People must agree with the idea that this could be an effective means of capturing and transferring tacit organizational knowledge.
2   Identify people in the organization willing to share how they learned from others about how to do their jobs.
3   Metaphors are a way to confront difficult organizational issues.
4   Stories can only transfer knowledge if the listener is interested in learning from them.

In fact, one of the strengths of stories is that they are clearly episodic in nature, which means related to events directly experienced. To the extent that the storyteller is able to provide a sufficiently vivid account for the listener to vicariously experience the story, many features of the story will be encoded in the listener's memory and later available for retrieval (Swap et al. 2001). In fact, the emphasis on the use of case studies at most business schools is related to the effectiveness of stories as a pedagogical tool. Much like case studies, Steve Denning (2000), who is best known for his efforts to implement communities of practice and storytelling at the World Bank, describes the importance of **springboard stories**. Springboard stories enable a leap in understanding by the audience in order to grasp how an organization may change by visualizing from a story in one context what is involved in large-scale organizational transformations. Springboard stories are told from the perspective of a protagonist who was in a predicament, which may resemble the predicament currently faced by the organization. As an example of a springboard story, consider the story used by Denning to convince his colleagues at the World Bank about the importance of knowledge management:

> In June of last year, a health worker in a tiny town in Zambia went to the Web site of the Centers for Disease Control and got an answer to a question about the treatment of malaria. Remember that this was in Zambia, one of the poorest countries in the world, and it was in a tiny place six hundred kilometers from the capital city. But the most striking thing about this picture, at least for us, is that the World Bank isn't in it. Despite our know-how on all kinds of poverty-related issues, that knowledge isn't available to the millions of people who could use it. Imagine if it were. Think what an organization we would become.
>
> (Denning 2005, p. 4)

An interesting question is the role storytelling plays with respect to analytical thinking. Denning (2000) supports the argument that storytelling supplements analytical thinking by enabling us to imagine new perspectives and new worlds. He sees storytelling as ideally suited to communicating change and stimulating innovation, because abstract analysis is easier to understand when seen through the lens of a well-chosen story and can of course be used to make explicit the implications of a story.

Finally, Denning (2000) describes the organizational areas where storytelling can be effective, including:

1   *Igniting action in knowledge-era organizations*: Storytelling can help managers and employees actively think about the implications of change and the opportunities for the future of their organization. Listeners actively understand what it would be like if things were done a different way, re-creating the idea of change as an exciting and living opportunity for growth.

2   *Bridging the knowing-doing gap*: This view proposes that storytelling can exploit the interactive nature of communication by encouraging the listener to imagine the story and to live it vicariously as a participant. The listener perceives and acts on the story as part of their identity.

3   *Capturing tacit knowledge*: Probably this line of reasoning is best captured in Denning's (n.d.) words:Storytelling relinquishes a straightforward journey from A to B, and in the end provides a vehicle for unveiling unseen tacit knowledge. Storytelling draws on deep-flowing streams of meaning, and on patterns of primal narratives of which the listeners are barely aware, and so catalyzes visions of a different and renewed future.

1   *To embody and transfer knowledge*: A simple story can communicate a complex multidimensional idea by actively involving the listeners in the creation of the idea in the context of their own organization.

2   *To foster innovation*: Innovation is triggered by the inter-relatedness of ideas. Storytelling enables to easily absorb and relate knowledge, the same spark that triggers innovation.

3   *Launching and nurturing communities*: In many large organizations, the formation of communities of practice enables the grouping of professionals who come together voluntarily to share similar interests and learn from each other. These communities of practice may be known under different names: *thematic groups* (World Bank), *learning communities* or *learning networks* (Hewlett-Packard Company), *best practice teams* (Chevron), and *family groups* (Xerox). Denning (2000) explains how a storytelling program provides a natural methodology for nurturing communities and integrating them to the organization's strategy and structure because:

   a   Storytelling builds trust—enabling knowledge seekers in a community to learn from knowledge providers through the sharing of candid dialogue.

   b   Storytelling unlocks passion—because they enable the members of the community to commit "passionately" to a common purpose, be it the engineering design of a new artifact, or sharing the discovery of a new medical remedy.

   c   Storytelling is nonhierarchical—because storytelling is collaborative, with the members of the community pooling resources to jointly create the story.

4   *Enhancing technology*: Most people agree that e-mail has made increasing demands in our lives, resulting in the expectation that we're available 24/7 to answer electronic requests that span from office memos to virtual garbage mail. Communities of practice and storytelling can enable us to interact with our neighbors and remain connected when we want to, providing us with "tranquility yet connectedness."

5   *Individual growth*: The world of storytelling is one that proposes avoiding adversarial contest and promotes a win-win situation for all: the knowledge seeker and the knowledge-provider.

Techniques for Organizing and Using Stories in the Organization

The power of narratives or stories as a knowledge capture mechanism in an organization lies in the fact that **narratives** capture the knowledge content as well as its context and the social networks that define the way "things are done around here." In order to capture organizational knowledge through narratives, it is best to encourage storytelling in a work context. In addition to the knowledge-elicitation techniques described in Chapter 6, here we present **knowledge-elicitation** techniques pertaining specifically to stories.

One technique described by Snowden (2000) for narrative knowledge capture is **anthropological observation**, or the use of naïve interviewers, citing an example where they used a group of school children to understand the knowledge flows in an organization. The children were naïve, therefore they asked innocent and unexpected questions which caused the subjects to naturally volunteer their anecdotes. They were also curious, which resulted in a higher level of knowledge elicitation.

He also describes a second technique, **storytelling circles**, formed by groups having a certain degree of coherence and identity such as a common experience in a project. Story circles are best recorded in video. Certain methods can be used for eliciting anecdotes such as:

1   **Dit-spinning**—or *fish tales*—represents human tendencies to escalate or better the stories shared previously.
2   **Alternative histories**—are fictional anecdotes which could have different turning points, based for example on a particular project's outcome.
3   **Shifting character or context**—are fictional anecdotes where the characters may be shifted to study the new perspective of the story.
4   **Indirect stories**—allow disclosing the story with respect to fictional characters, so that any character similarities with the real-life character are considered to be pure coincidence.
5   **Metaphor**—provides a common reference for the group to a commonly known story, cartoon, or movie.

Once a number of stories have been elicited and captured, the next problem is how to store the narratives so people will find them. **Narrative databases** can be indexed by the theme of the story, by the **stakeholders** of the story, or by **archetypal characters**. The theme could be, for example, innovative stories. The stakeholders could be the scientists, the marketing group, or the customers. The archetypal characters represent well-known characters that represent a virtue, for example, the extremely intelligent but obsessive-compulsive detective eccentric archetype represented by Tony Shalhoub in his TV role as Adrian Monk.

Designing the Knowledge Capture System

Typically, the documentation available in organizations is the result of applying expertise rather than expertise itself. For example, a radiologist interpreting high-precision functional images of the heart will have the results of his diagnosis captured in a document, but the reasoning process by which he reaches the diagnosis is not usually captured.

In addition, consider the process of engineering for complex systems. Traditional methods for documenting and representing the engineered designs include creating engineering drawings, specifications, and **computer-aided design (CAD)** models. But often the decisions leading to the design choices including the assumptions, constraints, and considerations, are not captured. Capturing these decisions is not only important but may lead to a more useful representation of the design, specifically when designing complex systems in an environment characterized by high uncertainty.

Knowledge-elicitation techniques have been studied and used extensively in AI for the development of expert systems (Chapter 6). The purpose of these techniques is to assist the knowledge-elicitation process based on interview sessions between a knowledge engineer and the domain expert, with the goal of jointly constructing an expertise model. Although computers may understand the resulting expertise models, these models may not directly meet the objective of capturing and preserving the expert's knowledge so it can be transferred to others, or in other words, so others can learn from it.

Next, we discuss how technology can facilitate capturing the knowledge of experts. We will describe two such systems based on different methodologies and intelligent technologies. The first system is based on the use of concept maps as a knowledge-modeling tool. The second system is based on the use of context-based reasoning (CxBR) to simulate human behavior. Each of these systems is best suited for certain specific situations. For example, the use of concept maps may be best suited to capture the knowledge of experts when supporting educational settings. On the other hand, CxBR is best suited to capture the tactical knowledge of experts, which requires assessment of the situation, selecting a plan of action, and acting on the plan. Both of these knowledge capture systems can then be used to construct simulation models of human behavior.

Concept Maps

Knowledge Representation through the Use of Concept Maps

One type of knowledge capture system that we describe in this chapter is based on the use of **concept maps** as a knowledge-modeling tool. Concept maps, developed by Novak (Novak 1998; Novak and Cañas 2008; Novak and Gowin 1984), aim to represent knowledge through *concepts* enclosed in circles or boxes of some types, which are related via connecting lines or *propositions*. Concepts are perceived regularities in events or objects that are designated by a label.

In the simplest form, a concept map contains just two concepts connected by a linking word to form a single *proposition*, also called a **semantic unit** or *unit of meaning.* For example, Figure 7.1 is a concept map that describes the structure of concept maps. Based on the concept map represented in Figure 7.1, the two concepts—concept maps and organized knowledge—are linked together to form the proposition: "Concept maps represent organized knowledge." Additional propositions expand the meaning of concept maps, such as: "Concepts are hierarchically structured."

In a concept map, the vertical axis expresses a hierarchical framework for organizing the concepts. More general, inclusive concepts are found at the top of the map with progressively more specific, less inclusive concepts arranged below them. These maps emphasize the most general concepts by linking them to supporting ideas with **propositions**. Concept maps represent meaningful relationships between concepts in the form of propositions. In addition, relationships between concepts (propositions) in different domains of the concept map are defined as *cross-links*. These cross-links help to visualize how different knowledge domains are related to each other.

Sometimes the difference between concept maps and semantic networks could be a source of confusion. **Semantic networks**, also called *associative networks*, are typically represented as a directed graph connecting the nodes (representing concepts) to show a relationship or association between them. This type of associative network can be useful in describing, for example, traffic flow in that the connections between concepts indicate direction, but directed graphs do not connect concepts through propositions. Furthermore, in a directed graph there's no assumption about the progression of generality to more

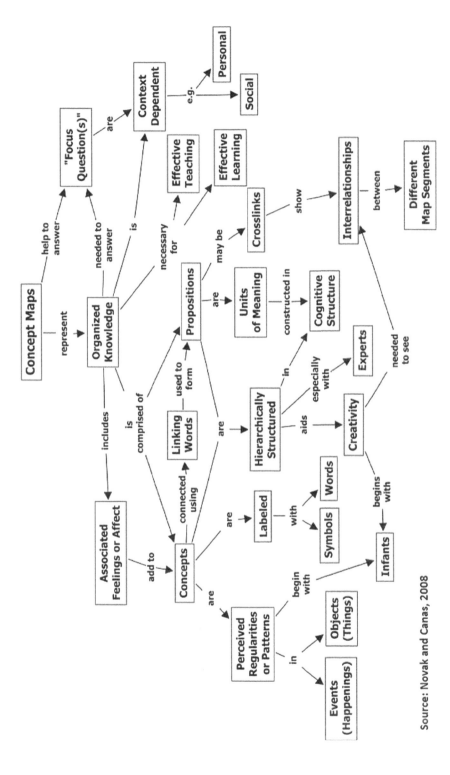

Source: Novak and Canas, 2008

Figure 7.1 Concept Map about Concept Maps

specific concepts as the nodes are traversed from the top of the network. The same holds true for associative networks in general.

Concept maps were developed based on Ausubel's (1963) learning psychology theory. Ausubel's cognitive psychology research provides us with the understanding that learning takes place through the assimilation of new concepts and propositions into existing concept frameworks by the learner. Ausubel's studies uncovered the conditions for meaningful learning to include (1) a clear presentation of the material, (2) the learner's relevant prior knowledge, and (3) the learner's motivation to integrate new meanings into their prior knowledge. Concept maps can be useful in meeting the conditions for learning by identifying concepts prior to instruction, building new concept frameworks, and integrating concept maps through cross-links.

In educational settings, concept-mapping techniques have been used in many fields, including as a teaching and learning tool for medical students (Baliga et al. 2021). Their rich expressive power derives from each map's ability to allow its creator the use of a virtually unlimited set of linking words to show how meanings have been developed. Consequently, maps having similar concepts can vary from one context to another. Also, concept maps may be used to measure a particular person's knowledge about a given topic in a specific context. Concept maps can help formalize and capture an expert's domain knowledge in an easy-to-understand representation of an expert's domain knowledge. Figure 7.2 shows a segment of a concept map from the domain of nuclear cardiology.

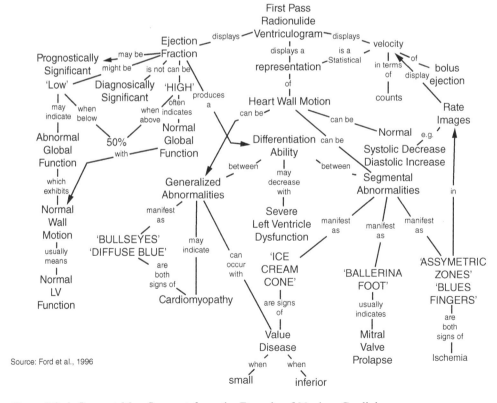

Source: Ford et al., 1996

Figure 7.2 A Concept Map Segment from the Domain of Nuclear Cardiology

Knowledge Capture Systems Based on Concept Maps

The goal of **CmapTools** (Cañas et al. 2004),[1] a concept map-based browser, is to capture the knowledge of experts. The navigation problem, an important concern in hypermedia systems, is alleviated by the use of concept maps, which serve as guides in the traversing of logical linkages among clusters of related objects. The CmapTools extend the use of concept maps beyond knowledge representation to serve as the browsing interface to a domain of knowledge.

Figure 7.3 shows the concept map-based browser as the interface for the explanation subsystem of a nuclear cardiology expert system (Cañas and Novak 2005; Cañas et al. 1997, 2001, 2003, 2004; Ford et al. 1996). Each of the concept nodes represents an abstraction for a specific cardiology pathology, which is fully described by the icons at the concept node. For the cardiologist, the image results of a Nuclear Medicine Radionuclide Ventriculogram[2] scan resembling a picture of "asymmetric blue fingers" (later depicted in Figure 7.4) is a sign of myocardial ischemia or chronic heart failure. An image resembling a "ballerina foot" is usually a representation of a mitral valve prolapse. Clearly the first patient will quickly need to be rushed to a hospital for emergency surgery, while the second may be given medication and a diet to relieve him of his symptoms.

The icons below the concept nodes provide access to auxiliary information that helps explain the concepts in the form of pictures, images, audio-video clips, text, Internet links, or other concept maps related to the topic. These linked media resources and concept maps can be located anywhere accessible via the Internet (Cañas et al. 2001).

The browser provides a window showing the hierarchical ordering of maps, highlights the current location of the user in the hierarchy, and permits movement to any other map

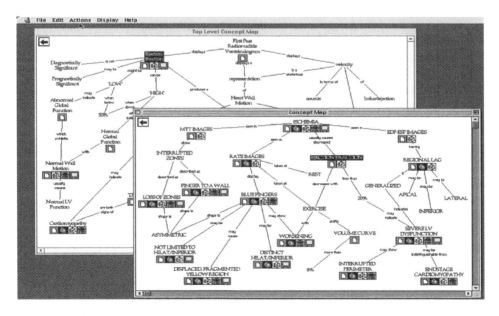

Source: Ford et al., 1996

Figure 7.3 Segment from Nuclear Cardiology using CmapTools

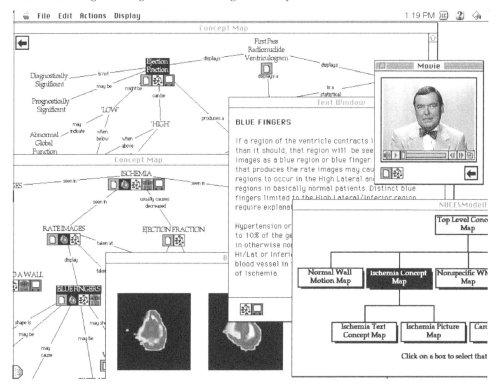

Figure 7.4 Explanation Subsystem using CmapTools

by clicking on the desired map in the hierarchy. This concept map-based interface provides a unique way of organizing and browsing knowledge about any domain.

CmapTools provides a practical application of the idea of utilizing concept maps to capture and formalize knowledge resulting in context-rich knowledge representation models that can be viewed and shared through the Internet. CmapTools takes advantage of the richness provided by multimedia, providing an effective platform for aspiring students to learn from subject-matter experts.

Concept maps provide an effective methodology to organize and structure the concepts representing the expert's domain knowledge. During the knowledge capture process, the knowledge engineer and domain expert interact to collaboratively construct a shared conceptual model of the domain which eventually becomes the concept map for the multimedia system. Users later browse this conceptual model through the CmapTools. Browsing enables the learner to implicitly gain the expert's view of the domain. In general, this model for knowledge representation provides a broad view of the domain as understood by that particular domain expert.

Links in concept maps are explicitly labeled arcs, and usually connect two concepts to form a concept-link-concept relation that may be read as a simple proposition. CmapTools users learn about the domain by clicking on the small icons depicted at the nodes in the concept map and directly navigate to other contexts (or subcontexts) through hyperlinks where other concepts are described. Figure 7.4 shows some of the different media windows opened from the windows in Figure 7.3.

Another advantage of using concept maps for knowledge representation is that, because of their hierarchical organization, concept maps can easily scale to large quantities of information. This particular characteristic can then enable the easy integration of domain concepts together.

CmapTools has been shown to facilitate virtual collaboration and the creation of concept maps at a distance (Cañas et al. 2003), which are stored on public servers that can be accessed via the Internet. Concept maps are the ideal mechanism to make explicit and capture ideas so they can later be shared to collaboratively create new knowledge. Studies also show that the use of concept maps has helped improve areas of knowledge such as reading comprehension and language (Liu et al. 2010).

In summary, concept-mapping tools like CmapTools can be an effective way to capture and represent the knowledge of domain experts in representation models that can later be used by potential students of the domain (Cañas and Novak 2005; Cañas et al. 2003; Correia et al. 2014). Practically speaking, the knowledge representation models illustrated in the aforementioned Figures 7.2, 7.3, and 7.4 could be used by students in the field of cardiology to effectively learn the practical aspects of the domain from one of the best experts in the field.

Context-Based Reasoning

Knowledge Representation through the Use of Context-Based Reasoning

Recall from Chapter 2 that tactical knowledge is defined as pertaining to the short-term positioning of the organization relative to its markets, competitors, and suppliers; and is contrasted to **strategic knowledge**, which pertains to the long-term positioning of the organization in terms of its corporate vision and strategies for achieving that vision. In the context of this example **tactical knowledge** refers to the human ability that enables domain experts to assess the situation at hand (therefore short-term) among a myriad of inputs, select a plan that best addresses the current situation, and execute that plan (Gonzalez and Ahlers 1998; Sodhani et al. 2021; Thorndike and Wescort 1984). Consider the following scenario:

> The commanding officer of the submarine is generally bombarded with a multitude of inputs when performing his job. He receives audio inputs such as engine noise, electronic noise, and conversations with others around him. He likewise receives visual inputs such as the radar and sonar screens, possibly the periscope and so forth, and tactile inputs such as vibrations of the submarine. He is able to cognitively handle these inputs rather easily when they are all in the normal expected range. However, if one of these should deviate from normal, such as abnormal noise and vibrations, the officer will immediately focus only on these inputs in order to recognize the present situation as, for instance, a potential grounding, collision, or engine malfunction. All other inputs being received, meanwhile, are generally ignored during the crisis.

Alternatively, consider an example more relevant to our daily lives:

> The daily routine drive to and from work is marked by a myriad of inputs while performing the task. A Dad driving to work with his children receives audio inputs

such as the noise from babies, siblings vying for attention, pop music, their spouse's conversation, and who could forget the cellular phone. In addition, he receives visual inputs like the gas gauge level (typically empty at this time), traffic signals (including those marking school zones), and the all-too-familiar police strobe lights. He's able to cognitively handle these inputs (even in the absence of coffee) when they're in the normal (albeit borderline chaotic) range. However, if any of these should deviate from normal—for example, the strobe signal from police following the car will signal to the driver that perhaps he has committed an infraction and needs to immediately pull over. At this point all other signals, including the screaming children, will be ignored during the crisis at hand.

Context-Based Reasoning (CxBR) helps to model this behavioral phenomenon. Context-based reasoning is a human behavior representation paradigm specifically designed to effectively represent human tactical behavior (Gonzalez et al. 1998, 2002, 2008). Tactical behavior is defined as: "The continual and dynamic process of decision making by a performing agent (human or otherwise) that interacts with its environment while attempting to carry out a mission in the environment" (Gonzalez et al. 2005, p. 146). In this sense tactical knowledge is associated with assessing a current situation, selecting a plan to address the current situation, and executing that plan. Tactical experts recognize and treat only the salient features of the situation and thus are able to abstract a small but important portion of the available inputs for general knowledge. Just like the nuclear cardiologist in Figure 7.3 is able to abstract a heart pathology that he describes as "blue fingers," the commanding officer is able to abstract and treat the key features of the situation at hand and act based on these features. CxBR is based on the following basic tenets (Gonzalez and Ahlers 1993):

1   A tactical situation calls for a set of actions and procedures that properly address the current situation. In the case of a driver, for example, these actions could include maintaining the car in its proper lane, stopping at a stop sign, and not exceeding the speed limit (by much). The set of actions and procedures is described as the context.

2   As the situation evolves, a transition to another context or set of actions and procedures may be required to address the new situation. For example, when a driver exits an interstate highway onto a city street, a different set of functions and procedures will be necessary to manage this new situation. In addition, one must be aware of cross traffic, traffic lights, and so forth that would not have to be considered when driving on an interstate highway.

3   What is likely to happen in a context or current situation is limited by the context itself. Continuing with the same example, one would not have to worry about operating the cruise control while waiting at a traffic light. However, that could be a potential action while driving on the interstate.

CxBR encapsulates knowledge about appropriate actions and/or procedures, as well as compatible new situations, into hierarchically organized contexts. Tactical behavior is action-based at low levels (e.g., keeping the car in the traffic lane), decision-and-action based at middle levels (stop or go at a traffic light), and decision-based at high levels (take the freeway or the back roads). In this sense, CxBR is hierarchical and modular and a sample hierarchy is depicted in Figure 7.5.

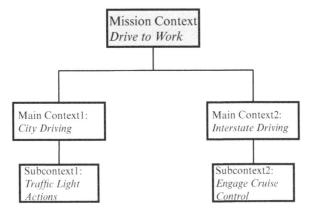

Figure 7.5 Knowledge Representation through CxBR

The **mission context** defines the scope of the mission, its goals, the plan, and the constraints imposed (time, weather, etc.). The **main context** contains functions, rules, and a list of compatible subsequent main contexts. Identification of a new situation can now be simplified because only a limited number of all situations are possible under the currently active context. **Subcontexts** are abstractions of functions performed by the main context, which may be too complex for one function or that may be employed by other main contexts. This encourages re-usability. Subcontexts are activated by rules in the active main context. They will deactivate themselves upon completion of their actions.

Decisions are heavily influenced by a sequence of main contexts, each of which, when active, controls behavior of an autonomous vehicle agent (either real or simulated) with an expectation for the future. Active main contexts change not only in response to external events or circumstances but also because of actions taken by the agent itself. One example of a main context could be driving in city traffic, called *City Driving*. Such a context would contain functions to maintain the vehicle on the road at a speed not to exceed the speed limit, the know-how to handle intersections, pedestrians, school zones, and so forth. It could call subcontexts to help it deal with traffic lights, school zones, and emergency vehicles.

One and only one specific main context is always active for each agent, making it the sole controller of the agent. When the situation changes, a transition to another main context may be required to properly address the emerging situation. For example, the automobile may enter an interstate highway requiring a transition to another main context, called *Interstate Driving*. Transitions between contexts are triggered by events in the environment—some planned, others unplanned. Expert performers are able to recognize and identify the transition points quickly and effectively.

Any situation, by its very nature, will limit the number of other situations that can realistically be followed. Therefore, only a limited number of things can be expected to happen within any one context. Using the domain of driving an automobile, a tire blowout is typically not expected while idling at a traffic light. However, getting rear-ended is a definite possibility. The converse is true when driving on an interstate highway. This can be used as an advantage in pruning the search space of the problem, since there is no need to monitor the simulation for blowouts when the driver is in the traffic light subcontext. If unexpected occurrences do take place, they introduce the element of surprise into the agent's behavior, which is highly consistent with actual human behavior.

CxBR has proven to be a very intuitive, efficient, and effective representation technique for human behavior. As such, it provides the important hierarchical organization of contexts. Additionally, it has the ability to incorporate any programming paradigm within the control activity (e.g., neural networks, a knowledge discovery technique described in Chapter 9, have been used as subcontexts). The presence of a mission context to define the mission and provide global performance modifiers is also a notable difference. CxBR provides the ability to perform complex reasoning to dictate the transitions between main contexts if necessary for the application. Transitions can be coded through the use of rules (described in Chapter 6). This flexibility and representational richness distinguishes CxBR not only from the traditional state transition paradigms but also from other commonly used modeling paradigms for human behavior. CxBR can be used to adequately capture and represent tactical knowledge. Potential applications include the capture and representation of the knowledge of airline pilots and of air traffic controllers. In addition, it can serve to capture and represent the knowledge of commercial pilots and bus drivers as well as of subway and train engineers. Also, CxBR can serve to represent knowledge related to military affairs (Gonzalez and Ahlers 1998) and even poker playing (Stensrud 2005). Finally, contextual reasoning can be used to monitor and supervise the collaborative work of knowledge workers working together on a project, and thus act as a competent project manager (Gonzalez et al. 2008). A full description of CxBR can be found in Gonzalez et al. (2008).

Knowledge Capture Systems Based on Context-Based Reasoning

As we discussed briefly in Chapter 6, knowledge engineers elicit the knowledge of experts primarily through detailed interview sessions with the subject-matter expert. Furthermore, the success of the knowledge elicitation process depends on many nontechnical factors such as the expert's personality, the knowledge engineer's experience, and her preparation. Ultimately, one of the goals of the field of artificial intelligence, which still remains unachieved, is to be able to build an expert's cognitive model directly via a query session between the expert and the intelligent system. Clearly, the advantages of accomplishing this would be many, the most important being the dramatic reduction in manpower required to capture the knowledge of experts and a significant reduction in the logical errors coded in the system.

Because of its hierarchical and modular nature, context-based reasoning lends itself well to automating the knowledge capture process. Here we describe a knowledge capture system based on CxBR known as **Context-Based Intelligent Tactical Knowledge Acquisition (CITKA)** (Gonzalez et al. 2002; 2005). CITKA uses its own knowledge base to compose a set of intelligent queries to elicit the tactical knowledge of the expert.

CITKA composes questions and presents them to the expert. The questions are designed to elicit tactical knowledge and represent it in the underlying CxBR paradigm. Upon responding to the questions, the result is a nearly complete context base which, when used with a CxBR reasoning engine, can be used to control someone performing the mission of interest in a typical environment (e.g., driving from New York to Boston, flying an airplane from Houston to Dallas). CITKA can be used by the expert or by the knowledge engineer. It is likely that both will need to use it to complete the context base. The query sessions only take place with the expert. The knowledge engineer is given direct edit access to the context base. Let us now look at how CITKA works.

The CITKA system consists of four modules of independent but cooperating subsystems. These modules are:

1   Knowledge engineering database back-end (KEDB)— A data structure that holds the evolving context base as it gradually becomes developed, either by the knowledge engineer or by the **subject matter expert (SME)**. The KEDB is subject to the hierarchical structure of mission, main, and subcontexts imposed by CxBR. To implement these data structures, a table is created for each context type.
2   Knowledge engineering interface (KEI)—Maps into the KEDB module. Data entry in the KEI is provided by eight interacting dialogs: Mission Context, Main Contexts, Subcontexts, Entity Objects, Helping Functions, Memory Variables, Transition Criteria, and Action Definitions. The KEI is designed in a table-driven fashion.
3   Query rule-based back-end (QRB)—A rule-based system containing the rules for executing the intelligent dialog with the subject matter expert (SME). A rule is provided for each SME interface input screen. These query rules have to be mapped to buttons, checkboxes, and menus by the SME Interface.
4   Subject matter expert interface (SMEI)—The graphical user interface (GUI) for the QRB. This environment allows a great deal of flexibility: the SMEI dynamically produces interfaces that correspond to the questions and rules that are put forth in the QRB.

The CITKA system was evaluated for its effectiveness. There were two main issues here: (1) estimating the reduction in person-hour effort to develop a context-based model for a particular mission, and (2) estimating the percentage of a context-based model that could conceivably be automatically developed through CITKA. The prototype was tested on a nontrivial mission for a submarine to monitor a port and protect surface assets against underwater threats emanating from the monitored port. This context base was first developed through the traditional interview methods, and the hours spent developing it were carefully documented. It was then estimated how long it would take to develop the same model with the CITKA tool. Its developers report that there could be as much as an 80 percent reduction in person-hour effort to build with a context-based system as compared to the current manual means (Gonzalez et al. 2002). Furthermore, they estimate that 50 to 80 percent of the context-based model could be developed directly through a query session in CITKA. Recent research aims to discover and identify the various contexts experienced by a human actor while performing tasks in a simulated environment, for the purpose of building autonomous tactical agents that may be able to perform the same tasks as the human actor (Trinh and Gonzalez 2013).

Barriers to the Use of Knowledge Capture Systems

This section discusses the barriers to the deployment of knowledge capture systems from two perspectives. The first perspective describes that of the knowledge engineer who seeks to build such systems. The second perspective is that of the subject matter expert, who would interact with an automated knowledge capture system to preserve his knowledge. First let's consider the barriers to the development of knowledge capture systems.

As discussed at the beginning of this chapter, there are two possible mechanisms to capture the knowledge of experts. The first mechanism is to simply ask the expert, through a knowledge-elicitation process (described in Chapter 6), that must be properly managed in order to maximize the results of the process. This is the essence of the externalization process. The second mechanism is to observe a person's behavior or performance while they're executing their tasks. This method, learning by observation, is essentially the internalization process. Perhaps in the not too far future, we may be able to connect a device to a person's brain that could sense and capture the neural firings of the brain that constitutes expertise, but clearly this is not yet a possibility. Undoubtedly, this futuristic possibility raises a host of ethical considerations as well. In fact, this possibility would clearly contradict the essence of KM that we described in Chapter 1—that is, KM should not distance itself from the knowledge owners but instead celebrate and recognize their position as experts in the organization.

One of the largest barriers to the automatic elicitation of an expert's knowledge is that in order to effectively accomplish this task, the knowledge engineer requires developing some idea of the nature and structure of the knowledge very early in the process. In this chapter, we have discussed how knowledge engineers must attempt to become versed in the subject matter, or the nature of knowledge, prior to the interview process. Familiarization with the structure of knowledge is an additional requirement, often a fairly difficult proposition, in the sense that the interviewer must quickly develop some idea of which paradigm would best represent the knowledge at hand. For example, while conducting the expert interviews, the knowledge engineer observes that the expert's knowledge is very conditional. In other words, if the expert describes it as "if A then B," this would be a good indication that his knowledge would best be represented as rules. If the expert describes the knowledge in terms of connections, in other words "A is related to B, B is related to C" as in describing an architecture, then perhaps the most adequate representation is the concept map paradigm. Furthermore, if the expert's knowledge is based on recollections "I remember when one such instance happened" then case-based reasoning is the most likely alternative. If the expert describes his knowledge in terms of a schedule of events, "this happens on A after B event," then a constraint-based paradigm may be the best alternative. Finally, if the expert's knowledge is described in tactical terms such as "how to drive a car," then context-based reasoning would be the best representation.

Only if the interviewer is able to develop an idea of the **type or nature of knowledge** early in the process, will she be able to adequately represent it. In theory, we could replace the knowledge engineer with an intelligent knowledge capture system that would develop a set of questions to adequately elicit the knowledge of the subject matter expert. The system would need to know the nature and structure of the knowledge and how to ask such questions accordingly. In other words, the intelligent knowledge capture system and the expert would need to be "in tune" with each other. This is several generations ahead of the CmapTools and CITKA systems described before. On the other hand, if the end result is only to elicit the expert's knowledge to capture it in a document or a story, the structure requirement may not be necessary.

In summary, developing an automated system for knowledge capture without *a priori* knowledge of the nature and structure of the knowledge in question is essentially not possible. Furthermore, developing a multiparadigm tool that could essentially define the appropriate knowledge capture technique is almost impossible. The knowledge acquisition process must be tailored to the specific type of knowledge, and making that assessment ahead of time could be difficult.

From the point of view of the expert who will be faced with the task of interacting with the knowledge capture system, this may pose additional barriers. The first one is that the expert will need to take the initiative of learning how to interact with the system, and he may need to be coached through the first few sessions until he's reached a certain comfort level with the technology. Naturally some people may be resistant to trying new things, and the proposition of interacting with a machine may be one that many experts may not necessarily look forward to. This barrier can be overcome with adequate training and the utilization of user-friendly interfaces. In the area of **graphical user interfaces**, current research examines the impact that "talking heads," even those that could portray emotion, could play on the user's feeling of ease with the technology.

Research Trends

Using Learning by Observation to Capture Knowledge

This section discusses some research trends about how learning by observation could be used to capture knowledge. Without a doubt, humans and many animals learn first by observation. Infants learn their language, what foods to eat and avoid, and the signs of danger including distinguishing prey from predators. Many animals have been shown to learn by observation including chimpanzees, dolphins, and some bird species. Research on how humans and animals learn through observation has been one important area of study in artificial intelligence. Learning by observation refers to a computing agent's ability to improve how it will act in the future, as the agent observes its interactions with the world and its own decision-making process (Russell and Norvig 2010).

Just like humans can learn by observing others perform a task, robots could improve their effectiveness by doing the same thing. Providing robots with such ability implies they would need to be equipped with vision. In addition, the movements required for a specific task would need to be encoded to "train" the robot. Exact emulation of human movement has been occurring since the 1970s. For example, a human could take a robot that paints automobile parts through his motions, and it could easily replicate exactly the same motions thereafter. What is much harder for the robot is to "understand" why the human is doing what he does so that it can extrapolate the learned tasks to slightly different situations. For example if a robot has to paint only the doorknob in a door forthcoming on the assembly line, as long as the doorknob is in exactly the same location every time, learning dumb moves suffices. But if the location of the doorknob varies with each door, and the robotic painting arm must look for it and paint it wherever it is that's more difficult. Even more difficult is to understand when a door comes along that doesn't have doorknobs, which means the robot should not paint anything at all. Clearly the benefits for the robot arm to learn by observation would be significant, since it would allow shortening its learning time while decreasing the required programming effort.

Learning through observation has been used successfully to automate the knowledge acquisition task. For example, Sammut et al. (1992) used learning by observation (which they term as *behavioral cloning*) to learn the knowledge required to fly a Cessna through observation of a human using a flight simulator to fly a predefined flight plan. In their research, observation logs were kept from a large set of training examples that recorded the sensor inputs and appropriate actions, which were used to create decision trees describing the pilot's behavior. Also, Pomerleau et al. (1994) developed an autonomous vehicle-driving system that they entitled Autonomous Land Vehicle In a Neural Network (ALVINN), using neural networks that were trained by observing how human drivers responded to diverse driving environments. ALVINN was trained to drive in a variety of conditions, including single-lane paved and unpaved roads, multilane roads, obstacle ridden on-road and off-road environments, and even under adverse environmental conditions like rain and snow, at speeds up to 55 miles an hour. Wang (1995) also described another system that learned to produce machine parts through observation. OBSERVER recorded each step the expert performed to generate the machine part and had the ability to learn operator preconditions and the corresponding actions for each step, even refining its actions through practice. Sidani and Gonzalez (1995) also captured the behavior of an expert automobile driver by observing his actions in a simulated task. In their work, they built a system based on neural networks and symbolic reasoning that learned by observing the expert driver's behavior. The system successfully operated a car at a traffic light as well as in the presence of a pedestrian crossing in front of the vehicle. Later van Lent and Laird (1999) defined a system they called OBSERVO-SOAR, which combined behavioral cloning with OBSERVER's behavioral representation in order to learn effectively in complex and dynamic domains such as a flight simulator domain.

More recently the term *cognitive imitation*, first introduced by Subiaul et al. (2004), is being used to denote "a type of observational learning in which a naïve student copies an expert's use of a rule" (p. 407). In this sense, cognitive imitation involves imitation with observational learning. Observational learning is not the same as cognitive imitation, because observational learning does not always involve imitation. For example, a student may learn via observation *what not to do*, which implies observational learning without imitation. But the reverse does hold in the sense that imitation requires observational learning.

The modern approach to learning by observation is "to design agents that already know something and are trying to learn some more" (Russell and Norvig 2010). In this sense, the agent must have some way to obtain the background knowledge that it will use to learn new episodes via incremental development. Although systems that learn by observation may still be in their infancy, the early success of these systems has proven the possibility of capturing knowledge from experts through nonintrusive interaction and observation of the behavior of the human expert. Perhaps the science fiction idea of plugging in expertise through an electronic socket behind our ears is not such a remote possibility after all. Do you want to be a rocket scientist? Just put on your rocket scientist eyeglasses, and voilà!

The next section discusses the role of radio frequency identification (RFID) technology in knowledge capture.

Radio Frequency Identification

Consider the following scenarios:

> On a snowy slope in Norway, a skier glides to the lift and goes right through the turnstile without slowing to show a ticket. In a Danish suburb, a woman's blood pressure is monitored as she weeds her garden. And during a safety drill at a Canadian oil refinery, over 200 workers are rapidly evacuated and instantly accounted for.
>
> (IBM 2007)

All of these scenarios have one thing in common: **radio frequency identification** or, in short, **RFID**. In the last two decades, RFID, a technology that was originally developed for radio and radar applications, has taken center stage in capturing information for the purpose of identification via radio waves. The first paper that explored RFID technology was the seminal paper by Harry Stockman in which he describes that

> point-to-point communication, with the carrier power generated at the receiving end and the transmitter replaced by a modulated reflector, represents a transmission system which possesses new and different characteristics. Radio, light, or sound waves (essentially microwaves, infrared, and ultrasonic waves) may be used for the transmission under approximate conditions of specular reflection.
>
> (Stockman 1948, p. 1196)

Even though Stockman states in that same paper that "considerable research and development work has to be done before the remaining basic problems in reflected-power communication are solved, and before the field of useful applications is explored" (Stockman 1948, p. 1204), the field of RFID has seen a dramatic surge of useful applications just in the last few years. Even though commercial activities would start in the 1960s, the 1980s saw the first significant implementations of RFID in the United States, primarily for transportation interests such as toll collection (Landt 2001). RFID is the combination of radio broadcast with radar technology, and consists of two parts: an RFID tag which is an integrated circuit that modulates and demodulates a radio frequency signal and processes and stores information. The second part is an antenna that receives and transmits the signal. There are three kinds of RFID tags: passive (which have no battery and the power is supplied by the reader),[3] active (which have a power supply),[4] and semi-passive (which have a power supply that powers the tag). The difference among the three lies in that for passive tags, the power level to power up the RFID circuitry must be 100 times stronger than with active or semi-active tag. In addition, condition-sensing tags include a battery and the electronic circuitry to read and transmit diagnostics back to the reader. The tags monitor the environmental conditions and communicate and collect data that are later transmitted to back-end systems using network software (IBM 2007).

The outlook for RFID is indeed promising. Despite certain unresolved challenges, such as the global macroeconomic downturn and shortages of chips and raw materials, the global RFID market is projected to continue expanding in 2023. According to IDTechEx, the market is estimated to reach US$14 billion in 2023 and US$24 billion in 2033, rising from US$12.8 billion in 2022 (Chang et al. 2023). This growth encompasses various RFID form factors, including labels, cards, fobs, and tags, along with readers, software, and services for both passive and active RFID technologies. This massive growth is largely due to the technology's widespread implementation across industries as diverse as retail, aerospace, pharmaceuticals, semiconductors, automotive, and mining, as well as various government institutions. Box 7.3 summarizes Walmart's journey with RFID.

Box 7.3 RFID Technology at Walmart

Walmart played a crucial role in bringing RFID technology into the public consciousness. Back in 2003, RFID was relatively unknown to the general public. However, Walmart changed that when they announced that their top 100 suppliers would be required to use RFID tags on all incoming shipments, including cases and pallets. Initially, Walmart piloted RFID-based inventory tracking in a few stores in Texas with the participation of eight product suppliers. Beyond shipments, Walmart also individually tagged high-value electronics like TVs, CDs, and stereos.

In 2005, Walmart mandated the use of RFID on all shipments in order to improve their supply chain and then Sam's Club, a Walmart division, announced that companies that supply them with goods that didn't meet their RFID tagging requirements would need to pay a service fee (Bachelor 2008).

The company aimed to expand the implementation of RFID technology gradually and have it fully deployed across all its stores by the end of 2006. Walmart's decision to adopt RFID stemmed from their belief that inaccurate stock numbers were impacting sales and customer satisfaction. They saw RFID as a solution to improve supply chain visibility and make more accurate ordering decisions.

This announcement by Walmart had a ripple effect, inspiring other major retailers like Best Buy, Target, Home Depot, Tesco, and Metro Stores to experiment with or adopt RFID technology as well. The move by Walmart marked a pivotal moment in RFID's journey toward becoming a widely-used technology in the retail industry.

Despite some challenges during Walmart's initial adoption of RFID, the technology continued to be used by Walmart and other retailers. By 2010, RFID technology had advanced, and Walmart expanded its use to track shipments to stores and goods within stores company-wide (Moore 2023). They also started using RFID tags to track specific sales floor items, beginning with men's jeans and underwear. This success prompted other major retailers like Bloomingdales and Macy's to adopt RFID for clothing tracking as well.

Walmart obtains excellent inventory accuracy from RFID. Shelly McDougal, Walmart's senior director of merchandising, remarked in early 2022 (CYBRA 2022):

> We have seen dramatic results in our ability to ensure product is available for our customers, leading to improved online order fulfillment and customer satisfaction.

In early 2022, Walmart made a significant announcement regarding its RFID mandate program. The company revealed its intention to expand the program to include additional products and departments. Suppliers will be required to tag home goods, sporting goods, electronics, and toys with RFID by September 2, 2022. The mandate is planned to be extended to more categories in the future. Being one of the world's largest retailers, this decision will have far-reaching consequences for virtually all of Walmart's manufacturers, distributors, and vendors. For organizations partnering with Walmart, it is crucial to understand the implications of this mandate and how it will impact their operations. To best prepare for Walmart's RFID mandate, here are the key details you need to know (CYBRA 2022).

With the RFID tagging mandate, Walmart's fulfillment and merchandising team is now targeting enhanced accuracy. By implementing RFID technology, Walmart joins the ranks of forward-thinking retailers seeking to optimize their supply chain processes and offer customers a seamless shopping experience.

Walmart reaps multiple benefits from its RFID initiative, as mentioned earlier: improved on-hand accuracy, enhanced consumer data collection, better tracking capabilities, reduced shrinkage, and more. Additionally, RFID brings an added advantage in supporting Walmart's online shoppers, enhancing the in-store experience for those who shop digitally. Suppliers within Walmart's supply chain have also seen a remarkable double-digit surge in demand, directly attributed to Walmart's RFID mandate.

Although in-store shopping remains relevant, Gen Z shoppers are revitalizing the brick-and-mortar experience. However, many customers still prefer to research products online before visiting physical stores. Here, RFID technology integrated with Walmart.com becomes valuable as it allows shoppers to check the availability of desired products in their local store. The increased inventory accuracy achieved through RFID empowers Walmart to truly function as an omnichannel retailer, seamlessly bridging the gap between online and in-store shopping experiences (8th and Walton, 2022).

Sources: Compiled from 8th and Walton (2022); Bachelor (2008); CYBRA (2022); Jenns (2023); Moore (2023)

Although apparel and footwear maintain their lead in the RFID market, other retail sectors are also witnessing significant growth. Retailers can reap significant benefits from adopting RFID technology. GS1 US reports that item-level tagging can enhance retail inventory accuracy by an impressive 95 percent. Moreover, RFID implementation has the potential to reduce out-of-stocks at the retail level by up to 50 percent. Precise inventory data is crucial for retailers to succeed both online and in physical stores, and RFID empowers them to achieve unprecedented accuracy throughout their entire supply chain. Notably, several prominent retailers, such as Target in 2016, H&M in 2021, and Nordstrom and Macy's in 2022, have recently integrated RFID into their supply chains (CYBRA 2022). These decisions reflect the industry's recognition of the importance of elevated inventory precision throughout their operations. Time and again, RFID has demonstrated its superiority in delivering accurate inventory numbers for retailers.

One example of government use of RFID technology is in passports, the chips contain all of the printed information on your passport (name, date of birth, age, etc.) as well as a digital copy of your passport photograph. Today, all new passports issued by the United States and a number of foreign governments are embedded with RFID chips. It is advocated that the use of this technology will prevent tampering and improve security. Another specific area where RFID is making a big impact is in asset management. For example, hospitals are increasingly using RFID technology to locate expensive equipment using real-time location systems (RTLS), in addition to using RFID to improve their surgical room throughput and patient flow. When paired with an indoor positioning system or RTLS, RFID tags allow healthcare providers to track newborns as well as prevent older patients with cognitive issues such as dementia from wandering away (Wong 2021). RFID systems implementation in healthcare has had truly transformational effects that span the elimination of paper-based processes to improved visibility of patients, all of them translating to higher financial performance, patient satisfaction, and improved decision-making. A case analysis of the benefits gained in the healthcare sector through RFID technology shows evident effects at the process level of organizations and thus substantial gains at the organizational level (Anand and Wamba 2013). For example, one hospital replaced a manually tracked process of hernia mesh patches, which frequently were expired or missing, by one where the meshes were tagged and stored in a smart shelf where an RFID interrogator continuously monitored and recorded the movement of the meshes. The pilot program not only had a ROI of over US$600K, but also brought improved patient care and safety, while eliminating waste processes in the hospital (Anand and Wamba 2013).

From the KM perspective, the promise of RFID will continue to generate huge returns in better inventory management for manufacturers, hospitals, and retail stores. RFID tags have also been implanted in animals, for example, to track livestock such as cattle (Gumpert and Pentland 2007) and also humans who are wary about abductions (Haines 2004). But the use of RFID implants in humans is also meeting great criticism as the debate grows about the privacy implications that this technology could pose in the hands of authoritarian governments that could use them to remove individuals' freedom (Monahan and Wall 2007). Should we then get a chip on our shoulders?

Summary

In this chapter, you learned the definitions and characteristics of knowledge capture systems and design considerations and various types of such systems. Specific attention was placed on the two knowledge capture systems based on different methodologies and intelligent technologies. The first system is based on the use of concept maps as a knowledge-modeling tool and is best suited to capture the knowledge of experts when supporting educational settings. The second system is based on the use of context-based reasoning to simulate human behavior and is best suited to capture the tactical knowledge of experts. Finally, the use of stories in organizational settings was discussed as a mechanism that can support knowledge capture.

Review

1 What is a concept map?
2 What is context-based reasoning?
3 How would you describe the domains that are best suited to be captured by concept maps versus context-based reasoning?
4 Describe the two techniques for knowledge elicitation via the use of stories.
5 What types of knowledge can be acquired through automated knowledge by observation?

Application Exercises

1 Pick a sample domain in which you're knowledgeable and build a concept map to represent that domain.
2 Define, using context-based hierarchy, the main contexts and subcontexts of the mission context that describes your particular driving pattern from home to work each day.
3 Define the rules that will cause the switch between main contexts and subcontexts in the aforementioned context hierarchy.

4 Describe a story that adequately embodies your organization's corporate culture.
5 Describe a specific type of knowledge that could adequately be captured through automated knowledge by observation.

Notes

1 CmapTools can be downloaded for free at http://cmap.ihmc.us. Last accessed July 24, 2023.
2 A medical procedure to assess how well the heart is beating when at rest and also when exercising. Also known as MUGA test. During the test, a small amount of radioactive material is injected into the patient so pictures can be taken of the blood in the heart. Experienced cardiologists are able to detect pathological conditions by abstracting a familiar shape from this image, which may resemble *asymmetric blue fingers*, a *ballerina's foot*, or an *ice cream cone*.
3 When the passive tag encounters radio waves from the reader, the coiled antenna within the tag forms a magnetic field that draws power to the tag, energizing the circuits in the tag. The tag then sends the data stored in the tag's memory (IBM 2007).
4 Active RFID tags are outfitted with a battery, which can serve as a partial or complete power source for the tag's circuitry and antenna. Some active tags are equipped with replaceable batteries for years of use while others are sealed (IBM 2007).

References

8th and Walton. 2022. Walmart RFID technology: What suppliers need to know, January 31.

Anand, A., and Wamba, S.F. 2013. Business value of RFID-enabled healthcare transformation projects. *Business Process Management Journal*, 19(1), 111–145.

Ausubel, D.P. 1963. *The psychology of meaningful verbal learning*. New York: Grune and Stratton.

Bachelor, B. 2008. Sam's Club tells suppliers to tag or pay. *RFID Journal*, January 11.

Baliga, S.S., Walvekar, P.R., and Mahantshetti, G.J. 2021. Concept map as a teaching and learning tool for medical students. *Journal of Education and Health Promotion*, 10(35), January 28.

Cañas, A., and Novak, J. 2005. *A concept map-centered learning environment*. Paper presented at the Symposium at the 11th Biennial Conference of the European Association for Research in Learning and Instruction (EARLI), Cyprus, August 24.

Cañas, A., Hill, G., Carff, R., Suri, N., Lott, J., and Eskridge, T. 2004. CmapTools: A knowledge modeling and sharing environment. In *Concept maps: Theory, methodology, technology: Proceedings of the First International Conference on Concept Mapping*, vol. I, ed. A.J. Cañas, J.D. Novak, and F.M. Gonzalez, 125–133. Pamplona, Spain: Unversidad Publica de Navarra.

Cañas, A., Hill, G., Granados, A., Perez, C., and Perez, J. 2003. The network architecture of Cmap tools. Technical Report No. IHMC CmapTools 2003–2001. Pensacola, FL: Institute for Human and Machine Cognition.

Cañas, A.J., Coffey, J., Reichherzer, T., Suri, N., and Carff, R. 1997. *El-Tech: A performance support system with embedded training for electronics technicians*. Eleventh Florida Artificial Intelligence Research Symposium, Sanibel Island, FL, May.

Cañas, A.J., Ford, N.J., Hayes, P., Reichherzer, T., and Suri, N. 2001. Online concept maps: Enhancing collaborative learning by using technology with concept maps. *The Science Teacher*, 68(4), 49–51.

Chang, Y.-H., Das, R., and Dyson, M. 2023. RFID forecasts, players and opportunities 2023–2033, *IDTechEx* (March). https://www.idtechex.com/en/research-report/rfid-forecasts-players-and-opportunities-2023-2033/927.

Clark, E. 2004. *Around the corporate campfire: How great leaders use stories to inspire success*. Sevierville, TN: Insight Publishing Co.

Correia, P., Cicuto, C., and Aguiar, J. 2014. Using Novakian concept maps to foster peer collaboration in higher education. In *Digital knowledge maps in education*, 195–217. Springer: New York.

CYBRA. 2022. What you need to know about Walmart's latest RFID tagging mandate, April 27. https://cybra.com/what-you-need-to-know-about-walmarts-latest-rfid-mandate/.

Denning, S. 2000. *The springboard: How storytelling ignites action in knowledge-era organizations.* Boston: Butterworth-Heinemann.

Denning, S. 2005. *The leader's guide to storytelling: Mastering the art and discipline of business narrative.* San Francisco: Jossey-Bass/Wiley.

Denning, S. n.d. How stories embody tacit knowledge. https://www.stevedenning.com/Business-Narrative/storytelling-to-capture-tacit-knowledge.aspx.

FINALCAD. n.d. www.finalcad.com (accessed July 24, 2023).

Ford, K.M., Coffey, J.W., Cañas, A.J., Andrews, E.J., and Turner, C.W. 1996. Diagnosis and explanation by a nuclear cardiology expert system. *International Journal of Expert Systems*, 9, 499–506.

Gonzalez, A., Stensrud, B., and Barret, G. 2008. Formalizing context based reasoning—A modeling paradigm for representing tactical human behavior. *Journal of Intelligent Systems*, 23(7), 822–847.

Gonzalez, A.J., and Ahlers, R.H. 1993. Concise representation of autonomous intelligent platforms in a simulation through the use of scripts. In *Proceedings of the Sixth Annual Florida Artificial Intelligence Research Symposium*, Ft. Lauderdale, FL, April.

Gonzalez, A.J., and Ahlers, R.H. 1998. Context based representation of intelligent behavior in training simulations. *Transactions of the Society of Computer Simulation*, 15(4), 153–166.

Gonzalez, A.J., Castro, J., and Gerber, W. 2005. Automating the acquisition of tactical knowledge for military missions. *The Journal of Defense Modeling and Simulation: Applications, Methodology, Technology*, 2(3), 145–160.

Gonzalez, A.J., Georgiopoulos, M., DeMara, R.F., Henninger, A.E., and Gerber, W. 1998. Automating the CGF model development and refinement process by observing expert behavior in a simulation. In *Proceedings of the 1998 Computer Generated Forces Conference*, Orlando, FL, May.

Gonzalez, A.J., Gerber, W.J., and Castro, J. 2002. Automated acquisition of tactical knowledge through contextualization. In *Proceedings of the Conference on Computer Generated Forces and Behavior Representation*, Orlando, FL, May.

Gonzalez, A.J., Nguyen, J., Tsuruta, S., Sakurai, Y., Takada, K., and Uchida, K. 2008. Using contexts to supervise a collaborative process. In *IEEE International Conference on Systems, Man and Cybernetics, 2008. SMC 2008*, October, 2706–2711. IEEE.

Guber, P. 2007. The four truths of the storyteller. *Harvard Business Review*, 85(12), 55–56.

Gumpert, D., and Pentland, W. 2007. USDA bets the farm on animal ID program. *The Nation*, December 14.

Haines, L. 2004. Kidnap-wary Mexicans get chipped—shot in the arm for RFID? *The Register*, July 14.

International Business Machines (IBM). 2007. Keeping tabs on RFID—It's way more than barcodes and it's changing the way the world works. *Ideas from IBM*, June 12. http://www.ibm.com/ibm/ideasfromibm/us/rfid/061207/images/RFID_061207.pdf.

Jenns, C. 2023. Did Walmart's RFID mandate successfully drive RFID adoption in retail? *Retail Insight Network*, June 9. https://www.retail-insight-network.com/news/walmarts-rfid-mandate-retail/.

Landt, J. 2001. Shrouds of time: The history of RFID. Association for Automatic Identification and Data Capture Technologies (AIM) Publications. http://www.aimglobal.orgon (accessed August 16, 2008).

Liu, P.L., Chen, C.J., and Chang, Y.J. 2010. Effects of a computer-assisted concept mapping learning strategy on EFL college students' English reading comprehension. *Computers & Education*, 54(2), 436–445.

Monahan, T., and Wall, T. 2007. Somatic surveillance: Corporeal control through information networks. *Surveillance and Society*, 4(3), 154–173.

Moore, L. 2023, Walmart and RFID: The relationship that put RFID on the map, February 15. https://www.atlasrfidstore.com/rfid-insider/walmart-and-rfid-the-relationship-that-put-rfi d-on-the-map.

Novak, J.D. 1998. *Learning, creating, and using knowledge: Concept maps as facilitative tools in schools and corporations*. Mahwah, NJ: Lawrence Erlbaum Associates.

Novak, J.D., and Cañas, A. 2008. The theory underlying concept maps and how to construct them. Technical Report IHMC CmapTools 2006–2001 Rev 01–2008, Florida Institute for Human and Machine Cognition. http://cmap.ihmc.us/Publications/ResearchPapers/TheoryUn derlyingConceptMaps.pdf.

Novak, J.D., and Gowin, D.B. 1984. *Learning how to learn*. New York: Cambridge University Press.

Phoel, C.M. 2006. Leading words: How to use stories to change minds and ignite action. *Harvard Management Communication Letter* (Spring), 3–5.

Pomerleau, D., Thorpe, D., Longer, J., Rosenblatt, K., and Sukthankar, R. 1994. *AVCS research at Carnegie-Mellon University*. *Proceedings of the Intelligent Vehicle Highway Systems America 1994, Annual Meeting*, 257–262.

Post, T. 2002. The impact of storytelling on NASA and EduTech. *Knowledge Management Review* (March/April).

Ready, D. 2002. How storytelling builds next-generation leaders. *Sloan Management Review*, 43 (4), 63–69.

Russell, S., and Norvig, P. 2009. *Artificial intelligence: A modern approach* (3rd ed). Upper Saddle River, NJ: Pearson Education.

Sammut, C., Hurst, S., Kedzier, D., and Michie, D. 1992. Learning to fly. In *Proceedings of the Ninth International Conference on Machine Learning*, ed. D. Sleeman, 385–393. San Francisco: Morgan Kauffmann.

Shaw, G., Brown, R., and Bromiley, P. 1998. Strategic stories: How 3M is rewriting business planning. *Harvard Business Review* (May–June), 41–50.

Sidani, T.A., and Gonzalez, A.J. 1995. IASKNOT: A simulation-based, object-oriented framework for the acquisition of implicit expert knowledge. In *Proceedings of the IEEE International Conference on System, Man and Cybernetics*, Vancouver, Canada, October.

Sodhani, S., Zhang, A., and Pineau, J., 2021. Multi-task reinforcement learning with context-based representations. In *International Conference on Machine Learning*, May, 9767–9779. PMLR.

Snowden, D. 1999. Three metaphors, two stories, and a picture. *Knowledge Management Review* (March/April).

Snowden, D. 2000. The art and science of story or are you sitting uncomfortably? Part 1: Gathering and harvesting the raw material. *Business Information Review*, 17(3), 147–156.

Stensrud, B.S. 2005. *FAMTILE: An algorithm for learning high-level tactical behavior from observation*. Doctoral Dissertation, Department of Electrical and Computer Engineering, University of Central Florida.

Sternberg, S. 1975. Memory scanning: New findings and current controversies. *Quarterly Journal of Experimental Psychology*, 27, 1–32.

Stockman, H. 1948. Communication by means of reflected power. *Proceedings of the Institute of Radio Engineers*, 36(10), 1196–1204.

Subiaul, F., Cantlon, J., Holloway, R.L., and Terrace, H.S. 2004. Cognitive imitation in Rhesus Macaques. *Science*, 305(5682), 407–410.

Swap, W., Leonard, D., Shields, M., and Abrams, L. 2001. Using mentoring and storytelling to transfer knowledge in the workplace. *Journal of Management Information Systems*, 18(1), 95–114.

Thorndike, P.W., and Wescort, K.T. 1984. Modeling time-stressed situation assessment and planning for intelligent opponent simulation. Final Technical Report PPAFTR-1124–1184–1, Office of Naval Research (July).

Trinh, V.C., and Gonzalez, A.J. 2013. Discovering contexts from observed human performance. *Human–Machine Systems, IEEE Transactions on*, 43(4), 359–370.

Tulving, E. 1983. *Elements of episodic memory*. New York: Oxford University Press.

van Lent M., and Laird, J. 1999. Learning hierarchical performance knowledge by observation. In *Proceedings of the Sixteenth International Conference on Machine Learning*, ed. I. Bratko and S. Dzeroski. San Francisco: Morgan Kaufmann.

Wang, X. 1995. Learning by observation and practice: An incremental approach for planning operator acquisition. In *Proceedings of the Twelfth International Conference on Machine Learning*, ed. A. Prieditis and S.J. Russell. San Francisco: Morgan Kauffman.

Wong, W. 2021. How RFID solutions improve patient safety and hospital workflow, January 5. https://healthtechmagazine.net/article/2021/01/how-rfid-solutions-improve-patient-safety-and-hospital-workflow.

Zendesk. n.d. https://www.zendesk.com/service/help-center/knowledge-capture-app/ (accessed July 24, 2023).

8 Knowledge Sharing Systems

Systems that Organize and Distribute Knowledge

In the last chapter, we discussed knowledge capture systems. In this chapter, we discuss what knowledge sharing systems are about, how they serve to organize and distribute organizational and individual knowledge, what constitutes their makeup, and provide examples of such systems. Knowledge sharing systems are designed to help users share their knowledge, both tacit and explicit. Most of the knowledge management systems in place at organizations are designed to share the explicit knowledge of individuals and organizations, and these are the focus of this chapter. These systems are also referred to as **knowledge repositories**. In this chapter we also discuss some guidelines on how to design knowledge sharing systems for practical use. The two types of explicit knowledge sharing systems most widely discussed in the KM literature are *lessons learned systems* and *expertise locator systems*; therefore, this chapter concentrates on those. Systems that support tacit knowledge sharing are those typically utilized by communities of practice, particularly those that meet virtually. Finally, we discuss issues about communities of practice and how KM systems can support tacit knowledge sharing.

Corporate memory (also known as an organizational memory) is made up of the aggregate intellectual assets of an organization. It is the combination of both explicit and tacit knowledge that may or may not be explicitly documented but which is specifically referenced and crucial to the operation and competitiveness of an organization. Knowledge management is concerned with developing applications that will prevent the loss of corporate memory. Such loss often results from a lack of appropriate technologies for the organization and exchange of documents, lack of adequate support for communication, and the proliferation of disparate sources of information. Often this results in the loss of explicit **organizational knowledge**. Another contributing factor to the loss of corporate memory is the departure of employees because of either turnover or retirement. The lost knowledge is typically the organization's tacit knowledge. A knowledge sharing system helps to organize and distribute an organization's corporate memory so that it can be accessed even after the original sources of knowledge no longer remain within the organization.

The standard communications medium upon which KM applications are based is the World Wide Web, a medium that facilitates the exchange of information, data, multimedia, and even applications among multiple distinct computer platforms. This characteristic of the Web is referred to as *platform independence*. Because the Web is pervasive and can interface with different computer platforms through a common user interface, it is often the base upon which knowledge sharing systems are created.

DOI: 10.4324/9781003364375-10

For a quick overview of what knowledge sharing systems are and how they are used, let us look at how two organizations view knowledge sharing. The following boxes explain how Ernst & Young, a professional services organization, and the Center for Advancing Microbial Risk Assessment (CAMRA), funded by the Environmental Protection Agency and Department of Homeland Security, successfully introduced knowledge sharing systems to share important knowledge. Box 8.1 discusses some of the KM experiences at a professional services organization in the business of providing its clients with the knowledge they require to effectively compete and succeed.

Box 8.1 Ernst & Young: The Development of a Knowledge Organization

In 1995, Ernst & Young underwent an important restructuring of their business strategy. This restructuring was designed to facilitate a move toward knowledge management. It included capturing and leveraging knowledge from consulting engagements. Another aspect of the revised strategy was to use knowledge to accelerate the process of providing consulting solutions for clients. This strategy led to the creation of several different KM initiatives within the company.

One such KM initiative was the establishment of the Center for Business Knowledge (CBK) and its network of local centers, with the goal of harvesting the knowledge of the firm's employees and enabling firm-wide knowledge sharing practices to meet their client needs and support their employees. The CBK served as a library for consulting methods and techniques as well as documents resulting from client engagements. Moreover, this center was created with the idea of distributing and integrating the knowledge of all the projects. The North American CBK employs 200 staff members that work to ensure that North American professionals have the required resources necessary to apply the experience and thought leadership of their colleagues throughout the world.

Ernst & Young's CBK uses many tools and methods to assist their client-serving professionals. The firm's Global Knowledge Steering group recognized early on that the key to leveraging knowledge capital is through the way people work together across business units and geographic boundaries, and the group focused its efforts on developing a knowledge sharing culture underpinned by a robust information and knowledge management infrastructure that included (Dellow 2004):

1   A collection of 22 standardized computer-mediated tools that support both synchronous as well as asynchronous collaboration. The KM infrastructure pivots on the firm's award-winning KnowledgeWeb (KWeb) which is home to thousands of databases and websites that provide employees with access to internal and external resources including business knowledge, intelligence, global news, and information.
2   A strong sociotechnical support system to help people effectively engage with these tools in practice. In fact, to better connect Ernst & Young professionals, the firm is renovating its people directories and experimenting with social network resources, for example using blogs as collaboration tools.
3   Knowledge centers around the world supported by hundreds of staff support employees.

At Ernst & Young the investments made in the development of the right collaborative infrastructure included more than the investment in the right technology, and the support provided by the CBK is what enabled the business to succeed. Knowledge management is a visible leadership priority and an integral part of the organization's business strategy. Ernst & Young's success is based on the successful development of the shared technology platforms coupled with the knowledge management function of the CBK (Dellow 2004). For its innovative workplace initiatives, Ernst & Young has been named year-over-year as one of the global Most Admired Knowledge Enterprises (MAKE), was recognized by *Fortune* magazine as one of "100 Best Companies to Work For," and won the "Best Information/Knowledge Team in a Business Environment" by the International Information Industry.

Note: We acknowledge Maria Thomas of Ernst & Young Center for Business Knowledge for contributing to this box.

Ernst & Young's KM initiatives specifically support knowledge sharing. These initiatives earned the firm many accolades for their leadership in KM in addition to a competitive advantage. In Box 8.2, we review how a group of diverse researchers share knowledge across different federal agencies. The CAMRA prototype system was designed to support the collaboration between the US Environmental Protection Agency (EPA) and the US Department of Homeland Security, in order to consolidate knowledge about bacterial agents of concern. Even though the CAMRA system is no longer in use as it was originally designed, the proof-of-concept as a platform for collaboration and integration of knowledge for a community of researchers across different organizations, still remain relevant today. For example, systems that allow researchers to uncover potential collaborators across different universities are of great utility today (see for example Chedid and Teixeira 2017).

Box 8.2 Sharing Scientific Knowledge at CAMRA

Following the anthrax attacks in Washington, DC, and Florida in 2001, the Environmental Protection Agency and Department of Homeland Security jointly funded the Center for Advancing Microbial Risk Assessment (CAMRA) to broaden and consolidate knowledge of Bacterial Agents of Concern. The CAMRA team is composed of researchers with diverse backgrounds: engineers, epidemiologists, and health, computer, and information scientists, working on five different projects and spread across seven different universities.

The CAMRA Knowledge Repository (KR) is a repository-based KM system built to meet the needs of this multidisciplinary user-base. Its design was based on knowledge engineering principles, lessons learned and best practices systems, and KM studies on failure prevention. The CAMRA KM approach is aimed at supporting the tasks of knowledge sharing and leveraging, collaboration, and integration (Weber et al. 2006). First, the CAMRA KR adopts a representation for knowledge artifacts that is both minimal and sufficient, which facilitates the transparency of research activities and encourages knowledge sharing and reuse among the community. Second, human intermediation is provided by knowledge facilitators who fill technological gaps by educating users on the importance of the approach, helping to build a culture of sharing and collaboration. Finally, users are asked to identify connections between their contributions and existing contributions by creating associations between knowledge artifacts.

Version 1.0 of the CAMRA KR was released in 2006. In the first two years of use, researchers contributed 177 knowledge artifacts and made 93 associations. As an indication that the CAMRA KR was successfully supporting the task of knowledge sharing and leveraging, 76 percent of associations were between artifacts contributed by different authors and 22 percent were between artifacts across different projects. Version 2.0 was released in early 2009 and supported the tasks of collaboration and integration by generating knowledge maps to demonstrate how researchers' contributions are connected to the rest of the community and to allow researchers to discover potential collaborators. The new version also included automatically generated reports to compensate researchers for the time and effort needed to share research activities.

Note: We acknowledge Sid Gunawardena, Rosina Weber, and Craig MacDonald for authoring this box.

What Are Knowledge Sharing Systems?

Knowledge sharing systems can be described as systems that enable members of an organization to acquire tacit and explicit knowledge from each other. The main purpose of these systems is to promote knowledge sharing for re-use by other members from the same organization, propagation of innovation, technology, and strategic management (Yoo and Ginzberg 2003). Knowledge sharing systems may also support sharing knowledge across organizations and may be viewed as *knowledge markets*: just as markets require adequate liquidity[1] to guarantee a fair exchange of products, knowledge sharing systems must attract a critical volume of knowledge seekers and knowledge owners in order to be effective (Dignum 2002). In a knowledge sharing system, knowledge owners will:

1 want to share their knowledge with a controllable and trusted group,
2 decide when to share and the conditions for sharing, and
3 seek a fair exchange, or reward, for sharing their knowledge.

By the same token, knowledge seekers may:

1 not be aware of all the possibilities for sharing, thus the knowledge repository will typically help them through searching and ranking, and
2 want to decide on the conditions for knowledge acquisition.

A knowledge sharing system is said to define a learning organization, supporting the sharing and reuse of individual and organizational knowledge. One tool frequently emphasized under the auspices of knowledge sharing systems is *document management*. At the core of a **document management system** is a repository, an electronic storage medium with a primary storage location that affords multiple access points. The document management system essentially stores information. This repository can be centralized or it can be distributed. Document management builds upon the repository by adding support to the classification and organization of information, unifying the actions of storage and retrieval of documents over a platform-independent system. A document management system aggregates relevant information through a common, typically Web-based, interface. The document management collaborative application increases communication, thus allowing the sharing of organizational knowledge. Document management systems support a wide range of file formats with features and tools for effective searches, multi-user access, multiple level security, auditing, and versioning. Among the systems in the market are GoogleDocs, Sharepoint, and others. The document management application increases the sharing of documentation across the organization, which helps in the sharing of organizational knowledge. Documents are typically organized or indexed following a standard hierarchical structure or classification taxonomy, much like the index catalog is used to organize the books in a library. Frequently, *portal* technologies are used to build a common entry into multiple distributed repositories, using the analogy of a "door" as a common entry into the organization's knowledge resources. Portals provide a common user interface, which can often be customized to the user's preferences such as local news, weather, and so forth. Many of these systems integrate workflow systems as well.

In its purest sense, workflow represents the automation of a business process. A **workflow management system (WfMS)** is a set of tools that support defining, creating, and managing the execution of workflow processes (Workflow Management Coalition 1999); in other words, they provide a method of capturing the steps that lead to the completion of a project within a fixed time frame. In doing so, they provide a method for illustrating such steps. WfMS have been around on factory assembly lines for some time. By automating many of their routine business processes, companies are able to save time and valuable human resources. Workflow systems can be useful for a project by enacting its elemental tasks, as well as by providing a mechanism for the analysis and optimization of the entire process detailing the project. Also, workflow systems provide a mechanism for the analysis and optimization of the entire process that make up a project. One benefit of using a WfMS is that it provides the user with an audit of necessary skills and resources prior to project initiation. Workflow systems also provide a platform for the replication and reuse of stored processes. Finally, WfMS can also serve as a training tool, since they provide a broad overview with detailed operations of tasks as well as an identification of possible "weak links" in a process.

WfMS can serve as the basis for **collaborative computing**, as evidenced by their growing popularity. A collaborative environment (which allows the informal exchange of ideas) combined with a detailed workflow (which captures process steps) is an efficient method for streamlining business practices. A document management system unifies an aggregate of relevant information conveniently in one location through a common interface. Categorizing and processing information for search purposes provides a detailed knowledge warehouse. The collaborative application increases communication, thus allowing the sharing of organizational knowledge. Information technology tools like document management systems, groupware, e-mail, databases, chat groups, discussion forums, videoconferencing technologies, and workflow management systems, which historically were used for singular unrelated purposes, are now typically integrated into knowledge sharing systems. Although there are benefits of using these tools independently of each other, their integration in a knowledge sharing system augments their individual contributions. The document management system essentially stores information. The electronic documents are usually organized and relevant to its hierarchical structure. The workflow, which details the steps involved in completing a project, combined with a central repository that contains information relevant to a project, provides added benefits. The most important benefits, according to KM theory, are the elicitation and capturing of organizational know-how that typically is not captured by most information systems, as well as an obvious user interface to access and reuse this organizational know-how. Collaborative computing provides a common communication space, improves sharing of knowledge, provides a mechanism for real-time feedback on the tasks being performed, helps to optimize processes, and results in a centralized knowledge warehouse.

Collaborative environments support the work of teams, which may not necessarily be present at the same time or same place. *Groupware* is an integrated package of applications used to support the informal exchange of ideas of remote collaborating teams who need to achieve a common deliverable (Hastings, 2009). Also, Groupware allows synchronous or asynchronous flows, and the informal exchange of ideas across multidisciplinary groups of people working from remote locations, increasing organizational communication, which in turn promotes knowledge sharing. Knowledge management mechanisms, discussed in Chapter 3, facilitate the use of knowledge sharing systems. For example, meetings and communities of practice facilitate knowledge sharing, as illustrated in Box 8.1 earlier in the chapter. This part of the chapter also examines the use of knowledge management mechanisms such as communities of practice for sharing tacit knowledge.

Traditional information systems are based on a consented interpretation based on the company's business culture and management's needs. Computer-generated information typically does not lend itself to interpretation that produces action, and knowledge implies action based on the information. Today's fast-paced, highly competitive business world forces the need for variety and complexity in the interpretation of information generated by computer systems. Group decision-making tools can help organizations make better decisions by capturing the knowledge from groups of experts. Furthermore, companies that capture their customers' preferences can improve their customer service, which translates to larger profits (Becerra-Fernandez 1998). In short, knowledge sharing systems integrate the capabilities of document management and collaborative systems along with knowledge management mechanisms. A document management system unifies an aggregate of relevant information through a common, typically Web-based, interface. Categorizing and processing organizational information for search and distribution purposes provides a detailed knowledge warehouse. A collaborative environment that includes workflow is an effective complement to a platform for sharing knowledge across the organization. These systems can later be used as the basis for organizations to further focus their efforts not only in gathering documentation, but also in discovering new knowledge, by mining the knowledge and experiences of their employees, customers, and competitors.

Next, we describe how information and computer technology enable knowledge sharing.

The Computer as a Medium for Sharing Knowledge

Much of knowledge management is about communicating knowledge among people. Certainly, knowledge must be applied in order to be useful. However, the wider the application of knowledge is, the more beneficial it is for the organization fostering that interchange of knowledge. Such widespread application comes from communicating the knowledge in its natural or electronically represented form. Furthermore, knowledge bases benefit from widespread contributions which are only possible through wide-ranging communications. In several chapters in this book, we discuss some of the leading technologies for capturing and applying knowledge. Now let's look at some of the communications technologies that permit and enhance this sharing of knowledge.

Prior to the information age, two-way communication relied on the telephone's synchronous capability which enabled parties to exchange information much like they did via face-to-face communications. Prior to the telephone, knowledge sharing required asynchronous communication via telegraph and written artifacts. Asynchronous communications allowed communicants to exchange ideas without the need for both parties to be present at the same time, which is one of the limitations offered by the telephone. In addition, the telephone did not facilitate communication of nonverbal multimedia information such as documents, photos, drawings, videos, and others. But the emergence of social media has completely revolutionized the concept of communications, and knowledge sharing, in the last two decades. Box 8.3 provides an illustrative example from REMA 1000, a Norwegian grocery chain (Sandino and Hull 2018).

Box 8.3 Knowledge Sharing through Social Media at REMA 1000

In 2017, REMA 1000, a Norwegian grocery chain that is a subsidiary of Reitangruppen, a private company, operated 600 grocery stores in Norway and 284 in Denmark. It employed 11,500 people serving about 3.5 million customers each week in Norway, and had reported sales of US$4.8 billion in 2016. Its stores were mostly franchises—the franchises had considerable autonomy, within the constraints of five-year franchise contracts, but were required to use company approved information systems. It positioned itself as a low-cost seller of quality products customized to local preferences. It did so by (a) empowering franchises and incentivizing them to pursue efficient store operations; and (b) developing technologies and systems that enabled franchises to focus on customers.

By 2016, franchisees and employees had at least ten digital tools, but information did not flow freely within the organization. The problem was compounded by security and privacy concerns as neither franchisees nor their employees had their own REMA e-mail addresses—they had to share one e-mail account per store. When REMA's Communications Director, Mette Fossum, learned about Facebook's new corporate social media platform, Workplace, she believed it would be an excellent fit for REMA. REMA's leaders and the HR team agreed to try Workplace. Workplace was a marked departure from REMA's highly structured apps. With Workplace, each user would have equal rights and privileges. Frederic Jahr, the HR Manager, felt the move to Workplace would be like having all of REMA's 11,500 employees in the same room. After a pilot test in April, Workplace was rolled out across the company in August 2016.

REMA benefitted from Workplace in several ways. Workplace engaged employees, with 90 percent participation. Franchisees and store managers used it to share and source ideas, leading to increase in sales. Headquarters could now directly communicate with frontline employees about product specifics such as product recalls. The viral nature of social networks also helped in conveying messages quickly. Moreover, employees could more easily reach out to peers who might have answers to their questions. Workplace also helped in promoting REMA's culture and values across franchise stores.

However, Workplace also posed some challenges. Because REMA's headquarters could directly communicate with frontline employees, franchise autonomy and store-level control seemed to be undermined. Also, employees sometimes felt overloaded by the information on Workplace, especially due to the lack of a search function. Finally, some franchisees were using Workplace only to source knowledge but not to share any of their own knowledge with others.

Source: Compiled from Sandino and Hull (2018)

Designing the Knowledge Sharing System

The main function of a knowledge sharing system is "to enhance the organization's competitiveness by improving the way it manages its knowledge" (Abecker et al. 1998). The creation of a knowledge sharing system is based on the organization of digital media, including documents, **hyperlinks**, and the like, which represent the explicit organizational knowledge. Khun and Abecker (1997) identify the crucial requirements for the success of a knowledge sharing system in industrial practice:

1   *Collection and systematic organization of information from various sources.* Most organizational business processes require information and data including CAD drawings, e-mails, electronic documents such as specifications, and even paper documents. This requisite information may be dispersed through the organization. This first step requires the organization and collection of this information throughout the organization.

2   *Minimization of up-front knowledge engineering.* Knowledge sharing systems must take advantage of explicit organizational information and data such that these systems can be built quickly, generate returns on investment, and adapt to new requirements. This information and data is mostly found in databases and documents.

3   *Exploiting user feedback for maintenance and evolution.* Knowledge sharing systems should concentrate on capturing the knowledge of the organization's members. This includes options for maintenance and user feedback so the knowledge can be kept fresh and relevant. Furthermore, knowledge sharing systems should be designed to support users' needs and their business process workflows.

4   *Integration into existing environment.* Knowledge sharing systems must be integrated into an organization's information flow by integrating with the IT tools currently used to perform the business tasks. Humans, by nature, will tend to avoid efforts to formalize knowledge (ever met a computer programmer that enjoys adding comments to her code?). In fact, as a rule-of-thumb, if the effort required in formalizing knowledge is too high, it should be left informal to be described by humans and not attempted to be made explicit. For instance, consider the possibility of capturing the "how-to" knowledge of how to ride a bicycle. Clearly an understanding of the laws of physics can help explain why a person stays on the bicycle while it's moving, but few of us recall these laws while we ride. Other than the proverbial "keep your feet on the pedals" which doesn't explicate much about the riding process, most of us learned to ride a bicycle through hours of practice, and many falls, when we were kids. It would be impractical to try to codify this knowledge and make it explicit. On the other hand, it might be useful to know who's a good bicycle rider, in particular if one is looking to put together a cycling team.

5   *Active presentation of relevant information.* Finally, the goal of an active knowledge sharing system is to present its users with the required information when and wherever it's needed. These systems are envisioned as intelligent assistants, automatically eliciting and providing knowledge that may be useful in solving the current task whenever and wherever it's needed.

Barriers to the Use of Knowledge Sharing Systems

Many organizations, specifically science- and engineering-oriented firms, are characterized by a culture known as the **not-invented-here syndrome (NIH)**. In other words, solutions that are not invented at the organizational subunit are considered worthless. Organizations suffering from this syndrome tend to essentially reward employees for "inventing" new solutions, rather than reusing solutions developed within and outside the organization. Organizations that foster the not-invented-here syndrome discourage knowledge seekers from participating in the knowledge market, since the organizational rewards are tied to creating knowledge and not necessarily to sharing and applying existing knowledge. Furthermore, organizations that do not reward their experts for sharing their knowledge or that try to disassociate the knowledge from those that create it will also discourage knowledge owners from participating in the knowledge market. The necessary critical volume can only be accomplished through adequate rewards to both knowledge creators and knowledge seekers to participate in the sharing of knowledge.

One of the impediments to nurturing the human component of KM is the lack of an institutionalized reward systems for knowledge sharing in most organizations. Typically, rewards exist at the individual level. When a group is rewarded, the reward is usually tied to contributions in *strong tie networks*, such as when people collaborate as a team to develop a new product. It is much more difficult to reward people who contribute in *weak tie networks*; for example, someone who pops into one discussion group and says something that makes people think a bit differently but who is not working in those groups on a long-term basis. Thus, organizations with significant intellectual capital recognize the importance of not only capturing knowledge for later reuse, but also ensuring that adequate reward systems are in place to encourage the sharing of ideas and the life-long learning by their employees.

Research has also pointed out some of the other reasons why knowledge sharing systems may fail (Weber 2007). They may fail:

1   If they don't integrate humans, processes, and technology—since technology alone will not achieve acceptance if both people and processes, the main component in delivering organizational goals, are not adequately associated with the knowledge sharing systems (Abecker et al. 2000). In fact, KM approaches are likely to fail if they are designed as stand-alone solutions outside of the process context (Weber and Aha 2003).

2   If they attempt to target a monolithic organizational memory— to be useful memories must be both an artifact that holds its state and an artifact embedded in organizational and individual processes. Furthermore, to be useful memory objects must be de-contextualized by the creator and re-contextualized by the user. Finally, to be useful memories must tag an authenticity marker (Ackerman and Halverson 2000).

3   If they don't measure and state their benefits—this is a requirement of any successful business initiative which we discussed at length in Chapter 5.

4   If they store knowledge in textual representations only—knowledge artifacts that are stored in textual format only may lack the adequate representation structure, including long texts that are hard to review, read, and interpret—therefore almost guaranteeing their lack of reusability due to their difficulty in comprehension (Weber and Aha 2003).

5   If they are outside the process context— users should be aware that a database exists to refer or contribute to. They should be able to reach, search, and trust that the repository contains re-usable data (Weber and Aha 2003).

6   If they do not support collaboration—lack of a collaborating environment hinders learning and sharing, which results in system failure. In fact, more than any other information systems, collaboration systems and processes must conform to the team culture and behavior or they simply won't work

7   If users are afraid of the consequences of their contributions—in addition to the importance of the organization to provide incentives for the employees' contributions to the knowledge repository, there may be some organizational barriers that act against knowledge sharing. For example, employees may be afraid that their contributions may be taken out of context, may aid competitors, may cause an information security breach, and may lack the necessary validation to be useful to others (Weber et al. 2001).

8   If users seek knowledge from others while not sharing their own knowledge—as done by some franchisees at REMA 1000 (Sandino and Hull 2018).

9   If users perceive a lack of leadership support, lack an understanding of the generalities that would make their knowledge useful, or just don't feel it's worth their time to make a contribution (Disterer 2002).

Specific Types of Knowledge Sharing Systems

Knowledge sharing systems are classified according to their attributes. These specific types of knowledge sharing systems include:

1   Incident report databases
2   Alert systems
3   Best practices databases
4   Lessons learned systems
5   Expertise locator systems

In this section, we briefly describe the differences among the first four systems. Specific attention is placed on the two knowledge sharing systems most frequently discussed in the knowledge management literature: lessons learned systems and expertise locator systems.

Incident Report Databases

Incident report databases are used to disseminate information related to incidents or malfunctions, for example of field equipment (like sensing equipment outages) or software (like bug reports). Incident reports typically describe the incident together with explanations of the incident, although they may not suggest any recommendations. Incident reports are typically used in the context of safety and accident investigations. Incident report databases are being widely adopted by complex and risky industries such as in the aviation industry, the military, nuclear power centers, the IT industry, and medical departments. As an example, the U.S. Department of Energy (DOE) disseminates chemical mishaps through their Chemical Occurrences Web page (U.S. DOE 2009). Also, the New Zealand Mountain Safety Council initiated the design of a database for collecting and analyzing incidents in outdoor sports for the safety of people or organizations participating in outdoor activities such as kayaking, ramping, and jet skiing, etc. (NZMSC 2013).

Alert Systems

Alert systems were originally intended to disseminate information about a negative experience that has occurred or is expected to occur. Alert systems could be used to report problems experienced with a technology, such as an alert system that issues recalls for consumer products. However, alert systems could also be used to share more positive experiences, such as Grants.gov, which offers registered users alerts to funding opportunities that match a set of user-specified keywords, as well as Google Alerts (google.com/alerts), which sends registered customers the latest information on the user-specified requested topics. Alert systems could be applicable to a single organization or to a set of related organizations that share the same technology and suppliers.

Best Practices Databases

Most organizational leaders are aware that a large percentage of an organization's corporate knowledge is largely tacit, hence the need for frequent managerial recommendations to emphasize the need to create *Best Practices* in the organization (Yoo and Ginzberg 2003). **Best practices databases** describe successful efforts, typically from the re-engineering of **business processes** (O'Leary 1999) that could be applicable to organizational processes. Best practices differ from lessons learned in that they capture only successful events, which may not be derived from experience. Best practices are expected to represent business practices that are applicable to multiple organizations in the same sector and are sometimes used to benchmark organizational processes. For example, the National Governors Association Center for Best Practices (NGA Center) develops innovative solutions to today's most pressing public policy challenges and is the only research and development firm that directly serves the nation's governors (NGA Center 2013). Microsoft Corporation offers a Web page that describes best practices for developers using their products (Microsoft Developer Network 2009), which provides helpful tips including how-to and reference documentation, sample code, and technical articles, for instance on how to prevent database corruption. Also, the Federal Transit Administration publishes a *Best Practices Procurement Manual* on the Web (U.S. DOT 2009). This manual describes procedures and practices for organizations wishing to pursue procurement opportunities with this agency.

Lessons Learned Systems (LLS)

The goal of lessons learned systems is "to capture and provide lessons that can benefit employees who encounter situations that closely resemble a previous experience in a similar situation" (Weber et al. 2001). LLS could be pure repositories of lessons or be sometimes intermixed with other sources of information (e.g., reports). LLS are typically not focused on a single task, for example, pure knowledge representations. In many instances, enhanced document management systems are supporting distributed project collaborations and their knowledge sources while actively seeking to capture and reuse lessons from project report archives.

The differences among these types of knowledge sharing systems are based upon:

- *Content Origin*—Does the content originate from experience like in lessons learned systems or from industry standards and technical documentation as in best practice databases?
- *Application*—Do the types of knowledge sharing systems describe a complete process or perhaps a task or a decision?
- *Results*—Do they describe failures, as in incident report databases or alert systems, or successes, as in best practices databases?
- *Orientation*—Do they support an organization or a whole industry?

Table 8.1 contrasts these knowledge sharing systems based on these attributes.

In Box 8.4, we describe how a small government contractor was able to achieve a competitive advantage through a business strategy that emphasizes knowledge sharing of its best practices. This box is important in that it proves that KM is not only important to large knowledge-intensive organizations but can also help small organizations gain a competitive advantage and succeed.

Table 8.1 Types of Knowledge Repositories

Knowledge Sharing System	Originates from experiences?	Describes a complete process?	Describes failures?	Describes successes?	Orientation
Incident Reports	Yes	No	Yes	No	Organization
Alerts	Yes	No	Yes	No	Industry
Lessons Learned System	Yes	No	Yes	Yes	Organization
Best Practices Databases	Possibly	Yes	No	Yes	Industry

Source: Weber et al. (2001).

Box 8.4 Small Business Knowledge Management Success Story

In January 1999, RS Information Systems, Inc. (RSIS) in McLean, Virginia, was a minority-owned 8(a)[1] small business with annual revenues of US$15 million and a total staff numbering 120[2] (Frey 2002). There were no institutional or even ad hoc processes in place to identify, audit, collect, archive, and leverage key business and technical knowledge within the company. In other words, it was just like the thousands of other small businesses that provided support services in the federal government market space. The practice of knowledge management was initiated within the company that same year. By the end of CY2001, RSIS closed its financial books with US $142 million in revenues and 1,200 staff members nationwide. Six years later, those numbers had rocketed to US$364 million in revenue and 1,965 people.

Were KM initiatives integral to the tangible success that RSIS enjoyed? Absolutely!

Their impact was important both at the business development and operations levels. For example, the company was able to develop more high-impact, client-focused winning proposals than ever before and do multiple proposals concurrently. Importantly, the company's bid and proposal (B&P) costs were also contained. By leveraging the business development knowledge base in a process called rapid proposal prototyping, RSIS proposal managers were able to generate first-draft proposal documents quickly with minimal B&P expenditure and little impact on billable technical staff. Direct-charge operations (technical) staff were able to stay focused on their client-support activities rather than be required to spend days at corporate headquarters writing proposals. This practice translated to enhanced customer satisfaction because RSIS' technical professionals stayed on their primary job.

Through knowledge management initiatives, RSIS' operations staff were able to harness best practices and lessons learned from across the company's contractual portfolio and apply these proven solutions quickly to address their specific client's technical and programmatic requirements. This knowledge sharing program facilitated near-real-time solutions and was conducted through a firewalled Intranet and e-mail system. Significantly, knowledge sharing was incentivized and also built into each person's annual performance evaluation.

There were four key ingredients in the RSIS KM success story: (1) a KM champion, an individual who understood and articulated the tangible benefits of knowledge management to executive management as well as business development and operations staff; (2) executive leadership, support, and vision necessary to grasp the value of KM and then fund the processes and clear the internal organizational impediments to knowledge sharing in order to institutionalize this critical business enabler; (3) disciplined and repeatable processes put into place enterprisewide within the company to leverage information and knowledge in near real time; (4) Web-based knowledge management tools, which included infoRouter by Active Innovations, Inc.

Experience has demonstrated the significant business value of launching your company's KM initiative as soon as possible within the corporate life of your firm. This approach does two things. First, there will be less explicit data and information as well as tacit knowledge to collect, review, and categorize. Second, the sooner your staff develop and hone knowledge-sharing behaviors and skills, the more quickly your firm will emerge as a learning organization—one that adapts and prospers in a high-velocity business environment of unpredictable change.

Notes:

1   The Small Business Administration (SBA) 8(a) Business Development Program assists in the development of small businesses owned and operated by individuals who are socially and economically disadvantaged. To be SBA 8a certified, the firm must be a small business (less than 500 employees); must be unconditionally owned and controlled by one or more socially and economically disadvantaged individuals (women or minority) who are of good character and citizens of the United States; and must demonstrate potential for success.

Federal acquisition policies encourage federal agencies to award a certain percentage of their contracts to small and disadvantaged (8a) businesses.

2　We acknowledge Robert S. Frey, author of Successful Proposal Strategies for Small Businesses: Using Knowledge Management to Win Government, Private-sector, and International Contracts (Boston: Artech House 2008), for this box.

Lessons Learned Systems

Lessons learned systems[2] have become commonplace in organizations and on the Web. The most complete definition of what constitutes a lesson learned is expressed by the American, European, and Japanese space agencies (Weber et al. 2001, p. 18, referring to Secchi et al. 1999):

> A lesson learned is knowledge or understanding gained by experience. The experience may be positive, as in a successful test or mission, or negative, as in a mishap or failure. Successes are also considered sources of lessons learned. A lesson must be significant in that it has a real or assumed impact on operations; valid in that is factually and technically correct; and applicable in that it identifies a specific design, process, or decision that reduces or eliminates the potential for failures and mishaps, or reinforces a positive result.

A second definition for LLS and what constitutes a lesson learned follows (Weber and Aha 2003, p. 34):

> Lessons learned systems (LLS) are knowledge management (KM) initiatives structured over a repository of lessons learned (LL). Lessons learned are knowledge artifacts that convey experiential knowledge that is applicable to a task, decision, or process such that, when reused, this knowledge positively impacts an organization's results. For this reason, LLS are ubiquitous in governmental organizations that need to leverage knowledge, such as the Department of Defense (DOD), where military operations may risk human lives, the Department of Energy (DOE), where accident prevention is a major concern, and space agencies (e.g., American space agency [NASA], European Space Agency [ESA], Japanese Space Agencies [NASDA]) due to their potential for incurring costly mission failures.

The purpose of LLS is to support organizational processes. Figure 8.1 describes the essential tasks of LLS as *collect, verify, store, disseminate*, and *reuse* (Weber et al. 2001).

1 Collect the Lessons

This task involves collecting the lessons (or content) that will be incorporated into the LLS. There are six possible lesson content collection methods:

a　Passive—the most common form of collection. Contributors submit lessons through a paper or Web-based form.

b　Reactive—where contributors are interviewed by a third party for lessons. The third party will submit the lesson on behalf of the contributor.

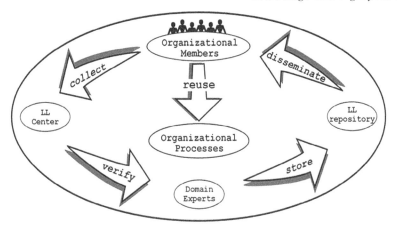

Figure 8.1 Lessons Learned Process

c After-action collection—where lessons are collected during a mission debriefing, as for example, in military organizations.

d Proactive collection—where lessons are automatically collected by an expert system, which may suggest that a lesson exists based on analysis of a specific content. For example, an expert system could monitor an individual's e-mail and prompt him/her when it understands that a lesson is described.

e Active collection—where a computer-based system may scan documents to identify lessons in the presence of specific keywords or phrases.

f Interactive collection—where a computer-based system collaborates with the lesson's author to generate clear and relevant lessons.

2 Verify the Lessons

Typically, a team of **domain experts** performs the task required by this component, which requires the verification of lessons for correctness, redundancy, consistency, and relevance. The verification task is critically important, but sometimes introduces a significant bottleneck in the inclusion of lessons into the LLS, since it's a time-consuming process. Some systems, for example Xerox's Eureka LLS, provide a two-stage process. The Eureka LLS, described in Box 8.5, was designed to support field engineers in solving hard-to-fix repair problems with the company's printers. Contributors enter fixes into the Eureka LLS. At that point, a team charged with the verification task receives an alert prompting their test of the solution to ensure that it works. If everything checks out, the fix is made available to the rest of the field engineers.

Box 8.5 Eureka: A Lessons Learned System for Xerox

In the mid-1990s, Xerox's customers reported the lowest customer satisfaction in the company's history. This prompted the company to look at the way the more than 20,000 copier field technicians serviced the machines. Xerox researchers realized field technicians would frequently share fixes over company-provided radios originating from a set of notes that each technician carried.

Researchers developed Eureka in 1996, the first LLS designed to help service technicians detect and solve problems on the road, by integrating each of these original sets of notes. Eureka allows Xerox technicians to share the knowledge about how to better fix Xerox's copy machines. Each service technician is provided with a notebook computer that contains the subset of the Eureka database that is pertinent to his area of expertise. Eureka has an alert system that delivers new fixes according to the subscriber's profile. When a technician uncovers a problem that is not addressed by Eureka, he will submit the fix to the system, including their point of contact. At this point the fix will be sent to a team tasked with verifying the solution to ensure it works. The team then rates and publishes the solution in Eureka. Useless tips were discarded; others were certified as valuable or edited as necessary.

It was agreed that tips would be validated within a few days, and the submitter's name would appear alongside the tip as both reward and incentive (Mitchell 2001). By 2002, the system supported field technicians in 71 countries and stored about 50,000 fixes, which have helped solve about 350,000 problems and has saved Xerox approximately US$15 million in parts and labor (Roberts-Witt 2002).

One interesting outcome of Eureka is that seven years after its development, the outcome of the development and deployment of a system for sharing knowledge from the front lines became a vehicle for organizational change (Bobrow and Whalen 2002). Even though in the beginning of the project, few people in the management ranks at Xerox believed there would be much value in what technicians could learn on their own in the field differently from other suggestions systems, local champions were able to assemble sufficient resources to make the system a go. As the system grew into a major corporate program it faced other challenges, namely that moving to a central organization required a uniform, worldwide approach which was opposite to the original paradigm that tried to adapt to local needs and practices. But one of the most significant outcomes of this system is that Xerox may have become a better learning organization as a result of the Eureka project (Bobrow and Whalen 2002). Other Eureka-like knowledge systems were created at other operational units. For example, LinkLite was developed to support the sales organization. And perhaps this learning organization "spirit" is the most important legacy of Eureka at Xerox (Bobrow and Whalen 2002).

Sources: Compiled from: Bobrow and Whalen (2002); Mitchell (2001);
Roberts-Witt (2002)

3 Store the Lesson

This task relates to the representation of the lessons in a computer-based system. Typical steps in this task include the indexing of lessons, formatting, and incorporating into the repository. In terms of the technology required to support this task, LLS could be based on structured relational or object-oriented databases as well as case libraries (case-based reasoning) or semi-structured document management systems. LLS can also incorporate relevant multimedia such as audio and video, which may help illustrate important lessons.

4 Disseminate the Lesson

This task relates to how the information is shared to promote its reuse. Six different dissemination methods have been identified:

a   Passive dissemination—where users look for lessons using a search engine.

b   Active casting—where lessons are transmitted to users that have specified relevant profiles to that particular lesson.

c   Broadcasting—where lessons are disseminated throughout an organization.

d   Active dissemination—where users are alerted to relevant lessons in the context of their work (for example by a software help-wizard that alerts a user of related automated assistance).

e   Proactive dissemination—where a system anticipates events to predict when the user will require the assistance provided by the lesson.

f   Reactive dissemination—when a user launches the LLS in response to a specific knowledge need, for example when he launches a Help system in the context of specific software.

5. *Apply the Lesson*

This is the most impactful step in the LLS. This task relates to whether the user has the ability to decide how to reuse the lesson. There are three categories of reuse:

a   Browsable—where the system displays a list of lessons that match the search criteria.

b   Executable—where users might have the option to execute the lesson's recommendation (as when the word processor suggests a specific spelling for a word).

c   Outcome reuse—when the system prompts users to enter the outcome of reusing a lesson in order to assess if the lesson can be replicated.

Today, many commercial as well as government organizations maintain LLS. Future LLS are expected to integrate advanced intelligent technologies that will alert the decision maker to available support in the form of explicit lessons in the context of the decision-making process. Furthermore, LLS are expected to integrate e-mail systems. E-mail messages could be a source for lesson extraction, as many contain historical archives of communications, often comprised of specific-case problems, and their solutions that could be mined for organizational lessons. At Xerox over 95 percent of their technicians use the Eureka LLS in support of their daily operations, saving the company over US$30 million annually. For example, a Brazilian service technician was having problems with a new Xerox product and was thinking of replacing it with a US$40,000 new piece of equipment, but once he consulted Eureka he found a tip from a Canadian service technician that described the problem he was having and to replace it with a US$90 connector (Gordon 2010).

Expertise Locator Knowledge Sharing Systems

Several different business organizations have identified the need to develop **expertise locator systems (ELS)** to help locate intellectual capital (Becerra-Fernandez 2006; Putrapratama et al. 2021; Rampisela et al. 2020). The main motives for seeking an expert are as a source of information and as someone who can perform a given organizational or social function (Kiani et al. 2020; Yiman-Seid and Kobsa 2003). The intent when developing these systems is to catalog knowledge competencies, including information not typically captured by human resources systems, in a way that could later be queried across the organization. Box 8.6 illustrates a sample ELS developed across different industries (Becerra-Fernandez 2006).

Box 8.6 Examples of Industry Expertise Locator Systems

Hewlett-Packard developed CONNEX, an expertise-locator KMS (Davenport and Prusak 1998). The goal of the project was to build a network of experts, available online, to provide a guide to human knowledge within HP. CONNEX consisted of a centralized database of user knowledge profiles with a Web-browser interface that allowed users to find profiles in multiple ways. Users' profiles contained a summary of their knowledge and skills, affiliations, education, and interests, as well as contact information. CONNEX users could easily find experts within Hewlett-Packard by searching the database using any combination of profile fields or by browsing through the different areas of knowledge, geographies, and/or names.

The National Security Agency (NSA) also took steps early on toward the implementation of a system to locate experts (Wright and Spencer 1999). The NSA is part of the "Intelligence Community," and their two missions are Foreign Signals Intelligence and National Information System Security. The goal of the implementation of the Knowledge and Skills Management System (KSMS) ELS was to catalog the talent pool within the agency to allow the precise identification of knowledge and skills and to take advantage of information technology. The NSA went through the development of the system by applying "database engineering" in order to solve the complexities of implementing an adequate, workable, and successful KMS. They also divided the execution of this project into several "Work Tasks" including the development of knowledge taxonomy applicable to their workforce.

The goal of Microsoft's Skills Planning und (and) Development, known as SpuD, was to develop a database containing job profiles available online across the IT group and to help match employee's competency with jobs and work teams. The following are the five major components of the SPuD project (Davenport and Prusak 1998): (1) developing a structure of competency types and levels, (2) defining the competencies required for particular jobs, (3) rating the employees' performance in particular jobs by the supervisors, (4) implementing the knowledge competencies in an online system, and (5) linking the competency models to learning offerings. Note that the validation of the data in this model rested with the supervisor who essentially assigned the competency criteria to each of the employees under his/her supervision.

Sources: Compiled from: Davenport and Prusak (1998), Wright and Spencer (1999)

Although ELS across organizations serve a similar purpose, a number of characteristics differentiate these systems:

1   *Purpose of the system*: An ELS may serve a different purpose across organizations. For example, the purpose could be to identify experts to help solve technical problems, or staff project teams, to match employee competencies with positions within the company, or to perform gap analyses that point to intellectual capital inadequacies within the organization. For instance, if a specific expertise domain is a critical knowledge area for an organization and the ELS points to only three experts, it may serve to identify the need to hire or internally train additional experts in that area.

2 *Access method*: Most company ELS are accessed via a company's Intranet. However inter-organizational systems such as *SAGE* (Searchable Answer Generating Environment, described later) are accessed via the Web. Systems accessed via the Web provide experts with an increased level of visibility, but organizations may fear that such increased visibility may be luring their experts to outside job opportunities.

3 *Self-assessment*: Most of the expertise locator KMS in place today rely on each employee completing a self-assessment of competencies, which is later used when searching for specific knowledge areas. Clearly there are some advantages to this approach, mainly that it allows building a repository of organization-wide competencies quickly. On the other hand, using self-assessment as the way to identify expertise presents an inherent shortcoming, in that the results are based on each person's self-perception and thus could be hard to normalize. Furthermore, employees' speculation about the possible use of this information could skew the results. Employees have been known to either exaggerate their competencies for fear of losing their position or downplay their duties so as not to have increasing responsibilities. For example, one particular organization conducted a skills self-assessment study during a period of downsizing. This resulted in employees' exaggeration of their competencies for fear they might be laid off if they did not appear maximally competent. On the other hand, another organization made it clear the self-assessment would be used to contact people with specific competencies to answer related questions. This resulted in employees downplaying their abilities in order to avoid serving as consultants for the organization. Microsoft's SPuD system addressed this problem by requiring supervisors to ratify their subordinates' self-perceptions and to assign a quantifiable value to it. Though this can be successful if adhered to, many organizations would find this requirement too taxing on their supervisors.

4 *Participation*: Defines whether the system represents expertise across the organization like at the National Security Agency (NSA), a department at Microsoft, or merely volunteer experts willing to share their knowledge with others.

5 *Taxonomy*: Refers to the specific taxonomy used to index knowledge competencies within the organization. Some organizations like Microsoft developed their own knowledge taxonomy—NSA's was based on O*NET, a standard published by the U.S. Department of Labor, and HP based their taxonomy on an existing standard published by the U.S. Library of Congress augmented by their own knowledge competencies.

6 *Levels of competencies*: Refers to expressing expertise as capability levels. Levels of competencies could be defined according to Wiig's (1993) levels of proficiency classifications:

    a   Ignorant—Totally unaware
    b   Beginner—Vaguely aware, no experience
    c   Advanced beginner—Aware, relatively unskilled
    d   Competent—Narrowly skilled
    e   Proficient—Knowledgeable in selected areas
    f   Expert—Highly proficient in a particular area, generally knowledgeable
    g   Master—Highly expert in many areas, broadly knowledgeable
    h   Grand Master—World-class expert in all areas of domain

Other differentiating characteristics for ELS may include technological differences, for example, the type of underlying database, the programming language used to develop the system, or the specifics about how the data are maintained current. Table 8.2 summarizes some of the major characteristics that differentiate the ELS described in Box 8.5 and in the case studies to follow.

The Role of Ontologies and Knowledge Taxonomies in the Development of Expertise Locator Systems

A significant challenge in the development of expertise locator KMS is the accurate development of a **knowledge taxonomy** or ontology. Taxonomy is the study of the general principles of scientific classification. **Ontology** is an explicit formal specification of how to represent the objects, concepts, and other entities that are assumed to exist in some area of interest and the relationships that hold among them. Taxonomies, also called classification or categorization schemes, are considered to be knowledge organization systems that serve to group objects together based on a particular characteristic. Knowledge taxonomies allow organizing knowledge or competency areas in the organization. In the case of ELS, the taxonomy is used to identify the critical knowledge areas used to describe and catalog people's knowledge, an important design consideration.

The development of adequate knowledge taxonomies and ontologies could be an expensive, time-consuming, and complex process. Typically, this exercise will require the collaboration of a cross-functional group tasked with defining the organization's most significant knowledge areas. In fact, this development requires consensus across a community whose members may have radically different visions of the domains under consideration (Gruninger and Lee 2002). In practice, organizations typically opt to create small lightweight ontologies that are later merged or seek to reuse formal ontologies developed by consortia and standards organizations (Gruninger and Lee 2002). But the latter solution also faces severe limitations in that it is difficult for users to understand the implicit assumptions and the distinctions between elements in the ontology, thus resulting in inappropriate modeling choices (Guarino and Welty 2002).

In addition, the process of developing knowledge taxonomies is complex because these decisions could play on organizational politics, since lack of representation in the knowledge taxonomy could be considered threatening to organizational subunits. Many ELS systems in place have addressed this consideration keeping in mind that taxonomies should easily describe a knowledge area, provide minimal descriptive text, facilitate browsing, and have the appropriate level of granularity and abstraction. If the level of granularity is too high then the knowledge taxonomy will be too difficult to use, but if the level is too low it will not properly describe the knowledge areas. Figure 8.2 depicts an excerpt from the competence taxonomy developed for NASA Goddard Space Flight Center. The complete taxonomy includes 57 competency areas, many of them with up to 12 additional subareas specified.

As we saw in the previous section, there exist a number of work classification standards that could be used to organize knowledge areas, such as the U.S. Library of Congress, INSPEC database, or the U.S. Department of Labor's O*NET. Using these standards may aid the development of knowledge taxonomies, but it may not be simple to apply any of these standards directly without some thought and further development of the taxonomy.

Table 8.2 Summary of Characteristics of Expertise Locator Knowledge Management Systems

ELS Categorization Dimensions	ELS Name				
	CONNEX (HP)	KSMS (NSA)	SPuD (Microsoft)	SAGE (FL Universities)	Expert Seeker (NASA)
Purpose of the System	To share knowledge for consulting and to search for experts	To staff projects and match positions with skills	To compile the knowledge and competency of each employee	To identify expert researchers within FL universities for possible research opportunities	To identify experts in the organization to staff projects and match positions with skills
Self-Assessment	Yes	Yes, supervisors also participate in data gathering	No, supervisors rate employee's performance	No, uses funded research data as the proxy for expertise	Both, self-assessment using competency assessment and database and Web content mining as proxy for expertise
Participation	Only those who are willing to share	Whole personnel	Whole personnel in the IT group	Profiles all researchers at universities (public and private) who are active in funded research in FL	Whole personnel
Knowledge Taxonomy	U.S. Library of Congress; INSPEC Index; Own	Department of Labor (O*NET)	Own	None required	Own for competency assessment, none required for database and Web content mining
Levels of Competencies	No	Yes	Yes	No	Yes
Data Maintenance	User (nagging)	User and Supervisor	Supervisor	Fusion of universities' funded research databases	Optional user maintenance for career summary and competency management, none required for database and Web content mining
Company Culture	Sharing, Open	Technology, Expertise	Technology, Open	Expertise	Technology, Expertise
Platform	HP-9000 Unix, Sybase, and Verity	OS/2, VMS, and Programming Bourne shell	SQL and MS Access	Coldfusion and MS Access	Coldfusion, MS Access, and multiple existing DB platforms

Source: Becerra-Fernandez (2006).

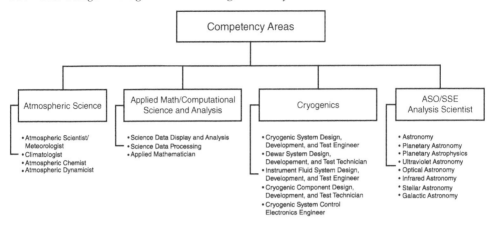

Figure 8.2 Competence Taxonomy for NASA Goddard Space Flight Center

Taxonomies and ontologies are related to other knowledge organization systems, including semantic networks and authority files. **Semantic networks** serve to structure concepts and terms in networks or webs versus the hierarchies typically used to represent taxonomies. Ontologies are relevant to knowledge management in that they are used to represent complex relationships between objects as rules and axioms, which are not included in semantic networks. **Authority files** are lists of terms used to control the variant names in a particular field, and link preferred terms to nonpreferred terms. Authority files are used to control the taxonomy vocabulary, in particular within an organization. In other words, authority files are used to ensure that everyone in the organization uses the same terms to organize similar concepts.

The use of **Web text data mining** can mitigate some of the problems inherent to relying on biased self-reporting required to keep employee profiles up to date, or the need to develop an accurate knowledge taxonomy *a priori*. This technique draws from an existing pool of information that provides a detailed picture of what the employee knows based on what she already publishes as part of her job, including her Web pages. Web data mining makes use of data mining techniques to extract information from Web-related data. An approach based upon Web data mining requires minimal user effort to maintain the accuracy of the records, eliminating the need for "nagging" systems that prompt users to maintain their profiles up to date. Through Web data mining the collection of expertise data is based on published documents, eliminating the need for possibly biased self-reporting. Using Web data mining this information can be collected automatically, and employee skill information can be kept up to date through periodic reprocessing of the document body for documents that are new or have been updated. Chapter 9 discusses Web data mining in more detail.

In the next four case studies, we explore how one premier knowledge organization successfully launched their first Web-based collaboration infrastructure to support teams working at a distance. Then the next three cases explore the development of innovative systems to identify experts either across organizations—in this case across universities in Florida—or within a large organization—in this case NASA and IBM respectively. We first look at the evolution of e-collaboration at NASA.

Case Studies

The Launch of Virtual Collaborative Decision Support at NASA

This section presents how one of the best-known knowledge intensive organizations, the National Aeronautics and Space Administration (NASA), was able to successfully develop a Web-based collaboration system, Postdoc, in order to be able to coordinate complex projects (Becerra-Fernandez et al. 2006, 2007b).

The pioneering research to develop Remote Agent,[3] the innovative software that operated the Deep Space 1 (DS-1) spacecraft and its futuristic ion engine, involved three teams of artificial intelligence experts (from Carnegie Mellon University in Pittsburgh, the Jet Propulsion Lab [JPL] in Pasadena, California, and the NASA Ames Research Center [ARC] in Moffett Field, Silicon Valley) who together developed the intelligent software that operated the DS-1 spacecraft more than 60 million miles away from Earth.

Remote Agent required innovations that were considered at that time as highly risky intelligent technologies for systems execution, fault tolerance and recovery, and autonomous planning systems. The Remote Agent design team could not work at the same location due to budget constraints. It was quickly recognized that e-mail would not provide an adequate infrastructure for group work at a distance, so in order to support the team's need for distributed collaboration the Postdoc Web-based collaborative document management system was developed. The first version of Postdoc supported the collaboration and project management needs of the 25-researcher team. As summarized by Kanna Rajan, a computer scientist who participated in the Remote Agent research project:

> Postdoc enabled the team to develop a common language that we used to share our design ideas and start talking about them. We created a token dictionary that enabled the defined team to establish clear semantics that were used to exchange comments among the team members.
>
> (Becerra-Fernandez et al. 2007b, p. 123)

The Postdoc collaborative system was developed by a team comprised of employees at NASA ARC and JPL as well as partners from Stanford University's Center for Design Research and from private industry. The design team recognized the following guiding principles for the collaborative structure: (1) it had to use the emerging Web infrastructure for document uploading, archiving, visualization, and integration; (2) it had to support agency-wide implementation with access controls and authentication capabilities; (3) it had to provide a portable application source; and (4) it had to provide users with features that allowed full control of their information anytime and anywhere. The Postdoc development effort required five-person-years of software coding and testing and became the collaborative infrastructure of choice to support teams throughout NASA in their cooperative research efforts with other NASA facilities, private industry, and academia.

NASA's use of the Postdoc software created agency-wide awareness about how virtual workspaces could be shared among geographically distributed teams. It was estimated that during the period of 1995 to 2004, the use of Postdoc as a collaboration infrastructure resulted in savings to the agency of over US$4 million a year. NASA programs across the organization estimated that the use of Web-based collaboration translated in savings in annual travel expenditures of at least US$100,000 and up to US$200,000. This did not consider the intangible efficiency gains achieved such as eliminating the hardships associated with attaching large documents to e-mails as well as increased document security and integrity.

Postdoc's use grew to support approximately 30 NASA programs, which even included partnerships across the federal government including programs at the Department of Defense, National Institutes of Standards and Technology, Naval Research Laboratories, and the National Imagery and Mapping Agency. Today Postdoc has been successfully migrated into NX, a new KM based technology that leveraged Postdoc's foundation of lessons learned and user requirements (Becerra-Fernandez et al. 2006, 2007b). Today, NASA continues to use NX to share non-sensitive data, information, and knowledge and MINX is used within the US Federal Government for sharing sensitive data which uses a separate security plan.

Overview of the Searchable Answer Generating Environment (SAGE) Expert Finder: Locating University Expertise

This section presents insights and lessons learned from the development of the **Searchable Answer Generating Environment (SAGE) Expert Finder**, which is in the category of ELS (Becerra-Fernandez 1999, 2000a, 2006). The motivation to develop SAGE was based on the National Aeronautics and Space Administration (NASA)–Kennedy Space Center's (KSC) requirement to partner with Florida experts, as the agency looks to develop new technologies necessary for the continuation of their space exploration missions. The purpose of SAGE was to create a searchable repository of university experts in the state of Florida. Each university in Florida keeps a database of funded research for internal use, but these databases are disparate and dissimilar. The SAGE Expert Finder created a single funded research data warehouse by incorporating a distributed database scheme that could be searched by a variety of fields including research topic, investigator name, funding agency, or university. Figure 8.3 represents the SAGE architecture. In this figure, the canisters in the Florida map represent each of the disparate databases at each of the Florida universities.

The content of each database was pulled by a file transfer protocol (FTP) client application that automatically obtained and transferred the database contents of each participating university. The file transfer took place according to a prescheduled transfer rule to the SAGE database server, represented by the canister DATABASE. The FTP client was customized to each university, and it is marked by the abbreviations that represent each university: University of West Florida (UWF), Florida Agricultural and Mechanical University (FAMU), University of North Florida (UNF), Florida State University (FSU), University of Florida (UF), University of Central Florida (UCF), Florida Atlantic University (FAU), Florida International University (FIU), and Florida Gulf Coast University (FGCU). After the information was in the SAGE server, the next steps involved the migration of the data to the SQL server format, followed by cleansing and transforming the data to a relational format.

The SAGE system combined the unified database by masking multiple databases as if they were one. This methodology provided flexibility to users and the database administrator, regardless of the type of program used to collect the information at the source. One of the advantages of SAGE was that it provided a single user a point of

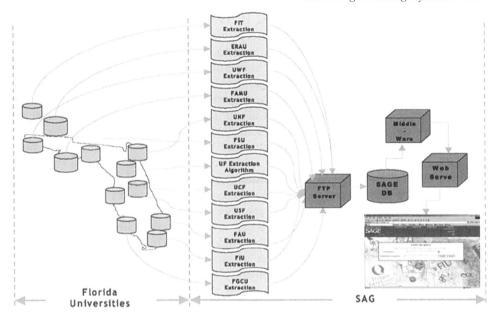

Figure 8.3 SAGE Architecture

entry at the Web-enabled interface. The main interfaces developed on the query engine used text fields to search the processed data for key words, fields of expertise, names, or other applicable search fields. The application processed the enduser's query and returned the pertinent information. The SAGE Expert Finder also included an interactive data dictionary or thesaurus and, upon user request, launched a query for similar words.

The development of SAGE was marked by two design requirements: a need to minimize the impact on each of the universities' offices of sponsored research that collect most of the required data and the need to validate the data used to identify experts. For this reason, the system was designed to receive the content in its native form, which made necessary data cleansing at the SAGE server site. SAGE's strength lies in the fact that it validated the data at the source, using the assumption that researchers who successfully obtained funded-research grants were indeed experts in their fields. At that point, a number of database systems existed on the Web that claimed to help locate experts with a defined profile, such as Community of Science. However, most of these tools relied on people assessing their own skills against a pre-defined taxonomy, which is inherently unreliable and hard to keep up to date.

One of the technical challenges faced during the design and implementation of this project was that the source databases of funded research from the various universities were dissimilar in design and file format. The manipulation of the source data was one of the most important issues, because the credibility of the system would ultimately depend on the consistency and accuracy of the information. Manipulating the data included the process of cleansing the data, followed by the data transformation into the relational model, and ultimately the databases' migration to a consistent format. One of the most important research contributions of SAGE was the merging of inter-organizational database systems.

SAGE made its online debut on August 16, 1999. NASA personnel have used SAGE to target university researchers for conferences and requests for proposals. SAGE has also been used by small businesses that need to identify research collaborators when pursuing contracts, businesses that need to identify experts who could assist in solving technical problems, and researchers who need to identify potential collaborators.

The SAGE system design required participating institutions to forward the most recent funded research data to a human agent. Then, this human agent uploaded the new data to keep the data repository current. Even though a file transfer protocol utility was developed to facilitate the maintenance of SAGE in a more automated fashion, using funded research as a proxy for expertise limited the SAGE system's ability to identify expertise as this is a limited criterion. To overcome this limitation, SAGE could have been integrated with other Web-based tools that could expand the criteria for defining domain expertise and thus generate a more complete list of experts. For example, SAGE could have been integrated with CiteSeer (Giles et al. 1998), an autonomous citation-indexing system, which indexes academic literature published on the Web. This functionality would have allowed SAGE to also consider expertise through publications in specific high-quality journals and number of citations. Although there are inherent limitations to this idea (e.g., CiteSeer is limited to only some scientific fields), it proposes to take advantage of other resources available on the Web to improve the scale of the search. Also, SAGE could have been redesigned to take advantage of intelligent agent techniques, which would increase the scope of researchers that SAGE would be able to identify (Becerra-Fernandez et al. 2005). In addition, many data source owners are resistant to providing their data to a "data broker" due to potential privacy issues. An agent approach could serve to overcome this crucial shortcoming by allowing a searching agent locating an expert to negotiate with a gatekeeper agent, guarding the data source. The gatekeeper would evaluate the request from the searching agent and only provide the necessary information to build the expert profile, eliminating the need for consolidating data from different sources in an overarching database. This enhancement would make it possible to represent data from a larger number of data sources, enabling the formulation of ELS that could search for experts at a national and even international level. Figure 8.4 depicts the agent-based approach to expertise location (Becerra-Fernandez et al. 2005).

Overview of Expert Seeker: Locating Experts at the National Aeronautics and Space Administration

What follows presents insights and lessons learned from the development of **Expert Seeker** (Becerra-Fernandez 2000b, 2001, 2006; Becerra-Fernandez and Sabherwal 2005), an organizational expertise locator KMS used to locate experts at NASA. The main difference between Expert Seeker and SAGE is that the former searched for expertise at NASA (KSC and GSFC—Goddard Space Flight Center), while the latter is on the Web and sought for expertise at various universities. Expert Seeker included an interface to SAGE, which allowed for specifying a search scope that was not bounded by the organization but included the base of researchers who work at different universities. Another important difference between SAGE and Expert Seeker is that the latter enables the user to search for much more detailed information regarding the experts' achievements including information, skills, and competencies as well as the proficiency level for each of the skills and competencies.

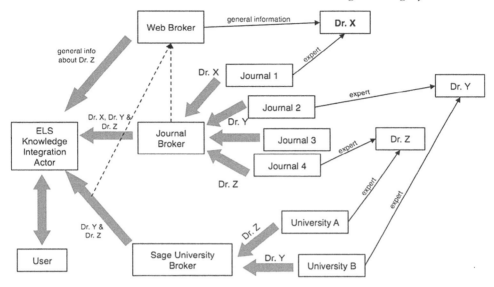

Figure 8.4 Event Diagram for an Actor Model-Based ELS

Previous knowledge management studies at Kennedy Space Center (KSC) affirmed the need for a center-wide repository that would provide KSC employees with Intranet-based access to experts with specific backgrounds (Becerra-Fernandez 1998; Becerra-Fernandez and Sabherwal 2005). To further create **synergies** between the efforts to develop Expert Seeker at KSC, a similar effort was funded to prototype Expert Seeker at GSFC. It was expected that the knowledge taxonomy for GSFC would differ from the one for KSC. However, this requirement did not pose a concern as Expert Seeker could be developed so the software could be "configured" with a customizable knowledge taxonomy. Expert Seeker offered NASA experts more visibility and at the same time allowed interested parties to identify available expertise within NASA, and this is especially useful when organizing cross-functional teams.

The Expert Seeker ELS was accessed via NASA's Intranet and provided a Web-based unified interface to access experts with specific competencies within the organization. The main interfaces on the query engine in Expert Seeker used text fields to search the repository by fields of expertise, names, or other applicable search fields. Expert Seeker unified a myriad of structured, semi-structured, and unstructured data collections to create an expert's profile repository that could easily be searched via a Web-based interface facilitating communication via a point of contact. The development of Expert Seeker required the utilization of existing structured data as well as semi-structured and unstructured Web-based information as much as possible. It used the data in existing human resources databases for information such as employee's formal educational background, the X.500 directory for point-of-contact information, a skills database that profiles each employee's competency areas, and the Goal Performance Evaluation System (GPES). Information regarding skills and competencies as well as proficiency levels for the skills and competencies needed to be collected, to a large extent, through self-assessment. Figure 8.5 depicts the architecture of Expert Seeker, and Table 8.3 describes the data sources for Expert Seeker. Furthermore, other related information deemed important in the generation of an expert profile not

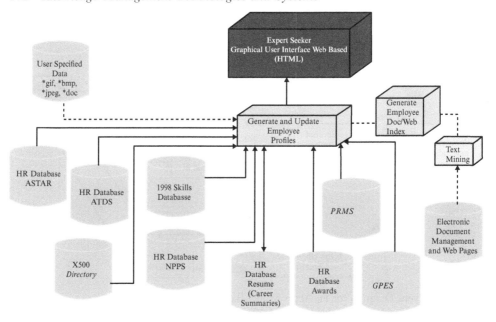

Figure 8.5 Expert Seeker Architecture

Table 8.3 Description of the Data Sources for Expert Seeker

User-Specified Data	This information is optionally user-supplied. For example, experts can opt to provide career summaries that will be used by Expert Seeker to augment the expertise search. A database table to hold this information was created and linked to the system, initially populated from the NPPS human resources database. Other user-supplied data could include pictures, publications, patents, hobbies, civic activities, etc.
ASTAR	This human resources database view provides the experts' in-house training courses.
ATDS	This human resources database view provides the experts' workshops and academic classes employees are planning to take.
X.500	This database view provides the experts' general employee data such as first name, last name, work address, phone, organization, fax, and e-mail. X.500's unique identifier is also used to cross reference employees in different databases.
Skills Database	This database view provides a set of skills and subskills that are used by Expert Seeker to index the expertise search. The KSC Core Competency team defined this set of skills and subskills as a refinement to a previous Center-wide skills-assessment.
NPPS Database	This human resources database view provides the experts' formal education, including professional degrees and the corresponding academic institutions. NPPS is also the source of the employee's department used for the directorate search. The contents of this database were also used to initially populate the career summary section table.
KPro	This database view will be populated with project participation information through a new project management system under development at NASA/KSC.

GPES	The Goal Performance Evaluation System (GPES) is a system developed at KSC. This database view serves as the data source for profile information such as employees' achievements. GPES will replace the Skills Database since GPES will also be populated with KSC's strategic competencies and levels of expertise.
Data Mining	Expert Seeker expertise search is augmented through the use of data-mining algorithms, which build an expert's profile based on information published by employees on their Web pages. Similarly, a document repository could be mined for expertise using these algorithms.
SAGE	The Searchable Answer Generating Environment (SAGE) is an expertise locator system developed and hosted at the Florida International University Knowledge Management Laboratory to identify experts within Florida's universities. Expert Seeker users can define the search scope to be within KSC or to expand it to universities in Florida. The latter means that Expert Seeker would launch an expert search to SAGE, and the results of this search will be integrated into one output at the Expert Seeker GUI.

Source: Becerra-Fernandez (2006).

currently stored in an in-house database system can be user-supplied such as employee's picture, project participation data, hobbies, and volunteer or civic activities.

Recognizing that there are significant shortcomings of self-assessment, the system relied on other systems' information in order to update employees' profiles, and thus was less dependent on self-assessed data. For example, Expert Seeker used the Global Performance Evaluation System, an in-house performance evaluation tool, to mine employees' accomplishments and automatically update their profiles. Typically, employees find it difficult to make time to keep their resumes updated, unless their job requires this activity, for example consultants. Performance evaluations, on the other hand, are without a doubt part of everybody's job. Therefore, it makes perfect sense to use this tool to unobtrusively keep the employees' profiles up to date. Future developments for expertise locator systems will incorporate advanced technologies, such as data mining and intelligent agent technologies, to automatically identify experts within as well as outside the organization.

Developments for expertise location at NASA include the use of Semantic Web technologies (Grove and Schain 2008). The deployment of the POPS ELS (People, Organizations, Projects, and Skills) combines Expert Seeker's original approach of reusing existing information sources with their integration via Resource Description Framework (RDF), a metadata data model, and other aggregation technologies. The system displays the social network between the user and the people who work on the same projects and people with the same skill sets and competencies. In addition, the system includes a know-who function that given the current user and target person will return an intermediate person related to both the user and the target person (see Figure 8.6). This functionality allows project managers to find intermediaries with whom to talk about potential project members, their abilities, interests, qualifications, and so forth.

Overview of BlueReach: A System to Facilitate Real-Time Knowledge Sharing, Capture, and Reuse

Large globally distributed organizations like IBM[4] continue the quest of how to adequately enable the sharing of expertise across organizational, geographic, and time boundaries. The motivation to develop and implement the *BlueReach* solution emerged

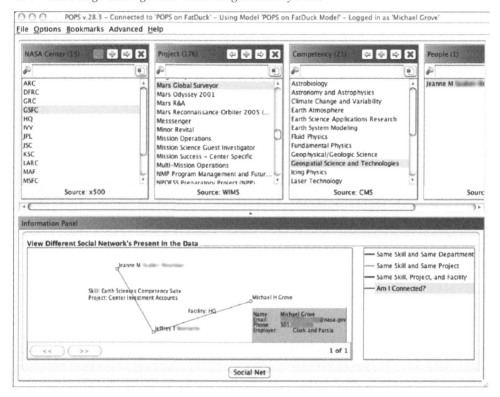

Figure 8.6 The POPS Expertise Locator System

initially from the immense growth in the global SAP consulting practice. A survey of SAP consultants in India revealed substantial shortcomings in terms of timely access to information for junior consultants. For example, of the 227 SAP respondents around 73 percent expressed they had to wait at least one day or longer for a typical question to be resolved, and 93 percent felt this wait was too long (Singley et al. 2008).

In order to respond to this need, the BlueReach Web-based system was built on the Lotus Sametime enterprise system. The goal of BlueReach is to provide the infrastructure for real-time expertise sharing and capture, to connect information-seekers (i.e., people with questions) to people with the expertise to answer them, while placing safeguards around the experts' time. The system was designed with two constraints in mind, the first being to provide sufficient controls for the experts regarding their visibility in the system to ensure that they are not overwhelmed by questions thus causing them to immediately drop out of the system. This first constraint must be balanced with the second requirement, which is to make the experts sufficiently accessible to information-seekers so as to create the vital "critical mass," that we described earlier as liquidity, necessary for collaborative systems. BlueReach gives users direct access to experts, by topic, in real time.

When a user selects a topic of interest, the application displays a taxonomy of expertise (with subtopics) for that topic area which the user can browse. The taxonomy is displayed as a simple tree structure that only goes a few levels deep. Once the question-asker has selected a subtopic, BlueReach does a real-time lookup of registered experts for that subtopic and displays only those who are available (see Figure 8.7). Some of the features of BlueReach include:

1   Multiple ways for the expert to control when they are "visible" in the system.
2   Ability for a question-asker to indicate if their question is urgent or can be deferred up to 90 minutes.
3   Logging of all chats and their associated ratings.
4   Browsable topic taxonomies for each of the supported service areas.
5   Support for composing a question before initiating chat with an expert, which can then be reused with other experts if immediate satisfaction is not obtained.
6   Full text search and browsing of stored questions with their associated answers.

Additionally, various types of export enrollment are supported by the tool. Enrollment can be specified as either: (a) open-enrollment model—anybody can volunteer, and it is up to the expert to designate his/her areas of expertise; (b) administrator-controlled model—only designated users can enroll experts in each of the topics; or (c) closed enrollment—when areas are saturated with experts, and no additional experts are accepted. A chat-harvesting tool allows experts to review and manage all the chats they have engaged in, quickly harvest and store important questions and answers that have value for reuse, and associate key words with the answers. One of the most valuable features of the tool is the reporting aspect. At any time BlueReach can report on the number of experts registered

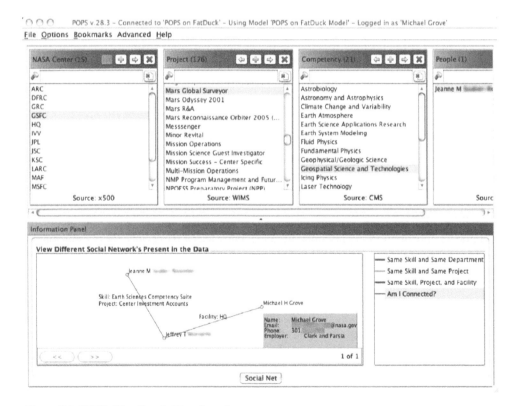

Figure 8.7 IBM's Blue Reach User Interface

for a given topic, how many questions being asked (by topic, by country, by expert, by practitioner), average ratings for each expert, and so on. This feature allows for companies to understand where they have concentrations of expertise and also to monitor emerging hot areas of interest as well as problem areas.

Load-balancing features in BlueReach enable the ability to view the number of experts visible in the system with a status of either available or idle. This can also be used for stress testing the system.

As part of the BlueReach initiative, the team of developers looked to understand the motivational aspects around this activity. Some of the findings showed that many junior practitioners are reluctant to ask a question of experts for fear of disturbing them at an inopportune time. This concern resulted in a feature to indicate the urgency of the question, allowing information-seekers to make their question less disruptive to the expert and thus making them more comfortable asking.

BlueReach was initially piloted with SAP consultants in India in the first quarter of 2007 and then rolled out to other global delivery centers around the world during the third quarter of 2007. More than 1,000 BlueReach experts registered in 16 different service areas supporting over 30,000 practitioners. Studies show that 60 percent of BlueReach users got their questions answered in less than an hour (as compared to 27 percent in the initial survey), and that half of the usage of BlueReach consisted of questions that would have normally been asked of a Team Lead. Additionally, 88 percent of practitioners said they would use it again, 85 percent found it easy to use, and 96 percent of experts said they would enroll again (Singley et al. 2008). IBM has migrated from BlueReach to Expertise Locator in early August 2010. The support of the Expertise Locator system was transferred to the IBM CIO Innovation Initiatives Organization who continue to support the current version of BlueReach while investigating possible integration with IBM's social networking tools (such as SmallBlue, SaND, Sonar) and other expertise location initiatives (e.g., ExCaliber) to create an enterprise-wide expert location solution.

Shortcomings of Knowledge Sharing Systems

Perhaps one of the biggest challenges for knowledge management systems is to make this knowledge meaningful across the organization (Becerra-Fernandez and Sabherwal 2008). For example, lessons learned systems were one of the first types of KMS that gained acceptance in organizations and many consulting agencies quickly adopted the implementation of such systems, which later they proposed to their clients. As the volume of information represented in these knowledge bases increased, information and knowledge overload, coupled with a lack of awareness about the lessons' context, became a significant problem (Davenport and Hansen 1998).

> One of the problems was that many documents failed to provide much information about the context in which the insight and experience embodied in the document was generated … Imagine … you start reusing the drawings for the development of an office building and notice that the elevators in the previous drawings were constructed to be very deep. You later discover that the previous drawings were for a hospital where elevators need to be deep to hold beds. Wouldn't it have been helpful if the document had stated up front that the drawings were only relevant for hospital elevators? Contextualizing … would involve … describing the context

in which the knowledge was generated and used, where it may be useful, and where it should—and should not—be used.

(Davenport and Hansen 1998, p. 9)

The lack of contextual components for most of the lessons learned systems severely limited the recipient's ability to realize the environment in which the knowledge was generated and furthermore restricted its reuse. In order to overcome this limitation, at the time of collection, lessons learned could be augmented with those attributes describing the identity, sensory, informational, and positioning components that could be detected in the background aided by the sensor network. These attributes could then be combined with the user's cognitive model, which could be used to stamp the lesson learned. This stamp could effectively describe where the lesson originated and under what physical and logical conditions. Subsequently, when lessons are being retrieved in order to ascertain their relevance to the current context, the system could match the stamp of the retrieved lessons to the user's current contextual components. Thus, using the example above, the system could proactively inform the user that the retrieved elevator design originated from the hospital architecture group and may not be applicable to an office building design (Becerra-Fernandez et al. 2007a).

In addition, organizations are still challenged by how to get more value from their own knowledge, in particular since it's estimated that 70 percent of the organizations with more than 10,000 employees have more than 100 separate information repositories (Weiss et al. 2004). This proliferation of repositories translates to lost productivity as employees often fall short at finding the knowledge they need. In order to improve the success of their knowledge sharing activities, organizations are encouraged to:

1   Develop one-stop access to content that emulates Google's one-stop search functionality. This requires companies to integrate their repositories, including effective back-end design. In addition, search functionality should be designed with content metadata or tags for each document including keywords, abstracts, author name, and document date.
2   Design dynamic classification systems and consistent formats that emulate eBay's classification system, which was developed based on what its customers want to buy and sell. Improving the browsing experience also requires consistency of formats of the information presented to the user, which allows people to spend less time analyzing the results.
3   Entice employees to find what they need much like Amazon helps people identify needed products based on their relevance to the user. Furthermore, Amazon's ability to support shoppers in assessing the quality of their products via customer-supplied reviews significantly improves the buyer's experience. More information on how Web 2.0 technologies support user-generated reviews is presented in Chapter 10. Additional attributes for the relevance and quality of knowledge could include an excerpt of the abstract, a snapshot of the content including who to contact for additional information, and a link to the author profiles.

Knowledge Management Systems that Share Tacit Knowledge

The systems discussed so far assist organizations in sharing explicit knowledge. In order to create a cultural environment that encourages the sharing of knowledge, some organizations are creating knowledge communities (Dignum 2002). As we discussed in

Chapter 3, a community of practice, also known as a *knowledge network*, is an organic and self-organized group of individuals who are dispersed geographically or organizationally but communicate regularly to discuss issues of mutual interest. Two examples of communities of practice mentioned in that chapter are a tech club at Daimler Chrysler, which includes a group of engineers who don't work in the same unit but meet regularly to discuss problems related to their area of expertise, and a strategic community of IT professionals at Xerox, who frequently meet to promote knowledge sharing among them.

Many studies have demonstrated that any technological support for knowledge exchange requires users to feel they know and can trust each other. One company that has already taken steps in this direction is Achmea Holding N.V., one of the top insurance and financial services companies in the Netherlands. The company encourages direct contacts among participants in their knowledge community through formalized workshops. Through these workshops the company assures the creation, maintenance, and uniformity of domain knowledge and at the same time enables members to appreciate other colleagues, thus contributing to a feeling of community. In Box 8.7 we describe how the World Bank developed a knowledge sharing culture through the development of communities of practice, which they called *thematic groups*. As we see, KM plays a significant role at the World Bank, an international organization funded by the governments of 188 countries.

Box 8.7 Sharing Knowledge at the World Bank

In 1996 James Wolfensohn, then president of the World Bank, outlined his vision for the Knowledge Bank, a partnership for creating and sharing knowledge, and making it a major driver of development. At the World Bank, KM is synonymous with sharing the experiences gained from staff, clients, and development partners and creating linkages between groups and communities. The World Bank recognizes that "fighting poverty requires a global strategy to share knowledge effectively and to ensure that people who need that knowledge get it on time, whether from the World Bank or others." The World Bank has concentrated its KM efforts in becoming a global development partner enabling the necessary knowledge exchange within and outside the Bank. Early on, the World Bank developed a matrix structure to combine local country knowledge with world-class technical expertise along communities of practice that they called *Thematic Groups* (TGs). TGs refer to voluntary groups of people who are passionate about a common subject. Leadership and membership in any Thematic Group is open to all staff and may also include external partners enabling knowledge sharing seamlessly across the group via e-mail distribution lists and websites. The role of TGs has been to bring together, online and face-to-face, experts from within and outside the Bank and across all its regions. TGs receive funding from their sector board(s) based on work program agreements which tie their work to the sector strategy. The activities of the thematic groups include:

1   Production of knowledge collections (good practices, knowhow, sector statistics, etc.).
2   Dissemination and outreach to staff and partners (brown bag lunches, clinics, workshops, study tours, websites, newsletters, etc.).
3   Support to task teams, thus enabling staff to apply and adapt the global knowledge to the local situation.

4   Raising additional funds for specific work program activities.

Currently, there are 79 TGs at the World Bank, and a list of these groups and their leaders can be accessed via the World Bank website.

The Bank also implemented a number of advisory services that functioned as help desks, as an interface for connecting people and answers. The Bank also launched a knowledge management system for the purpose of sharing lessons and best practices. Other KM initiatives at the World Bank included starting a Global Knowledge Partnership conference, linking all its local offices to global communications and establishing an innovation marketplace to share ideas, talents, and resources that address development challenges. This level of success would not have been accomplished if the organization had not rewarded knowledge sharing, which in 1998 became part of their annual performance evaluation system. In 2000, the bank launched the Global Development Learning Network, which provided 17 countries with simultaneous videoconferencing and Internet facilities for distance learning. Also, the World Bank established the Knowledge for Development program, to help developing countries better understand how to exploit the knowledge revolution to help reduce poverty. For all its KM efforts, the American Productivity and Quality Center recognized the World Bank as a best practice partner.

Current efforts at the World Bank include increased awareness about the role of metrics in the implementation of KM programs (Carayannis and Laporte 2002), and the importance of knowledge for long-term economic growth (Chen and Dahlman 2006).

Knowledge sharing at the World Bank is now a mainstream activity that has required significant investments in infrastructure, communities of practice, global networks, training, and in understanding the role of knowledge in development. As a result, the role of the World Bank is now considered to be catalytic, ensuring effective integration of internal and client knowledge. The World Bank now understands that capacity building is about creating environments in which local and global knowledge can inform action and influence the change necessary to end poverty.

Sources: Compiled from Carayannis and Laporte (2002); Chen and Dahlman (2006)

Communities are groups of people who come together to share and learn from one another and who are held together by a common interest in a body of knowledge. Communities come together either face-to-face or virtually and are driven by a desire and need to share problems, experiences, insights, templates, tools, and best practices (McDermott 2000). This section concentrates on systems used to share tacit knowledge, specifically to support **communities of practice (CoPs)**. According to McDermott, people come together in communities of practice because they're passionately interested in the topic and will receive direct value from participating in the community, or because they're emotionally connected to the community, or to learn new tools and techniques. Communities grow out of its members' natural networks, and follow five stages of development: planning, start-up, growth, sustenance, and closure. Although communities of practice are not new phenomena, the Internet has enabled the proliferation of virtual communities facilitated through the same collaborative technologies. In 1995, IBM started supporting the growth and development of communities of practice focused on the competencies of the organization. By the year 2000 at IBM the number of CoPs numbered around 60, and more than 20,000 employees had participated in a community (Gongla and Rizzuto 2001).

While knowledge repositories support primarily codified and explicitly captured knowledge, virtual communities of practice are supported through technology that enables interaction and conversations among its members. Interaction technology can support structured (and perhaps more explicated) communication such as in discussion groups and Web-based forums to unstructured (and perhaps more tacit) communication such as in videoconferencing.

For example, in Box 8.7 presented in this section, we mentioned the World Bank's initiative to establish CoPs, as a powerful venue for sharing global experiences while at the same time adapting them to meet local challenges. For example, the Knowledge for Development (K4D) Community combines experts from across sectors, networks, and regions of the Bank to share knowledge related to capacity development in each of the different regions of the world. At the World Bank, technology is considered a critical building block for CoPs but only as support for the social aspects of sharing knowledge which are building trust, personal communication, and face-to-face meetings. At the World Bank, technology is adapted to the needs of the community and the tools that support their CoPs include document repositories, debriefings to identify lessons learned, an Internet-based broadcasting station, newsletters and printed publications, and websites. Specifically, the World Bank developed a website that supports virtual discussions called The Development Forum (DevForum), an electronic venue for dialogue and knowledge sharing on issues of sustainable development. Participants of this forum must adhere to a set of rules, namely:

1   *Personal Identification*: Participants should include their name in all messages posted to the discussion and never represent themselves as another person.
2   *Conduct*: Participants may not post libelous or defamatory messages or materials or links to such materials. They may not post messages or materials that are obscene, violent, abusive, threatening, or designed to harass or intimidate another person.
3   *Liability and Responsibility*: Participants are legally responsible, and solely responsible, for any content posted to a discussion. They may only post materials that they have the right or permission to distribute electronically. The sponsors of the Development Forum are not responsible for any liability arising from users' posting of any materials to the Forum Dialogues.
4   *Accuracy*: The World Bank, as sponsor of the Development Forum, cannot and does not guarantee the accuracy of any statements made in or materials posted to the Forum by participants.
5   *Attribution*: Participants in the Development Forum, including participants in the Development Dialogues and the authors of contributions to the Speakers' Corner, are assumed to be speaking in their personal capacity, unless they explicitly state that their contribution represents the views of their organization. For this reason, participants in the Forum should not quote the postings of other participants as representing the views of the organizations to which those other participants belong.
6   *Copyright and Fair Use*: As a participant in the Development Forum, participants retain copyright of any materials that is their own creation that is posted to the Forum. However, users authorize other participants in the Forum to make personal and customary use of that work, including creating links to or reposting such materials to other Internet discussion sites but not otherwise to reproduce or disseminate those materials unless you give permission. Participants must always identify the source and author of materials downloaded from the Forum if it's reposted elsewhere.

CoPs have been observed to impact organizational performance (Lesser and Storck 2001) in four areas:

1   Decreasing new employee's learning curves—CoPs can help new employees identify subject matter experts in the organization who can guide them to the proper resources and thus foster relationships with more senior employees. CoPs can help develop mentor-protégé relationships that can help employees with career development and to understand the larger organizational context of their individual tasks.
2   Enabling the organization to respond faster to customer needs and inquiries— CoPs can help identify experts that can address customer issues. Furthermore, since many communities maintain electronic document repositories, relevant codi- fied knowledge can often be reused.
3   Reducing rework and preventing to "reinvent the wheel"—CoPs are able to locate, access, and apply existing knowledge in new situations. Repositories serve as common virtual workspace to store, organize, and download presentations, tools, and other valuable materials. Metadata is used to identify authors and subject matter experts. Most repositories include human moderation. For example, the sponsors of the World Bank's Development Forum retain the right to refuse to post any message that they consider to be in violation of the rules, and may opt to publish the messages posted to the Forum in whole or in part. CoPs help create trust within the organization by helping individuals build reputations both as experts and for their willingness to help others.
4   Spawning new ideas for products and services—CoPs serve as a forum in which employees are able to share perspectives about a topic. Discussing diverse views within the community can often spark innovation. Furthermore, CoPs provide a safe environment where people feel comfortable about sharing their experiences.

In short, CoPs are effective mechanisms for tacit knowledge sharing that can provide significant value to organizations. The role of management is to carefully craft inter- ventions that are likely to support the formation and development of CoPs. Box 8.8 describes the use of the Department of Defense's Network (APAN), a community of unclassified Web portals to enhance partnership building and collaboration during humanitarian assistance and disaster relief. The box describes how the community helped support the disaster relief mission of the U.S. Southern Command in the after- math of the 2010 Haiti earthquake.

Box 8.8 Department of Defense's All Partners Access Network: Leverages Community Technology

The All Partners Access Network (APAN) is a community of unclassified Web portals, which offer information exchange in a collaborative planning environment to enhance partnership building, security cooperation initiatives, humanitarian assistance, disaster relief, and even planning. APAN provides a unique military operation capability to multi-agency operations, bridging government (U.S. military and non-U.S. military) and non-government during complex operations. APAN is hosted by Commander, U.S. Pacific Command (USPACOM), and was first developed in 1999. The original plan was to use APAN to communicate across borders, particularly in countries without sophisticated communication technology.

In January 2009, APAN initiated the design of a software application built on easy-to-use community social networking principles for unstructured exchange of data, with tools like file sharing applications, chat, blogs, calendar tools, and wikis to enable and optimize the communication between both government and non-government units and people across the globe. In January 2010 with the unfortunate earthquake in Haiti, U.S. Southern Command (USSOUTHCOM), charged with coordinating the humanitarian response, decided to launch the new APAN ten months ahead of its scheduled launch date. SOUTHCOM decided to use APAN as the primary non-military information exchange and collaboration portal during the emergency operation period in Haiti, to support all Haiti relief unclassified coordination operations.

The use of APAN community during Haiti relief operations shifted the "top-down" structured data architecture to a more horizontal collaborative unstructured data communication technology in US military communications. The new APAN community collaboration tools included forums (to set up dialog on specific issues), a chat tool (to allow for real time collaboration), wikis (for ease of dissemination and retrieval), a mobile mail gateway (to make APAN services accessible to mobile users through e-mails and SMS texts), and a file sharing system (to enable the exchange of more than 3,500 files such as imagery, photos, and documents). APAN was also integrated with various features of other data sources and application systems such as Google Relief Mapping, Sahana (disaster management system), Ushahidi (crowdsource crisis information), and bio-surveillance tracking.

Some of the examples of how APAN was able to support the relief efforts after the earthquake in Haiti include:

1   A post in the APAN Haiti community forum indicated family members were receiving SMS messages from a victim buried in the rubble. Within 30 minutes, a replay was posted to the APAN Haiti forum that provided contact information for assistance.
2   A forum post identified the need for emergency access to a brain scan machine. The request was answered by a donor in Miami who had a functional machine that could be donated if transportation was provided, which was addressed and coordinated in the same thread.
3   A hospital in Milot, which had not been affected by the earthquake and was fully staffed, tried unsuccessfully to reach out to the responder community through several channels. Four days into the crisis, only six patients were admitted. Immediately after a post in APAN, injured survivors started being transported to the hospital. Within a week, the hospital admitted around 250 victims and conducted 42 rooftop helicopter landings.
4   An APAN post stated that one Haitian encampment's rations of food and water were depleted. A quick response to the post indicated that there was a U.S. and Canadian forces relief camp nearby.

These are only a few examples of how APAN enhanced the relief efforts after the earthquake in Haiti. The result of the implementation of APAN was faster response, improved resource allocation, and ultimately lives were saved. Because of the great success achieved by the APAN during the relief operations following the earthquake in Haiti, APAN became the first responder destination for the disaster relief community worldwide.

Source: Compiled from Goggins et al. (2012)

Summary

In this chapter, we discussed what knowledge sharing systems are, including design considerations and specific types of such systems. Specific attention was placed on the two systems most frequently discussed in the KM literature: lessons learned systems (LLS) and expertise locator systems (ELS). The lessons learned process was discussed, and knowledge sharing using social media was illustrated. Also, we discussed LLS and ELS in further detail, including design considerations and three representative case studies. The experience gained from the development of four such systems was presented: Postdoc—a collaborative system to support dispersed teams at NASA; SAGE Expert Finder—an ELS to locate experts in universities in Florida; Expert Seeker—an ELS used to identify experts at NASA; and BlueReach—a system to locate and share expertise at IBM. The chapter concludes with a discussion of systems used to share tacit knowledge through communities of practice.

Review

1 Describe the crucial requirements for the successful implementation of knowledge sharing systems.
2 Discuss the different types of knowledge sharing systems.
3 Explain the lessons learned process.
4 Explain the role that taxonomies play in knowledge sharing systems.
5 Explain the differentiating characteristics of the ELS developed at HP, NSA, Microsoft, state of Florida universities, and NASA.
6 Discuss the role that communities of practice play in sharing tacit knowledge.

Application Exercises

1 Identify examples of knowledge sharing systems in use in your organization. What are some of the intelligent technologies that enable those systems?
2 Design a knowledge sharing system to support your business needs. Describe the type of system and the foundation technologies that you would use to develop such a system.
3 Describe the nontechnical issues that you will face during the implementation of the system designed in the previous question.
4 Design the system architecture for the system described in question 2 above.
5 Identify three recent examples in the literature of knowledge sharing systems.

Notes

1 Liquidity refers to the number of trades made in the market — the greater the volume of trades, the greater the liquidity.
2 For a comprehensive survey of lessons learned systems, including capabilities, limitations, design issues, and the role of artificial intelligence in the creation of these systems, please refer to Weber et al. (2001).
3 Remote Agent was a complex software system for controlling and monitoring of autonomous spacecraft.
4 We acknowledge IBM, in particular Jennifer Lai of the IBM T.J. Watson Research Center, for the support in creating this section.

References

Abecker, A., Bernardi, A., Hinkerlmann, K., Kuhn, O., and Sintek, M. 1998. Towards a technology for organizational memories. *IEEE Intelligent Systems and Their Applications*, 13(3) (May/June).

Abecker, A., Decker, S., and Maurer, F. 2000. Organizational memory and knowledge management. *Information Systems Frontiers*, 2(3–4), 251–252.

Ackerman, M., and Halverson, C. 2000. Reexamining organizational memory. *Communications of the ACM*, 43(1), 59–64.

Becerra-Fernandez, I. 1998. Corporate memory project. Final Report, NASA grant No. NAG10–0232, 12–25.

Becerra-Fernandez, I. 1999. Searchable answer generating environment (SAGE): A knowledge management system for searching for experts in Florida. In *Proceedings of the Twelfth Annual International Florida Artificial Intelligence Research Symposium*, ed. A.N. Kumar and I. Russell. Orlando, Florida, May.

Becerra-Fernandez, I. 2000a. The role of artificial intelligence technologies in the implementation of people-finder knowledge management systems. *Knowledge-Based Systems*, 13(5) (October).

Becerra-Fernandez, I. 2000b. Facilitating the online search of experts at NASA using Expert Seeker People-Finder. In *Proceedings of the Third International Conference on Practical Aspects of Knowledge Management*, ed. U. Reimer. Basel, Switzerland.

Becerra-Fernandez, I. 2001. Locating expertise at NASA—Developing a tool to leverage human capital. *Knowledge Management Review*, 4(4), 34–37.

Becerra-Fernandez, I. 2006. Searching for experts on the Web: A review of contemporary expertise locator systems. *ACM Transactions on Internet Technology*, 6(4), 333–355.

Becerra-Fernandez, I., and Sabherwal R. 2005. Knowledge management at NASA–Kennedy Space Center. *International Journal of Knowledge and Learning*, 1(1/2), 159–170.

Becerra-Fernandez, I., and Sabherwal R. 2008. Individual, group, and organizational learning: A knowledge management perspective. In *Knowledge management: An evolutionary view, advances in management information systems*, vol. 12, ed. I. Becerra-Fernandez and D. Leidner, 13–39. Armonk, NY: M.E. Sharpe.

Becerra-Fernandez, I., Cousins, K., and Weber, R. 2007a. Nomadic context-aware knowledge management systems: Applications, challenges, and research problems. *International Journal of Mobile Learning and Organisation*, 1(2), 103–121.

Becerra-Fernandez, I., Del Alto, M., and Stewart, H. 2006. A case study of Web-based collaborative decision support at NASA. *International Journal of e-Collaboration*, 2(3), 49–63.

Becerra-Fernandez, I., Del Alto, M., and Stewart, H. 2007b. The launch of Web-based collaborative decision support at NASA. In *E-collaboration in modern organizations: Initiating and managing distributed projects*, ed. N. Kock, 113–125. Hershey, PA: Information Science Reference.

Becerra-Fernandez, I., Wang, T., Agha, G., and Sin, T. 2005. Actor model and knowledge management systems: Social interaction as a framework for knowledge integration. *Lecture Notes in Computer Science*, 3782, 19–31.

Bobrow, D., and Whalen, J. 2002. Community knowledge sharing in practice: The eureka story. *Journal of the Society for Organizational Learning*, 4(2), 47–59.

Carayannis, E., and Laporte, B. 2002. By decree or by choice? A case study-implementing knowledge management and sharing at the education sector of the World Bank Group. Stock No. 37206. http://www.worldbank.org/reference/ (accessed August 19, 2008).

Chedid, M., and Teixeira, L. 2017. The knowledge management culture: An exploratory study in academic context. In *Enhancing academic research with knowledge management principles*, ed. D. Deshpande, N. Bhosale, and R. Londhe, 1–24. IGI Global. https://doi.org/10.4018/978-1-5225-2489-2.ch002.

Chen, D., and Dahlman, C. 2006. The knowledge economy, the KAM methodology, and World Bank operations. Stock No. 37256. http://www.worldbank.org/reference/ (accessed August 19, 2008).

Davenport, T., and Hansen, M. 1998. *Knowledge management at Andersen Consulting*. Case No. 9-499-032. Boston: Harvard Business School Press.

Davenport, T., and Prusak, L. 1998. *Working knowledge: How organizations manage what they know.* Boston: Harvard Business School Press.

Dellow, J. 2004. Success at Ernst & Young's center for business knowledge: Online collaboration tools, knowledge managers, and a cooperative culture. In *Knowledge management tools and techniques*, ed. M. Rao. London: Elsevier.

Dignum, V. 2002. A knowledge sharing model for peer collaboration in the non-life insurance domain. In *Proceedings of the 1st German Workshop on Experience Management*, ed. M. Minor and S. Staab. Berlin, Germany.

Disterer, G. 2002. Management of project knowledge and experiences. *Journal of Knowledge Management*, 6(5), 512–520.

Frey, R.S. 2002. Small business knowledge management success story—This stuff really works! *Knowledge and Process Management*, 9(3), 172–177.

Frey, R.S. 2008. *Successful proposal strategies for small businesses: Using knowledge management to win government, private-sector, and international contracts.* Boston: Artech House.

Giles, C., Bollacker, K., and Lawrence, S. 1998. CiteSeer: An automatic citation indexing system. In *Proceedings of the ACM Conference on Digital Libraries*. New York: Association for Computing Machinery.

Goggins, S., Mascaro, C., and Mascaro, S. 2012. Relief work after the 2010 Haiti earthquake: Leadership in an online resource coordination network. *In Proceedings of the ACM 2012 Conference on Computer Supported Cooperative Work*, 57–66, Seattle, Washington, February.

Gongla, P., and Rizutto, C. 2001. Evolving communities of practice: IBM global services experience. *IBM Systems Journal*, 4(4), 842–862.

Gordon, 2010. Innovation from field observation—The Xerox eureka story, http://helixcomm erce.blogspot.com/2010/02/innovation-from-field-observation-xerox.html (accessed December 30, 2013).

Grove, M., and Schain, A. 2008. Semantic Web use cases and case studies. W3C Semantic Web. http://www.w3.0rg/2001/sw/sweo/public/UseCases/ (accessed September 12, 2008).

Gruninger, M., and Lee, J. 2002. Ontology applications and design. *Communications of the ACM*, 45(2), 39–41.

Guarino, N., and Welty, C. 2002. Evaluating ontological decisions with Ontoclean. *Communications of the ACM*, 45(2), 61–65.

Hastings, R, 2009, *Groupware Library Technology Reports*, 45(4), 28–30.

Kiani, K., Chilana, P., Bunt A., Grossman, T., and Fitzmaurice, G. 2020. *"I would just ask someone": Learning feature-rich design software in the modern workplace.* 2020 IEEE Symposium on Visual Languages and Human-Centric Computing (VL/HCC), Dunedin, New Zealand, 1–10, doi:10.1109/VL/HCC50065.2020.9127288.

Khun, O., and Abecker, A. 1997. Corporate memories for knowledge management in industrial practice: Prospects and challenges. *Journal of Universal Computer Science*, 3(8), 929–954.

Lesser, E., and Storck, J. 2001. Communities of practice and organizational performance. *IBM Systems Journal*, 40(4), 831–841.

McDermott, R. 2000. Community development as a natural step. *Knowledge Management Review* (November/December).

Microsoft Developer Network. 2009. MSDN library. http://msdn.microsoft.com/en-us/library/default.aspx.

Mitchell, M. 2001. Share and share alike. *Darwin Magazine* (February).

National Governors Association (NGA Center). 2013. http://www.nga.org/cms/center (accessed December 30, 2013).

New Zealand Mountain Safety Council (NZMSC). 2013. http://www.incidentreport.org.nz NID_Report_2012.pdf (accessed December 30, 2013).

O'Leary, D.E. 1999. Knowledge Management for best practices. *Intelligence*, 10(4), 12–21.

Putrapratama, Y, Adjandra, W., Wiraguna, A., Sensuse, D., and Safitri, N. 2021. *Knowledge reuse evaluation in software development: A case study on a startup company.* Sixth International Conference on Informatics and Computing (ICIC), Jakarta, Indonesia, 1–7, doi:10.1109/ICIC54025.2021.9632904.

Rampisela, T., Elisabeth, D., and Sensuse, D. 2020. *Characteristics of expertise locator system in academia: A systematic literature review.* 2020 International Seminar on Intelligent Technology and Its Applications (ISITIA), Surabaya, Indonesia, 186–193, doi:10.1109/ISITIA49792.2020.9163671.

Roberts-Witt, S. 2002. A "eureka!" moment at Xerox. *PC Magazine* (March).

Sandino, T., and Hull, O. 2018. Knowledge sharing at REMA 1000 (A), Case 9–118–072, Harvard Business School Publishing.

Secchi, P., Ciaschi, R., and Spence, D. 1999. A concept for an ESA lessons learned system. In *Proceedings of Alerts and LL: An effective way to prevent failures and problems* (Technical Report WPP-167), ed. P. Secchi. Noordwijk, The Netherlands: ESTEC.

Singley, K., Lai, J., Kuang, L., and Tang, J. 2008. *Blue reach: Harnessing synchronous chat to support expertise sharing in a large organization.* Conference on Human Factors in Computing Systems (CHI), Florence, Italy, April.

Telligent. n.d. Telligent.com.

U.S. Department of Energy. 2009. Chemical occurrences. Office of Health, Safety, and Security Web site. http://www.hss.energy.gov/HealthSafety/WSHP/chem_safety/chemstart.html.

U.S. Department of Transportation. 2009. Best practices procurement manual. Grants and Financing, Federal Transit Administration website. http://www.fta.dot.gov/funding/thirdpartyprocurement/grants_financing_6037.html.

Weber, R. 2007. Addressing failure factors in knowledge management. *Electronic Journal of Knowledge Management*, 5(3), 333–346.

Weber, R., Aha, D.W., and Becerra-Fernandez, I. 2001. Intelligent lessons learned systems. *International Journal of Expert Systems Research and Applications*, 20(1), 17–34.

Weber, R., and Aha, D. 2003. Intelligent delivery of military lessons learned. *Decision Support Systems*, 34(3), 287–304.

Weber, R.O., Morelli, M.L., Atwood, M.E., and Proctor, J.M. 2006. Designing a knowledge management approach for the CAMRA community of science. In *Proceedings of the Sixth International Conference on Practical Aspects of Knowledge Management*, LNAI vol. 4333, ed. U. Reimer and D. Karagiannis, 315–325. Heidelberg: Springer-Berlin.

Weiss, L., Capozzi, M., and Prusak, L. 2004. Learning from the internet giants. *MIT Sloan Management Review*, 45(4), 79–84.

Wiig, K. 1993. *Thinking about thinking—How people and organizations create, represent, and use knowledge.* Arlington, TX: Schema Press.

Workflow Management Coalition. 1999. WFMC-TC-1011, Issue 2. Terminology and glossary. http://www.huihoo.org/jfox/jfowfbw/specfication/03.Terminology.glossary.pdf.

Wright, A., and Spencer, W. 1999. *The National Security Agency (NSA) networked knowledge and skills management system.* Presentation at Delphi's International Knowledge Management Summit (IKMS), San Diego, CA.

Yiman-Seid, D., and Kobsa, A. 2003. Expert finding systems for organizations: Problem and domain analysis and the DEMOIR approach. *Journal of Organizational Computing and Electronic Commerce*, 13(1), 1–24.

Yoo, Y., and Ginzberg, M. 2003. *One size doesn't fit all: knowledge management systems and knowledge sharing practices in global learning organizations.* Case Western University.

9 Knowledge Discovery Systems

Systems that Create Knowledge

In the last chapter, we discussed knowledge sharing systems. In this chapter we introduce **knowledge discovery systems**. Knowledge discovery dates back to the time before the existence of the word "researcher." Certainly, popular lore contends that Galileo discovered knowledge while dropping objects from the Tower of Pisa and observing the time each took to reach the ground. The Wright brothers, Alexander Graham Bell, Thomas Edison, and thousands of other, less well-known researchers and inventors throughout history have discovered knowledge that has helped our understanding of how things work in nature. Cumulatively, their contributions have shaped our present lives in many ways. But how is knowledge discovered? For the purposes of this chapter, we focus on two significant ways:

1 Synthesis of new knowledge through socialization with other knowledgeable persons; and
2 Discovery by finding interesting patterns in observations, typically embodied in explicit data.

As we saw in Chapter 4, knowledge discovery systems support the development of new tacit or explicit knowledge from data and information or from the synthesis of prior knowledge. Knowledge discovery systems rely on mechanisms and technologies that can support the combination and the socialization processes. For the purpose of the discussions in this chapter we don't distinguish between knowledge creation and knowledge discovery, and we consider both to describe the same thing: the innovation and advancement of knowledge. We do distinguish knowledge creation from knowledge capture, the latter activity presumes that knowledge has already been created and may exist tacitly in the minds of experts, which was the topic of Chapter 7. Knowledge creation assumes knowledge didn't exist before the activity that catalyzed the innovation.

You may recall from Chapter 4 that **knowledge discovery mechanisms** involve socialization processes. In the case of tacit knowledge, **socialization** facilitates the synthesis of tacit knowledge across individuals and the integration of multiple streams for the creation of new knowledge, usually through joint activities rather than written or verbal instructions. For example, one mechanism for socialization is research conferences, which enable researchers to develop new insights through sharing their own findings. Also, when colleagues brainstorm and do **"back-of-the-napkin" diagrams**, leading to the discovery of new knowledge that didn't exist individually before the group activity, knowledge is created or discovered by the team. We expand on the topic of socialization as a mechanism for knowledge discovery in the next section.

DOI: 10.4324/9781003364375-11

On the other hand, technologies can support knowledge discovery systems by facilitating combination processes. New explicit knowledge is discovered through **combination**, wherein the multiple bodies of explicit knowledge (and/or data and/or information) are synthesized to create new, more complex sets of explicit knowledge. Existing explicit knowledge may be **re-contextualized** to produce new explicit knowledge, for example during the creation of a new proposal to a client that is based upon existing prior client proposals. Knowledge discovery mechanisms and **technologies** can facilitate socialization and combination within or across organizations (Bratianu 2015). **Knowledge creation systems** can be enabled by the use of data mining technologies, such as those discussed later in this chapter. These may be used to uncover new relationships among explicit data, which in turn can serve to develop models that can predict or categorize highly valuable assets in business intelligence.

Mechanisms to Discover Knowledge: Using Socialization to Create New Tacit Knowledge

Socialization, as defined in Chapter 4, is the synthesis of tacit knowledge across individuals, usually through joint activities rather than written or verbal instructions. Socialization enables the discovery of tacit knowledge through joint activities between masters and apprentices, or between researchers at an academic conference. Many Japanese companies, for example Honda, encourage socialization through "**brainstorming camps**" to resolve problems faced in R&D projects (Nonaka and Takeuchi 1995). The format for these meetings is outside the workplace, much like the ones spearheaded at Westinghouse, as presented in Box 9.1. The idea is to encourage participants to meet outside their normal work environment, perhaps at a resort, where they are able to discuss their problems in an informal and relaxed environment. These meetings serve not only as a medium for creativity to flourish but also to share knowledge and build trust among the group members. Socialization as a means of knowledge discovery is a common practice at many organizations, pursued either by accident or on purpose.

Box 9.1 The Westinghouse Innovation Group

George Westinghouse, considered by many as one of the world's leading inventor-engineers, founded Westinghouse Electric Corporation in 1886 and eventually 59 other companies, receiving over 100 patents for his work. Westinghouse Electric Corporation established one of the nation's first industrial research laboratories in 1886 with the invention of the transformer, which enabled the transmission of electricity over large distances by increasing the voltage of alternating current electricity.

The company had established a reputation for developing advanced technology products. Its Transmission and Distribution (T&D) business unit was a relatively small segment of the corporation's product range and sales volume and was comprised of several product divisions. These divisions were fairly independent. They manufactured products for electric utilities and large industrial complexes, and each division addressed different (noncompeting) product lines within the same industries. The products ranged from the world's largest power transformers, power circuit breakers, and electronic voltage regulators for large electrical generators all the way to the more mundane pole-mounted transformers and standard house meters.

In 1979, the Westinghouse T&D Business Unit (comprising all the divisions that built and marketed products for the T&D market segment) realized that its product offerings were rather mature and in serious need of upgrading. The president of the T&D Business Unit, in cooperation with the Westinghouse Headquarters technical staff, instituted and sponsored the T&D Innovation Group to foster innovation and creativity in its technical offerings. Its mission was to creatively apply new ideas to solve old problems, and more specifically, to inject a measure of high technology into its product line. Furthermore, through this group, it sought to "upgrade the competence" (that is, enhance the knowledge) of the technical staff at their home divisions. One senior engineer from each T&D division was selected to participate in this twelve-member group. In addition, the sponsoring manager from corporate headquarters, who arranged the meetings, suggested the agenda, and provided guidance to the group and also served as the communication link to the T&D president and his staff. Each selected engineer would communicate directly with his own division general manager, bypassing the three or four hierarchical levels in the chain of command. This communication involved briefing the general manager on the proceedings of the group, as well as obtaining from him any problems that he would like to have addressed by the group.

The T&D Innovation Group meetings took place once per quarter and lasted for two-and-a-half days (and three nights), typically in a resort hotel near one of the participating division headquarters or factories that served as the host for that meeting. This location ensured freedom from interruptions from the members' daily responsibilities. While some of the problems to be addressed were defined by the business unit staff or the division general managers, others originated within the group itself. In the early meetings, most of the problems addressed were of a technical nature. As the group matured and the operating procedures became more streamlined, the discussions shifted to problems of an organizational nature. The group always addressed each problem using the technique of creative brainstorming (described below), until a consensus was reached on a set of recommendations for the individual presenting the problem, typically during the same two- or three-hour meeting.

The T&D Innovation Group continued to meet for three years before reorganizations, divestitures, promotions, transfers, retirements, and such took a toll on those individuals who had a vested interest in this concept. Nevertheless, in its relatively short existence, the group succeeded in generating a few dozen patent disclosures many of which later became valuable corporate patents. In addition, several products were upgraded as a direct result of the group's work. Moreover, several recommendations were made to senior management, which were either implemented, or at the very least, seriously considered. Lastly, the T&D Innovation Group had some success in injecting advanced technology into the technical staff of the divisions.

In September 2022, the company signed an agreement to sell the Power Delivery business (then BHI Energy Co) to United Utility Services. The Power Delivery business provides industry-leading specialty services in design, construction, maintenance, and storm restoration to the T&D end markets.

Note: We acknowledge Avelino Gonzalez of the University of Central Florida for this box.

Source: Business Wire (2022)

Simple discussions over lunch among friends discussing their daily problems often lead to knowledge discovery. Cocktail napkins have been known to contain descriptions of critical new ideas. Organizations interested in fostering discovery of knowledge take steps to formalize this socialization among their employees. This process promotes innovation and creativity, which in turn leads to advances in knowledge. For example, Wei et al. (2022) explore how mentoring relates to tacit-to-tacit knowledge transfer among middle school novice teachers in China, and that job crafting (which includes both task crafting and skill crafting) help mediate this knowledge transfer. Task crafting refers to altering the form or number of activities one engages in while doing the job, while skill crafting is about improving strategies or techniques of teaching (Wei et al. 2022). Therefore, for mentoring to actually effect tacit-to-tacit knowledge transfer, novice teachers interacted with their mentors and engaged in continuous improvement of their teaching techniques.

The following boxes describe formal mechanisms instituted by two major U.S. corporations, starting back before knowledge management had become a household word. Box 9.2 describes the use of the **creative brainstorming** process, which involves a customer (the person with the problem or need), a **facilitator** (the person controlling the process), and the **innovators** (who will brainstorm solutions to the customer's problem or need). The process begins by having the facilitator establish the ground rules, which are not many. The main one is that one person speaks at a time and there are no such things as crazy, dumb, wild, or silly ideas. The latter ensures the creative freedom of the innovators to generate solutions, which may at first glance appear silly or wild. The customer then takes her turn explaining the problem briefly, without discussing what has already been tried. Then the main part of the process begins. The innovators voice ideas out loud to the facilitator. These ideas are described in one or two sentences. The facilitator displays them each in a way that is visible to the participants (a flipchart, a whiteboard, a computer with a projection device, etc.). This process runs unabated until the ideas cease to flow (typically, 30 to 45 minutes depending on the size of the group and the complexity of the problem). The customer is then once again given the floor and asked to select a few (three to five) ideas that appeal to her. The appealing ideas are then further examined in order to make them viable. Lastly, those ideas showing the greatest potential are even further examined and the potential drawbacks are identified. The process ends at this point, and the customer departs with some innovative potential solutions to her problem. It should be mentioned that the problem does not need to be technical or scientific in nature. Any kind of problem is eligible for this approach.

Box 9.2 Creative Brainstorming

Westinghouse Electric Corporation was a major manufacturer of home appliances before White Consolidated Industries acquired the product line in 1974 (now called White-Westinghouse). Once upon a time, they built washing machines that stood on four small metal legs on each corner at the bottom of the box-like structure that we commonly recognize as a washing machine. The legs were fitted with built-in screws to stabilize the machine during operation and avoid vibrations. These small legs protruded from the basic box-like design of the washing machine. Unfortunately, when these appliances were shipped in boxes, their movement (and often dropping of the boxes from trucks) caused these small legs to bend. Bent legs destabilized the washing machine and caused annoying as well as damaging vibrations when the machine was in operation. This resulted in significant warranty expenses to Westing-house when a serviceman had to be called to fix the bent legs.

The manager of engineering at the product division that built the washing machines was told to solve the problem. He assembled his best design engineers and told them to go into a room and not come out until they had solved the problem. The lore goes that the engineers labored night and day for three days and finally emerged from the room proudly with a new design that greatly strengthened the legs by adding steel thickness and additional bracing. The manager looked at the solution and saw that this would add significant cost to the product, which was deemed unacceptable. The leader of the group, angry that their three days of captivity had gone for naught screamed, "What do you want us to do, stand on our heads?" Immediately, another member of the group, one who apparently had gotten some sleep the night before, immediately said "I've got it! We ship the washing machines upside down." They proceeded to do an analysis of whether the top of the box could withstand the shocks and whether there were any components that would be damaged by the upside-down shipment. They found out there were none. The problem was solved without adding any cost to the product.

Note: We acknowledge Avelino Gonzalez of the University of Central Florida for this box.

The process addresses two important aspects of problem-solving and decision-making. One is to identify the real problem. In many situations, problem-solvers are not addressing the real problem but a perceived one. Even if the perceived problem is solved, it does not address the real problem. Group thinking may be able to identify the real problem and address it. The second aspect is what is referred to as **lateral thinking**. This is when an entirely different approach is taken to solve a problem. Identifying wild, crazy, or silly ideas may trigger ideas (new knowledge) in the other innovators that may not be wild, crazy, or silly and which may actually solve the problem.

Box 9.2 describes an anecdotal experience of the successful application of the collaboration process fostered in creative brainstorming. This box shows that the engineering task force was solving the wrong problem. The problem was in the shipment of the washing machines, not in their design. The legs were well designed for their purpose. There was no need to design them for anything else. Furthermore, it shows how seemingly silly ideas can become realistic and provide a way to solve the problem in unintended ways. This, of course, is new knowledge!

In the next section, we describe how technologies can support the discovery of new knowledge.

Technologies to Discover Knowledge: Using Data Mining to Create New Explicit Knowledge

The technologies that enable the discovery of new knowledge uncover the relationships from explicit information. Knowledge discovery technologies can be very powerful for organizations wishing to obtain an advantage over their competition. Recall that **knowledge discovery in databases (KDD)** is the process of finding and interpreting patterns from data, involving the application of algorithms to interpret the patterns generated by these algorithms (Fayyad et al. 1996). Another name for KDD is **data mining (DM)**. Although the majority of the practitioners use KDD and DM interchangeably, for some KDD is defined to involve the whole process of knowledge discovery including the application of DM techniques.

Although data mining systems have made a significant contribution in scientific fields for years, for example in breast cancer diagnosis (Kovalerchuk et al. 2000), perhaps the recent proliferation of e-commerce applications providing reams of hard data ready for analysis presents us with an excellent opportunity to make profitable use of these techniques. The increasing availability of computing power and integrated DM software tools, which are easier than ever to use, have contributed to the increasing popularity of DM applications to businesses. Many success stories have been published in the literature describing how data mining techniques have been used to create new knowledge. Here we briefly describe some of the more mature and/or specifically relevant applications of data mining to knowledge management for business.

Over the last decade, data mining techniques have been applied across business problems.[1] Examples of such applications are as follows:

1 *Marketing*: **Predictive DM techniques**, like **artificial neural networks (ANN)**, have been used for target marketing including market segmentation. This allows the marketing departments using this approach to segment customers according to basic demographic characteristics such as gender, age group, and so forth, as well as their purchasing patterns. They have also been used to improve direct marketing campaigns through an understanding of which customers are likely to respond to new products based on their previous consumer behavior.

2 *Retail*: DM methods have likewise been used for sales forecasting. These take into consideration multiple market variables, such as customer profiling based on their purchasing habits. Techniques like **market basket analysis** also help uncover which products are likely to be purchased together. Box 9.3 describes how Amazon takes advantage of this technique to improve the user's shopping experience and increase their sales.

3 *Banking*: Trading and financial forecasting have also proven to be excellent applications for DM techniques. These are used to determine derivative securities pricing, futures price forecasting, and stock performance. Inferential DM techniques have also been successful in developing scoring systems to identify credit risk and fraud. An area of recent interest is attempting to model the relationships among corporate strategy, financial health, and corporate performance.

4 *Insurance*: DM techniques have been used for segmenting customer groups to determine premium pricing and to predict claim frequencies. **Clustering techniques** have also been applied to detecting claim fraud and to aid in customer retention.

5 *Telecommunications*: Predictive DM techniques, like artificial neural networks, have been used mostly to attempt to reduce **churn**, that is, to predict when customers will attrition to a competitor. In addition, predictive techniques like neural networks can be used to predict the conditions that may cause a customer to return. Finally, market basket analysis has been used to identify which telecommunication products customers are likely to purchase together.

6 *Operations management*: Neural networks have been used for planning and scheduling, project management, and quality control.

Box 9.3 Amazon Making Use of Market Basket Analysis

Amazon.com takes advantage of market basket analysis techniques to provide its customers with high quality recommendations of products that they're most likely to buy. How does it work? Amazon uses advanced algorithms to analyze its customer's activity once they logon to their website. The company analyzes what items the customer views, searches for, purchases and rates, as well as the shopping cart activity. For example, Amazon keeps track of any items added and removed from the shopping carts as well as those left unpurchased. By doing so, the company is able to optimize the shopping experience and customize each webpage as if it were personally tailored for its customers.

After processing all of this data with its market-basket algorithms, Amazon can then combine this information from each customer's current and past shopping sessions with that of other customers. The company's patented algorithm, *item-to-item collaborative filtering*, matches each of the customer's purchased and rated items to similar items, then combines those similar items into a recommendation list. By leveraging this data, Amazon is able to present its customers with additional purchasing recommendations that are most likely to be of interest and are most likely to lead to a sale.

In the market-basket analysis report, vendors have the option to apply various filters like category, subcategory, brand, and select a specific time period. Once vendors set the filters, a table is generated, presenting valuable information. Within the chosen time frame, the report displays the top three products most frequently purchased together with the vendor's product. This breakdown provides insights into what other items were present in the customers' shopping carts during checkout. The metrics used in the report are further elucidated below.

The Cart Analysis report enables vendors to discover product relationships and associations. Vendors in the marketplace can gain insights into what customers often purchase alongside their products and the percentage of these joint purchases. A small percentage (e.g., 1 percent) may indicate random purchases, so it's important to pay attention to these product connections. Sometimes, customers might buy unrelated items together, not directly linked to a vendor's product. Generally, a solid percentage guideline for meaningful relationships using market-basket analysis among products in the shopping cart is around 10 percent, but this should be considered in the context of critical content engagement.

Once vendors identify products frequently bought together, they can leverage this knowledge for combined product offers or cross-marketing strategies. For instance, if customers commonly purchase matching filter cartridges with a specific vendor's water filter, vendors can seek to bundle these items as a set for sale.

Additionally, the market basket analysis report can help optimize product targeting. Vendors can create a new Sponsored Products campaign, specifically targeting the products often bought together with special offerings. This can potentially lead to increased sales, as products may be seen more frequently in both paid and free placements on the product detail page, enhancing their visibility and appeal to customers. It can also increase sales through the display of items the customers who bought this item also bought.

The market-basket analysis report holds significant importance within Amazon Brand Analytics. Leveraging the data from this report effectively can lead to increased sales and added value for retail business. By understanding the product associations, vendors can make suitable product suggestions to potential customers, ultimately enhancing their shopping experience and driving more sales.

Sources: Fries (2021), Linden et al. (2003)

Diagnosis is a fertile ground for mining knowledge. Diagnostic examples typically abound in large companies with many installed systems and a wide network of service representatives. The incidents are typically documented well, and often in a highly structured form. Mining the incident database for common aspects in the behavior of particularly troublesome devices can be useful in predicting when they are likely to fail. Having this knowledge, the devices can be preventatively maintained in the short-range and designed or manufactured in a way to avoid the problem altogether in the long-term. Witten (2000) mentions a specific example where diagnostic rules were mined from 600 documented faults in rotating machinery (e.g., motors, generators) and compared to the same rules elicited from a diagnostic expert. It was found that the learned rules provided slightly better performance than the ones elicited from the expert.

In the electric utility business, neural networks have been used routinely to predict the energy consumption load in power systems. The load on a power system depends mostly on the weather. In hot weather areas, air conditioners during the summer represent the biggest load. In cold regions, it is the heating load in the winters. Knowing the weather forecast and how that maps to the expected load can help forecast the load for the next 24, 48, and 72 hours, and thereby place the appropriate generating capacity in readiness to provide the required energy. This is particularly important because efficient power stations cannot be turned on and off within minutes if the load is greater than expected. Nuclear power stations (the most efficient) take several days or weeks to place online from a cold state. Coal- or oil-fired stations (the next most efficient) take the better part of one day to do the same. Although other types of generating equipment can be turned quickly on and off, they are highly inefficient and costly to operate. Therefore, utilities greatly benefit if they can bring their efficient units online in anticipation of energy load increases, yet running them unnecessarily can also be expensive.

All major electric utilities have entire departments expressly dedicated to this load-forecasting function. The expected temperature is the most influential factor. However, other attributes such as the day of the week, the humidity, and wind speed have some influence as well. Data mining in this context consists of training neural networks to predict the energy load in a certain area for a specified period of time. This is considered supervised training. The relations are embedded in the weights computed by the training algorithm, typically the **back-propagation algorithm**. By mining a database containing actual recorded data on ambient temperatures, wind speed, humidity, day of the week (among others), and the actual power consumed per hour, the network can be trained. Then, the forecast values can be fed the same attributes and it can predict the load on a per hour basis for 24, 48, and 72 hours. Positive results in this arena have led the Electric Power Research Institute to offer neural network-based tools to perform this specific function.

Witten (2000) describes a use of data mining for credit applications. In this project, a credit institution undertook a project in data mining to learn the characteristics of borrowers who defaulted on their loans in order to better identify those customers who are likely to default on their loans. Using 1,000 examples and 20 attributes, a set of rules was mined from the data, which resulted in a 66 percent successful prediction rate. Back in the mid-1990s, 95 percent of the top banks in the United States were already utilizing data mining techniques (Smith and Gupta 2000). For example, back in the mid-1990s, Bank of Montreal was facing increased competition and the need to **target-sell** to its large customer base. Earlier telemarketing attempts had proven unsuccessful, therefore the bank embarked on an attempt to develop a knowledge discovery system to determine a customer's likelihood of purchasing new products. As a result, the bank could segment its customers for more targeted product marketing campaigns (Stevens 2001).

A more recent example by Li et al. (2012) describes a use of data mining for identifying fraudulent bank accounts. In this project, the authors collected transaction data from 10,216 accounts from a bank in Taiwan. They analyzed metrics such as transaction type, transaction time, on-line banking activity, and transaction amount and found that the system had an effectiveness of about 65 percent.

Nevertheless, the most common and useful applications are in product marketing and sales and in business operations. Every time someone purchases a product, a sales record is kept. Often, these records contain demographic information on the buyer and other times not. In any case, obtaining a **personal profile** of the purchasers of the product can serve to better direct the product to this cross-section of consumers or expand its appeal to other cross-sections not currently purchasing the product. This is true for not only hard products but also for services such as mobile services, Internet service providers, banking and financial services, and others.

For example, Proflowers is a Web-based flower retailer. Flowers perish quickly; therefore, Proflowers must level its inventory as the day progresses in order to adequately serve its customers. Proflowers has achieved better management of its customer traffic via inventory optimization that downplays the better-selling products on their Web-storefront while highlighting the slower-selling ones. Based on their analysis of Web purchases, Proflowers is able to change their website throughout the day and therefore effectively attract attention to lower-selling items through their website (Stevens 2001). Proflowers has been innovative in their use of Customer Relationship Management (CRM) software. By connecting growers to customers via the Proflowers website and eliminating the middleman, Proflowers is able to guarantee fresh flowers to its customers. Their CRM software is highly scalable and flexible because it's easily able to communicate with its suppliers' systems to ensure fast and accurate order processing (PR Newswire 2012).

Another example is eBags, a Web-based retailer of suitcases, wallets, and related products. Through the use of **Web content mining**, the company is able to determine which Web pages result in higher customer purchases. This information is used to adequately determine how Web content can drive the sales process. Finally, eBags uses the results from their Web content mining to help them personalize their retailing Web pages on the fly, based on customer's buying preferences and even geographic location. For example, capturing the Web visitor's zip code could be used to infer how affluent the online shopper is. If she comes from an affluent neighborhood, the website may feature designer items. If the online shopper comes from a zip code marked by a large number of apartments, discounted offers would be made prominent in the user's view of the Web store (Stevens 2001).

Data mining techniques have also been used in areas as diverse as facilitating the classification of a country's investing risk based on a variety of factors and identifying the factors associated with a country's competitiveness (Becerra-Fernandez et al. 2002). For example, let us look at Box 9.4, which shows how DHL uses data mining techniques. In Box 9.5, we describe the role that data mining can play in detecting money laundering and terrorist financing.

The KDD process is viewed as both an interactive and iterative process that turns data into information and information into business knowledge. Next, we discuss the steps in the KDD process.

Box 9.4 Data Mining by DHL

Throughout the package logistics process, DHL gathers ambient temperature data, which is then stored in a database. Before using a data mining tool, retrieving and preparing this data was a time-consuming task, taking up to a week to complete. The process involved cleaning the data, transferring it to an Excel file, and creating pivot tables to share with DHL's team. Recognizing the need for a more efficient solution, DHL sought a business analytics tool to transform this data into actionable insights.

The data mining tool provides DHL with several benefits:

1   Actionable information: Thanks to the data mining tool, DHL has the flexibility to merge data in any way they desire. By importing all of their data into the data mining tool, they can easily manipulate it as per its own requirements. The data mining tool significantly enhances their data handling capabilities relative to their previous methods.
2   Visualization: The interface is highly intuitive, offering a comprehensive overview of the needed information, both at a high-level and in-depth.
3   Troubleshooting issues: Using the data mining tool, DHL can now identify and pinpoint issues that were previously hidden from view. For instance, they can quickly spot recurring problems with a specific product on a particular lane at a certain station. The creation of a visualization heat map in the data mining tool allows them to gain clarity and understand the specific issues in ways that were not readily available before.
4   Better customer engagement: The data mining tool empowers DHL to provide its customers with reports and insights regarding their shipments that were previously unavailable. DHL's employees can now clearly understand the story behind the data and effectively communicate it to its valued customers.Source: DOMO (n.d.)

---

preferred by terrorists and money launderers because they avoid the use of financial institutions, involve purchasing products at market price for cash and then exporting to a colluding importer at below market prices which resells the goods for their true value. All of these activities can translate to customs fraud, income tax evasion, and money laundering (Zdanowicz 2004, 2009).

A data mining study of the 2001 U.S. import and export transactions produced by the U.S. Department of Commerce reported suspicious prices that translated to overvalued imports and undervalued exports to the tune of US$156.22 billion in 2001. Money laundered from the United States to countries appearing in the U.S. State Department Al Qaeda watch list was estimated to be around US$4.27 billion that same year (Zdanowicz 2004, 2009). In this respect, data mining is without a doubt critical in order to win the war against terrorism. More recently, neural networks have been shown to be effective in detecting money laundering and terrorism financing (Rocha-Salazar et al. 2021).

Sources: Compiled from Rocha-Salazar et al. (2021); Zdanowicz (2004, 2009)

Designing the Knowledge Discovery System

Discovering knowledge can be different things for different organizations. Some organizations have large databases, while others may have small ones. The problems faced by the users of data mining systems may also be quite different. Therefore, the developers of DM software face a difficult process when attempting to build tools that are considered generalizable across the entire spectrum of applications and corporate cultures. Early efforts to apply data mining in business operations faced the need to learn, primarily via trial and error, how to develop an effective approach to DM. In fact, as early adopters of DM observed an exploding interest in the application of techniques, the need to develop a standard process model for KDD became apparent. This standard should be well-reasoned, nonproprietary, and freely available to all DM practitioners.

In 1999, a consortium of vendors and early adopters of DM applications for business operations—consisting of Daimler-Chrysler (then Daimler-Benz AG, Germany), NCR Systems Engineering Copenhagen (Denmark), SPSS/Integral Solutions Ltd. (England), and OHRA Verzegeringen en Bank Groep B.V. (The Netherlands)—developed a set of specifications called **Cross-Industry Standard Process for Data Mining (CRISP-DM)** (Brachman and Anand 1996; Chapman et al. 2000; Edelstein 1999; Hotz 2023). CRISP-DM is an industry consortium that developed an industry-neutral and tool-neutral process for data mining. CRISP-DM defines a hierarchical process model that defines the basic steps of data mining for knowledge discovery as follows:

Business Understanding

The first requirement for knowledge discovery is to **understand the business problem**. In other words, to obtain the highest benefit from data mining, there must be a clear statement of the business objectives. For example, a business goal could be "to increase the response rate of direct mail marketing." An economic justification based on the return of investment of a more effective direct mail marketing may be necessary to justify the expense of the data mining study. This step also involves an assessment of the current situation, for example:

> The current response rate to direct mail is 1 percent. Results of the study showed that using 35 percent of the current sample population for direct mail (the one that is likely to buy the product), a marketing campaign could reach 80 percent of the prospective buyers.

In other words, the majority of the people in a marketing campaign who receive a target mail do not purchase the product. This example illustrates how you could effectively isolate 80 percent of the prospective buyers by mailing only to 35 percent of the customers in a sample marketing campaign database. Identifying the most likely prospective buyers from the sample and targeting the direct mail to those customers could save the organization significant costs, mainly those associated with mailing a piece to 65 percent of the customers who are the least likely to buy the new product offering. The maximum profit occurs from mailing to the 35 percent of the customers that are most likely to buy the new product. Finally, this step also includes the specification of a project plan for the DM study.

Data Understanding

One of the most important tenets in data engineering is "know thy data." Knowing the data well can permit the designers to tailor the algorithm or tools used for data mining to their specific problem. This maximizes the chances for success as well as the efficiency and effectiveness of the knowledge discovery system. This step, together with preparation and modeling, consumes most of the resources required for the study. In fact, data understanding and preparation may take from 50 percent to 80 percent of the time and effort required for the entire knowledge discovery process. Typically, data collection for the data mining project requires the creation of a database, although a spreadsheet may be just as adequate. Data mining doesn't require data collection in a **data warehouse** and in the case the organization is equipped with a data warehouse, it's best not to attempt to manipulate the data warehouse directly for the purpose of the DM study. Furthermore, the structure of the data warehouse may not lend itself to the type of data manipulation required. Finally, the construction of a data warehouse that integrates data from multiple sources into a single database is typically a huge endeavor that could extend a number of years and cost millions of dollars (Gray and Watson 1998). Most data mining tools enable the input data to take many possible formats, and the data transformation is transparent to the user. The steps required for the data understanding process are as follows:

1 Data Collection

This step defines the data sources for the study, including the use of external public data (e.g., real estate tax folio) and proprietary databases (e.g., contact information for businesses in a particular zip code). The **data collection** report typically includes the following: a description of the data source, data owner, who (organization and person) maintains the data, cost (if purchased), storage format and structure, size (e.g., in records, rows, etc.), physical storage characteristics, security requirements, restrictions on use, and privacy requirements.

2 Data Description

This step describes the contents of each file or table. Some of the important items in this report are number of fields (columns) and percent of records missing. Also, for each field or column: data type, definition, description, source, unit of measure, number of unique values, list and range of values. Also, some other valuable specifics are about how the data were collected and the time frame when the data were collected. Finally, in the case of relational databases, it is important to know which attributes are the primary or foreign keys.

3 Data Quality and Verification

In general, good models require good data; therefore, the data must be correct and consistent. This step determines whether any data can be eliminated because of irrelevance or lack of quality. In addition, many data mining packages allow specifying which columns in a table will be ignored (for the same reasons) during the modeling phase. Furthermore, missing data can cause significant problems. Some data mining algorithms (e.g., C5.0) can handle the missing data problem by automatically massaging the data and using **surrogates** for the missing data points. Other algorithms may be sensitive to missing values. In that case, one approach would be to discard the data sample if some of the attributes or fields are missing which could cause a substantial loss of data. A better approach is to calculate a substitute value for the missing values. Substitute values could consist of the mode, median, or mean of the attribute variable depending on the data type.

4 Exploratory Analysis of the Data

Techniques such as visualization and online analytical processing (OLAP) enable preliminary data analysis. This step is necessary to develop a hypothesis of the problem to be studied and to identify the fields that are likely to be the best predictors. In addition, some values may need to be derived from the raw data, for example factors such as per capita income may be a more relevant factor to the model than the factor income.

Data Preparation

The steps for this task are:

1 Selection

This step requires the selection of the predictor variables and the **sample set**. Selecting the predictor variables is necessary because typically data mining algorithms don't work well if all the variables (fields or database columns) are considered as **potential predictors**. In essence, that's why data mining requires an understanding of the domain and the potential variables influencing the outcome in question. As a rule-of-thumb, the number of predictors (columns) must be smaller than the number of samples (rows) in the data set. In fact, the number of simple observations should be at least 10 to 25 times the number of predictors. As the number of predictors increases, the computational requirement to build the model also increases. Selecting the sample set is necessary because when the data set is large, a sample of the data set can be selected to represent the complete data set. In selecting the sample, attention must be paid to the constraints imposed by sampling theory in order for the sample to be representative of the complete data set.

2 Construction and Transformation of Variables

Often, new variables must be constructed to build effective models. Examples include ratios and combination of various fields. Furthermore, some algorithms, like market basket analysis, may require data to be transformed to categorical format (integer) when in fact the raw data exist in continuous form. This may require transformations that group values in ranges like *low, medium*, and *high*.

3 Data Integration

The data set for the data mining study may reside on multiple databases, which would need to be consolidated into one database. Data consolidation may require redefinition of some of the data fields to allow for consistency. For example, different databases may relate to the same customer with different names; for instance, one database may refer to the "National Aeronautics and Space Administration" while other database fields may just use "NASA". These incompatibilities must be reconciled prior to data integration.

4 Formatting

This step involves the reordering and reformatting of the data fields as required by the DM model.

Model Building and Validation

Building an accurate model is a trial-and-error process. The process often requires the data mining specialist to iteratively try several options until the best model emerges. Furthermore, different algorithms could be tried with the same data set and the results then compared to see which model yields the best results. For example, both neural network and **rule induction algorithms** could be applied to the same data set to develop a predictive model. The results from each algorithm could be compared for accuracy in their respective predictive quality. Following the model development, the models must be evaluated or validated. In constructing a model, a subset of the data is usually set aside for validation purposes. This means that the validation data set is not used to develop or train the model but to calculate the accuracy of predictive qualities of the model. The most popular validation technique is n-fold cross-validation, specifically ten-fold validation. The **ten-fold validation** divides the population of the validation data set into ten approximately equal-sized data sets and then uses each of the ten holdout sets a single time to evaluate the models developed with the remaining nine training sets. For each of the ten models (the last model includes using the whole data set) the accuracy is determined, and the overall model accuracy is determined as the average of each of the model samples.

Evaluation and Interpretation

Once the model is determined, the validation data set is fed through the model. Because the outcome for this data set is known, the predicted results are compared with the actual results in the validation data set. This comparison yields the accuracy of the model. As a rule-of-thumb, a model accuracy of around 50 percent would be insignificant because that would be the same accuracy as for a random occurrence.

Deployment

This step involves implementing the "live" model within an organization to aid the decision-making process. A valid model must also make sense in the real world, and a pilot implementation is always warranted prior to deployment. Also, following implementation it's important to continue to monitor how well the model predicts the outcomes and the benefits that this brings to the organization. For example, a clustering model may be deployed to identify fraudulent Medicare claims. When the model identifies potential instances of fraud, and these instances are validated as indeed fraudulent, the savings to the organization from the deployment of the model should be captured. These early successes will then act as champions and will result in continued implementation of knowledge discovery models within the organization.

Figure 9.1 summarizes the CRISP-DM process methodology. Figure 9.2 illustrates the iterative nature of the CRISP-DM process.

Business Understanding	Data Understanding	Data Preparation	Modelling	Evaluation	Deployment
Determine **Business Objectives** *Background* *Business Objectives* *Business Success* *Criteria*	**Initial Data Collection** *Intial Data Collection Report*	*Data Set* *Data Set Description*	**Generate Test Design** *Test Design*	**Evaluate Results** *Approved Models* *Asseement of Data Mining Results w.r.t.* *Business Success* *Criteria*	**Plan Deployment** *Deployment Plan*
Situation Assessment *Inventory of Resources* *Requirements* *Assumptions* *Constraints* *Risks and Comingencies* *Terminology* *Costs and Benefits*	**Data Description** *Data Description Report* **Data Quality** **Verification** *Data Quality Report* **Exploratory Analysis** *Exploratory Analysis Report*	**Selection** *Rationale for Inclusion / Exclusion* **Cleaning** *Data Cleaning Report* **Construction** *Derived Variables* *Generated Records* *Transformation*	**Build Model** *Parameter Settings* *Models* **Model Evaluation** *Model Description* *Assessment*	**Review Process** *Review of Process* **Determine Next Steps** *List of Possible Actions* *Decision*	**Produce Final Report** *Final Report* *Final Presentation* **Plan Monitoring and** **Maintenance** *Maintenance Plan* **Review Project** *Experience* *Documentation*
Determine **Data Mining Goal** *Data Mining Goals* *Data Mining Success* *Criteria* **Produce Project Plan** *Project Plan*		**Intergration** *Merging* *Aggregation* **Formatting** *Rearranging Attributes* *Reording Records* *Withing-Value* *Reformatting*			

Figure 9.1 CRISP-DM Data Mining Process Methodology

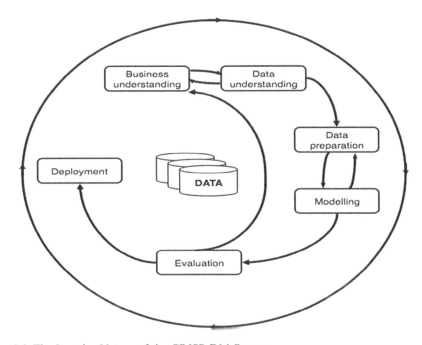

Figure 9.2 The Iterative Nature of the CRISP-DM Process

CRISP-DM is only one of the institutions that have ongoing efforts toward streamlining the KDD process. Other similar efforts include:

1 **Customer Profile Exchange (CPEX):** offers a vendor-neutral, XML-based open standard for facilitating the privacy-enabled interchange of customer information across disparate **enterprise** applications and systems.
2 **Data Mining Group (DMG):** is an independent, vendor-led group, which develops data mining standards, such as the Predictive Model Markup Language (PMML).

In general, the goal that these standards pursue is to facilitate the planning, documentation, and communication in data mining projects and to serve as a common reference framework for the DM industry. Many of these standards were developed based on practical experience resulting from the implementation of DM projects. In fact, the purpose of these standards is to help people involved in the process to communicate.

The next section describes in detail step four in the KDD process, which is building and validating the data mining predictive model.

Guidelines for Employing Data Mining Techniques

Once the goal of the data mining system is understood (step 1 of the CRISP-DM process) and the data have been collected (step 2) and prepared (step 3), the next step involves building and validating the data mining model (step 4). In terms of defining the adequate data mining techniques to be used, the nature of the data will play the deciding role as to which technique is most appropriate. Input variables (also called predictors) and output variables (also called outcomes) could be continuous or discrete (also called categorical). In addition, the data could also be textual, which commands a different set of data mining techniques.

In general, the first step in defining the data mining technique to be used involves defining if the study is of a predictive nature, meaning there is an outcome in mind. For example, to build a model to predict credit risk for customers seeking a loan from a bank, a data set must exist that includes for each customer their corresponding characteristics (such as credit score, salary, years of education, etc.), which will serve as the predictors or inputs to the model as well as the outcome variable credit risk. In this example, there is an outcome in mind: credit risk. This is also called **inferential techniques** or supervised learning. In unsupervised learning, there is not a previously known outcome in mind, and we describe these methods later as the descriptive techniques that appear in Table 9.4.

Data mining techniques include both statistical as well as nonstatistical techniques. Statistical techniques are known as traditional data mining methods including regression, logistic regression, and multivariate methods. Nonstatistical techniques, also known as intelligent techniques or data-adaptive methods, include memory-based reasoning, decision trees, and neural networks.

Table 9.1 summarizes the different inferential statistic techniques and their applicability pertaining to the characteristics of the input and output variables. Inferential statistical techniques are differentiated from descriptive statistics. Inferential statistics are used to generalize from data and thus develop models that generalize from the observations. Descriptive statistics (which appear in Table 9.4) are used to find patterns or define classes of similar objects in the data collected.

Table 9.1 Summary of Applicability of Inferential Statistical Techniques

Goal	Input Variables (Predictors)	Output Variables (Outcomes)	Statistical Technique	Examples (SPSS, 2000)
Find linear combination of predictors that best separate the population	Continuous	Discrete	Discriminant Analysis	• Predict instances of fraud • Predict whether customers will remain or leave (churners or not) • Predict which customers will respond to a new product or offer • Predict outcomes of various medical procedures
Predict the probability of outcome being in a particular category	Continuous	Discrete	Logistic and Multinomial Regression	• Predicting insurance policy renewal • Predicting fraud • Predicting which product a customer will buy • Predicting that a product is likely to fail
Output is a linear combination of input variables	Continuous	Continuous	Linear Regression	• Predict expected revenue in dollars from a new customer • Predict sales revenue for a store • Predict waiting time on hold for callers to an 800 number • Predict length of stay in a hospital based on patient characteristics and medical condition
For experiments and repeated measures of the same sample	Most inputs must be discrete	Continuous	Analysis of Variance (ANOVA)	• Predict which environmental factors are likely to cause cancer
To predict future events whose history has been collected at regular intervals	Continuous	Continuous	Time Series Analysis	• Predict future sales data from past sales records

The key difference between using statistical techniques and nonstatistical techniques is that the statistical techniques require a hypothesis to be specified beforehand. In addition, statistical techniques often are subject to stringent assumptions such as normality of the sample data, uncorrelated error, or homogeneity of variance. In particular when the number of explanatory variables is large, model specification and selection is increasingly difficult, making it harder to work with statistical techniques. However, statistical techniques provide for a more rigorous test of hypotheses. Table 9.2 summarizes the predictive nonstatistical techniques and their applicability pertaining to the

Table 9.2 Summary of Applicability of Non-Inferential Predictive Techniques

Goal	Input (Predictor) Variables	Output (Outcome) Variables	Statistical Technique	Examples (SPSS, 2000)
Predict outcome based on values of nearest neighbors	Continuous, Discrete, and Text	Continuous or Discrete	Memory-based Reasoning (MBR)	• Predicting medical outcomes
Predict by splitting data into subgroups (branches)	Continuous or Discrete (Different techniques used based on data characteristics)	Continuous or Discrete (Different techniques used based on data characteristics)	Decision Trees	• Predicting which customers will leave • Predicting instances of fraud
Predict outcome in complex non-linear environments	Continuous or Discrete	Continuous or Discrete	Neural Networks	• Predicting expected revenue • Predicting credit risk

characteristics of the input and output variables. Memory-based reasoning (MBR) is a DM technique that looks for the nearest neighbors of known data samples and combines their values to assign classification or prediction values for new data samples. It is very similar to Case-based Reasoning as described in Chapter 6. Like CBR, MBR uses a distance function to find the nearest element to a new data sample, and a combination function to combine the values at the nearest neighbors to make a prediction. For more information on MBR refer to Berry and Linoff (2011).

Among the techniques described in Table 9.2, decision trees (or rule induction methods) are used to predict the outcome by splitting data into subgroups. Different decision tree and rule induction methods are applicable depending on the characteristics of the data. Table 9.3 summarizes the various methods.

Table 9.4 summarizes the different descriptive techniques, including both association and clustering methods, and their applicability pertaining to the characteristics of the input variables. Note that for all these techniques, the outcome or output variable is not defined. Market basket or association analysis can include the use of two techniques: Apriori is an association rule algorithm that requires the input fields to be discrete. Apriori is generally faster to train than Generalized Rule Induction (GRI). Apriori allows only the specification of logical (or dichotomies) for the input variables, such as (True, False) or (1,0) to indicate the presence (or absence) of the item in the market basket. Generalized rule induction is an association rule algorithm, capable of producing rules that describe associations between attributes to a symbolic target and is capable of using continuous or logical data as its input.

Typically, several methods could be applied to any problem with similar results. The knowledge discovery process is an **iterative** process as we will describe in the next section. Once the model has been developed, the results must be evaluated. The potential for errors and their consequences must be carefully considered when performing a data mining exercise. An intelligent computer system can make two types of errors when trying to solve a problem. To simplify the argument, let's assume that the possible

Table 9.3 Summary of Applicability of Decision Tree Techniques

Goal	Input (Predictor) Variables	Output (Outcome) Variables	Statistical Technique	Examples (SPSS, 2000)
Predict by splitting data into more than two subgroups (branches)	Continuous, Discrete, or Ordinal	Discrete	Chi-square Automatic Interaction Detection (CHAID)	• Predict which demographic combinations of predictors yield the highest probability of a sale • Predict which factors are causing product defects in manufacturing
Predict by splitting data into more than two subgroups (branches)	Continuous	Discrete	C5.0	• Predict which loan customers are considered a "good" risk • Predict which factors are associated with a country's investment risk
Predict by splitting data into binary subgroups (branches)	Continuous	Continuous	Classification and Regression Trees (CART)	• Predict which factors are associated with a country's competitiveness • Discover which variables are predictors of increased customer profitability
Predict by splitting data into binary subgroups (branches)	Continuous	Discrete	Quick, Unbiased, Efficient, Statistical Tree (QUEST)	• Predict who needs additional care after heart surgery

solutions can only be "yes" or "no." One instance of this could be in a medical diagnosis of a serious disease, such as cancer. The two possible errors are: (1) an indication of "no" when the true answer is "yes," and (2) an indication of "yes" when the true answer is "no." The former is called the user's risk, while the latter is called the developer's risk. Depending on the application of the system, one type of error may be tolerable while the other may not be. For example, in the case of medical diagnosis such as cancer, a false positive ("no" when the answer is truly "yes") can be very costly in terms of the seriousness of the error. On the other hand, a system designed to select a type of wine for a meal may tolerate such an error quite acceptably.

The cost of errors must be carefully evaluated when the model is examined. For example, Table 9.5 presents the results of a study to predict the diagnosis of patients with heart disease based on a set of input variables. In the table, the columns represent predicted values for the diagnostic and the rows represent actual values for diagnostics of patients undergoing a heart disease examination. Actual values are coded in the cells, with percentages coded in parentheses along the actual values. In this table, the predictions made along the quadrant (*Actual No Disease/Predicted No Disease*) represent patients that were correctly predicted as being healthy. That means that 118 patients (or 72 percent of a total of 164 patients) were diagnosed with *No Disease* and they were indeed healthy. On the other hand, looking at the quadrant (*Actual Presence*

Table 9.4 Summary of Applicability of Clustering and Association Techniques

Goal	Input Variables (Predictor)	Output Variables (Outcome)	Statistical Technique	Examples (SPSS 2000)
Find large groups of cases in large data files that are similar on a small set of input characteristics	Continuous or Discrete	No outcome variable	K-means Cluster Analysis	• Customer segments for marketing • Groups of similar insurance claims
To create large cluster memberships			Kohonen Neural Networks	• Cluster customers into segments based on demographics and buying patterns
Create small set associations and look for patterns between many categories	Logical	No outcome variable	Market Basket or Association Analysis with Apriori	• Identify which products are likely to be purchased together • Identify which courses students are likely to take together
Create small set associations and look for patterns between many categories	Logical or numeric	No outcome variable	Market Basket or Association Analysis with GRI	• Identify which courses students are likely to take together
To create linkages between sets of items to display complex relationships	Continuous or Discrete	No outcome variable	Link Analysis	• To identify a relationship between a network of physicians and their prescriptions

Table 9.5 Classification Table Results

Heart Disease Diagnostic	Predicted No Disease	Predicted Presence of Disease
Actual: No Disease	118 (72%)	46 (28%)
Actual: Presence of Disease	43 (30.9%)	96 (69.1%)

of Disease/Predicted Presence of Disease) 96 patients (or 69.1 percent of a total of 139 patients) were diagnosed with *Presence of Disease* and they were indeed sick. So, for the patients in these two quadrants the classification algorithm correctly predicted their heart disease diagnosis. But the patients whose diagnosis falls off this diagonal were incorrectly classified. In this example, 46 patients (or 28 percent of a total of 164 patients) were diagnosed with the disease when in fact they were healthy. Furthermore, 43 patients (or 30.9 percent of a total of 139 patients) were incorrectly diagnosed with no disease when in fact they were sick.

In summary, 70.6 percent of the patients in this example were correctly classified with the prediction algorithm. Note that in this example, the cost of incorrectly giving a patient a sound bill of health, when in fact she is sick, is considered much higher than incorrectly predicting the patient to be sick, when in fact he is healthy. The former may cause the patient to die without the proper care, while the latter will give the patient a jolt but further tests are likely to exonerate him.

Discovering Knowledge on the Web

Business organizations profit greatly from mining the Web. Web-based companies discover considerable knowledge from the logs maintained by their Web servers, which provide data such as customer relationship management (CRM) data, email marketing data, web traffic, and customer service data (InformationWeek 2020). The expectation is that a customer's path through the data may enable companies to customize their Web pages, increase the average purchase amount per customer visit to the site, and in a nutshell increased profitability.

Certainly, e-business provides a fertile ground for learning market trends as well as what the competitors are up to. Therefore, learning to mine the Web can lead to a tremendous amount of new knowledge. Web pages and documents found on the Web can provide important information at a minimal cost to develop or maintain. Text mining refers to automatically "reading" large documents (called *corpora*) of text written in natural language and being able to derive knowledge from the process. Web mining is "Web crawling with on-line text mining" (Zanasi 2000). Zanasi reports about Online Analyst, a system that can mine the Web to provide competitive intelligence—a term that indicates knowledge leading to competitive advantages for a business organization. This system provides the user with an intelligent agent that surfs the Web in an intelligent fashion, and reads and quickly analyzes documents that are retrievable online. This system has the advantage that it can review many more documents than a human analyst can, even working 24 hours per day. Some of the documents may be well hidden (unintentionally or otherwise), and often times the relevant information can be found deeply buried within one document. Zanasi does not describe the techniques behind Online Analyst, probably to protect its own secrets. The system was developed by IBM-Bologna in Italy and is used as a tool for consulting.

Unfortunately, the information and data in the Web are unstructured. This can lead to difficulties when mining the Web. Conventional data mining techniques described earlier are not all applicable to Web mining, because by their nature they are limited to highly structured data. There are several differences between traditional data mining and Web mining. One significant difference is that Web mining requires linguistic analysis or natural language processing (NLP) abilities. It is estimated that 80 percent of the world's online content is based on text (Chen 2001). Web mining requires techniques from both information retrieval and artificial intelligence domains. Therefore, Web text mining techniques are rather different from the DM techniques described previously.

Web pages are indexed by the words they contain. Gerald Salton (1989) is generally considered the father of **information retrieval (IR)**. IR indexing techniques consist of calculating the function **term frequency inverse document frequency (TFIDF)**. The function consists of the product of a term frequency and its inverse document frequency, which depends on the frequency of occurrence of a specific keyword-term in the text and the number of documents it appears in. The term frequency (TF) refers to how frequently a term occurs in the text, which represents the importance of the term. The inverse document frequency (IDF) increases the significance of terms that appear in fewer documents, while downplaying terms that occur in many documents. TFIDF then highlights terms that are frequently used in one document but infrequently used across the collection of documents. The net effect is that terms like cryogenics which may occur frequently in a scientist's Web page, but infrequently across the whole domain of Web pages in an organization, will result in a good indexing term.

Web Mining Techniques

Web mining techniques can be classified into four main layers (Chen 2001):

1 Linguistic Analysis/NLP

Linguistic Analysis/NLP is used to identify key concept descriptors (the *who, what, when*, or *where*), which are embedded in the textual documents. In NLP the unit of analysis is the word. These functions can be combined with other linguistic techniques such as *stemming, morphological analysis, Boolean, proximity, range*, and *fuzzy search*. For example, a **stemming algorithm** is used to remove the suffix of a word. **Stoplists** are used to eliminate words that are not good concept descriptions, such as prepositions (e. g., *and, but*, etc.). Linguistic techniques can be combined with statistical techniques, for example to represent grammatically correct sentences. Also, **semantic analysis** is used to represent meaning in stories and sentences.

2 Statistical and Co-Occurrence Analysis

Statistical and co-occurrence analysis is similar to the TFIDF function mentioned before. For example, **link analysis** is used to create conceptual associations and automatic thesauri for keyword concepts. Also, **similarity functions** are used to compute co-occurrence probabilities between concept pairs.

3 Statistical and Neural Networks Clustering and Categorization

Like those discussed previously in "Designing the Knowledge Discovery System" section, statistical and neural networks clustering and categorization are used to group similar documents together as well as communities into domain categories. Kohonen NN techniques work well for large-scale Web text mining tasks and its results can be graphically visualized and intuitive.

4 Visualization and Human Computer Interfaces

Visualization and **human computer interfaces (HCI)** can reveal conceptual associations, which can be represented in various dimensions (one-, two-, and three-dimensional views). Furthermore, interaction techniques, such as zooming, can be incorporated to infer new knowledge.

Uses for Web Data Mining

There are three types of uses for Web data mining. They are as follows:

1 Web Structure Mining

Mining the Web structure examines how the Web documents are structured and attempts to discover the model underlying the link structures of the Web. **Intra-page structure** mining evaluates the arrangement of the various HTML or XML tags within a page; **inter-page structure** refers to hyperlinks connecting one page to another. Web structure mining can be useful to categorize Web pages, and to generate relationships and similarities among websites (Jackson 2002).

2 Web Usage Mining

Web usage mining, also known as **clickstream analysis**, involves the identification of patterns in user navigation through Web pages in a domain. Web usage mining tries to discover knowledge about the Web surfer's behaviors through analysis of their interactions with the website including the mouse clicks, user queries, and transactions. Web usage mining includes three main tasks: *preprocessing, pattern discovery*, and *pattern analysis* (Jackson 2002):

1   Preprocessing: Converts usage, content, and structure from different data sources into data sets ready for pattern discovery. This step is the most challenging in the data mining process, since it may involve data collection from multiple servers (including **proxy servers**), cleansing of extraneous information, and using data collected by cookies for identification purposes.
2   Pattern analysis: This step takes advantage of visualization and **Online Analytical Processing (OLAP)** techniques, like the ones discussed earlier, to aid understanding of the data, notice unusual values, and identify possible relationships between the **variables**.
3   Pattern discovery: Based on the different DM techniques discussed earlier except that certain variations may be considered. For example, in a market basket analysis of items purchased through a Web storefront, the click-order for the items added to the shopping cart may be significant, which is not typically studied in brick-and-mortar settings.

3. Web Content Mining

Web content mining is used to discover what a Web page is about and how to uncover new knowledge from it. Web content data include what is used to create the Web page including the text, images, audio, video, hyperlinks, and metadata. Web content mining is based on text mining and IR techniques, which consist of the organization of large amounts of textual data for most efficient retrieval—an important consideration in handling text documents. IR techniques have become increasingly important, as the amount of semistructured as well as unstructured textual data present in organizations has increased dramatically. IR techniques provide a method to efficiently access these large amounts of information.

Mining Web data is by all means a challenging task, but the rewards can be great including aiding the development of a more personalized relationship with the virtual customer, improving the virtual storefront selling process, and increasing Web-site revenues.

Data Mining and Customer Relationship Management

Customer relationship management (CRM) is the mechanisms and technologies used to manage the interactions between a company and its customers. Database marketers were the early adopters of CRM software, in order to automate the process of customer interaction. CRM implementations can be characterized as being operational and/ or analytical. **Operational CRM** includes sales force automation and call centers. Most global companies have implemented such systems. The goal of operational CRM is to provide a single view and point of contact for each customer. On the other hand, **analytical CRM** uses data mining techniques to uncover customer intelligence that serves to better understand and serve the customer.

In particular, the financial services, retailing, and telecommunications industry among others, facing increasing competitive markets, have turned to analytical CRM in order to (Schwenk 2002):

1   Integrate the customer viewpoint across all touchpoints: since many CRM solutions combine infrastructure components such as **enterprise application integration (EAI)** technology and data warehouses, as well as OLAP and data mining. The CRM promise is to build an integrated view of the customer, to understand the customer touchpoints, and resulting customer intelligence that will enable organizations to better recognize and service the needs of the customer.
2   Respond to customer demands in "Web time": because the Web has changed the dynamics of decision-making, and competitive environments require organizations to react to increasingly complex customer requests at faster speeds. Also, the analysis and interpretation of Web data can be used to enhance and personalize customer offerings. Analysis of Web data can uncover new knowledge about customer behavior and preferences, which can be used to improve website design and content.
3   Derive more value from CRM investments: since data mining analysis can be used to perform market segmentation studies that determine what customers could be targeted for certain products, to **narrowcast** (send out target e-mails) customers, and to perform other related studies such as market basket analysis.

For example, Rede (formerly known as Redecard, www.usrede.com), a company that captures and transmits MasterCard, Diners Club, and other credit and debit card transactions in Brazil, uses CRM to analyze transaction and customer data. The company performs market segmentation analysis to determine which customers to target for certain products (Lamont 2002). Also, Soriana (www.soriana.com), a Mexican grocery retailer, uses the market basket analysis capability of its CRM product to study promotion effectiveness and the impact of price changes on purchasing behavior (Lamont 2002).

The first step in the CRM process involves identifying customer market segments with the potential of yielding the highest profit. This step requires sifting through large amounts of data in order to find the "gold nuggets"—the mining promise. CRM software automates the DM process to find predictors of purchasing behaviors. In addition, CRM technology will typically integrate the solution of the DM study into **campaign management software** used to manage the targeted marketing campaign. The goal of campaign management software is to effectively manage the planning, execution, assessment, and refinement of myriad marketing campaigns at an organization. Campaign management software is used to manage and monitor a company's communications with its customers, including direct mail, telemarketing, customer service, point of sale, and Web interactions.

In CRM applications, the data mining prediction models are used to calculate a score, which is a numeric value assigned to each record in the database to indicate the probability that the customer represented by that record will behave in a specific manner. For example, when using DM to predict customer attrition or the likelihood that the customer will leave, a high score represents a high probability that the customer will indeed leave. The set of scores is then used to target customers for specific marketing campaigns.

Perhaps one of the best-known innovative implementations of CRM is Harrah's Entertainment, one of the most recognized brand names in the casino entertainment industry. Harrah's comprehensive data warehouse and CRM implementation enabled them to keep track of millions of customers' activities, allowing them to market more effectively, thus increasing the attraction and retention of targeted customers. Armed with deep knowledge about their customers' preferences, they customized their customer rewards program and were able to target promotions based on individual preferences. As an example, Harrah's provided hotel vouchers to their out-of-town guests and free show tickets to day-trip visiting customers. Harrah's CRM implementation won them national recognition in addition to an increase of their share of the gaming budget from 36 percent to 42 percent between 1999 and 2002 as well as 110 percent increase in their earnings per share between 1999 and 2002 (Lee et al. 2003). More recently, Hilton Hotels launched their "Customers Really Matter" (also abbreviated as CRM) strategy aimed at improving service delivery and consistency across the Hilton brand. The CRM strategy was viewed as "a way to use technology to give you the power to solidify relationships with our best customers" (Applegate et al. 2008, p. 3) via the consolidation of far-flung customer data to produce comprehensive arrival reports of their top customers. This strategy aimed to achieve a "holistic view" of the customer and thus improve their experience at every one of their **customer touchpoints** and recognize them properly. The online gambling industry has also made an entry into the CRM business, as it seeks to predict *churn* in order to understand customer retention. Churn prediction refers to the process of identifying gamblers with a high probability of leaving based on their prior behavior (Coussement and DeBock, 2013).

Consider the following scenario: the result of a DM study at a large national bank revealed that many of its customers only take advantage of the checking account services it provides. A typical customer at this institution would deposit their check, quickly moving the funds once they became available to mutual funds accounts and other service providers outside the bank. Using the integrated capabilities for campaign management, the software automatically triggers a direct marketing piece for those customers with a sizable deposit to encourage them to keep their money at the bank. DM and campaign management software can work together to sharpen the focus of prospects, therefore increasing marketing response and effectiveness. For more details about the relationship between DM and CRM, please refer to Berson et al. (2000).

Even in times of economic slowdown, worldwide CRM software revenue grew to a total of US$12 billion in 2011, showing an 82 percent increase from 2006 revenue of US$6.6 billion (Columbus 2012; Gartner 2008). The CRM market is expected to continue to expand in the foreseeable future. According to Gartner (2023): "In 2022, the value of CRM sales software market was $20.1 billion, an increase of over 65% from the 2011 values".

Barriers to the Use of Knowledge Discovery Systems

Possibly two of the barriers that prevented earlier deployment of knowledge discovery in the business arena, versus what we have witnessed in the scientific realm, relate to the prior lack of data in business to support the analysis and the limited computing power to perform the mathematical calculations required by the DM algorithms. Clearly, with the advent of more powerful computers at our desktops and the proliferation of relational databases, data warehouses, and data marts, these early barriers have been overcome. In fact, according to the **Storage Law** (Fayyad and Uthurusamy 2002), the capacity of digital data storage worldwide has doubled every nine months for the last decade at twice the rate predicted by **Moore's Law** for the growth of computing power. But by and large, this growing capacity has resulted in phenomena called **data tombs** (Fayyad and Uthurusamy 2002) or **data stores** where data are deposited to "merely rest in peace." This means there's no possibility that these data will be used and the opportunity to discover new knowledge that could be used to improve services, profits, or products, will be lost.

In addition, although many of the DM techniques have been around for more than ten years for scientific applications, only in the past few years have we witnessed the emergence of solutions that consolidate multiple DM techniques in a single software offering. Probably one of the most significant barriers to the explosion of the use of knowledge discovery in organizations relates to the fact that still today implementing a data mining model is still considered an art. Although a number of software packages exist that bundle data mining tools into one software offering, adequately implementing the knowledge discovery models requires intimate knowledge of the algorithmic requirements in addition to familiarity of how to use the software itself and a deep understanding of the business area and the problem that needs to be solved. In addition, a successful DM study typically requires a number of actors to partake in the activity including the project leader, the DM client, the DM analyst, the DM engineer, and the IT analyst (Jackson 2002). The project leader has the overall responsibility for the management of the study. The DM client understands the business problem, but in general doesn't have the adequate technical skills to carry out the study. The DM analyst translates the business needs into technical requirements for the DM model. The DM engineer develops the DM model together with the DM client and analyst. The IT analyst provides access to hardware, software, and data needed to carry out the project. In some large projects, a number of DM analysts and engineers may be involved. Clearly managing the number of actors involved in the study is indeed a challenging task that must be carefully coordinated by the project leader.

Perhaps one of the most interesting dilemmas facing KDD today is its basic definition of being an "interactive" process versus the notion that for the technology to be successful it must become "invisible." KDD can't be both interactive and invisible at the same time. Advocates of making KDD invisible argue that DM is primarily concerned with making it easy, convenient, and practical to explore very large databases without years of training as data analysts (Fayyad and Uthurusamy 2002). In fact, according to this view this goal requires that the following challenges be addressed:

1   *Scaling analysis to large databases*: Current DM techniques require that data sets be loaded into the computer's memory to be manipulated. This requirement offers a significant barrier when very large databases and data warehouses must be scanned to identify patterns.

2   *Scaling to high-dimensional data and models*: Typical statistical analysis studies require humans to formulate a model and then use techniques to validate the model via understanding how well the data fit the model. But it may be increasingly difficult for humans to formulate models *a priori* based on a very large number of variables, which increasingly add dimension to the problem. Models that seek to understand customer behavior in retail or Web-based transactions may fall in this category. In general, current solutions require humans to formulate a lower dimensional abstraction of the model, which may be easier for humans to understand.

3   *Automating the search*: DM studies typically require the researcher to enumerate the hypothesis under study *a priori*. In the future, in may be possible for DM algorithms to be able to perform this work automatically.

4   *Finding patterns and models understandable and interesting to users*: In the past, DM projects focused on measures of accuracy (how well the model predicts the data) and utility (the benefit derived from the pattern, typically money saved). New benefit measures like understandability of the model and novelty of the results must also be developed. Also, DM techniques should incorporate the generation of meaningful reports resulting from the study.

Some of these current challenges are being resolved today through the increasing availability of "verticalized" solutions. For example, in CRM software, KDD operations are streamlined through the use of standardized models which may include the most widely used data sources. For instance, a standardized model for financial services would most likely include customer demographics, channel, credit, and card usage as well as information related to the promotion and actual response. In order to streamline the KDD process, the metadata type for each table must be predefined (nominal, ordinal, interval, or continuous) while subsequent KDD operations are based on this information including the prespecification of algorithms that are appropriate to solve specific business problems (Parsa 2000). For example, based on the results presented earlier in Table 9.5, a verticalized application to predict which loan customers are considered a "good" risk will automatically implement the C5.0 algorithm if the input **variables** are continuous and the outcome is discrete.

An additional limitation in the deployment of DM today is the fact that the successful implementation of KDD at any organization may require the integration of disparate systems, since there are few plug-and-play solutions. All of these requirements translate into dollars, making many DM solutions sometimes quite expensive. Making the business case based on realistic estimations of ROI is essential for the success of the knowledge discovery initiative. Finally, effective application of the KDD to business applications requires the solution to be seamlessly integrated into existing environments. This requirement makes the case for vendors, researchers, and practitioners to adopt standards like the CRISP-DM standard discussed earlier.

A more recent preoccupation for many CIOs is the relentless growth of data in most organizations, which has been observed to be growing by 35 to 50 percent each year. Organizations are said to be processing more than 60 terabytes of data annually, which represents about one-thousand times more than what they did ten years ago (Beath et al. 2012). Interviews with Information Technology leaders revealed that they are faced with two serious challenges: (1) dealing with the increased granularity of data and (2) an explosion of unstructured data which makes it increasingly challenging to fully exploit. Not surprisingly, the majority of the organizations interviewed appeared to be unsatisfied with their ability to generate significant value from the data. IT leaders must learn to control data management costs and risks, and take steps toward promoting innovation in data utilization, including making other complementary business changes that will enable them to unlock the significant value inherent in the stored data (Beath et al. 2012).

Case Studies

An Application of Rule Induction to Real Estate Appraisal Systems

In this section we describe an example of how data mining, specifically rule induction, can be used to infer new knowledge, specifically the contribution of an individual piece of data on a data set or the incremental worth of the individual component on an aggregate set (Gonzalez et al. 1999). For example, when performing real estate appraisals, it is necessary to know the incremental worth that a specific feature may have on a house—say for example a swimming pool or garage. Property appraisers face this dilemma, and typically it is the market and not the feature construction cost that determines the incremental worth of the feature on the house. For instance, the incremental worth of an additional bedroom when going from three to four bedrooms may be different from the incremental worth of going from four to five bedrooms.

Property appraisals estimate property values via market analysis, which means comparing a house with other similar houses sold recently in the same area. Property appraisers typically use databases of recently sold properties to establish a basis of sales comparables. Market changes are reflected on these databases, although there may be a lag before the market effects are reflected. Sometimes, depending on market conditions, it may be difficult to make such comparisons. For example, during the economic downturn of the housing market it may have been hard to find comparable sales because homes were just not selling. On the flipside, during the height of the housing market bubble, past sales comparables didn't match what the market, based on supply and demand, estimated were adequate property values.

The technique that we focus on here is described as calculating the *incremental* or *relative* worth of components of **aggregate sets**, where an aggregate set represents a collection, assembly or grouping of member components that have a common nature or purpose (Gonzalez et al. 1999). Based on this definition, a house constitutes an aggregate set of features such as number of bedrooms, number of bathrooms, living area, and so forth. In this example, the term *worth* is used to represent the price of the house, and discovering the incremental worth that a particular feature (e.g., an extra bedroom) will contribute to the price of a house.

In the research cited in this case study, the authors use a technique called difference-based induction (DBI)[1] to calculate the incremental worth of a feature, given the database has similar attributes (e.g., bedrooms) that may have dissimilar impact on the price of the house. The induction algorithm used in this example identifies aggregate sets in the database that contribute slight differences in their attributes' values, thereby identifying which are the most significant attribute/value combination of nearly similar aggregate sets of individual houses. In this example, *value* is associated with each attribute (or feature) in the database, while *worth* is associated with the value of the aggregate set (or house). For each house attribute, the *value* of the attribute is specified (for example area = 1,500 square feet, or number of bedrooms = four) as well as how each one contributes to the house's *worth*. In this example, the individual worth of an attribute is the amount that it contributes to the overall worth of the house.

The procedure to create the decision tree based on the induction techniques presented earlier is as follows:

1 **Data preparation** and preprocessing: For example, there may be missing values in the database, there could be data-entering errors, or lack of consistency with other sets. Therefore, they will need to be identified and eliminated, otherwise they could have a distorting effect on the outcome worth of the house.
2 **Tree construction**: Houses are progressively assigned to each of the nodes at each of the tree levels. Branches represent each range of values of the attribute represented in that node, and the branch through which each house is routed depends on the value that each particular house has for the attribute represented in the parent node.
3 House pruning: **Heuristics** are applied to identify and discard those houses whose worth is not consistent with that of other houses in the same leaf-level group.
4 **Paired leaf analysis**: Any difference in worth between houses in two sibling leaves is directly caused by the difference in their values of the critical attribute. For example, two houses are identical in all features, but one has three bedrooms and the other four. If the four-bedroom house sells for US$75,000 and the three-bedroom one for US$73,000, the extra bedroom is attributed the difference of US$2,000.

Figure 9.3 and Table 9.6 represent the partial decision tree resulting from the induction algorithm applied to a small sample database of 84 sold homes. The incremental worth

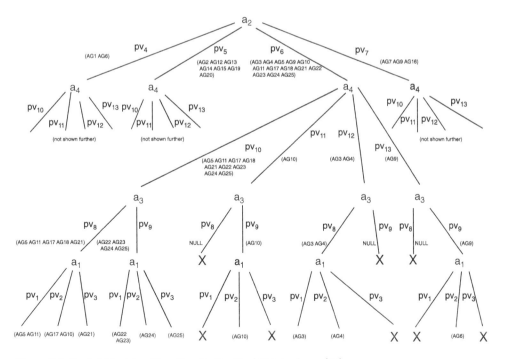

Figure 9.3 Partial Decision Tree Results for Real Estate Appraisal

Table 9.6 Summary of Induction Results

Attribute	Induction Results	Expert Estimate	Difference (%)
Living Area	$15–$31	$15–$25	0–2.4
Bedrooms	$4,311–$5,212	$2,500–$3,500	49–72
Bathrooms	$3,812–$5,718	$1,500–$2,000	154–186
Garage	$3,010–$4,522	$3,000–$3,500	0.3–29
Pool	$7,317–$11,697	$9,000–$12,000	2.5–19
Fireplace	$1,500–$4,180	$1,200–$2,000	25–109
Year Built	1.2–1.7%	1.0–1.2%	20–42

Source: Gonzalez et al. (1999).

computed with the induction algorithm was validated by opinions of real estate appraisal experts. For additional details on this case study, please refer to Gonzalez et al. (1999).

An Application of Web Content Mining to Expertise Locator Systems

One application of Web content mining methods is in the construction of **expertise locator knowledge management systems**. A KM system that locates experts based on published documents requires an automatic method for identifying employee names, as well as a method to associate employee names with skill keywords embedded in those documents. Although we discuss expertise locator systems in general in Chapter 8, we include in this section a discussion of the system's Web text mining component.

An example of an expertise locator KM system is the NASA Expert Seeker Web Miner,[2] which required the development of a name-finding algorithm to identify names of NASA employees. Traditional IR techniques[3] were then used to identify and match skill keywords with the identified employee names. An IR system typically uses as input a set of inverted files, which is a sequence of words that reference the group of documents in which the words appear. These words are chosen according to a selection algorithm that determines which words in the document are good index terms. In a traditional IR system, the user enters a **query** and the system retrieves all documents that match that keyword entry. Expert Seeker Web Miner is based on an IR technique that goes one step further. When a user enters a query, the system initially performs a document search based on user input. However, since the user is looking for experts in a specific subject area, the system returns the names of those employees whose names appear in the matching documents (excluding Webmasters and curators). The employee name results are ranked according to the number of matching documents in which each individual name appears. The employee information is then displayed to the user.

The indexing process was carried out in four stages. First, all the relevant data were transferred to a local directory for further processing. In this case, the data included all the Web pages on the NASA-Goddard Space Flight Center domain. The second stage identifies all instances of employee names by programmatically examining each HTML file. The name data are taken from the personnel directory databases (based on the X.500 standard). All names in the employee database are organized into a map-like data structure beforehand that is used in the Web content mining process. This map consists of all employee names referenced by their last name key. In addition, each full name is stored in every possible form it could appear. For example, the name John A. Smith is stored as

- John A. Smith
- J. A. Smith
- J. Smith
- Smith, John A.
- Smith, J.A.
- Smith J.

An individual document is first searched for all last name keys. Subsequently, the document is again searched using all values of the matching keys. Name data organized in this way can increase the speed of the text search. Using one long sequence containing all names in every possible form as search criteria would slow down processing time.

The third stage involves identifying keywords within the HTML content. This is done using a combination of word stemming and frequency calculation. First the text is broken up into individual words through string pattern matching. Any sequence of alphabetical characters is recognized as a word while punctuation, numbers, and whitespace characters are ignored. The resulting list of words is processed to determine if a word was included in a stoplist. The resulting list of words was then processed with a **stemming algorithm**. This is done to group together words that may be spelled differently but have the same semantic meaning. A person who types "astronomical" as a query term would most likely also be interested in documents that match the term "astronomy." Once the stemming process is completed, the algorithm calculates the frequency of each term. Word frequency was used during the keyword selection process in the determination of good index terms. However, other indexing algorithms could have been used instead with comparable results.

It is important to note that the degree of relation between an employee name and a keyword within an individual document is not considered. Rather, expertise is determined based on the assumption that if an employee recurrently appears in many documents along with a keyword, then that person must have some knowledge of that term. Theoretically, a large document count for a search query should produce more accurate results.

The chosen keywords have a twofold purpose. First, they are used to quickly associate employees with recurring skill terms. These keywords can also be used in future work for clustering similar documents into topic areas. Finally, **knowledge taxonomy** can be constructed from the mined keywords such that an appropriate query relevance feedback system can be developed that suggests **query terms** that are related to the query entered by the user. Details about the role of taxonomies on the development of expertise locator systems are presented in Chapter 8.

Next, we discuss the role that the Web and search engines play in knowledge discovery.

Novel-Knowledge Discovery on the Web

The Web is a rich source of information for knowledge discovery.[4] Organizations and individuals search the Web for different types of knowledge and to answer different types of questions. For example, individuals typically use the Web to find specific answers—also known as focused search—and to uncover patterns and trends about a topic—also known as scanning. Google (www.google.com) is the most popular Web-searching tool and is most suited to focused searching and discovering deep knowledge. Tools such as Kartoo (www.kartoo.com) and Yippy (www.yippy.com), which provide knowledge maps and clustered categories, are more suitable for scanning and discovering broad knowledge.

In addition to deep and broad knowledge, individuals and organizations sometimes seek to discover novel knowledge—knowledge that is surprising and unknown to them yet interesting and relevant. The challenge with discovering novel knowledge on the Web is that the question posed in the search is usually very vague, therefore creating appropriate search terms may be virtually impossible. Essentially, it's like searching for "what you don't know you don't know!" In addition, novel knowledge may be difficult to locate among the vast amount of content returned; one of the many challenges posed by the information overload that may result from the Web search. In most instances, the content returned may be highly related to the search terms provided. Thus, discovering novel knowledge may be more like looking for a needle in a haystack—except you may not know what the needle looks like. In other words, because of its novelty, individuals have a difficult time differentiating purely irrelevant results ("junk") from surprising and interesting results ("novel knowledge"). Furthermore, what's interesting, surprising, and relevant differs from individual to individual based on what they already know; novel knowledge to one person may be considered deep knowledge to another person. Thus, novel knowledge is basically "in the eye of the beholder."

Novel knowledge can be valuable to organizations for many reasons, for example, for the discovery of new strategic opportunities, for development of learning capabilities, and to support the creative thinking leading to innovation or solving "wicked" problems (for more on wicked problems see Chapter 16). Researchers at Queen's University in Kingston, Ontario, have been investigating the importance of novel knowledge to organizations and how they currently go about discovering novel knowledge. Their findings show that organizations do consider novel knowledge important, especially in industries where innovation is critical. However, in many of the organizations investigated, the discovery of novel knowledge was purely serendipitous. Unlike deep and broad knowledge, they found that there are currently no specialized tools to support the discovery of novel knowledge on the Web, motivating the development of Athens (Jenkin 2008a; Jenkin et al. 2007; Vats and Skillicorn 2004a; Vats and Skillicorn 2004b). The Athens prototype uses text and data mining techniques such as clustering, singular-value decomposition, and spectral graph partitioning to find content on the Web that is indirectly connected yet contextually related to what the individual knows. In essence, the individual specifies to Athens the specific topic of interest and Athens finds content on the Web that is literally two steps away from it, that is, related to the area of knowledge familiar to the individual. Thus, Athens tries to find what you don't know you don't know but would find interesting and relevant.

An example using a popular knowledge discovery case will help to illustrate how Athens works. Don Swanson, an information scientist, made an important discovery about Raynaud's Syndrome (a condition that results in intermittent restriction of blood flow to fingers and toes) by exploring the medical literature (Gordon and Lindsay 1996; Swanson 1986; Swanson 1990). Swanson did not know what to look for specifically, so he began by reviewing the Raynaud's literature and found a connection between Raynaud's Syndrome and blood viscosity. He then reviewed the blood-viscosity literature and found that dietary fish oil lowers blood viscosity. He then hypothesized that fish oil may be a useful dietary supplement to help decrease the blood viscosity in humans and therefore alleviate symptoms of Raynaud's Syndrome (Swanson 1986). At the time, this was novel knowledge and not explicitly mentioned in any of the source documents Swanson had previously reviewed. Using this manual approach, Swanson spent a significant amount of time reviewing different bodies of literature in order to make this important novel-knowledge discovery.

If Don Swanson had used Athens for this task rather than a manual approach, he would have provided Athens with terms to describe what he knows or, rather, his focal topic—*Raynaud's Syndrome*. Athens, using an iterative clustering approach, would discover content that is directly connected to Raynaud's Syndrome—in this case, *blood viscosity*. Next, Athens would repeat this iterative clustering step, using blood viscosity as the starting point, in order to find content that is indirectly connected to the original topic of Raynaud's Syndrome—in this case, *fish oil*. Thus, the final result is content that is two steps away from original topic area. It would be up to the user to hypothesize how Raynaud's Syndrome and fish oil might be related.

The Athens prototype is an example of a tool to discover novel knowledge. However, current research findings show that the innovative aspects of the tool may present some problems. For most individuals and organizations, the concept and task of searching for novel knowledge is new. The popularity of Web-search tools like Google has trained us to view Web searching as a focused search activity. Thus, the initial reaction when using Athens is to view it as a focused search tool yielding a specific result, essentially comparing its features and output to those of Google. Despite these challenges, organizations that have been experimenting with the Athens prototype see the potential of the tool's capabilities. For example, they were impressed with how quickly they were able come up with new and innovative ideas for the topics investigated—something that would have taken a lot of time, effort, and serendipity to do before (Jenkin 2008b). Athens promises to be a useful tool for organizations interested in discovering novel knowledge on the Web or within their own internal information repositories.

Summary

In this chapter you learned what knowledge discovery systems are, the design considerations for such systems, and specific types of data mining techniques that enable such systems. Also, the chapter discusses the role of DM in customer relationship management. Three case studies that describe the implementation of knowledge discovery systems are presented, each based on different methodologies and intelligent technologies. The first system is based on the use of decision trees, or rule induction, as a knowledge-modeling tool, and is described in the context of a real estate appraisal system. The second system is based on the use of Web-content mining to identify expertise in an expertise locator system. The third tool presents the use of an innovative tool used to improve the discovery of novel knowledge on the Web. Finally, the use of socialization in organizational settings is discussed as a mechanism to help discover new knowledge and catalyze innovation.

Review

1   How do socialization techniques help to discover tacit knowledge?
2   Describe the six steps in the CRISP-DM process.

3   Why is understanding of the business problem essential to knowledge discovery?
4   Describe the three types of Web DM techniques. Which one is used in the Expert Seeker case study?
5   Describe some of the barriers to the use of knowledge discovery.

Application Exercises

Identify which DM techniques would be selected to solve the following problems. Explain your answer. Include a description of the input and output variables that would be relevant in each case. Note that more than one technique may apply for each of these problems.

(A)   Predict fraudulent credit card usage based on purchase patterns.
(B)   Predict instances of fraud related to Medicare claims.
(C)   Predict which customers are likely to leave their current mobile service provider.
(D)   Predict whether a person will renew their insurance policy.
(E)   Predict who will respond to a direct mail offer.
(F)   Predict that a generator is likely to fail.
(G)   Predict which specialized voice services a person is likely to purchase from their local telecommunications provider.
(H)   Identify factors resulting in product defects in a manufacturing environment.
(I)   Predict the expected revenue from a customer based on a set of customer characteristics.
(J)   Predict cost of hospitalization for different medical procedures.
(K)   Create customer segments in a marketing campaign.
(L)   Segment among university graduates those that are likely to renew their alumni membership.

Notes

1   For additional details on DBI, please refer to Gonzalez et al. (1999).
2   This version of Expert Seeker was developed to support the needs of Goddard Space Flight Center. Expertise locator systems in general are discussed in detail in Chapter 8.
3   See for example Selection by Discriminant Value in Frakes and Baeza-Yates (1992), an algorithm for selecting index terms.
4   We acknowledge Tracy Jenkin, Yolande Chan, and David Skillicorn of Queen's University for this case study.

References

Applegate, L., Piccoli, G., and Dev, C. 2008. Hilton Hotels: Brand differentiation through customer relationship management. Harvard Business School Case Study #809029, July 23.
Beath, C., Becerra-Fernandez, I., Ross, J., and Short, J. 2012. Finding value in the information explosion. *MIT Sloan Management Review*, 53(4), 18.
Becerra-Fernandez, I., Zanakis, S., and Walczak, S. 2002. Knowledge discovery techniques for predicting country investment risk. *Computers and Industrial Engineering*, 43(4), 787–800.
Berry, M., and Linoff, G. 2011. *Data mining techniques for marketing, sales, and customer relationship management*. New York: John Wiley & Sons.
Berson, A., Smith, S., and Thearling, K. 2000. *Building data mining applications for CRM*. New York: McGraw-Hill.

Brachman, R., and Anand, T. 1996. The process of knowledge discovering in databases. In *Advances in knowledge discovery and data mining*, ed. U.M. Fayyad et al., 37–57. Menlo Park, CA: AAAI Press.

Bratianu, C. 2015. *Organizational knowledge dynamics: Managing knowledge creation, acquisition, sharing, and transformation.* Hershey: IGI Global.

Business Wire. 2022. Westinghouse completes sale of power delivery business. https://www.busi nesswire.com/news/home/20220928005736/en/Westinghouse-Completes-Sale-of-Power-Delivery -Business (accessed July 24, 2023).

Chapman, P., Clinton, J., Kerber, R., Khabaza, T., Reinartz, T., Shearer, C., and Wirth, R. 2000. CRISP-DM 1.0: Step-by-step data mining guide. SPSS Technical Report.

Chen, H. 2001. Knowledge management systems: A text mining perspective. Tucson, AZ: The University of Arizona.

Columbus, L. 2012. Gartner hype cycle for CRM sales, 2012: Sales turns to the cloud for quick relief. *Forbes.com.* http://www.forbes.com/sites/louiscolumbus/2012/07/27/gartner-hype-cycle-for-crm-sales-2012-sales-turns-to-the-cloud-for-quick-relief/ (accessed January 3, 2014).

Coussement, K., and De Bock, K.W. 2013. Customer churn prediction in the online gambling industry: The beneficial effect of ensemble learning. *Journal of Business Research* 66(9), 1629–1636.

DOMO. n.d. DHL ordered a week's worth of data collection in an instant. Domo delivered. https://www.domo.com/customers/dhl.

Edelstein, H.A. 1999. *Introduction to data mining and knowledge discovery*, 3rd ed. Potomac, MD: Two Crows Corporation.

Edelstein, H.A. 2001. Pan for gold in the clickstream. *Information Week*, March 12.

Fayyad, U., and Uthurusamy, R. 2002. Evolving data mining into solutions for insights. *Communications of the ACM*, 45(8), 28–21.

Fayyad, U., Piatetsky-Shapiro, G., Smyth, P., and Uthurusamy, R. 1996. From data mining to knowledge discovery: An overview. In *Advances in knowledge discovery and data mining*, ed. U.M. Fayyad et al., 1–33. Menlo Park, CA: AAAI Press.

Frakes, W., and Baeza-Yates, R. 1992. *Information retrieval: Data structures and algorithms.* Upper Saddle River, NJ: Prentice Hall.

Fries, T. 2021. The Market Basket Analysis report explained in detail. *Amalytix*, March 26. https://www.amalytix.com/en/knowledge/controlling/aba-market-basket-analysis/.

Gartner. 2008. Gartner says worldwide customer relationship management market grew 23 percent in 2007. Press release, *Gartner.com*, July 7. http://www.gartner.com/it/page.jsp?id=715308 (accessed January 3, 2009).

Gartner. 2023. Market share analysis: CRM sales software worldwide 2022. Press release, *Gartner. com*, October 3. https://www.gartner.com/en/documents/4801131.

Gonzalez, A., Daroszweski, S., and Hamilton, H.J. 1999. Determining the incremental worth of members of an aggregate set through difference-based induction. *International Journal of Intelligent Systems*, 14(3), 275–294.

Gordon, M.D., and Lindsay, R.K. 1996. Toward discovery support systems: A replication, re-examination, and extension of Swanson's work on literature-based discovery of a connection between Raynaud's and fish oil. *Journal of the American Society for Information Science*, 47(2), 116–128.

Gray, P., and Watson, H.J. 1998. *Decision support in the data warehouse.* Upper Saddle River, NJ: Prentice Hall.

Hotz, N. 2023. What is CRISP DM?https://www.datascience-pm.com/crisp-dm-2/ Data Science Process Alliance (accessed July 24, 2023).

InformationWeek. 2020. Align your data architecture with the strategic plan. September 22. https://www.informationweek.com/data-management/align-your-data-architecture-with-the-strategic-plan.

Jackson, J. 2002. Data mining: A conceptual overview. *Communications of the Association for Information Systems*, 8, 267–296.

Jenkin, T.A. 2008a. How IT supports knowledge discovery and learning processes on the Web. In *Proceedings of the 41st Hawaii International Conference on System Sciences* (HICSS). Waikoloa, HI.

Jenkin, T.A. 2008b. *Using information technology to support the discovery of novel knowledge in organizations.* PhD Thesis (Management), Queen's University.

Jenkin, T.A., Chan, Y.E., and Skillicorn, D.B. 2007. Novel-knowledge discovery—Challenges and design theory. In *Proceedings of the Annual Conference of the Administrative Sciences Association of Canada.* Ottawa, Canada.

Kovalerchuk, B., Triantaphyllou, E., Ruiz, J., Torvik, V., and Vityaev, E. 2000. The reliability issue of computer-aided breast cancer diagnosis. *Journal of Computers and Biomedical Research*, 33(4), 296–313.

Lamont, J. 2002. CRM around the world. *KM World*, 11(9) (October).

Lee, H., Whang, S., Ahsan, K., Gordon, E., Faragalla, A., Jain, A., Mohsin, A., and Shi, G. 2003. Harrah's Entertainment Inc.: Real-time CRM in a service supply chain. Harvard Business School Case Study #GS50, October 27.

Li, S., Lu, W., Wang, C., and Yen, D. 2012. Identifying the signs of fraudulent accounts using data mining techniques. *Computers in Human Behavior*, 28(3), 1002–1013.

Linden, G., Smith, B., and York, J. 2003. Amazon.com recommendations item-to-item collaborative filtering. *Internet Computing, IEEE*, 7(1), 76–80.

Nonaka, I., and Takeuchi, H. 1995. *The knowledge creating company.* New York: Oxford University Press.

Parsa, I. 2000. Data mining: Middleware or middleman, panel on KDD process standards (position statement). In *Proceedings from the Sixth ACM SIGKDD International Conference on Knowledge Discovery and Data Mining*, ed. R. Ramakrishnan and S. Stolfo. New York: ACM.ProFlowers.

PR Newswire. 2012. ProFlowers honored with top customer satisfaction award from J.D. power and associates. http://www.prnewswire.com/news-releases/proflowers-honored-with-top-custom er-satisfaction-award-from-jd-power-and-associates-182983321.html.

Rocha-Salazar, J.-d.-J.Segovia-Vargas, M.-J., and Camacho-Miñano, M.-d.-M. 2021. Money laundering and terrorism financing detection using neural networks and an abnormality indicator, *Expert Systems with Applications*, 169(1) (May).

Salton, G. 1989. *Automatic text processing.* Reading, MA: Addison-Wesley.

Schwenk, H. 2002. Real-time CRM analytics: The future of BI? *KM World*, 11(2), (February).

Smith, K.A., and Gupta, J.N.D. 2000. Neural networks in business: Techniques and applications for the operations researcher. *Computers and Operations Research*, 27, 1023–1044.

SPSS. 2000. Data mining: Modeling. Chicago, Illinois.

Stevens, L. 2001. IT sharpens data mining's focus. *Internet Week*, August 6.

Swanson, D.R. 1986. Fish oil, Raynaud's Syndrome, and undiscovered public knowledge. *Perspectives in Biology and Medicine*, 30(1), 7–18.

Swanson, D.R. 1990. Medical literature as a potential source of new knowledge. *Bulletin of the Medical Library Association*, 78(1), 29–37.

Vats, N., and Skillicorn, D.B. 2004a. The ATHENS system for novel information discovery. Department of Computing and Information Science, Queen's University, Technical Report 2004–2489.

Vats, N., and Skillicorn, D.B. 2004b. Information discovery within organizations using the Athens system. In *Proceedings of the 2004 Conference of the Centre for Advanced Studies on Collaborative Research*, ed. H. Lutfiyya, J. Singer, and D.A. Stewart, 282–292. Markham, Ontario.

Wei X., Hisrich R., Yu M., and Li X. 2022. Mentoring and tacit knowledge transfer in novice teachers from Chinese middle schools: Mediating effect of job crafting. *Front. Educ.* 7.

Witten, I. 2000. Adaptive text mining: inferring structure from sequences. In *Proceedings of the 34th Conference on Information Sciences and Systems.* Princeton University, NJ, March 15–17.

Zanasi, A. 2000. Web mining through the Online Analyst. In *Proceedings of the first Data Mining Conference*. Cambridge University, Cambridge, UK.

Zdanowicz, J. 2004. Detecting money laundering and terrorist financing via data mining. *Communications of the ACM*, 47(5).

Zdanowicz, J. 2009. Trade-based money laundering and terrorist financing. *Review of Law and Economics*, 5(2), 854–878.

Part III

Management of Knowledge Management

10 Factors Influencing Knowledge Management

In the last chapter, we discussed some of the emerging trends in knowledge management. Earlier, in Chapter 5, we examined the impacts KM can have on companies and other private or public organizations. These impacts result either directly from KM solutions or indirectly through knowledge created by KM solutions. KM solutions include KM processes and systems, which were discussed in Chapter 4. In this chapter, we argue that various KM solutions may have different impacts on performance depending on the circumstances, and we examine the key factors affecting the suitability of KM solutions. This perspective, which is called *contingency perspective*, is discussed next and the overall approach in this chapter is outlined. The subsequent sections examine the effects of several important factors.

A Contingency View of Knowledge Management

Previous literature on knowledge management promoted a universalistic view of knowledge management (Becerra-Fernandez et al. 2004). A universalistic view of knowledge management would imply that there is a single best approach of managing knowledge, which should be adopted by all organizations in all circumstances. This seems to be implicit in the literature on knowledge management; for example, knowledge sharing is recommended as being useful to all organizations, although we believe that the use of direction may sometimes represent an equally effective but more efficient alternative. In contrast to this prior universalistic view, a **contingency theory**, which has previously been used in the literature on organization design, suggests that no one approach is best under all circumstances. Whereas a universalistic view focuses on identifying a single path to successful performance, a contingency theory considers the path to success to include multiple alternative paths, with success being achieved only when the appropriate path for an organization is selected. For instance, an organization design with few rules or procedures is considered appropriate for small organizations, whereas one with extensive rules and procedures is recommended for large organizations.

Similarly, other research findings support that not all knowledge management efforts would necessarily end in better result in terms of firm performance (Sabherwal and Sabherwal 2007). Instead, this research argues that a KM effort that is aligned to the firm's business strategy would lead to an improvement in the firm's business performance whereas a KM effort that is not aligned with the firm's business strategy would not. Based on an empirical study of the stock market responses to the announcement of KM efforts, the researchers found this expectation to be empirically

DOI: 10.4324/9781003364375-13

supported. More specifically, the stock market reacted better to the announcement of a KM effort as the alignment between the announced KM effort and the firm's business strategy increased.

We recommend the use of an approach based on contingency theory for identifying KM processes and solutions. When asked what kind of a KM solution should an organization use, we often find ourselves responding, "it depends," rather than unequivocally recommending a specific solution. We need to understand the specific circumstances within the organization and the ones surrounding it in order to identify the KM solution that would be most beneficial for those circumstances. This indicates that each KM solution is contingent upon the presence of certain circumstances—hence the name. A contingency perspective for KM is supported by prior empirical research (Becerra-Fernandez and Sabherwal 2001; Sabherwal and Sabherwal 2005). For example, based on a detailed study of Nortel Networks Corporation, Massey et al. (2002, p. 284) conclude: "Thus, a key finding of our study is that successful KM initiatives like Nortel's cannot be disentangled from broader organizational factors and changes."

Figure 10.1 summarizes the way in which the relationship between the contingency factors and KM solutions is examined in this chapter. As discussed in Chapters 3 and 4, KM solutions include KM systems and KM processes. Much of this chapter focuses on **knowledge management processes**, with the choice of appropriate KM process depending on contingency factors, as shown by arrow 1 in Figure 10.1. Once the appropriate KM processes are recognized, the KM systems needed to support them can be identified as well. Thus, the contingency factors indirectly affect KM systems and the mechanisms and technologies enabling KM systems, as shown using arrows 2 and 3. Moreover, the KM infrastructure supports KM mechanisms and technologies (arrow 4), which in turn affect KM systems (arrow 5) and KM systems support KM processes (arrow 6). Thus, the KM infrastructure indirectly affects KM processes (arrow 7).

Several contingency factors influence the choice of KM processes. They include characteristics of the tasks being performed, the knowledge being managed, the organization, and the organization's environment. Figure 10.2 summarizes these categories of contingency factors affecting KM processes. In the forthcoming sections, we will examine the

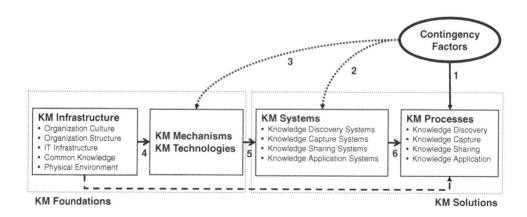

7

Figure 10.1 Contingency Factors and Knowledge Management

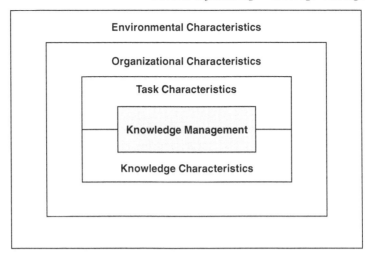

Figure 10.2 Categories of Contingency Factors

effects of task characteristics and knowledge characteristics, respectively. And, we will also describe the effects of organizational and environmental characteristics.

In general, the contingency factors and KM infrastructure affect the suitability of KM processes in two ways: (a) by increasing or reducing the need to manage knowledge in a particular way; and (b) by increasing or reducing the organization's ability to manage knowledge in a particular way. For example, larger organizations have a greater need to invest in knowledge sharing processes, whereas an organization culture characterized by trust increases the organization's ability to use knowledge sharing processes. Consequently, the benefits from a KM process would depend on the contingency factors (Sabherwal and Sabherwal 2005). Box 10.1 summarizes insights from two empirical studies adopting such an approach.

Box 10.1 Two Empirical Studies of Factors Affecting Benefits from Knowledge Management

Using data collected from 141 Korean firms that have implemented enterprise-wide KM initiatives, researchers Kim et al. (2014) sought to answer the following question: how does the effect of KM strategies on KM performance differ depending on a firm's external and internal contexts, i.e., the degree of environmental knowledge intensity and the level of organizational IS maturity? They focused on four KM strategies: internal codification, internal personalization, external codification, and external personalization. Their results indicate that:

1   The external codification strategy is most effective for firms with high knowledge intensity and IS maturity. Organizations in this situation can combine internal and external knowledge, convert tacit knowledge to explicit knowledge, and transfer it to members through system-oriented channels.
2   For organizations with high IS maturity but low knowledge intensity, the internal codification strategy is more suitable. These firms focus on routine activities and

incremental innovations, relying on their internal IS capabilities to develop and accumulate knowledge.

3   Firms with low IS maturity and high knowledge intensity benefit from the external personalization strategy. They primarily rely on human-based networks for knowledge sources and import knowledge through face-to-face interactions to thrive in knowledge-intensive environments.

Another survey-based study (Handzic et al. 2016) investigates the impact of two different types of KMS, technical and social, and the impact on the decision makers' behavior and performance in different decision contexts: simple and complex. Their results indicate that:

1   In complex contexts, social KMS is the best fit based on the individuals' performance.
2   In simple contexts, both KMS are an equally good fit based on individuals' performance, but social KMS is preferred in terms of adoption.

As these studies confirm, a universalistic view to KM might not be appropriate. In order to maximize the outcome of launching a KMS, organizations should understand certain characteristics, both external and internal to the organization. Some of these characteristics include the organization's environmental knowledge intensity, the organization's IS maturity, as well as the organization's decision context.

Sources: Compiled from Handzic et al. (2016); Kim et al. (2014)

The Effects of Task Characteristics

The underlying argument here is that the KM processes that are appropriate for an organizational subunit (e.g., a department, a geographic location, etc.) depend on the nature of its tasks (Becerra-Fernandez and Sabherwal 2001; Haas and Hansen 2005). This involves viewing each subunit at the aggregate level based on the predominant nature of its tasks. This approach has considerable support in prior literature. For example, Van de Ven and Delbecq (1974) offered a contingency view of the relationship between subunit tasks and organization structure. They suggested that the structure appropriate for a subunit depends on task difficulty, or on the problems in analyzing the work and stating performance procedures and task variability, or on the variety of problems encountered in the tasks. Lawrence and Lorsch (1967) also focused on a task characteristic—**task uncertainty**—at the subunit level, and found subunits that perform certain, predictable tasks to be more effective when they were formally structured. Thus, a number of task characteristics have been studied at the level of organizational subunits. Here, two task characteristics—task uncertainty and task interdependence—are considered as influencing the appropriate KM processes (Spender 1996).

Consistent with Lawrence and Lorsch (1967), greater task uncertainty is argued to reduce the organization's ability to develop routines, and hence knowledge application would depend on direction. Moreover, when task uncertainty is high, **externalization** and **internalization** would be more costly due to changing problems and tasks. Under such circumstances, knowledge is more likely to remain tacit, inhibiting the ability to use combination or exchange. Therefore, under high task uncertainty, direction or socialization would be recommended. For example, individuals responsible for product design when customer tastes are expected to change frequently would benefit most from socializing with, and receiving directions from, each other.

On the other hand, when the tasks are low in uncertainty routines can be developed for the knowledge supporting them. Moreover, the benefits from externalizing or internalizing knowledge related to any specific task would accumulate through the greater occurrence of that task. Finally, exchange and combination would be useful due to the externalization of potentially tacit knowledge. Therefore, under low task uncertainty, routines, exchange, combination, internalization, or externalization would be recommended. These conclusions are summarized in the bottom part of Figure 10.3.

For example, for individuals performing tasks related to credit and accounts receivables, considerable benefits would be obtained from the use of routines (e.g., those for credit-checking procedures), exchange (e.g., sharing of standards and policies), combination (e.g., integration of explicit knowledge that different credit analysts may have generated from their experiences), and from externalization and internalization (e.g., to facilitate training and learning of existing policies by new credit analysts).

The second important task characteristic is **task interdependence**, which indicates the extent to which the subunit's achievement of its goals depends on the efforts of other subunits (Jarvenpaa and Staples 2001). Performing tasks that are independent of others primarily requires the knowledge directly available to the individuals within the subunit. These tasks rely mainly on distinctive units of knowledge, such as "functional knowledge embodied in a specific group of engineers, elemental technologies, information processing devices, databases, and patents" (Kusonaki et al. 1998, p. 670). They often require deep knowledge in a particular area. With internalization, such as when individuals acquire knowledge by observing or by talking to others, as well as with externalization, such as when they try to model their knowledge into analogies, metaphors, or problem-solving systems, the learning processes are personal and individualized. Through externalization,

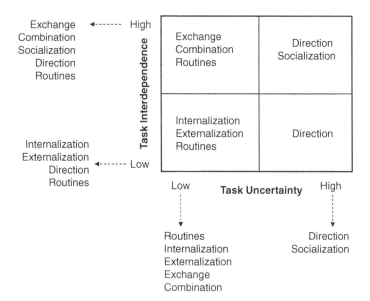

Figure 10.3 Effects of Task Characteristics on KM Processes

the individual makes the knowledge more agreeable and understandable to others in the group while through internalization the individual absorbs knowledge held by others in the group (Maturana and Varela 1987). Internalization and externalization are thus fundamental to KM in an independent task domain. Performance of interdependent tasks relies mainly on dynamic interaction in which individual units of knowledge are combined and transformed through communication and coordination across different functional groups. This creates greater causal ambiguity, since knowledge is being integrated across multiple groups that may not have a high level of shared understanding. Socialization and combination processes, both of which help synthesize prior knowledge to create new knowledge, are therefore appropriate for interdependent tasks (Grant 1996).

The left portion of Figure 10.3 shows that internalization and externalization should be preferred for independent tasks whereas **exchange, combination**, and **socialization** should be preferred for interdependent tasks. Moreover, **directions** and **routines** can be used for independent as well as interdependent tasks; their suitability depends more on task uncertainty, as already discussed.

Combining the arguments regarding the effects of task uncertainty and task interdependence, we obtain the four-cell matrix in Figure 10.3. As shown in the matrix, direction is recommended for uncertain, independent tasks; direction and socialization are recommended for uncertain, interdependent tasks; exchange, combination, and routines are recommended for certain, interdependent tasks; and internalization, externalization, and routines are recommended for certain, independent tasks.

The Effects of Knowledge Characteristics

Three knowledge characteristics—explicit versus tacit, procedural versus declarative, and general versus specific—were examined in Chapter 2. The first two of these knowledge characteristics directly affect the suitability of KM processes. The underlying contingency argument is that certain KM processes may have greater impact on the value that one type of knowledge contributes to the organization, while some other KM processes might affect the value of another type of knowledge (Spender 1996).

Figure 10.4 shows the KM processes that were presented earlier in Chapter 3 while also depicting the effects of the two knowledge classifications. The difference between KM processes appropriate for explicit and tacit knowledge is based directly on the main difference between these knowledge types.

For **knowledge discovery**, combination would be appropriate for integrating multiple streams of explicit knowledge, for example with knowledge discovery systems, where socialization would be suitable for integrating multiple streams of **tacit knowledge**. For **knowledge capture**, externalization would be appropriate for tacit knowledge as it helps convert tacit knowledge into **explicit knowledge**, for example in knowledge capture systems; whereas internalization would be appropriate for explicit knowledge, as it helps convert explicit knowledge into tacit knowledge, for example in learning. For **knowledge sharing**, exchange helps transfer explicit knowledge whereas socialization is needed for tacit knowledge. These intuitively obvious recommendations are also based on the logic that a KM process would contribute much to the value of knowledge if it is both effective and efficient for managing that knowledge (Gupta and Govindarajan 2000). Some KM processes might not contribute to the value of a given type of knowledge either because they are not effective in managing it (e.g., combination and exchange would not be effective for managing tacit knowledge), or because they are too

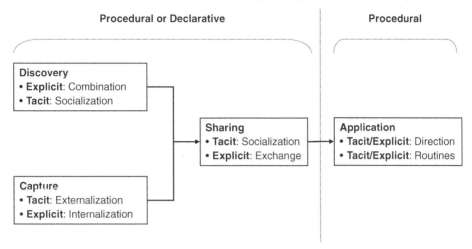

Figure 10.4 Effects of Knowledge Characteristics on KM Processes

expensive or too slow—that is, an alternative process would be able to integrate it more quickly or at a lower cost (e.g., socialization would be too expensive and slow for sharing explicit knowledge, especially in comparison to exchange).

No difference between the suitability of direction and routines is expected between tacit and explicit knowledge. In other words, either direction or routines could be used to apply either tacit or explicit knowledge. This is the case because no knowledge is being transferred in either direction or routines; only recommendations based on the expert's knowledge (whether tacit or explicit) are being transferred. Both direction and routine processes are appropriate to be used mainly for **procedural knowledge**, or "know-how," which focuses on the processes or means that should be used to perform the required tasks—for instance how to perform the steps in performing a specific process, such as installing a piece of software. This is shown in the right portion of Figure 10.4. Procedural knowledge differs from **declarative knowledge**, substantive knowledge, or "know what," which focuses on beliefs about relationships among variables, as we discussed in Chapter 2. As shown in the left part of Figure 10.4, all the KM processes supporting knowledge discovery, capture, and sharing can be used for both declarative and procedural knowledge.

Thus, either direction or routines could be used to apply procedural knowledge, whether tacit or explicit. KM processes used to discover, capture, or share knowledge are the same for both procedural and declarative kinds of knowledge. However, these processes differ between tacit and explicit knowledge, as discussed and shown in Figure 10.4 within the boxes for knowledge discovery, capture, and sharing.

The Effects of Organizational and Environmental Characteristics

Two organizational characteristics—size and strategy—and one environmental characteristic—uncertainty—affect the suitability of various knowledge management processes. Table 10.1 summarizes the effects of environmental and organizational characteristics.

Organization size affects KM processes by influencing the choice between the two processes supporting **knowledge application** (direction, routines) and the two processes

Table 10.1 Effect of Environmental and Organizational Characteristics on KM Processes

Characteristic	Level/Type	Recommended KM Processes
Organization Size	Small	• Knowledge sharing (socialization)
		• Knowledge application (direction)
		• Knowledge discovery (combination, socialization)
		• Knowledge capture (externalization, internalization)
	Large	• Knowledge sharing (exchange)
		• Knowledge application (routines)
		• Knowledge discovery (combination)
		• Knowledge capture (externalization, internalization)
Business Strategy	Low cost	• Knowledge application (direction, routines)
		• Knowledge capture (externalization, internalization)
		• Knowledge sharing (socialization, exchange)
	Differentiation	• Knowledge discovery (combination, socialization)
		• Knowledge capture (externalization, internalization)
		• Knowledge sharing (socialization, exchange)
Environmental Uncertainty	Low	• Knowledge sharing (socialization, exchange)
		• Knowledge capture (externalization, internalization)
	High	• Knowledge discovery (combination, socialization)
		• Knowledge application (direction, routines)

supporting knowledge sharing (socialization, exchange). For knowledge application, large and more bureaucratic organizations would benefit more from routines because of their greater use of standards and their potential for reuse of these routines. Small organizations, on the other hand, are usually not very bureaucratic and have less potential for reusing processes and procedures coded as routines. They would therefore benefit more from direction, which does not rely on standardization and rules. The circumstances needed for direction—for example, the knowledge user's trust in the individual providing direction (Conner and Prahalad 1996)—are also more likely to exist in smaller organizations. Large organizations are often globally distributed, therefore knowledge sharing across greater distances would be needed; whereas knowledge is more likely to be shared across shorter distances in smaller co-located organizations. Therefore, knowledge sharing through exchange is recommended for large distributed organizations while socialization is recommended for small co-located organizations (Boh 2007). Socialization for knowledge discovery is also recommended for small organizations, although combination could be used in either small or large organizations. Finally, small and large organizations do not differ in terms of the suitability of the alternative knowledge capture processes (externalization, internalization).

For example, a small financial consulting firm with 25 employees would have only a few experts in any area—for instance, customer relations practices. Consequently, others in the organization are likely to trust these experts and depend on their direction. Moreover, the small number of employees would have frequent opportunities to interact with each other thereby enabling greater use of socialization for knowledge discovery as well as knowledge sharing. On the other hand, a large consulting firm with over 5,000 employees would find it infeasible or overly expensive to rely on socialization, especially across large distances. Instead, in such an organization, knowledge sharing would rely more on exchange of knowledge explicated in reports, lessons learned documents, and so on. In addition, large organizations may find it more likely to reuse knowledge that has been explicated previously, for example in lessons learned systems or best practices databases as described in Chapter 8. Furthermore, this firm would find it beneficial to develop and use routines for applying knowledge. Routines would be more economical due to their greater frequency of use in such larger firms and also needed by more individuals within the organization who may be seeking help.

The effect of **business strategy** may be examined using Porter's (1980, 1985) popular typology of low cost and differentiation strategies.[1] Organizations pursuing a low-cost strategy should focus on applying existing knowledge rather than creating new knowledge, whereas organizations following a differentiation strategy are more likely to innovate (Langerak et al. 1999), seek new opportunities (Miles and Snow 1978), and frequently develop new products (Hambrick 1983). They would therefore benefit more from knowledge discovery and capture processes (combination and socialization). Organizations pursuing either low-cost or differentiation strategy would benefit from knowledge capture and sharing processes, as these processes can be used to capture or share knowledge on ways of reducing costs as well as innovating with products or services.

For example, a supermarket chain competing through a low-cost strategy would seek to reuse prior knowledge about ordering, inventory management, supplier relations, pricing, and so on. This company would therefore use organizational routines (in case the company is large) or direction (if the company is small) to support the application of prior knowledge. In contrast, an exclusive fashion boutique, trying to differentiate itself from its competitors, would seek new knowledge about attracting competitors' customers and retaining its own customers, developing innovative products, and so on. This boutique would significantly benefit from socialization and combination processes for creating new knowledge about these aspects, using prior tacit and explicit knowledge, respectively.

The environmental uncertainty encountered by the organization also affects knowledge management (Hsu and Wang 2008), and the suitability of various KM processes (Sabherwal and Sabherwal 2005). Environmental uncertainty, which refers to the business context in which the firm operates, should not be confused with task uncertainty which refers to not having *a priori* knowledge of details involved in the steps required by a task. When the organization faces low levels of uncertainty, knowledge sharing and knowledge capture processes would be recommended because the captured and shared knowledge would be relevant for longer periods of time. On the other hand, under higher uncertainty, knowledge application and discovery would be recommended. Knowledge application contributes in an uncertain environment by enabling individuals to address problems based on existing solutions indicated by those possessing the knowledge, instead of more time-consuming processes like sharing knowledge (Alavi and Leidner 2001; Conner and Prahalad 1996). Knowledge discovery processes contribute by enhancing the organization's ability to develop new innovative solutions to emergent problems that may not have been faced before (Davenport and Prusak 1998).

For example, the environment would be rather certain and predictable for an automobile-manufacturing firm that has a relatively stable product line and competes with a small number of competitors, especially when each firm has its own clear market niche. For such an organization, knowledge about product design, manufacturing, marketing, sales, and so forth would be generally stable, benefiting from the sharing of prior knowledge through socialization or exchange and the capture of knowledge through internalization and externalization. Knowledge sharing, as well as internalization and externalization, would have long-term benefits, as the knowledge remains inherently stable. On the other hand, an international mobile phone manufacturer having a dynamic product line and evolving customer base would face a highly uncertain environment. This organization would seek to create new knowledge and quickly apply existing knowledge by investing in combination and socialization for knowledge discovery and routines and direction for knowledge application. For example, Canon Inc.'s success has been attributed to both creating new innovations, for example in the photography industry, and quickly applying these innovations to other relevant products like fax and copy machines.

The effects of contingency factors on the selection of knowledge management solutions at one leading consumer-goods company, Groupe Danone, is described in Box 10.2.

Box 10.2 Networking Attitude Fosters Knowledge Sharing and Creation at Danone

Groupe Danone is a leading consumer-goods company, with headquarters in Paris. Known as Dannon in the United States, it is among the world's leading producers of dairy products, bottled water, cereals, and baby foods. Danone is a fast-moving and entrepreneurial company, emphasizing differentiation rather than cost reduction. Although it is spread across 120 countries, it is smaller than its competitors and operates in a decentralized fashion with considerable emphasis on responsiveness to the needs of local markets. Most of the knowledge used at Danone is held in tacit form by its employees. Danone's business strategy (differentiation), environmental uncertainty (which is high because of its operating in numerous countries with changing products), and focus on tacit knowledge make it important for the company to share knowledge across countries and across divisions. However, the use of exchange through IT did not seem promising due to the tacit nature of their knowledge. Moreover, Danone's employees did not make much use of portals and information technologies in general.

Senior executives at Danone, including Frank Mougin, Danone's executive vice president of human resources, recognized that using IT to share knowledge would not work as well for the company. Therefore, they have concentrated their KM efforts on using socialization for sharing existing knowledge as well as creating new knowledge using processes akin to their firm's characteristics. As a result, they launched the Networking Attitude Conference in the Fall of 2002. Networking Attitude was presented to the company's general managers as a mechanism for people in units distant from each other to share their knowledge. It focused on the following initiatives:

- "Marketplaces" were special events focusing on a theme, and involving "takers" who "pay" for best practices obtained from "givers," using a "check" and a facilitator tracking the number of checks acquired by each giver and using it as a way of evaluating the relevance of each best practice.

- A "message-in-a-bottle" session brought "takers" facing problems to a smaller audience of potential "givers," and with no observer to facilitate more spontaneous networking.
- A "T-shirt session" was incorporated into meetings or conferences, with the participants writing suggestions and problems on the front and back of their T-shirts, respectively.
- "Who's Who" was an internal directory on the company's Intranet.
- "Communities" were smaller networks (with a leader and about 10 to 15 members) who met regularly (every six months or so).

Although there was no formal tracking of its impact, the Networking Attitude Conference appears to have worked well for Danone, with people participating actively by sharing important knowledge and providing each other recommendations on directions. People seemed to like it, and marketplaces had become especially popular in Mexico and Hungary. From 2004 to 2007, Danone employees shared about 640 best practices with each other and made useful knowledge available to about 5,000 (out of a total of about 9,000) Danone managers around the world.

The success of Networking Attitude led to a demand for introducing additional networking opportunities. Danone was considering three ways of extending Networking Attitude: *deeper* (i.e., involving all the employees rather than only managers), *wider* (i.e., extending the use of networks to customers, consumers, suppliers, and partners), and *richer* (i.e., using it more explicitly for innovation by inviting employees to network with each other with the goal of identifying new products or processes).

Sources: Compiled from Edmondson et al. (2011); Groupe Danone (n.d.); Mougin and Benenati (2005)

Identification of Appropriate Knowledge Management Solutions

Based on the above discussion, we recommend a **methodology** for identifying appropriate KM solutions. The methodology includes the following seven steps:

1 Assess the contingency factors.
2 Identify the KM processes based on each contingency factor.
3 Prioritize the needed KM processes.
4 Identify the existing KM processes.
5 Identify the additional needed KM processes.
6 Assess the KM infrastructure and identify the sequential ordering of KM processes.
7 Develop additional needed KM systems, mechanisms, and technologies.

These seven steps are now discussed.

Step 1. *Assess the Contingency Factors*

This step requires assessing the organization's environment in terms of the contingency factors—characterizing the tasks, the knowledge, the environment, and the organization—and how they contribute to uncertainty.

The variety of tasks for which KM is needed should be characterized in terms of task interdependence and task uncertainty. Furthermore, the kind of knowledge those tasks require should be classified as general or specific, declarative or procedural, and tacit or explicit. Environmental uncertainty may arise from changes in the firm's competition, government regulations and policies, economic conditions, and so on.

Additionally, the organization's business strategy—low-cost or differentiation—should be identified. Lastly, the organization should be classified as small or large relative to its competitors. In some instances, it may be labeled as midsized, in which case the KM processes would be based on considerations of both small and large organizations.

In using these contingencies, it is important to use the appropriate unit of analysis, which could be either the entire organization or a subunit depending on the specific context for which the KM solution would be developed. When deciding on KM processes that are intended to improve KM within a subunit, such as the accounting department of the organization, the contingency factors should be evaluated for that subunit. On the other hand, when deciding on KM processes that are intended to improve KM for the entire company, the contingency factors should be evaluated for the entire company.

Step 2. Identify the KM Processes Based on Each Contingency Factor

Next, the appropriate KM processes based on each contingency factor should be identified. In doing this, Table 10.2, which summarizes the effects of various contingency factors,

Table 10.2 Appropriate Circumstances for Various KM Processes

Contingency factors	KM Processes							
	Combination	Socialization for knowledge discovery	Socialization for knowledge sharing	Exchange	Externalization	Internalization	Direction	Routines
Task uncertainty	Low	High	High	Low	Low	Low	High	Low
Task interdependence	High	High	High	High	Low	Low	High/low	High/low
Explicit (E) or tacit (T) knowledge	E	T	T	E	T	E	T/E	T/E
Procedural (P) or declarative (D) knowledge	P/D	P/D	P/D	P/D	P/D	P/D	P	P
Organizational size	Small/large	Small	Small	Large	Small/large	Small/large	Small	Large
Business strategy (Low cost—LC; Differentiation—D)	D	D	LC/D	LC/D	LC/D	LC/D	LC	LC
Environmental uncertainty	High	High	Low	Low	Low	Low	High	High

should be useful. This table shows the seven contingency factors and the effects they have on the KM processes. It is important to note, however, that this table only provides some of the most important factors that need to be considered in making this choice. There are several other factors, such as the information intensity of the organization's industry, that would also affect the appropriateness of KM processes, but they have been excluded to simplify the presentation.

Step 3. Prioritize the Needed KM Processes

Once the KM processes appropriate for each contingency factor have been identified, they need to be considered together in order to identify the needed KM processes. In doing so, it is useful to assign a value of 1.0 to situations where a KM process is appropriate for a contingency variable and 0.0 where it is not appropriate. Moreover, where a KM process is appropriate for all possible states of a contingency variable, a value of 0.5 could be assigned. As a result, a prioritization of the importance of various KM processes can be developed, and a Cumulative Priority Score can be computed. For example, if KM process A has a composite score of 6.0 based on the seven contingency factors whereas another one (B) has a composite score of 3.0, greater attention is needed toward KM process A rather than B. This computation is shown in greater detail using an illustrative example in the next section.

Step 4. Identify the Existing KM Processes

Next, the KM processes that are currently being used should be identified. In doing so, a short survey of some of the employees assessing the extent to which each KM process is being used may be helpful. Possible approaches for such assessments are discussed in detail in the next chapter.

Step 5. Identify the Additional Needed KM Processes

Based on the needed KM processes (identified in step 3) and the existing KM processes (identified in step 4), the additional needed KM processes can be identified. This comparison might also find some of the existing KM processes to not be very useful. In other words, if a KM process is identified as needed (step 3) but it is not currently being used (step 4), it should be added; whereas if a KM process is not identified as needed (step 3) but it is currently being used (step 4), it could potentially be dropped— at least based on knowledge management considerations.

Step 6. Assess the KM Infrastructure and Identify the Sequential Ordering of KM Processes

The KM infrastructure indirectly affects the KM processes as we discussed earlier. Specifically, organization culture, organization structure, and the physical environment can facilitate or inhibit knowledge sharing and creation. Additionally, information technologies can support all KM processes, and organizing knowledge can help enhance the efficiency of knowledge sharing (e.g., through common language and vocabulary) and application processes (e.g., by enhancing recognition of individual knowledge domains). These aspects of the KM infrastructure should be considered with respect to the additional KM processes needed (as identified in step 5) to identify the KM processes for which supporting infrastructure, mechanisms, and technologies currently exist. This step is especially important when deciding the sequence in which KM processes that are nearly equal in importance (step 3) should be developed.

Step 7. Develop Additional Needed KM Systems, Mechanisms, and Technologies

Steps 1 through 6 have helped identify the KM processes and the order in which they should be developed. Now the organization needs to undertake steps to initiate the creation of KM systems, **mechanisms**, and technologies that would support those KM processes. This might require creation of teams, acquisition of technologies, development of systems, and so on. In the long run, these systems, mechanisms, and technologies would also contribute to the KM infrastructure.

Illustrative Example

As an illustration, which is kept somewhat simple to prevent this discussion from becoming overly complex, let us consider the fictional Doubtfire Computer Corporation, a manufacturer of low-end personal computers for home users. A small player in this industry, Doubtfire has recently undergone some difficult times due to new competition for its product line. Competitors make frequent changes in technology in an attempt to gain the upper hand in the marketplace with more state-of-the-art products. Having belatedly recognized this, Doubtfire recently hired a new president and a new sales manager to turn the situation around. The new president called a meeting of the staff to discuss possible strategies for the financial turnaround of the company. The main thrust of this presentation was that the staff needed to better manage knowledge so as to creatively identify areas where new technology could improve the company's products and operations. Based on inputs from the senior management, the president hired a knowledge management consulting firm, KM-Consult Inc., to help improve its KM strategy.

A team of consultants from KM-Consult Inc. conducted an in-depth study of Doubtfire, using interviews with several employees and examination of company documents. Based on their investigation, they concluded that Doubtfire is a small organization that has pursued a low-cost business strategy to operate in an uncertain environment as is typical of high-tech firms. Knowledge management is needed for its tasks, which are highly interdependent and also highly uncertain due to changing components in the computer industry. Doubtfire relies mainly on the tacit, procedural knowledge possessed by its employees rather than seeking the explication of that knowledge or management of declarative knowledge. Then, based on Table 10.2, the consulting team arrived at the following conclusions.

First, based on Doubtfire's small organization size, socialization (for knowledge sharing or knowledge discovery) and direction processes would be appropriate. In addition, combination, internalization, and externalization could be used regardless of organization size. However, exchange and routines would be inappropriate due to Doubtfire being a small organization.

Moreover, considering Doubtfire's low-cost business strategy, direction and routines would be appropriate. In addition, socialization (for knowledge sharing), exchange, internalization, and externalization could be used regardless of strategy. However, combination and socialization (for knowledge discovery) would be inappropriate because they are not suitable for firms pursuing a low-cost strategy.

The consulting team also concluded that, based on the uncertain environment in which Doubtfire operates—which is characteristic of firms in the high-tech sector—direction, combination, and socialization (for knowledge discovery) would be appropriate. However, the remaining processes would be inappropriate as they are more suitable for certain, predictable environments.

The high task interdependence in Doubtfire suggests that socialization (for knowledge sharing or knowledge discovery), combination, and exchange would be appropriate. In addition, direction and routines could be used regardless of task interdependence. However, externalization and internalization would not be as useful. The high task uncertainty suggests that socialization (for knowledge sharing or knowledge discovery) and direction would be appropriate. However, the remaining processes would be less suitable.

The procedural nature of knowledge indicates that direction and routines would be useful for managing this knowledge. The tacit nature of knowledge suggests that socialization (for knowledge sharing or knowledge discovery) and externalization would be appropriate. In addition, direction and routines could be used regardless of tacit or explicit nature of knowledge.

Table 10.2 shows the results of this analysis by KM-Consult Inc. The cells in the columns for each contingency factor show the suitability of the KM process in that row for that contingency variable. More specifically, "Yes" indicates that the KM process in that row is appropriate for the contingency variable in that column, which converts to a score of 1.0; "No" indicates that the KM process in that row is inappropriate for the contingency variable in that column, which converts to a score of 0.0; and "OK" indicates that the KM process in that row can be used for all possible values of the contingency variable in that column, which converts to a score of 0.5.

The last four columns of the table show the computation of the Cumulative Priority Score for each KM process, based on the number of "Yes," "OK," and "No" responses for the suitability of that KM process for the seven contingency variables. Based on this analysis, direction has the highest Cumulative Priority Score (6.0), followed by socialization for knowledge discovery (5.5) and then socialization for knowledge sharing (5.0). Routines are at an intermediate level of priority with a Cumulative Priority Score of 4.0, whereas combination, externalization, exchange, and internalization have low Cumulative Priority Scores (3.0 or less).

Thus, the consideration of the contingency variables led KM-Consult Inc. to conclude that Doubtfire should focus its KM efforts primarily on direction and socialization (for both knowledge discovery and knowledge sharing), with attention being given to combination and routines if the resources so allow. However, recognizing the financial difficulties Doubtfire was facing, KM-Consult Inc. recommended that Doubtfire should focus its efforts on direction and socialization. Moreover, KM-Consult Inc. had found that the current KM initiative at Doubtfire was making little use of both socialization and direction. Therefore, KM-Consult Inc. recommended that Doubtfire should try to enhance the use of direction and socialization for knowledge management. Their report also identified the specific technologies and systems for Doubtfire to pursue. It recommended the establishment and use of communities of practice to support socialization and an expertise locator system to support direction. It also recommended that Doubtfire should enhance socialization through more frequent meetings, rituals, brainstorming retreats, and more. The consultants argued that this socialization would also enhance mutual trust among Doubtfire's employees, thereby increasing their willingness to provide and accept direction. Moreover, KM-Consult Inc. found Doubtfire to be currently making considerable use of internalization, and spending considerable resources on employee training programs. In the light of the low cumulative score for internalization, KM-Consult Inc. advised Doubtfire to consider reducing the budget allocated toward employee training.

Summary

Following our discussion of knowledge management impacts in Chapter 5, we have described how an organization can seek to enhance these impacts by targeting its KM solutions according to the circumstances in which KM is being used. In doing so we have examined the variety of KM processes, systems, mechanisms, as well as technologies discussed in Chapters 3 and 4, while focusing mainly on the KM processes. Table 10.2 summarizes the conclusions regarding the suitability of the KM processes under various circumstances. A methodology for effectively targeting the KM solutions has also been described and illustrated using a detailed example. The next chapter examines how we can evaluate the contributions of KM solutions.

Review

1   What is the contingency view of knowledge management? How does it differ from the universalistic view of knowledge management?
2   What do you understand by the terms task uncertainty and task interdependence?
3   What are the knowledge characteristics that affect the appropriateness of knowledge management processes? Explain why.
4   How does organizational size affect knowledge management processes?
5   In what way do organizational strategy and environmental uncertainty affect knowledge management processes?
6   What steps would one take in identifying appropriate knowledge management solutions? Briefly describe them.
7   Explain how a large organization operating in a highly uncertain environment should pursue a low-cost business strategy using knowledge management. State the assumptions made to arrive at your answer.
8   In the seven steps of identifying appropriate KM solutions, Cumulative Priority Score was computed. Describe the function of the score and its application.

Application Exercises

1   Visit local area companies to study their knowledge management practices. Determine how they decided on the type of KM solution they use.
2   Consider reasons why an organization would choose the universalistic view of KM over the contingency view.
3   Visit an organization with a high level of task uncertainty in their business. Explore the extent to which KM is helping or could help them.

4   Similarly, visit an organization with high levels of task interdependence among the subunits. Explore the ways in which they have implemented KM to the benefit of the organization.

5   Visit any three organizations and identify their major areas of organizational knowledge and the prominently used KM processes. Next, classify the characteristics of their organizational knowledge into: explicit or tacit; procedural or declarative; and general or specific. Based on the data you collect, determine how appropriate their KM processes are.

6   Collect information from the Internet, *Business Week, Fortune,* and others on either Toyota Motor Corporation or Apple Inc. about the nature of these organizations. Based on this information and the contingency approach presented in this chapter, identify how knowledge should be managed at this company.

7   You are a KM consultant for BP (www.bp.com). BP is one of the world's largest petroleum and petrochemicals groups. Its main activities are exploration and production of crude oil and natural gas; refining, marketing, supply, and transportation of oil and gas; and selling fuels and related products. Due to current worldwide financial problems, environmental uncertainty is said to be relatively high these days.

   a   Gather information on BP and decide whether its task uncertainty and task interdependence are high or low. Provide the reasons for your decision.

   b   What types of knowledge does BP use most? Suggest the appropriate KM process for each of these types of knowledge?

   c   Assess (i) the organization size of BP (small or large); (ii) business strategy (low cost or differentiation); and (iii) environmental uncertainty (high or low).

   d   Next, compute the Cumulate Priority Score of each KM processes discussed in this chapter. Based on this analysis, what is your recommendation to BP of appropriate KM solutions?

Note

1   Another popular classification of business strategy focuses on classifying firms into Defenders, Analyzers, and Prospectors (Miles and Snow 1978). Defenders, Analyzers, and Prospectors have been found to differ according to the kind of KM efforts that would be most suitable in terms of their effects on the firm's stock market performance (Sabherwal and Sabherwal 2007).

References

Alavi, M., and Leidner, D. 2001. Knowledge management and knowledge management systems: Conceptual foundations and research issues. *MIS Quarterly*, 25(1), 107–136.

Becerra-Fernandez, I., and Sabherwal, R. 2001. Organizational knowledge management processes: A contingency perspective. *Journal of Management Information Systems*, 18(1) (Summer), 23–55.

Becerra-Fernandez, I., Gonzalez, A., and Sabherwal, R. 2004. *Knowledge management: Challenges, solutions, and technologies*, vol. 2. Upper Saddle River, NJ: Prentice Hall.

Boh, W.F. 2007. Mechanisms for sharing knowledge in project-based organizations. *Information and Organization*, 17, 27–58.

Conner, K.R., and Prahalad, C.K. 1996. A resource-based theory of the firm: Knowledge versus opportunism. *Organization Science*, 7(5), 477–501.

Davenport, T.H., and Prusak, L. 1998. *Working knowledge: How organizations manage what they know.* Boston: Harvard Business School Press.

Edmondson, A., Moingeon, B., Dessain, V., and Jensen, D. 2011. Global knowledge management at Danone (A). *Harvard Business Publishing*, 9–608–107, September 6.

Grant, R.M. 1996. Toward a knowledge-based theory of the firm. *Strategic Management Journal*, 17 (Winter), 109–122.

Groupe Danone. n.d. https://www.danone.com/.

Gupta, A.K., and Govindarajan, V. 2000. Knowledge management's social dimension: Lessons from Nucor steel. *Sloan Management Review* (Fall), 71–80.

Haas, M.R., and Hansen, M.T. 2005. When using knowledge can hurt performance: The value of organizational capabilities in a management consulting company. *Strategic Management Journal*, 26, 1–24.

Hambrick, D.C. 1983. Some tests of the effectiveness and functional attributes of Miles and Snow's strategic types. *Academy of Management Journal*, 26(1), 5–26.

Handzic, M., Ozlen, K., and Durmic, N. 2016. A contingency approach to knowledge management: Finding the best fit, *International Journal of Knowledge Management*, 12(1), 31–44.

Hsu, I-C., and Wang, Y-S. 2008. A model of intraorganizational knowledge sharing: Development and initial test. *Journal of Global Information Management*, 16(3), 45–73.

Jarvenpaa, S.L., and Staples, D.S. 2001. Exploring perceptions of organizational ownership of information and expertise. *Journal of Management Information Systems*, 18(1) (Summer), 151–184.

Kim, T.H., Lee, J-N., Chun, J.U., and Benbasat, I. 2014. Understanding the effect of knowledge management strategies on knowledge management performance: A contingency perspective. *Information & Management*, 51(4), 398–416.

Kusonaki, K., Nonaka, I., and Nagata, A. 1998. Organizational capabilities in product development of Japanese firms: A conceptual framework and empirical findings. *Organization Science*, 9(6), 699–718.

Langerak, F., Nijssen, E., Frambach, R., and Gupta, A. 1999. Exploratory results on the importance of R&D knowledge domains in businesses with different strategies. *R&D Management*, 29(3), 209–217.

Lawrence, P.R., and Lorsch, J.W. 1967. *Organization and environment: Managing differentiation and integration*. Cambridge: Harvard University Press.

Massey, A.P., Montoya-Weiss, M.M., and O'Driscoll, T.M. 2002. Knowledge management in pursuit of performance: Insights from Nortel Networks. *MIS Quarterly*, 26(3) (September), 269–289.

Maturana, H., and Varela, F. 1987. *The tree of knowledge*. Boston: New Science Library.

Miles, R.E., and Snow, C.C. 1978. *Organizational strategy, structure, and process*. New York: McGraw-Hill.

Mougin, F., and Benenati, B. 2005. Story-telling at Danone: A Latin approach to knowledge management. Report by Sylvie Cherier, trans. Rachel Marlin. Report, École de Paris du management. http://innovation.zumablog.com/images/186_uploads/Networking_at_Danone.pdf (accessed February 16, 2009).

Porter, M.E. 1980. *Competitive strategy*. New York: Free Press.

Porter, M.E. 1985. *Competitive advantage*. New York: Free Press.

Sabherwal, R., and Sabherwal, S. 2005. Knowledge management using information technology: Determinants of short-term impact on firm value. *Decision Sciences*, 36(4), 531–567.

Sabherwal, R., and Sabherwal, S. 2007. How do knowledge management announcements affect firm value? A study of firms pursuing different business strategies. *IEEE Transactions on Engineering Management*, 54(3), 409–422.

Spender, J.C. 1996. Making knowledge the basis of a dynamic theory of the firm. *Strategic Management Journal*, 17 (Winter), 45–63.

Van de Ven, A., and Delbecq, A. 1974. The effectiveness of nominal, delphi, and interacting group decision-making processes. *Academy of Management Journal*, 17, 314–318.

11 Leadership and Assessment of Knowledge Management

In Chapter 3 we discussed knowledge management foundations including infrastructure, mechanisms, and technologies, and how organizations manage it. In Chapter 4, we examined how organizations manage KM solutions, including KM systems and processes. In Chapter 10, we examined how organizations should consider the contingency factors in selecting KM solutions. We also examined the management of specific KM systems in Chapters 6, 7, 8, and 9. To complement these chapters and better understand the overall management of KM in an organization, this chapter examines the leadership of KM and the ways in which the value of KM can be assessed in an organization.

This chapter begins with a discussion of the overall leadership of KM in an organization. Next, it examines the reasons why a KM assessment is needed. It subsequently describes the alternative approaches to assessing KM in the organization, first for evaluating various aspects related to KM and then for the overall evaluation of KM effectiveness.

Leadership of Knowledge Management

The **Chief Executive Officer (CEO)** and the executive board have a direct impact on how the organization views KM. In order for KM to be practiced across the organization, leaders at the top must endorse and stress the importance of KM programs (DeTienne et al. 2004). The CEO must be involved in the knowledge sharing efforts so that others in the organization can follow (Kluge et al. 2001). Also, "if KM doesn't permeate all levels of an organization, beginning at the top, it is unlikely that KM programs will ever catch on or be effective" (DeTienne et al. 2004, p. 34). In summary, the role of the CEO is critical to the success of KM in the organization: first, to articulate a "grand theory" of the organization's vision for KM; second, to incorporate this vision into the organization's objectives; and third, to identify which KM initiatives support that strategy (Takeuchi 2001).

The CEO designates the leadership of the knowledge management function to another senior executive who could be the **Chief Knowledge Officer (CKO)**, Chief Learning Officer, and in some cases the Chief Information Officer. The Chief Knowledge Officer is usually expected to balance social and technical aspects of KM, while the Chief Learning Officer and the Chief Information Officer are generally charged with KM in organizations where the emphasis is on the social aspects and technical aspects, respectively.

DOI: 10.4324/9781003364375-14

Some CEOs might consider adding that responsibility of leading KM to the role of the **Chief Information Officer (CIO)**. However, this may not be an appropriate decision:

> While some CIOs might have the capabilities for the model CKO—entrepreneur, consultant, environmentalist, and technologist—most will score high on the technologist and consultant dimensions but be less accomplished on the entrepreneur and environmentalist dimensions. And CIOs are oriented toward directing a substantial function, rather than toward nurturing and leading a transitory team. Most CIOs have demanding enough agendas without adding the ambiguities of the CKO role.
>
> (Earl and Scott 1999, p. 38)

The **Chief Learning Officer (CLO)** is the "business leader of corporate learning" (Bersin 2007). At organizations like CIGNA Corporation (Conz 2008), HP (Kiger 2007), PriceWaterhouseCoopers LLP (Cencigh-Albulario 2008), Accenture Ltd (Meister and Davenport 2005), and many others the CLO is the business executive who leads the organization's learning and development strategy, processes, and systems. Thus, the CLO usually focuses on human resource development and employees' learning and training. For example, PriceWaterhouseCoopers hired a Chief Learning Officer in 2007 to work with its human resource development team and to lead the further study and training of its personnel (Cencigh-Albulario 2008). CLOs usually focus on people and on social aspects of KM, although the CLO's role increasingly involves utilizing ITs to improve KM, often in collaboration with the CIO.

Organizations that recognize the importance of knowledge management as a critical function that goes beyond either information management or human resource development appoint a CKO and charge that individual with the management of the organization's intellectual assets and knowledge management processes, systems, and technologies (Kaplan 2007). Appointing a CKO is "one way of galvanizing, directing, and coordinating a knowledge management program" (Earl and Scott 1999, p. 37).

A study of twenty CKOs in North America and Europe (Earl and Scott 1999) found that many of the CKOs were appointed by CEOs more through intuition and instinct than through analysis or logic, based on the understanding about the increasing importance of knowledge in value creation and the recognition that companies are not good about managing it. Therefore, CKOs were named with the purpose of correcting a perceived corporate deficiency: lack of formal management of knowledge in operations, failure to leverage knowledge in business development, inability to learn from past failures and successes, and not creating value from existing knowledge assets. This study also found that many CKOs did not have a formal job description and that their position was perceived as somewhat transient (three to five years), culminating in the expectation that KM would be embedded in all organizational work processes. Many of these individuals were tasked first with articulating a customized KM program. This study characterized a model CKO as being both a technologist and an environmentalist. CKOs are technologists because they invest in IT, and they are environmentalists because they also create social environments that stimulate conversations and knowledge sharing. In addition, the model CKOs are also entrepreneurs, because they are visionary and starting a new activity; and at the same time they are consultants, because they match new ideas with managers' business needs.

Two other studies, one based on a survey of 41 organizations in the United States and Canada (McKeen and Staples 2003) and the other based on announcements of 23 newly created CKO positions during the period 1995–2003 (Awazu and Desouza 2004), found additional insights regarding the backgrounds, roles, and challenges for CKOs. They found that CKOs usually possess postgraduate education in business or an allied discipline and include many former academics, mainly professors in the areas of information and knowledge management (Awazu and Desouza 2004). An analysis of the background of CKOs revealed that most had a nice blend of technical and management skills. Many CKOs spent their formative years in areas such as KM, management consulting, corporate planning, change management, customer research, marketing, human resource planning, and IT. Organizations were equally likely to promote from within for the CKO position or make an external hire for the job. In either case, the average CKO had about ten years of experience in the industry in which the organization operates (Awazu and Desouza 2004).

CKOs' budgets and staff are modest, because KM initiatives are typically corporately funded and they may have divisional knowledge managers appointed on a dotted-line basis (Earl and Scott 1999; McKeen and Staples 2003). But the most important resource for CKOs is CEO support and sponsorship. The critical success factors for CKOs to achieve their goal of managing knowledge in organizations are (Awazu and Desouza 2004; Earl and Scott 1999):

- Having high-level sponsorship that extends beyond the CEO support.
- Institutionalizing knowledge sharing incentives.
- Breaking knowledge bottlenecks in the organization that impede smooth knowledge flows.
- Embedding knowledge into the work practices and processes.
- Organizational slack time to think, dream, talk, and sell.
- Creating reference projects that demonstrate the value of KM.
- Documenting visible successes for their own performance.

The CKO continues to be an important position in contemporary organizations. It is sometimes combined with other important positions. For example, at Colliers International, the president of U.S. Brokerage Services also serves as the Chief Knowledge Officer and was instrumental in setting up Colliers University, which is the company's business development and training division (Business Wire 2009). Similarly, global management consulting firm Booz & Company announced the position of Chief Marketing and Knowledge Officer and the Symbio Group in China, which provides outsourced software development for companies such as IBM, Mercedes-Benz (a division of Daimler AG), and MasterCard, announced the appointment of their Chief Knowledge Officer (Knowledge Management Review 2008).

Box 11.1 describes the experience of the Chief Knowledge Officer (CKO) and Chief Operating Officer (COO) at Atlantis Systems International.

Box 11.1 Management of KM at Atlantis Systems International

In an interview in September 2006, Blake Melnick, the chief knowledge officer (CKO) and chief operating officer (COO) of Atlantis Systems, discussed his role in the company's knowledge management efforts and the way in which Atlantis deployed its strategic knowledge advantage to recover following the September 11 terrorist attacks. Melnick stated that he has "always been an active knowledge builder," but his formal KM work started in 1995 during graduate studies at the University of Toronto, where he helped to found the Institute for Knowledge Innovation and Technology. He served as the head of external relations and workplace research for this institute for five years before joining Atlantis.

After September 11, 2001, the company faced difficult financial times and changed ownership in 2004. The new CEO, Andrew Day a strong supporter of KM, hired Melnick as CKO and COO to develop and deploy KM initiatives intended to achieve internal change management. Melnick considered measuring and demonstrating the ROI associated with KM to be a major challenge. Another challenge related to externalizing KM and using it as a discriminator in Atlantis' current and targeted markets.

Melnick described an integrated systems approach to KM, Knowledge Exchange (KX), which has been developed at Atlantis. The KX system integrates facilities for content management, collaborative discourse, performance management, mentoring, and employee and customer satisfaction and is the key to KM at Atlantis. The KX system is supported by several analytic tools that track usage, idea development, knowledge clusters, and so forth.

Melnick champions several established KM methods at Atlantis:

- Democratization of knowledge by providing every employee with the ability to influence the company's direction.
- Iterative improvement by encouraging each employee to strive to progress beyond best practices and capture ideas for improvement as they perform their tasks and activities.
- Rewards and recognition for employees, which contribute to the company's collective knowledge.
- Incorporation of the customer into the improvement process by encouraging them to contribute to the company's knowledge base.
- Flattening of organizational hierarchy, thereby enabling people to talk to each other.

Melnick has learned three lessons about KM that might be valuable to others:

1 KM is not all about technology. Instead, it involves both information management (technology) and knowledge-building (people).
2 We cannot really "manage knowledge," but we can manage the process that helps convert information into knowledge.
3 For KM in any organization, it is essential to address the employees' primary concern, such as, "What's in it for me?"

Melnick believes that since he joined Atlantis, KM at the company has progressed in terms of a greater appreciation for the "human dynamic" as an essential ingredient to successful KM implementation. Atlantis became more successful after making the various improvements in KM. The revenues grew by over 200 percent during the three years prior to 2007. During the same period the number of employees increased from 102 to 210, the retention rates remained stable at 3 percent, and the company successfully leveraged its knowledge of the aerospace sector to enter the nuclear energy sector.

Sources: Compiled from Knowledge Management Review (2006); Melnick (2006); Melnick (2007)

Another important component in the management of an organization's KM is the **management of knowledge communities of practice** within the organization. Two aspects are important in this realm—the management of a knowledge community of practice at the broad level, and leadership from within the community (Fallah 2011). Management is important in terms of the sponsorship of the community to enable the resources, technologies, infrastructure, and incentives needed for the launch and sustained use of the community, whereas leadership within the community, which is often distributed, is crucial for the exchange of knowledge within the community in a cooperative and respectful fashion (Denning 2009).

Moreover, knowledge management requires reducing **knowledge hiding**. Box 11.2 examines knowledge hiding, how individuals and organizations are affected by it, and how organizations can reduce it.

Box 11.2 How to Reduce Knowledge Hiding

Open communications and transparency are crucial elements of a successful work environment. A recent report (Great Place to Work 2016) highlights that firms fostering a high-trust environment, where employees collaborate and transparently exchange knowledge, experience stock returns two to three times higher than the industry average and 50 percent lower employee turnover compared to their competitors.

Another report (Panopto 2023) found that a significant number of employees, around 60 percent, find it difficult, very difficult, or nearly impossible to obtain the necessary information from their colleagues to perform their job duties. This leads to employees spending an average of 5.3 hours per week waiting for the necessary information to do their work, causing delays in project schedules. A substantial 66 percent of projects experience delays of up to a week, while 12 percent face delays lasting a month or even more. The lack of access to crucial information frustrates a majority of employees, with 81 percent expressing frustration when they cannot access the data they need to effectively carry out their job responsibilities. These findings highlight the significant impact that lack of effective knowledge sharing has on employee productivity and overall project efficiency. Indeed, by preserving and sharing knowledge, smaller enterprise-size businesses might save US$2 million in employee productivity, while larger firms could save US$200 million or more.

Despite the above clear benefits of sharing knowledge, many individuals conceal knowledge due to concerns about potential costs, such as losing power (the old adage that "knowledge is power") or fear of judgment based on what they know (Jiang 2019). This could be because individuals worry about losing status or their perceived power by sharing their knowledge, given their status as subject matter experts (SMEs) with unique knowledge in the organization. Other potential reasons for SMEs not wanting to share knowledge include perceiving their knowledge as personal property, being afraid to be judged based on what they know, or not liking or trusting those who seek that knowledge.

However, knowledge hiding doesn't help. Three studies examined the consequences of knowledge hiding and revealed that those who engage in such behavior are approximately 17 percent less likely to thrive at work, experiencing limited learning and growth opportunities. Furthermore, knowledge hiding makes employees feel psychologically unsafe (Jiang 2019). Suggestions for organizations to reduce knowledge hiding include (Jiang 2019): work toward developing a culture where employees feel comfortable to openly share their concerns; use third party, anonymous surveys to identify why employees might be withholding information; educate employees regarding the consequences of knowledge hiding. All these actions require sound leadership of the organization's knowledge management.

Sources: Compiled from Great Place to Work (2016); Jiang (2019); Panopto (2023)

Importance of Knowledge Management Assessment

In any aspect of organizational or individual task performance, it is imperative to track whether the efforts are enabling the organization or the individual to achieve the underlying objectives. Without such assessment, it would be impossible to determine either the contribution of those efforts or whether and where improvements are needed. More specifically, a **knowledge management assessment** is aimed at evaluating the need for KM solutions—the knowledge these solutions can help discover, capture, share, or apply—and the impact they will have on individual or organizational performance. A KM assessment can help establish the baseline for implementing those KM solutions, including the existing infrastructure and technologies that can help support those efforts.

Overall, the assessment of knowledge management is a critical aspect of a KM implementation; what is not measured can't be managed well. A survey by Ernst & Young (1997) indicated that measuring the value and contribution of knowledge assets ranks as the second most important challenge faced by companies, with changing people's behavior being the most important. However, only 4 percent of the firms surveyed by Ernst & Young claimed to be good or excellent at "measuring the value of knowledge assets and/or impact of knowledge management." Several reasons attest to the need for conducting a KM assessment, as described below.

1   A KM assessment helps identify the contributions being currently made by KM. It helps answer the question: Is KM improving the individual's or the organization's ability to perform various tasks and thereby enhancing efficiency, effectiveness, and/or innovativeness?

2   A KM assessment enhances the understanding of the quality of the efforts being put into KM as well as the intellectual capital produced through these efforts. It helps answer the questions: Are the KM solutions being employed adequate for the needs of the individual or the organization? Do these efforts produce the intellectual capital required to perform individual or organizational tasks?

3   A KM assessment helps understand whether the costs of the KM efforts are justified by the benefits they produce. It helps answer the question: Do the direct and indirect benefits from KM together exceed or equal the various costs incurred? This is an important benefit for the overall KM solutions as well as the solutions pursued in a specific KM project. Thus, the overall KM solutions as well as specific KM projects can be cost-justified through careful KM assessment.

4   A KM assessment helps recognize the gaps that need to be addressed in the KM efforts by individuals or the organization. It helps answer the question: What kind of potentially valuable KM solutions do the individual and the organization currently lack? What potentially important knowledge is not adequately supported by the KM efforts?

5   Finally, a KM assessment can also help in making a business case to senior executives in an organization for additional investments in KM efforts. Based on

the benefits currently provided by the organization's KM solutions (Point 1 above) and the gaps in the organization's KM efforts (Point 4 above), a business case can be built for the development of solutions that address these gaps.

Thus, knowledge management assessments are important because of several reasons, as described above. We next examine the different types of KM assessments and then examine the alternative KM assessment approaches in some detail.

Types of Knowledge Management Assessment

KM assessments can be classified in a number of different ways. Three possible ways of considering alternative KM assessments are described here. They are related to the following aspects: (1) When is KM assessed? (2) How is KM assessed? (3) What aspects of KM are assessed?

The Timing of KM Assessment

A KM assessment can be performed on different occasions. Three possibilities are especially noteworthy. First, a KM assessment may be performed *periodically for an entire organization or a subunit*. The objective of such an assessment is to evaluate the overall quality of KM solutions, intellectual capital, and their impacts. This could help identify any areas that need improvement in KM. Such an assessment can be performed, for example by surveying employees and inquiring about their degree of agreement with statements such as in Box 11.3.

Box 11.3 An Illustrative Tool for Assessing KM

Please indicate your level of agreement with each of the following statements by selecting a number from 1 (Strongly Disagree) to 5 (Strongly Agree).

1   I am satisfied with the availability of knowledge for my tasks.
2   It is easy for me to locate information I need to perform my job.
3   I always know where to look for information.
4   The available knowledge improves my effectiveness in performing my tasks.
5   My supervisor encourages knowledge sharing within my subunit.
6   The members of my group consistently share their knowledge.
7   I am satisfied with the management of knowledge in my subunit.
8   The available knowledge improves my subunit's effectiveness.
9   The organization directly rewards employees for sharing their knowledge.
10   The organization publicly recognizes employees who share their knowledge.

Responses to the above statements may be averaged across a number of employees from various subunits of the organization. Averages for each subunit and the entire organization would then show where the individual subunits, as well as the overall organization, perform in terms of the overall quality of KM. Each assessment would be in terms of a number ranging from 1 (poor KM) to 5 (excellent KM).

KM assessments may also be conducted at *the start of a KM project* to build a business case for it. The purpose of such an assessment is to identify the gap in current KM at the organization and delineate the potential benefits of the proposed KM project. For example, for a firm focusing on new products and increasing market share, so that R&D represents a major cost center, the business plan might include the following statement describing the value of the proposed KM project:

> The target for the KM project will be to cut cycle time on specific new projects by 20 percent. In addition, ... The project will identify cost savings and time savings for scientists in the unit of 25 percent.
>
> (Wilson 2002, p. 17)

The above example illustrates the outcome of a KM assessment conducted at the start of the project. It indicates there are currently problems in KM within the R&D function, which is a critical component of the organization, and that addressing these problems through the proposed project would be highly beneficial.

A KM assessment may also be done *following the conclusion of a KM project*. Such assessment aims to determine the impacts of the KM project and may focus on the entire organization or a specific subunit. It may be necessary to establish historical KM performance in order to evaluate the effects produced by the KM project. Following are some of the aspects that can be evaluated during such a post-project assessment:

- Perceptions of improved knowledge management in the area focused on by the project.
- Perceptions of greater availability of knowledge in the area focused on by the project.
- Some evidence of financial return (e.g., cost savings, increased returns, ROI, etc.), either for KM function itself or for the entire organization.
- Increased awareness of the importance of knowledge management.
- Increased recognition of the different areas of knowledge and their importance to the organization.
- Greater knowledge sharing throughout the organization.
- Greater comfort level throughout the organization with the concepts of knowledge and knowledge management.

For example, a KM project at one large consulting firm caused a major transformation of the organization. This transformation was significant in both breadth and depth of impact across the organization. The KM project required line managers to re-engineer their business processes to draw heavily from the organization's centralized knowledge by accessing earlier client presentations, work plans, system specifications, and other important documents. Consequently, the consulting firm's "win rate" in client proposals increased as well (Davenport and Prusak 1998, p. 152). Box 11.4 describes a KM assessment that relies on measuring the effectiveness of one specific KM mechanism—communities of practice.

Box 11.4 Assessment of KM through Communities of Practice

1   What was the overall value of this community to you and your team?
2   When your community discussed "topic A," what specific knowledge, information, or data did you use?

3   What was the value of this knowledge, information, or data for you as an indivi-
    dual? Can you express the value in numeric terms such as time saved?

4   Can you estimate the value of this knowledge, information, or data to your busi-
    ness unit in cost savings, reduced cycle time, improved quality of decision-
    making, or lower risk?

5   What percentage of this value was obtained directly from the community? What is
    the likelihood you would have learned it without the community?

6   How confident are you of the above estimate?

7   Who else in your team used this knowledge, information, or data?

Source: Compiled from Wilson (2002)

The Nature of KM Assessment

KM assessments are also differentiated on the basis of the way in which KM assessment is done. There are two distinct and important methods to perform KM assessments: qualitative and quantitative.

Qualitative KM assessments aim to develop a basic understanding of whether the KM efforts are producing positive results. Qualitative assessments focus on signs, text, language, and so on instead of focusing on numbers, as is the case with quantitative assessments. Qualitative assessments involve such simple tasks as walking around the halls and buildings of the organization and informally chatting with the employees about how things are going for them. They also include more formal **interviews** based on semi-structured or structured interview guides, individually conducted with a carefully selected set of employees. Regardless of the formality of these conversations, they are inherently qualitative, surfacing anecdotes about how well the KM efforts seem to be working as well as examples of situations where the KM efforts did not produce the desired results. Such anecdotes of successes (or problems) may concern the quality of decisions, innovations, and technology transfer at the organizational level. In addition, they may point out issues related to career development, visibility, confidence, and staying up-to-date technologically at the individual level. Furthermore, such qualitative assessments can be performed at certain periodic intervals, such as at the start of a project or at the conclusion of a project as discussed before. Consequently, they may focus on the organization's overall strategy for KM or on more specific aspects, such as the development of a KM system like a community of practice or an expertise locator system.

Quantitative KM assessments, on the other hand, produce specific numerical scores indicating how well an organization, an organizational subunit, or an individual is performing with respect to KM. Such quantitative assessments may be based on a survey, such as the one described in Box 11.3. Alternatively, such quantitative KM assessments may be in financial terms, such as the ROI or the cost savings from a KM project. Finally, quantitative measures also include such ratios or percentages as employee retention rate (i.e., the percentage of employees most essential to the organization retained during the preceding year) or training expenditures as a proportion of payroll (i.e., total expenditures on training as a percent of the organization's annual payroll).

Quantitative measures are more difficult to develop during an organization's early experiences with knowledge management. During initial stages, qualitative assessments should be preferred, with greater use of quantitative measures as the organization gains experience with knowledge management. This is depicted in Figure 11.1. However, it is

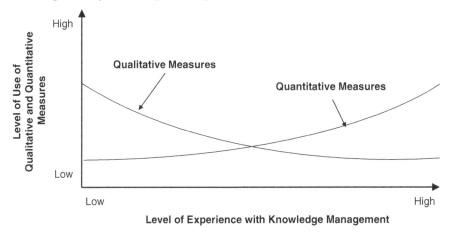

Figure 11.1 Qualitative and Quantitative Assessments of KM

important to note that even when an organization is very experienced with KM, it can obtain considerable benefits from using qualitative assessment, especially in uncertain environments that reduce the benefits from quantitative measurement.

Differences in the Aspects of KM Assessed

The third way of viewing knowledge management assessments, which is used to structure the rest of this chapter, focuses on the aspect being assessed. As discussed in Chapter 5, KM can directly or indirectly impact organizational performance at several levels: people, processes, products, and the overall organizational performance. These impacts either come about directly from the KM solutions or from the knowledge produced and shared through the KM solutions. Therefore, the KM assessment can focus on: (a) the KM solutions, as discussed in the next section—"Assessment of KM Solutions"; (b) the knowledge produced or shared through KM solutions, as discussed in the section entitled "Assessment of Knowledge"; and (c) the impacts of KM solutions or knowledge on performance (including individuals or employees, processes, products, and the overall organizational performance), as discussed in the section entitled "Assessment of Impacts."

Assessment of Knowledge Management Solutions

Assessment of knowledge management solutions involves evaluating the extent to which knowledge discovery, capture, sharing, and application processes—discussed in Chapter 3—are utilized and how well they are supported by KM technologies and systems. Table 11.1 provides some illustrative measures of the four aspects of KM solutions—discovery, capture, sharing, and application. Although most of the measures given in this table are easy to quantify, some (e.g., extent of use of learning by doing) involve perceptions to some extent. Moreover, further research is needed to establish these measures, but some of them are based on prior empirical research.

Table 11.1 Illustrative Measures of Key Aspects of KM Solutions

Dimension	Illustrative Measures
Knowledge Discovery	• Number of cooperative projects across subunits divided by the number of organizational subunits
	• Extent of use of apprentices and mentors to transfer knowledge
	• Employee rotation, i.e., number of employees who move to a different area each year
	• Annual number of brainstorming retreats or camps as a proportion of the total number of employees
	• Number of patents published per employee
Capture	• Average number of annual hits on each document in the document repository
	• Number of subscriptions to journals per employee
	• Attendance at group presentations as a proportion of invited attendees
	• Number of annual presentations per employee
	• Extent of use of learning by doing
Sharing	• Proportion of information used that is available on Web pages (Intranet and Internet)
	• Proportion of organizational information that resides in databases
	• Level of use of groupware and repositories of information, best practices, and lessons learned
	• Size of discussion databases
	• Annual number of shared documents published per employee
Application	• Frequency of advice seeking per employee
	• Corporate directory coverage, i.e., proportion of employees whose expertise areas are listed in the corporate directory
	• Annual number of improvement suggestions made per employee
	• Level of use of decision-support systems and expert systems
	• Frequency of hits on KM Web sites

Collison and Parcell (2001) describe another way of viewing KM solutions, especially for knowledge sharing in organizations that focus on organizational subunits and the key activities they perform. Such organizational activities include increased morale and motivation; plan, schedule, and work execution; management of spare parts and stores; and more. Once these activities are identified for the organization, interviews with managers from each subunit are used to evaluate each subunit's target performance as well as actual performance for each activity. This process helps identify, for each combination of subunit and activity, the gap between actual and target performance. For each activity, actual as well as target performance for various subunits can then be placed along a matrix as shown in Figure 11.2. Subunits that show a high level of actual performance and a high level of target performance, such as SU-1 in Figure 11.2, are the ones that both consider that activity as important and perform it well. These subunits should be emulated by subunits, such as SU-2, that consider that activity as important but perform it poorly as shown by a high level of

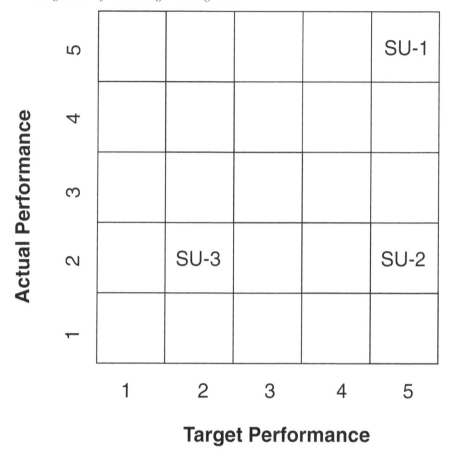

Figure 11.2 Identifying Knowledge Sharing Opportunities

target performance combined with a low level of actual performance. Therefore, the organization would benefit from knowledge sharing between these two kinds of sub-units (SU-1 and SU-2), which both consider that activity as important (high level of target performance) but differ in actual performance. Subunits (such as SU-3) that consider the activity as less important (low level of target performance) may also benefit from knowledge sharing with subunits that consider that activity as important in case the focus of their operations changes.

Some specific tools for assessing KM solutions have also been proposed. One example is "Metrics that Matter"[1] from Knowledge Advisors, a Chicago-based company (PR Newswire 2001b), which provides a comprehensive solution to help training organizations measure their learning investments. This approach using **metrics** has three components—learner-based, manager-based, and analyst-based. Each component helps measure learning across five levels of evaluation: (1) did they like it? (2) did they learn? (3) did they use it? (4) what were the results? and (5) what is the return on investment?

Assessment of Knowledge

Assessment of knowledge requires: (a) the identification of the various areas of knowledge that are relevant to the organization or a specific subunit, followed by (b) an evaluation of the extent to which knowledge in each of these areas is available. The first of these steps—*identification of the relevant areas of knowledge*—may be performed using interviews with managers and other employees of that organization or subunit. In this step, it may be useful to first identify the *critical success factors* for the organization or the subunit. Critical success factors have been defined as "the limited number of areas in which results, if they are satisfactory, will ensure successful performance for the organization" (Rockart 1979, p. 85). Organizations should therefore give special attention to them, trying to perform exceedingly well in the few areas they represent rather than seeking to perform a larger number of tasks only reasonably well. Asking the senior executives to identify six to eight critical success factors, and then asking them to identify the knowledge needed to succeed with respect to each critical success factor can thus obtain the most important knowledge areas.

Once the relevant knowledge areas have been identified, *the extent and quality of available knowledge* in each area needs to be assessed. This is often a very tricky issue, for such knowledge can reside in individuals' minds, corporate databases and documents, organizational processes, and so on. To some extent, such measurement of available knowledge may be conducted through surveys or interviews of organizational employees, asking them to evaluate items such as the ones in Box 11.5.

Box 11.5 Assessment of Available Knowledge

Likert scale survey can be used in measuring the availability of knowledge. For instance, on a 5-point scale, (ranging from 1 = Strongly disagree to 5 = Strongly agree), I can easily access knowledge in this area. Statements 1–4 are coded such that a *high* score indicates excellent availability of this knowledge, whereas statements 5 and 6 are reverse-coded so that a *low* score on these items indicates excellent availability of this knowledge. Therefore, ratings on items 5 and 6 should be subtracted from 6 and the results can then be averaged with the ratings on items 1 to 4. The resulting average would range from 1 to 5, with 5 indicating excellent availability of this knowledge.

1   I can easily access knowledge in this area.
2   Everyone in the organization (or the subunit) recognizes the experts in this area of knowledge.
3   Available knowledge in this area is of a high quality.
4   Available knowledge in this area helps improve the organization's (or subunit's) performance.
5   I often have to perform my tasks without being able to access knowledge in this area.
6   The performance of this organization (or subunit) is often adversely affected due to the lack of knowledge in this area.

Another important aspect of KM assessment is the value each area of knowledge contributes to the organization. *Assessment of value of knowledge* is one way of attributing a **tangible measure** of benefits resulting from knowledge, which is often intangible (Sullivan 2000). In general, value has two monetary measures—cost and price. Price represents the amount a purchaser is willing to pay in exchange for the utility derived from that knowledge, whereas cost is the amount of money required to produce that knowledge. Both cost and price are direct, quantitative measures of value, but there are also other nonmonetary or indirect measures of value, such as the improvement in the quality of decisions enabled by this knowledge. Some of these benefits of knowledge are discussed in the next section. The Intangible Assets Monitor approach focuses on **intangible measures** of knowledge. This approach, and its use to evaluate the value of intellectual capital, is discussed later in the section entitled "Overall Approaches for KM Assessment."

Assessment of Impacts

As we discussed in Chapter 10, KM solutions and the knowledge they help to create, capture, share, and apply can impact individuals, products, processes, and the overall performance of organizations. A KM assessment, therefore, involves not only the evaluation of KM solutions and knowledge but also an evaluation of their impacts. This section describes how these impacts may be assessed.

Assessment of Impacts on Employees

KM can impact an organization's employees by facilitating their learning from each other, from prior experiences of former employees, and from external sources. KM can also enable employees to become more flexible by enhancing their awareness of new ideas, which prepares them to respond to changes and also by making them more likely to accept change. These impacts, in turn, can cause the employees to feel more satisfied with their jobs due to the knowledge acquisition and skill enhancement and their enhanced market value. Thus, KM can enhance learning, adaptability, and job satisfaction of employees. Some illustrative measures of impacts on each of these three dimensions are given in Table 11.2.

Assessment of Impacts on Processes

KM can improve organizational processes—for example marketing, manufacturing, accounting, engineering, public relations, and so forth. These improvements can occur along three major dimensions: **effectiveness, efficiency**, and degree of **innovation** of the processes as discussed in Chapter 4. For example, at HP, a KM system for computer resellers enhanced efficiency by considerably reducing both the number of calls for human support and the number of people needed to provide this support (Davenport and Prusak 1998). Table 11.3 lists some illustrative measures of the impacts that KM and organizational knowledge can have along each of these dimensions.

Assessment of Impacts on Products

KM can also impact the organization's products by helping to produce either value-added products or inherently knowledge-based products. Value-added products are new or improved products that provide a significant additional value as compared to earlier

Table 11.2 Illustrative Measures of Impacts on People

Dimension	Illustrative Measures
Employee learning	• Average amount of time annually spent by an employee in being trained
	• Average number of conferences or seminars annually attended by each employee
	• Average amount of time annually spent by an employee in training others within the organization
	• Average of employees' annual assessment of their learning during the year
Employee adaptability	• Proportion of employees who have worked in another area (other than the area in which they currently work) for more than one year
	• Average number of areas in which each employee has previously worked
	• Number of countries in which each senior manager has worked as a proportion of the total number of countries in which the organization conducts business
Employee job satisfaction	• Proportion of employees who express a high level of satisfaction with the organization and their jobs
	• Percentage of critical employees retained during the previous year
	• Percentage of openings requiring advanced degrees or substantial experience filled in the previous year

Table 11.3 Illustrative Measures of Impacts on Organizational Processes

Dimension	Illustrative Measures
Efficiency	• Reduced ratio of manufacturing costs to annual sales
	• Shortening proposal times
	• Quicker decisions
	• Faster delivery to market
Effectiveness	• Enhanced customer service
	• Improved project management
	• Fewer surprises due to external events
	• Percentage of customers reporting complaints about products/services
Innovativeness	• Percentage of all current products/services introduced in the previous year
	• Greater number of patents per employee
	• Organizational changes precede, rather than follow, competitors' moves
	• Number of new ideas in KM databases

products. Inherently **knowledge-based products** refer for example to products from the consulting and software development industries. These impacts were discussed in Chapter 4. Table 11.4 provides some examples of possible measures of the impacts that knowledge management can have on these two dimensions.

Table 11.4 Illustrative Measures of Impacts on Organizational Products

Dimension	Illustrative Measures
Value-added Products	• Increased rate of new product launch
	• More frequent improvements in products
	• Average of the ratio of profit margin to price across the range of products offered by the organizations
Knowledge-based Products	• Increased information content in products
	• Greater product-related information provided to customers
	• Proportion of customers accessing product-related knowledge that the organization places on the Internet

Assessment of Impacts on Organizational Performance

KM can impact overall organizational performance either directly or indirectly. Direct impacts concern revenues and/or costs, and can be explicitly linked to the organization's vision or strategy. Consequently, direct impact can be observed in terms of increased sales, decreased costs, and higher profitability or **return on investment**. For example, Texas Instruments Inc. generated revenues by licensing patents and intellectual property (Davenport and Prusak 1998). However, it is harder to attribute revenue increases to KM than cost savings (Davenport et al. 2001). Indirect impacts on organizational performance come about through activities that are not linked to the organization's vision, strategy, or revenues and cannot be associated with transactions. As discussed in Chapter 5, indirect impacts include **economies of scale and scope**, and sustainable **competitive advantage**. Table 11.5 provides some examples of possible measures of these direct and indirect impacts that knowledge management can have on overall organizational performance.

The value of a KM investment should be evaluated based on how it affects discounted cash flow. Improved problem-solving, enhanced creativity, better relationships with customers, and employees' more meaningful work can all eventually be linked to real cash flows. Therefore, organizations can enhance their cash flow in the following ways:

- Reduce expenses by decreasing costs.
- Enhance margins by increasing efficiency to improve profit.
- Increase revenue through the sale of more products or services.
- Reduce taxes using smart strategies to minimize tax liabilities of the organization.
- Reduce capital requirements by lowering amount of capital needed by regulation.
- Reduce cost of capital by lowering the cost of loans, equity, and other financing.

(Clare 2002; Wilson 2002)

It is important to keep the above drivers in mind during the implementation of knowledge management projects. In other words, if KM initiatives are observed to help increase the company's cash flow, executives will listen and therefore find a viable way to fund them.

Conclusions about Knowledge Management Assessment

We have examined and provided illustrative measures for KM assessments. We also discussed the direct and indirect impacts that KM assessments can have on the overall

Table 11.5 Illustrative Measures of Impacts on Organizational Performance

	Illustrative Measures
Direct Impacts	• Revenues: Increase in total revenues per employee compared to the previous year
	• Costs: Increase in total annual costs per employee compared to the previous year
	• ROI: Increase in ROI compared to the previous year
Indirect Impacts	• Economy of scale: Average (across all products offered by the organization) change in total cost per unit sold as compared to the previous year
	• Economy of scope: Average (across all products offered by the organization) change in the number of different products a salesperson can sell as compared to the previous year
	• Economy of scale: Average (across all products offered by the organization) of the difference between the price of the organization's product and the mean price of competing products
	• Economy of scope: Difference between the average number of different products produced in the organization's manufacturing plants and the average number of different products produced in the manufacturing plants of its main competitors
	• Competitive advantage: Difference between return on investment for the organization and its key competitors
	• Competitive advantage: Average number of years existing customers have been buying the organization's products/services
	• Competitive advantage: Percentage of top customers ending sales contracts in the previous year

organizational performance. In this section, we examine and provide a broader discussion of KM assessment including a discussion of who performs KM assessment, some overall approaches for KM assessment, the approach for the implementation of a KM assessment, and some caveats regarding KM assessments.

Who Performs KM Assessment?

In order to perform a KM assessment, it is helpful to form a team that includes internal and external members. The internal members provide the necessary context and help retain within the organization the knowledge acquired from the assessment, whereas the external members can help identify KM-related assumptions and opportunities that may be missed by internal members. Overall, a KM assessment should incorporate: (a) peer review of internal performance; (b) external appraisal (by customers, suppliers, etc.) of the organization and its outputs; (c) business evaluation of effectiveness, efficiency, and innovativeness; and (d) evaluation of the knowledge assets created (Quinn et al. 1996).

The following example illustrates how these perspectives could be included and effectively integrated. Following each project, a major investment banking firm asks all team members, the team leader, and its customer group to rank all project participants in terms of their exhibited knowledge, specific contributions to the project, and support for the team. Customers also rate their overall satisfaction with the firm as well as with the specific project. Annual surveys, ranking the firm against competitors on 28 key dimensions, complement these evaluations. The firm also measures costs and profits for each project and allocates them among participating groups based on a simple, pre-established formula. Annually, for each division the firm computes the net differential between its market value (if sold) and its fixed asset base. This net intellectual value of the division is tracked over time as an aggregate measure of how well the division's management is building its intellectual assets.

Overall Approaches for KM Assessment

In the preceding sections we have discussed a number of measures that can be used for KM assessment. Overall KM assessment approaches usually combine several of these measures, as illustrated above with the investment banking firm's example. One such approach involves the use of **benchmarking**, or comparing KM at an organization or subunit with other organizations or subunits. Adopted as a systematic technique for evaluating a company's performance in reaching its strategic goals, benchmarking is based on the recognition that best practices are often the same within a company or even within an industry. Benchmark targets could therefore include other units within the same company, competing firms, the entire industry, or in some cases, successful companies in other industries. For example, a leading manufacturer identifies out-standing operating units, formally studies them, and then replicates their practices throughout the rest of the company. This approach produced sales that exceed goals by 5 percent (PR Newswire 2001a). Box 11.6 provides information on a cross-industry survey that may be used as a benchmark in the arena of KM.

Box 11.6 The Most Innovative Knowledge Enterprise Survey

The Annual Most Innovative Knowledge Enterprises (MIKE) survey by the International Global MIKE Study Group, is based on the original Most Admired Knowledge Enter-prise (MAKE) Award, launched by Rory Chase of Teleos in 1998. The MIKE award is based on a ranking of firms by a panel of CKOs and leading KM practitioners along eight criteria, which together cover human capital, relational capital, innovation capital, and process capital:

1   Empowerment of knowledge workers
2   Transformative leadership
3   User experience
4   Knowledge network
5   Innovative culture
6   Knowledge-based offerings
7   Knowledge creation processes, and
8   Creative spaceSource: Compiled from Rao (2020)

Another overall approach for KM assessment utilizes the **Balanced Scorecard**, which was originally developed by Kaplan and Norton (1996) to provide a more "balanced view" of internal performance rather than for KM assessment. The Balanced Scor-ecard provides a way of maintaining a balance between short-term and long-term objectives, financial and nonfinancial measures, lagging and leading indicators, and external and internal perspectives. It examines the goals, metrics, targets, and initiatives for the following four different perspectives (Tiwana 2002):

1 *The Customer Perspective*: How should our customers perceive us?
2 *The Financial Perspective*: What is the face that we want to present to our shareholders?
3 *The Internal Business Perspective*: Are our internal operations efficient and effective and performing at their best?
4 *The Learning and Growth Perspective*: How can we sustain our competitive advantage over time?

In employing the Balanced Scorecard for KM assessment, the above four perspectives are used in a series of four steps performed over time. The first step involves translating the KM vision (i.e., Why are we managing knowledge, and what is our vision for KM?). In the second step, this vision is communicated within the organization with rewards linked to knowledge use and contribution. The third step involves business planning, including the establishment of goals and the alignment of metrics and rewards to them. The fourth step—learning and feedback on whether KM is working and whether it can be improved—then feeds back to the first step to begin the cycle again. The above four complementary criteria from the Balanced Scorecard are used during each of these steps.

Like the Balanced Scorecard, the Intangible Assets Monitor Framework (Sveiby 2000) also recognizes the importance of examining **intangible knowledge** assets rather than focusing only on financial or monetary assets. The Intangible Assets Monitor considers a firm's market value to depend on tangible net book value and **intangible assets** which include external structure (including relationships with customers and suppliers, brand names, trademarks, and image or reputation); internal structure (including the patents, concepts, models, and systems); and the competence of the organization's individual employees (including skills, education, experience, values, and social skills). Based on these factors, WM-Data, a Swedish computer software and consulting company,[2] designed a set of nonmonetary indicators that top management uses to supervise their operations on a weekly, monthly, and annual basis. The **Intangible Assets Monitor Framework**[3] evaluates growth, renewal, efficiency, and stability for tangible assets (financial value), external structure (customer value), internal structure (organizational value), and individuals' competence (individual value). Following are some of the questions that may be used to evaluate growth:

1 Is the existing customer base growing in value?
2 Are the support staff and administrative management improving their competence?
3 Are our tools and processes growing in value?

The **Skandia Navigator method** is another approach to KM assessment that gives considerable attention to intangible assets (Edvinsson and Malone 1997). The Swedish company, Skandia Insurance Company Ltd., developed this method in 1993 under the leadership of Leif Edvinsson, although it preferred using the term intellectual capital rather than knowledge. The Skandia Navigator included a number of ratios in which it looks at the past, present, and future. In the Skandia Navigator approach, the past is examined with an emphasis on financial aspects, the present is examined by focusing on customers, people, and processes, and the future is examined in terms of renewal and development.[4]

KM assessment can also benefit from the **real options approach**, which views KM initiatives as a **portfolio of investments** (Tiwana 2002). This approach focuses on the value-to-cost ratio—that is, the ratio of the net value to the total cost for each investment and the volatility faced by each investment. Using this approach, KM projects can be placed on an option space as shown in Figure 11.3. A clockwise move from region 1 to region 3 in the option space implies a shift from projects that are low-risk and attractive to projects that are fairly attractive. Continuing further to region 6, the projects reduce further in attractiveness. Thus, projects A and B in the figure are attractive, and projects C and D are not, with project A being the most attractive and project D being the least attractive. Such real options analysis combines strategic and financial approaches to evaluating investments. In positioning projects on the option space, it can benefit from the techniques discussed earlier in the chapter, especially for identifying the value-to-cost ratio. To conclude this section on overall KM assessment, Box 11.7 provides a summary of KM assessment at Siemens AG.

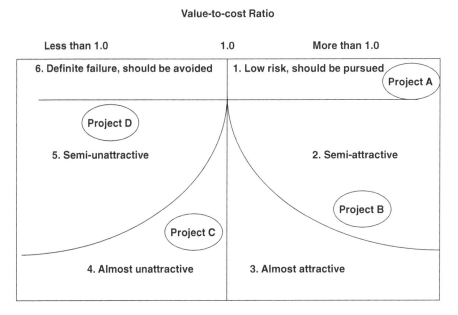

Figure 11.3 KM Projects Mapped on the Option Space

Box 11.7 KM Assessment at Siemens

Siemens, a large firm in the electronics industry, has benefited considerably over the years from one of its knowledge sharing systems. Called "ShareNet," this system serves as the foundation for several communities of practice. To estimate ROI, Siemens computes the costs of a community of practice including labor, meetings, facilities, and the effort spent by KM experts. It also considers costs of the incentive program. Siemens then decides how much effort has been saved through the sharing of solutions in the community.

Siemens also considers subcommunities and their generation of solutions in terms of community projects. If a group needs a solution and embarks on a knowledge-creation effort, it can determine the savings in time-to-market, competitive positioning, and so forth. To further determine the value of KM, Siemens has developed a master plan of KM metrics that contains measures for each of four dimensions of its holistic KM system:

- *Knowledge community*: the organization, community, and people dimensions
- *Knowledge marketplace*: the IT involved in knowledge management
- *Key KM processes*: sharing and creation
- *Knowledge environment*: all of the above

Siemens has realized that it can assess the success of its communities and market-places with measures such as how much knowledge comes in or out of the community and the quality of feedback. Contracts that had been gained with the support of other divisions, or savings obtained through knowledge shared using the knowledge communities, were also included in the benefits. A contribution key, determined through a survey form that the ShareNet Managers fill out, indicated the proportion that ShareNet had contributed to the success of each initiative.

Siemens believes communities are the heart of their KM systems, and it has spent a great deal of time on communities-of-practice assessments—questionnaires for community members that provide ideas on how to improve each of the communities. Siemens has tried to check the health of KM processes to determine the performance of the sharing process. Ideally, the measures evaluate whether a person has managed the process correctly and set the right limits on it. This provides Siemens a good way to look at the marketplace and also to examine how much sharing and creation is taking place.

To monitor the entire KM systems, Siemens performs a KM maturity assessment that defines whether KM is still *ad hoc* and chaotic or has progressed to an optimized state. To do this, Siemens measures its four dimensions and 16 enablers, each of which has a set of questions.

Sources: Compiled from Davenport and Probst (2002); MacCormack et al. (2002); Voelpel et al. (2005)

Finally, another overall approach for KM assessment is to evaluate the organization in terms of the **maturity of its KM**. For example, Yokell (2010) views an organization's KM as being in one of five stages of maturity: (1) initiation, where awareness of KM is growing within the organization; (2) development, where the organization introduces localized and repeatable practices; (3) standardization, where the organization moves toward common processes and approaches; (4) optimization, where the organization measures the consequences of KM and accordingly adapts its KM approach; and (5) innovation, where the organization continually improves its KM practices. Using archival data from the American Productivity and Quality Center (APQC), Yokell found firms that were higher in KM maturity to significantly outperform those with lower KM maturity in terms of return on sales as well as return on assets.

Further Recommendations for KM Assessment

So far in this chapter we have described a number of KM metrics and assessment approaches. In developing these measures and approaches, the following eight suggestions should be carefully considered (Tiwana 2002; Wilson 2002):

1   *Remember why you are doing KM*: When proposing a KM project, it is critical to define its measures of success based on things the organization cares about, such as: reducing waste, lowering costs, enhancing the customer experience, and so forth.

2   *Establish a baseline*: It is important to identify and develop a baseline measure when you begin efforts, rather than scrambling after the effort is completed to try to determine measures of success. Establishing a baseline is essential to prove successful results down the line.

3   *Consider qualitative methods*: KM is a qualitative concept and qualitative methods of measurement, such as analyzing the value of social networks, telling success stories, and others, should not be ignored.

4   *Keep it simple*: An organization does not need hundreds of measures. A handful of the relevant, robust, and easily assessable ones are better in demonstrating to yourself and your organization that KM is indeed adding value.

5   *Avoid KM metrics that are hard to control*: KM assessment should use metrics that are specific and within the control of the organization's employees. Broad and grand statements, such as "enable the firm to become one of the top learning organizations in the world by 2010" are visionary but impossible to control or measure.

6   *Measure at the appropriate level*: Measure at the project or application level in the beginning. Organizations that have implemented KM initiatives for a long time can then try to measure the total organizational value of KM or their program.

7   *Link rewards to KM assessment results*: KM assessment should not be an end in itself. Instead, it's the results of KM assessments that should be used to provide rewards and incentives thereby motivating improved KM results in the future.

8   *Be conservative in your claims*: When calculating a figure like ROI for KM projects, it is better to err on the higher side when estimating costs and to err on the lower side when estimating value in order to make the results more believable to management.

Summary

This chapter complements our earlier discussion of management of KM foundations and KM solutions in Chapters 3 and 4, respectively; the effects of contingency factors on KM solutions; and the management of specific KM systems in Chapters 6, 7, 8, and 9. To better understand the overall management of knowledge management in an organization, we have examined in this chapter the leadership of KM and the ways in which the value of KM can be assessed in an organization. We have discussed the assessment of KM systems and the impacts that assessments can have. We have also summarized some overall KM assessment approaches and how a KM assessment can be implemented.

Review

1   Distinguish between the roles of Chief Knowledge Officer and Chief Learning Officer.
2   Why is it important to perform KM assessment? Identify and discuss any three reasons.

3 Describe the different types of KM assessment in terms of (a) the timing of KM assessment; and (b) the aspects assessed.

4 What are the differences between quantitative and qualitative assessments of KM assessment? How does their use depend upon the organization's experience with KM?

5 Briefly describe some financial measures that can be used for KM assessment.

6 Briefly describe some nonfinancial measures that can be used for KM assessment.

7 Briefly discuss how the different impacts of KM on employees can be assessed.

8 How can the impacts of KM on efficiency, effectiveness, and innovation be evaluated?

9 What is KM maturity? Identify the various stages from one KM maturity model.

10 How do the measures of the direct impacts of KM differ from the measures of its indirect impacts?

Application Exercises

1 Visit a local area firm to study its KM assessment process. Determine how they decided on the type of KM solution they use.

2 How would you conduct KM assessment at the firm you visited? Describe the suggested approach in some detail, making sure to connect this approach to the approaches described in this chapter.

3 Study how knowledge is managed at either your family physician's office or your dentist's office through 15-minute conversations with a few individuals who work at that office. Then recommend an approach for assessing KM at this office. Discuss the suggested approach with some senior employees (e.g., the family physician or the dentist) at this office, and seek their feedback concerning your suggestions.

4 Visit any three organizations of varying sizes and different industries. Identify who leads the KM function at each organization, and examine how these organizations perform their KM assessments. Compare the three organizations in terms of whether they use a Chief Knowledge Officer, a Chief Learning Officer, a Chief Information Officer, or an individual in some other position to lead the KM function. Discuss why the organizations might differ or be similar with respect to the leaders of their KM function.

5 For each of the organizations you visited in Question 4 above, examine how consistent the organization's KM assessment approach is with the recommendations in this chapter. Which organization seems most consistent with the recommended approach? Of the three organizations, is this organization the one that has the most experience with KM?

Notes

1 More details about this approach may be found at www.knowledgeadvisors.com/metrics-that-matter/.

2 Since October 10, 2006, WM-Data has become a subsidiary to LogicaCMG (www.logica.com).

3 See www.sveiby.com/articles/EmergingStandard.html#TheIntang.

4 Edvinsson left Skandia in 1999. Although intellectual capital remained an important focus of Skandia's corporate philosophy until early 2000, Skandia has undergone considerable changes as a company, with a merger with Storebrand in 1999, followed by its acquisition by Old Mutual in 2006. See www.valuebasedmanagement.net/methodsskandianavigator.html and www.skandia.com/about/history.asp.

References

Awazu, Y., and Desouza, K. 2004. The knowledge chiefs: CKOs, CLOs and CPOs. *European Management Journal*, 22(3), 339–344.

Bersin, J., 2007. The new Chief Learning Officer: 2008 and beyond. Bersin and Associates, July 21. http://joshbersin.com/2007/07/21/the-new-chief-learning-officer-2008-and-beyond/ (accessed February 17, 2009).

Business Wire. 2009. Colliers International appoints top executives to its USA management team. *Business Wire*, February 2.

Cencigh-Albulario, L. 2008. Now everyone is joining the rush to learn. *Weekend Australian*, November 22, 11.

Clare, M. 2002. Solving the knowledge-value equation: Part one. *Knowledge Management Review* (May/June).

Collison, C., and Parcell, G. 2001. *Learning to fly*. Milford, CT: Capstone Publishing.

Conz, N. 2008. CIGNA has launched a series of public-facing e-learning modules that leverage Web technologies to teach consumers about the basics of the health insurance system. *Insurance and Technology*, December 1, 13.

Davenport, T.H., and Probst, G. (Eds.). 2002. *Knowledge management case book: Siemens best practises*, 2nd ed. New York: John Wiley & Sons.

Davenport, T.H., and Prusak, L. 1998. *Working knowledge: How organizations manage what they know*. Boston: Harvard Business School Press.

Davenport, T.H., Harris, J.G., De Long, D.W., and Jacobson, A.L. 2001. Data to knowledge to results: Building an analytic capability. *California Management Review*, 43(2), 117–138.

Denning, S. 2009. Communities for knowledge management. http://www.stevedenning.com/Knowledge-Management/communities-of-practice.aspx (accessed January 31, 2014).

DeTienne, K., Dyer, G., Hoopes, C., and Harris, S. 2004. Toward a model of effective knowledge management and directions for future research: Culture, leadership and CKOs. *Journal of Leadership and Organizational Studies*, 10(4), 26–43.

Earl, M., and Scott, I. 1999. What is a chief knowledge officer? *Sloan Management Review* (Winter), 29–38.

Edvinsson, L., and Malone, M.S. 1997. *Intellectual capital: The proven way to establish your company's real value by measuring its hidden values*. London: Piatkus.

Ernst & Young. 1997. *Executive perspectives on knowledge in the organization*. Cambridge, MA: The Ernst & Young Center.

Fallah, N. 2011. Distributed form of leadership in communities of practice (CoPs), *International Journal of Emerging Science*, 1(3) (September), 357–370.

Great Place to Work. 2016. The business case for a high-trust culture. https://s3.amazonaws.com/media.greatplacetowork.com/pdfs/Business+Case+for+a+High-Trust+Culture_081816.pdf.

Jiang, Z. 2019. Why withholding information at work won't give you an advantage. Harvard Business Review Web Article, November 14.

Kaplan, B. 2007. Creating long-term value as chief knowledge officer. *Knowledge Management Review* (September/October), 30–33.

Kaplan, R.S., and Norton, D.P. 1996. *The balanced scorecard*. Boston: Harvard Business School Press.

Kiger, P.J. 2007. Precision-targeted development at HP. *Workforce Management*, June 25, 38.

Kluge, J., Shein, W., and Licht, T. 2001. *Knowledge unplugged: The McKinsey and Company Global Survey on knowledge management*. New York: Palgrave Macmillan.

Knowledge Management Review. 2006. Using knowledge as a competitive differentiator at Atlantis Systems. *Knowledge Management Review*, 9(4), 4.

Knowledge Management Review. 2008. Recent appointments demonstrate KM's continued influence. *Knowledge Management Review*, 11(5) (November/December), 4.

MacCormack, A., Volpel, S., and Herman, K. 2002. *Siemens ShareNet: Building a knowledge network*. Boston: Harvard Business School Publishing, Case 9–603–036, November 5.

McKeen, J.D., and Staples, D.S. 2003. Knowledge managers: Who they are and what they do. In *Handbook on knowledge management*, vol. 1, ed. C.W. Holsapple, 21–41. Berlin: Springer.

Meister, D., and Davenport, T. 2005. Knowledge management at Accenture. Ivey Management Services, University of Western Ontario.

Melnick, B. 2006. Using knowledge as a competitive differentiator at Atlantis Systems. *Knowledge Management Review*, 9(5), 8–13.

Melnick, B. 2007. Case study: Atlantis System International—Using KM principles to drive productivity and performance, prevent critical knowledge loss and encourage innovation. *International Atomic Energy Agency*. http://www.iaea.org/inisnkm/nkm/documents/nkm Con2007/fulltext/ES/IAEA-CN-153–2-P-17es.pdf (accessed February 20, 2009).

Panopto. 2023. Workplace knowledge and productivity report. https://panopto.docsend.com/view/pzjpwm6.

PR Newswire. 2001a. Knowledge management: Best practice sharing overcomes barriers. *PR Newswire*, November 1.

PR Newswire. 2001b. Microsoft teams with knowledge advisors to measure training investments. *PR Newswire*, November 27.

Quinn, J.B., Anderson, P., and Finkelstein, S. 1996. Leveraging intellect. *Academy of Management Executive*, 10(3), 7–27.

Rao, M. 2020. Knowledge and innovation excellence: CII summit presents tips from winners of the Most Innovative Knowledge Enterprise awards. *YOURSTORY*, July 18. https://yourstory.com/2020/07/knowledge-innovation-excellence-cii-mike-awards.

Rockart, J.H. 1979. Chief executives define their own data needs. *Harvard Business Review*, 57(2), 81–92.

Sullivan, P.H. 2000. *Value-driven intellectual capital*. New York: John Wiley & Sons.

Sveiby, K-E. 2000. Measuring intangibles and intellectual capital. In *Knowledge management: classic and contemporary works*, ed. D. Morey, M. Maybury, and B. Thuraisingham, 337–353. Cambridge, MA: The MIT Press.

Takeuchi, H. 2001. Toward a universal management concept of knowledge. In *Managing industrial knowledge*, ed. I. Nonaka and D. Teece, 314–329. London: Sage Publications.

Tiwana, A., 2002. *The knowledge management toolkit: Orchestrating IT, strategy, and knowledge platforms*. Upper Saddle River, NJ: Prentice Hall.

Voelpel, S.C., Dous, M., and Davenport, T.H. 2005. Five steps to creating a global knowledge-sharing system: Siemens' ShareNet. *Academy of Management Executive*, 19(2) (May), 9–23.

Yokell, M.R. 2010. *A quantitative correlational study of the relationship between knowledge management maturity and firm performance*. Unpublished doctoral dissertation, University of Phoenix. ProQuest, UMI Dissertations Publishing. http://search.proquest.com/docview/878892492.

Wilson, J. (Ed.). 2002. *Knowledge management review: The practitioner's guide to knowledge management*. Chicago: Melcrum Publishing.

Part IV

Emergent Trends in Knowledge Management

12 Knowledge Management through Cloud Computing

Throughout this book, we have documented how KM systems and processes are utilized to discover, capture, share, and apply knowledge. Information systems and technologies, as well as human intervention, are essential elements of KM systems and processes. In this chapter, we explore the relationship between cloud-computing technologies and KM systems and processes. Cloud computing uses computer networks to provide shared, on-demand, and usually subscription-based computing services to clients and users. Such computing services include applications, physical and virtual servers, data storage, development tools, and network infrastructure. Usually, these services are hosted in a data center managed by a cloud service provider (CSP). Cloud-computing technologies are enablers of KM systems and processes by facilitating access to computing resources which are critical elements of KM systems and processes. Cloud-computing technologies are not dedicated KM systems, but they enable KM systems and processes. The case studies on AT&T and Fish & Paykel demonstrate how cloud computing enables KM systems and processes. In Box 12.1, we explore e-mail as a cloud-hosted messaging and communication application and explain how it enables KM systems and processes.

In the rest of this chapter, we explore the components and structure of cloud computing and explain how they influence KM systems and processes. In the next section, we review and explain some of the technologies, components, and structures of cloud computing.

What is Cloud Computing?

Cloud-computing technologies have evolved since the 1950s as the underlying technologies leverage the advances in technology and respond to the demands of a digitized economy. Virtualization and network technologies are fundamental to current cloud-computing technologies. Cloud computing utilizes virtualization and other supporting technologies to pool, divide, and share computing resources. These technologies enable a single server to be divided into shared multiple virtual servers that provide access to computing resources shared among multiple clients using a variety of devices and interfaces. Cloud-computing architecture is made up of several components in the front-end and back-end. As illustrated in Figure 12.1 clients can use multiple devices, such as mobile devices, personal computers, and tablets, to access cloud-computing resources. Figure 12.1 illustrates the cloud-computing architecture; the front-end elements are visible to the user through a variety of application interfaces and devices.

The front-end enables users to interact with cloud services by sending queries and requesting services. The back-end of the cloud-computing architecture provides

DOI: 10.4324/9781003364375-16

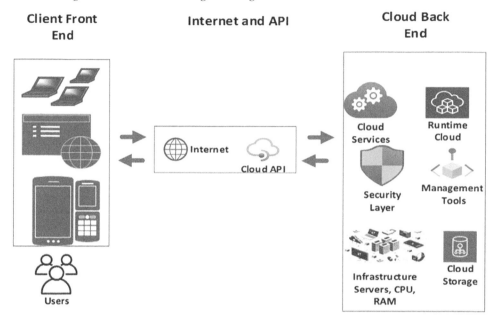

Figure 12.1 Cloud-Computing Architecture

dedicated servers, storage, network infrastructure, operating systems, and other computing resources. The back-end relies on virtualization technologies to deploy and scale computing resources to meet the needs of users based on available capacity. The cloud services and runtime cloud deliver and manage the execution of the shared computing resources as services. Additionally, the security layer and management tools in the back-end implement security controls; and monitor, control, govern, and connect all services and applications. The infrastructure and cloud storage provide the physical hardware and software to host on-demand and time-shared computing resources. Virtualization, containerization, and microservices are some of the technologies used in the back-end of cloud-computing systems to pool, divide, and share computing environments among multiple users.

E-mail is one of the most popular messaging and communication tools to receive and transmit messages on electronic devices. In 2021, 319.6 billion e-mails were sent and received a day, and this has increased to 347 billion by 2023. As e-mail users increase globally, e-mail service providers, such as Google, Microsoft, and Amazon are increasingly using cloud-computing technology to deploy e-mail as a software as a service (SaaS) to make e-mail services easily accessible, scalable, and device independent. In Box 12.1 we explore the capabilities of Gmail.

Box 12.1 Gmail: A Popular E-mail Platform

Google is the service provider for Gmail, one of the most popular e-mail platforms, with about 1.8 billion users worldwide in 2023 (Wise 2023). Google e-mail is a cloud-based e-mail application that is delivered through cloud computing. Gmail has all the features of cloud-native applications and embodies some of the critical features of cloud-computing technologies and can also facilitate KM process, especially the sharing of knowledge.

Like most cloud-based SaaS, Gmail is a subscription-based service with multiple levels of subscription. The free subscription provides users with a limit of 15 gigabyte of storage and comes with Google Drive and Google Photos. Like most SaaS and on-demand computing, users can increase the storage limit by paying for the Google One service which provides expanded cloud storage starting from 100 gigabytes to 20 terabytes. Gmail service comes with several add-ons which users can access using a Web browser, a mobile application, or an e-mail client. Like most SaaS, it is scalable and device agnostic. Thus, users can access e-mail if they have access to the Internet and an electronic device.

Users can receive e-mails up to 50 megabytes in size and send up to 25 megabytes of e-mail including attachment. Larger e-mails can be sent using file links from Google drive. Gmail uses a conversation view to group e-mails threads between individuals and groups. Gmail provides search capabilities with filters that can search e-mail labels, senders, recipients, e-mail messages, and attachments for specific e-mails.

Source: Compiled from Google Mail (n.d.)

Although e-mail is not a KM system, it is an important tool for knowledge sharing because of its ability to connect people asynchronously and provide a platform for interpersonal and group interactions. E-mail users are more attentive and responsive to e-mail messages; thus, it is a veritable tool for sharing information and messages that can crystallize into knowledge. KM processes involve the exchange and combination processes of sharing knowledge, converting tacit knowledge to explicit knowledge, and enabling users to internalize the shared knowledge. E-mail communication enables and promotes these KM processes.

Interpersonal communication, messages, and team interaction through e-mail can support and simplify knowledge-sharing processes. E-mail messages are informal flows of information in the form of messages and electronic documents that are sometimes embedded with knowledge. E-mail conversations may form around an initial message that becomes part of message threads, that others may contribute and respond to. The evolving dialogue and communication between two or more users can enable knowledge sharing and discovery.

E-mail makes it easy for users to codify and share expertise and can promote and encourage knowledge sharing among experts. Knowledge sharing is critical to any successful KM process; if the knowledge is not shared then those who need the knowledge may not have access to the knowledge, and the value of the knowledge is not realized. Conversations and dialogues in e-mail facilitate and promote knowledge sharing and discovery. Some of these e-mail interactions may lead to the discovery of new organizational knowledge which is shared among e-mail correspondence.

E-mail usage illustrates how cloud-computing technologies enable KM processes, especially sharing and discovering knowledge (Saratchandra and Shrestha 2022). However, basic e-mail subscriptions with functionality like Google Drive and Google Photos are not suitable for a centralized capture, storage, retrieval, and transfer of knowledge. Furthermore, knowledge in e-mail is not centrally managed, thus some of the knowledge embedded in e-mail correspondence and attached electronic documents may not be easily shared without an effective KM system and processes.

History and Background of Cloud Computing

Cloud-computing technologies emerged in the mid-2000s, but the concept of time-shared computing using grid computing and virtualizations has been around much longer. In the 1950s and 1960s, virtualization and computer networks enabled large mainframe computers to share centralized computing resources among multiple clients using simple and basic terminals. In the late 1960s, the Advanced Research Projects Agency (ARPA) of the U.S. Department of Defense, created the ARPNET, a host-to-host computer network that linked time-sharing computers. Then, in the 1970s, IBM introduced virtual machines, a process of creating virtual computing resources with dedicated amounts of CPU, memory, and storage, provided by a physical host computer.

Virtualization promoted and encouraged rented computing resources and utility computing. As illustrated in Figure 12.2, a virtual machine configuration can provide multiple computing resources encompassing an operating system and applications that meet the needs of clients and users. As illustrated in Figure 12.2, through virtualization a physical server can spawn multiple virtual machines that are dedicated to a user and are loosely coupled with other virtual machines. For example, in Figure 12.2, physical server 1 uses virtualization software to spawn three virtual computing environments with its corresponding operating systems and applications that can be shared among multiple users or clients.

Beyond virtualization and virtual machine technologies, the Internet and worldwide network of computers also spurred the development of cloud computing as we know it today. The nature of shared and on-demand computing requires that each client or user has access to a reserved and isolated computer environment that is time-shared. Virtualization technologies enable cloud computing to manage these independent and decoupled IT environments and simplify the delivery of applications and computing environments that are managed separately and independently. Cloud-computing technologies integrate a variety of virtualization technologies to manage the complexities of a computing environment with multiple isolated and decoupled computing resources for multiple users.

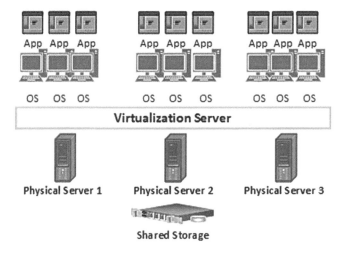

Figure 12.2 Structure of Virtualization

Virtualization: Containerization and Microservices

Cloud-computing technologies are adopting *containerization* and *microservices* to abstract computing resources and services that are pooled, shared, and tailored to needs of multiple users. Containers are mechanisms for isolating computing resources and services with shared physical infrastructure. They abstract computing resources and deliver them using microservice technologies that decouple shared computing resources from other pooled computing environments (IBM Market Development & Insights 2020).

Containers are lightweight application components that combine the application and operating system dependencies libraries into a unit that can operate in any computer environment. Containerization enables the development and deployment of productivity applications as microservices in containers. These microservices are flexible, portable, scalable, platform-agnostic, nimble, and suitable for digitized business environments. For example, when you want to use visualization and charts in Microsoft Excel 2022, you must install the appropriate Windows Operating System that supports MS Excel 2022. This dependence on the Windows Operating System (platform) can be addressed through containerization. Containerization of application and microservices can create a single software package/container that is platform-independent (i.e., does not require a platform like the Windows Operating System) and will run on any device or system and deliver Microsoft Excel 2022 visualization features specific to users' needs.

Microservices decompose complex software applications into collection of small, independent, and loosely coupled services. For example, microservices architecture can decompose a monolithic learning management system (LMS) into student services, faculty services, learning activities, and assessment. These collections of smaller, self-contained services are autonomous and specialized and can be developed, deployed, and scaled independently. Moreover, these loosely coupled services are fault tolerant. Failure of a component of the LMS only degrades functionality but does not crash the whole learning management system. Each microservice focuses on a specific domain of the LMS (Beltre et al. 2019). These containerized microservices are more lightweight and portable than virtual machines, thus they have become the foundation and drivers of cloud-computing technologies.

Container orchestration is an intelligent technology to manage and coordinate service interactions and ensure data consistency across services. Container orchestration tools automate deployment and implementation, and provide storage and network connection among containers. These tools automatically start, stop, and manage containers in the back-end of a cloud computer. Container orchestration software, such as, Kubernetes (https://kubernetes.io/), Docker Swarm (www.docker.com), and Apache Mesos (https://mesos.apache.org/), automate the management and coordination of containerized microservices, including operational tasks, deployments, and running containerized applications and services.

Configurations files schedule container deployments to the appropriate host based on capacity and requirements and constraints dictated in the configuration file. The ability of the container orchestration tool to automate host selection and resource allocation in the configuration file maximizes efficient use of computing resources (Pahl and Lee 2015). Container orchestration maximizes resource availability through automated system health monitoring and relocation of containers. Once containers are deployed, their lifecycle is managed and monitored to provide scalability and availability.

Cloud-Computing Deployment Models

The growth in demand for cloud-computing technologies is fueled by an increasing demand for flexible computing as businesses continuously innovate to stay competitive in a global and digitized economy. According to IBM Research (Comfort et al. 2020), 90 percent of global businesses have adopted cloud-computing solutions in 2019. Cloud computing offers several benefits to organizations, including the ability to access current and up-to-date technologies without the challenges of procurement, configuration, and deployment. Furthermore, on-demand cloud-computing resources enable flexibility, efficiency, and agility. When businesses opt for cloud computing, they must also decide what deployment models are suitable for their business environment. There are three types of cloud-computing deployment models. Cloud computing can be deployed as public clouds, private clouds, or hybrid clouds.

Public clouds are hosted and managed by third-party cloud service providers. These deployment models offer computing services and resources accessible over the Internet through a subscription plan. Access and usage of public clouds are controlled by fee-based subscriptions, thus only users with subscription plans can access resources on public clouds. Public clouds can provide an array of computing services including applications, storage, database services, networking, analytics, artificial intelligence, and machine learning. Public cloud services enable organizations to access shared on-demand computing resources that meet their unique requirements and goals. Fee-based subscription enables organizations to scale resource utilization based on their needs. Public clouds may offer minimal services for free that are only suitable for home use. For most businesses, public cloud models are cost effective because they eliminate the initial capital expenditures for servers and hardware, especially in an era of fast-paced advances in technology that render technologies obsolete in a short period of time. For many businesses, public cloud computing is cost-effective and a viable cloud computing deployment model.

Private clouds provide computing resources dedicated to an organization or entity. Thus, the owners of private cloud-computing resources have exclusive access and exclude other users and the public from access. Private cloud services can be hosted by third-party vendors or on-premises. On-premises cloud services are privately hosted and managed by organizations using their own data centers. On-premises private cloud computing restricts access to an organization or entity. Private cloud computing can be hosted by third-party vendors that dedicate computing resources exclusively for an entity or organization. Regulatory compliance, security, privacy, and other enterprise requirements drive some organizations to deploy on-premises, or third-party hosted private clouds.

Hybrid clouds combine public and private cloud-deployment models. In the hybrid model, parts of the shared computing resources are hosted by third-party vendors and other parts are privately hosted on-premises or by third-party vendors with dedicated physical systems. This model enables enterprises to take advantage of the benefits of both private and public cloud services. These hybrid cloud-deployment models are portable and enable organizations to maintain some level of control over their computing resources. When computing resource demand increases beyond capacity and workload, excess demand can be moved between public and private cloud environments to minimize time and cost of purchasing, installing, and maintaining new servers that may be underutilized most of the time.

Many organizations are opting for cloud services because of the fast-paced changes in technologies and the inability of on-premises computing resources to keep up with continuous changes in technologies. For example, the on-premises installation of Microsoft Office applications in a large organization and the management of updates, security, and storage can be challenging. Cloud computing eliminates many of these challenges. Through cloud computing, organizations can access current and up-to-date technologies without the challenges of procurement, configuration, and deployment. These benefits enable flexibility, efficiency, and agility. Cloud computing increases resource accessibility. Users and clients can access computing resources anytime and anywhere through the Internet. For example, Dropbox or Google Drive users can have access to data and files anytime and anywhere regardless of device or operating system.

Cloud Service Models

Cloud services are hosted by third-party providers and made available to users through the Internet. Cloud services facilitate the flow of user data from front-end clients (e.g., users' tablets, desktops, laptops, and mobile devices), through the Internet, to the back-end systems. There are three main cloud service models, infrastructure as a service (IaaS), platform as a service (PaaS), and software as a service (SaaS).

IaaS provides access to cloud-hosted physical and virtual servers, storage, and networking. Thus, IaaS provides the IT infrastructure for running applications and workloads in the cloud. Through paid subscriptions client and customers access these computing resources over the Internet. IaaS provides a platform for businesses to set up physical or virtual hardware, install and configure software, such as operating systems and applications, integrate middleware applications, configure networks and storage components. IaaS may include options to manage user and identity controls, and setup network hardware, such as routers and switches, and allocate IP addresses. IaaS enables organizations to implement and setup computing resources in a cloud environment. Amazon Web Services, Google Cloud, IBM Cloud, and Microsoft Azure are some of the cloud service providers that host IaaS. IaaS eliminates the need for organizations to procure, configure, install, and maintain physical servers.

PaaS provides access to an on-demand platform comprising of the hardware and software stack to build, deploy, and manage applications. Cloud-hosted platforms provide servers, network infrastructure storage, operating system, and databases. Developers use these services to create applications: code, run, build, test, deploy, maintain, and scale application containers and container orchestration software to deploy the software. PaaS is a useful cloud service model for organizations with multiple vendors or developers working on a project. The PaaS provides the necessary infrastructure, and developers can focus on developing the code and the application and not be concerned about the underlying infrastructure. AWS Elastic Beanstalk (http s://aws.amazon.com) is an example of a PaaS. PaaS doesn't eliminate the need for developers, but it streamlines development, deployment, and operations and integrates them with the hosting infrastructure. PaaS can improve efficiency by eliminating the physical resource procurement, capacity planning, software maintenance and patching required for software development. PaaS can be more attractive when an organization wants to get applications out to production quickly.

SaaS provides access to cloud-hosted application software. Users and clients use desktop clients, application programming interface (API), or Web interface to access and use software applications. Users can subscribe to these applications services or use them on a pay-as-you-go basis. Most commercial software applications have options for cloud delivery. SaaS enables immediate implementation, thus making new technology available to users quickly. Web-based e-mail is a good example of SaaS. Once you sign up and provide some personal information you can start using e-mail immediately and you don't have to worry about storage or compatibility, as long as you have Internet connection and a Web browser. Another typical example is Microsoft Office 365SaaS, which provides multiple types and categories of subscriptions. There are home and business subscriptions with options for monthly or yearly paid subscriptions that may prescribe the number of users and/or devices in the subscription plan. Many of these SaaS providers complement these services with other cloud services such as cloud storage. With Microsoft Office 365Saas software services, users also have access to Microsoft's storage services.

Cloud Computing and Knowledge Management

Cloud-computing technologies are not dedicated KM systems, but they can support and enhance KM systems and processes. Information technologies are critical to KM systems, thus access to current technologies through cloud computing can support the discovery, capture, and sharing of knowledge (Gupta et al. 2022). Hence, cloud-computing technologies are enablers of KM systems and processes (Boamah et al. 2022). In Figure 12.3, the three main cloud services, IaaS, PaaS, and SaaS are enablers of KM systems and processes. These cloud services influence the use of KM processes and systems.

Using a cloud-based KM system can improve KM process and enterprise performance (Shehzad et al. 2022). Cloud-based KM systems can eliminate the cost of acquiring hardware and software and speed up development and implementation of KM systems (Younas et al. 2022). In this section, we focus on how cloud-computing resources enable KM systems and processes.

The capacity of cloud-computing technologies to provide access to innovative technologies makes cloud services an enabler of KM systems and processes (Anshari et al. 2016; Sultan 2013). As illustrated in Figure 12.3, the cloud-computing services, IaaS, PaaS, and SaaS, are enablers of KM systems and processes. The case study on using Dropbox cloud storage is an example of how SaaS enables KM systems and processes. For example, users can share and combine knowledge when they use cloud

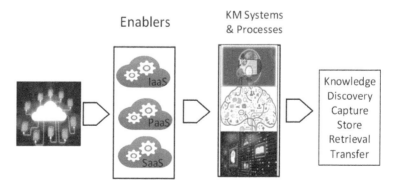

Figure 12.3 Cloud Services Enable KM and Processes

collaboration software, such as Zoom (www.zoom.us) or Webex (www.webex.com), to interact with associates and co-workers. Through these interactions, explicit knowledge can be captured and shared, and then combined with other forms of explicit knowledge to create new knowledge (Arpaci 2017). The case studies on AT&T and Fisher & Paykel provide practical examples of how cloud services enable KM systems processes.

Figure 12.3 illustrates the relationship between cloud services as enablers of KM systems and processes. Thus, by making technology easily accessible, cloud services facilitate knowledge management process.

Case Studies

We present the three case studies below to demonstrate how cloud-computing technologies enable KM processes. The first case study describes how Dropbox, a cloud storage service can support and promote the use of KM systems and processes. The case studies on AT&T and Fisher & Paykel illustrate how cloud-computing technologies are supporting KM systems and processes.

Dropbox Cloud Storage Service and KM

Dropbox cloud storage is a SaaS that is very popular among users and enterprises. Some of the popular cloud storage service providers include Dropbox (www.dropbox.com), OneDrive (www.microsoft.com/en-us/microsoft-365/onedrive/online-cloud-storage), Google Drive (www.google.com/drive), and iCloud (www.icloud.com). In this case study we explore the use of Dropbox as SaaS and how its usage facilitates KM systems and processes. Cloud storage services, such as Dropbox, enable businesses and individuals to manage their electronic data on remote storage servers and avoid the challenges of storing data on local devices.

Dropbox was launched in 2008, and by 2021 it had 700 million users. Dropbox integrates with Windows Operating System, Google Workspace, Adobe, and Amazon Web Services and has apps for personal computers, mobile devices, and smartphones, as well as a Web interface. The apps enable automatic photo upload from storage devices, such as USB drives, or tablets, and backup and restore services.

Dropbox is an on-demand, subscription-based cloud storage service. Dropbox cloud storage services include additional services for commercial and private usage. The Dropbox *freemium* services provide free accounts with limited storage, and the paid subscriptions provide additional storage capacity and other features. For the free subscriptions, users get two gigabytes of storage for free, and can expand the storage limit through a referral program. The paid subscription, Dropbox Plus, provides users with two terabytes of storage space. Dropbox Business and Dropbox Enterprises are subscription services for small and large organizations. Commercial subscriptions add more functionality for teams and collaboration (Dropbox n.d.). Commercial and paid subscription services include productivity and sharing tools that enable users to perform various tasks including full text search, viewer history, and Web previews. According to a Forrester study (Forrester Research Inc. 2022) commissioned by Dropbox, businesses that adopt Dropbox increase team and individual productivity through faster team collaboration.

The Dropbox workspace collaboration features include Dropbox *DocSend* and Dropbox *Sign*. DocSend enables users to share trackable links and provides insights on shared documents. Users can also sign documents with Dropbox Sign. These features promote collaboration in Dropbox among team members working on electronic documents. Content protection and other features enable users to backup data, recover files, control shared links, meet regulatory compliance, and secure files against cyberattacks.

Although Dropbox cloud storage services and the functionality it provides is not dedicated to KM systems, many of the benefits of using cloud storage services can support and promote KM systems and processes (Gunadham 2015). The digital assets of the organization are embedded with knowledge and Dropbox workspace provides a platform to manage electronic documents and digital assets. This capability enhances the capacity of the organization to capture and share knowledge from electronic documents. The digital workspace provided by Dropbox facilitates the management and control of documents which are embedded with organizational knowledge.

Dropbox workspace promotes team collaboration that can support the capture, sharing, combination, and discovery of knowledge through the sharing of electronic documents among individuals and team members. For example, a user may codify tacit knowledge into a document and then share the document with other users or team members. Other users with access to the document may combine that explicit knowledge with other existing knowledge to create new knowledge. Similarly, as team members engage and collaborate on a document and update and review the document, a context and history of team member interactions is captured and can provide additional insights that may lead to the discovery of new knowledge. For example, the coauthors of this book used Dropbox to collaborate to create this new edition of the book. In the past, book authors collaborated by sharing files via e-mail, which often resulted in version control issues. Therefore, collaborating via Dropbox contributes to increased team productivity by properly supporting version control, among other features.

All these features are supported by back-end and front-end technologies linked together by the Internet. As illustrated in Figure 12.4, the architecture of the cloud

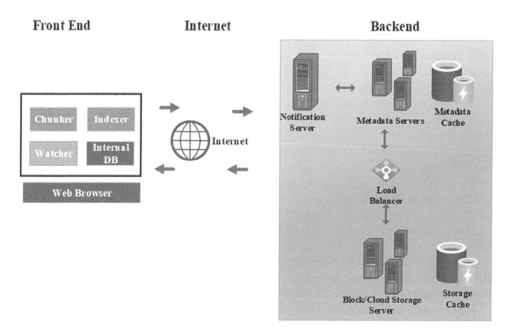

Figure 12.4 Dropbox Architecture

storage service consists of a back-end and a front-end. Users typically interact with the front-end through client software or Web browsers on a variety of devices. The back-end consists of software, servers, storage, and network. The front-end client provides a graphical interface that users interact with to access files and folders on the back-end through the Internet.

The front-end of the Dropbox cloud architecture provides an interface for a Web browser that renders the content of the workspace as a webpage with links to folders, files, and other workspace functionality. Users can also use client software that runs on mobile devices and personal computers to access the contents of a workspace. There are several software components on the front-end that work together to provide users with an effective and efficient workspace to manage electronic documents and team interactions.

The client interface monitors and synchronizes files in the users' workspace folder using the watcher, chunker, indexer, and internal database components within the client interface as shown in Figure 12.4. The watcher monitors the local workspace folders and notifies the indexer of any changes to the workspace folders and files. To handle file transfer efficiently, the chunker breaks each file into smaller chunks to speed file transfer to the back-end. The files are split into chunks by the chunker using a chunking algorithm. The chunker splits and reconstructs files, identifies modified chunks, and transmits only modified chunks to the cloud storage. The internal database keeps tracks of version history and file location.

The back-end of the Dropbox architecture consists of notification server, metadata servers, and block/cloud storage servers as illustrated in Figure 12.4. The metadata server stores information on chunks, files, devices, and users, and provides synchronization services to maintain a consistent view across devices and interfaces. The synchronization services update files and folders and synchronize with the client local database. The synchronization services use the notification server to inform users on the synchronization processes. The cloud/block storage stores chunks of files. When users upload chunks to the block/cloud storage, the block server updates the metadata server and commits the changes, and the notification server informs clients about the changes. Qualified clients get metadata updates and can download updated chunks. The back-end architecture uses cache to reduce latency, increase throughput, and improve client access to chunks and files.

Although cloud storage services such as Dropbox are not KM systems, the workspace it provides for collaboration and group management of documents and interaction supports and promotes KM system and processes. Organizations can also integrate Dropbox into their KM systems and processes to take full advantage of the benefits of cloud storage services.

AT&T Cloud First Policy with Microsoft Azure

American Telephone and Telegram (AT&T) is a telephony and communication company established in 1885 with headquarters in Dallas TX, US. Over the years, telephone and communication technologies have evolved. Communication technologies have changed from digital subscriber lines to broadband and fifth-generation broadband cellular networks. Telephone technologies have also changed with mobile phone subscription outpacing landline phone subscription and the adoption of Voice over Internet protocol (VoIP) technologies. As technology changes, the needs and demands of customers are also changing (Microsoft Azure n.d.).

AT&T has grown, adapted, and innovated its IT infrastructure to keep up with the changes in telephony and communication technologies and meet the needs of a growing customer base. In the process, AT&T developed a complex Web of IT environment and applications. In 2019, there were about 7,500 applications in a complex IT environment of mainframes and midrange servers supported by 34 data centers. The complexity of the IT environment hampered the ability of AT&T to respond quickly to customer needs and market changes. The IT environment also includes a myriad of productivity and collaboration tools to manage workflows and communication across its global operations. The environment was further complicated with decades of old home-grown applications that were not necessary, but part of the IT infrastructure. Thus, the AT&T IT environment was made up of legacy, outdated, innovative, and sophisticated applications that were not integrated. Furthermore, some of the data centers supporting these numerous applications were underutilized and inefficient.

Besides the cost and expense of maintaining a complex IT environment with redundant systems, AT&T was hampered in the discovery, capture, sharing, and application of organizational knowledge. The collective knowledge of the organization was scattered across disparate systems, and the complexities of these systems hindered AT&T's abilities to efficiently apply its collective knowledge. For example, it took AT&T a long time to develop new applications or enhance a product, because it took a significant amount of time and resources to secure the necessary infrastructure to test and deploy new products given its complex IT environment. Thus, the complexity of the IT environment hindered the timely application of the collective knowledge of AT&T.

AT&T's response was to adopt a "cloud first" policy that moved the company away from focusing on on-premises hosted applications. With this new focus, any new application is reviewed for possible cloud deployment if possible. The IT team strategically reviewed the 7,500 applications, retired about 2,500 and deployed another 2,500 in the Microsoft Azure cloud and retained the remaining applications. With a simplified number of applications, AT&T retired twenty-eight data centers and kept six data centers to support the on-premises hosted applications. To further simplify the IT environment AT&T reduced the number of collaboration and productivity tools and implemented SaaS solution with Microsoft 365, Exchange Online, and Teams as the main collaboration and productivity platform. Through SaaS, Microsoft Azure provides most of the business-critical productivity and collaboration tools for AT&T.

Knowledge is embedded in organizational artifacts, processes, routines, and documents. Thus, when an organization is saddled by a complex IT environment, it is unable to capture, share, and apply the knowledge scattered across all these systems. Furthermore, when the knowledge is discovered and captured, transferring the knowledge to where it is needed is challenging if the systems are not well integrated. Lack of integrated systems hampers knowledge retrieval, transfer, and application.

This case study demonstrates that although cloud-based systems are not dedicated KM systems, the benefits of cloud computing can minimize the barriers to effective KM systems and processes. Furthermore, the benefits of scalability, security and agility that come with a cloud service helped AT&T focus on using its collective knowledge to meet the changing needs of customers and remain competitive. By adopting a cloud first policy and deploying cloud-based applications, AT&T has minimized the barriers for efficiently leveraging its collective knowledge.

Service Cloud at Fisher & Paykel

As noted in this chapter, cloud-computing technologies are enablers of KM systems and processes. In this case study, Fisher & Paykel's implementation of cloud marketing by Salesforce illustrates how cloud-computing technologies enable knowledge sharing and application to improve customer experience. Fisher & Paykel is an appliance manufacturer established in 1934 in New Zealand, and now operates in over 30 countries. The mission of Fisher & Paykel is to create products that are tailored to human needs; hence, it is important, indeed critical, to Fisher & Paykel to understand and anticipate the needs of its customers. Fisher & Paykel manufactures and markets human-centered home appliances for homeowners, home builders, contractors, home designers, retail partners, and retail customers. Thus, Fisher & Paykel has multiple marketing channels and functional units that provide pre-sale and post-sale support for a wide range of customers. Since 2017, the company has been pursuing a strategy to improve engagement with all its multiple customer bases (Salesforce n.d.-a, n.d.-b).

Global operations and multiple types of customers with diverse and unique needs have resulted in multiple customer support systems siloed by functional units and locations of operations. Customers were frustrated with the need to provide the same information multiple times to customer service technicians, as these technicians switched between systems and escalated calls to other departments for assistance. Furthermore, customers did not think that the support system adequately addressed their needs. For example, customers did not have the means to track when a technician would arrive to service an appliance; thus, customers may spend hours waiting for a technician. Additionally, the support staff were exasperated because they did not have comprehensive tools and access to information to support the needs of all customers.

In 2021, Fisher & Paykel implemented Service Cloud from Salesforce to address these challenges. Service Cloud uses cloud-computing technologies to host customer information systems that are accessible to all support staff regardless of locations or departments. Through the Service Cloud, Fisher & Paykel was able to integrate all customer knowledge into a central database and create a single view of the customer across its sales and service operations. Centralizing customer interaction data provides a complete view of the customer. Service Cloud provided customer case management using omni-channel routing to match calls with the appropriate technician with the best skillset, and track customer assets, orders, and support history. The Service Cloud also supported technicians by integrating data across departments, back-end systems, and legacy systems. The customer services process was automated to create and update records, log calls, and guide technicians through dynamic and adaptive screens.

Centralizing customer interaction data enables technicians to optimize article search and access customer knowledge that drives quick case resolution. The Service Cloud systems provide the platform for support staff to engage more efficiently with customers and gain more knowledge about the customers. Support staff can use their knowledge about the customer to serve them better, providing a seamless experience personalized to the needs of customers. For example, customers could track when a technician would arrive using a link to get live updates on the arrival time of the technicians. The Service Cloud provided a more tailored support for customers all over the world. Through the Service Cloud, Fisher & Paykel was able to personalize and streamline customer experiences, and provided the sales team with better tools, including more up-to-date information on customers. Customers could also use the system to rate representatives and if the ratings are unfavorable, Fisher & Paykel is able to take steps to address the customer's concern. These cloud technologies have also made a remarkable change in the post-sales experience. Technicians and support staff can spend more of their time helping customers as the Service Cloud provides them with the knowledge to assist customers.

The case of Fisher & Paykel illustrates the enabling capabilities of cloud-computing technology. Although Service Cloud is not a dedicated KM system, it enables and facilitates KM process in several ways. Improving and enhancing the interaction between the pre-sale and the post-sale teams, and customers, Service Cloud provided a platform for the conversion of tacit knowledge to explicit knowledge and the combination of explicit knowledge to create new knowledge. As technicians and support staff use these systems to document their interaction with customers, technicians can codify and convert tacit knowledge to explicit knowledge, which eventually becomes part of the collective knowledge of Fisher & Paykel. Additionally, the Service Cloud systems improved the storage and retrieval and application of knowledge to personalize the customer experience. This illustrates the enabling characteristics of cloud-computing technologies and how they enable and support KM systems and processes.

Service Cloud enabled Fisher & Paykel to better leverage the collective knowledge of the organization which was previously siloed and scattered across multiple systems. Through cloud computing, Fisher & Paykel has undertaken a digital transformation that is putting the appliance manufacturer in more regular contact with happy customers that will continue to buy its products.

Summary

In this chapter, we have reviewed the history of cloud computing to explain some of the underlying technologies for cloud computing. Cloud computing has become a popular mechanism to provide computing services due to the benefits associated with lower cost, and increased scalability and efficiency. In this chapter we demonstrated the benefits of cloud computing in the case studies on AT&T and Fisher & Paykel. Although KM systems can be deployed in the cloud and as cloud services, cloud-computing technologies, per se, are not dedicated KM systems; however, the benefits that they bring to the organization is to provide the infrastructure to promote and support the deployment of KM systems and processes. As demonstrated in the Dropbox case study, the digital workspace and the document management processes enable interpersonal and team interactions which are essential to KM processes of knowledge discovery, capture, and sharing. However, because cloud-computing technologies are not a dedicated KM system, it may not have the capacity to support all the processes necessary for efficient and effective KM systems and processes. Thus, cloud-computing technologies can complement organizational efforts to leverage the organization's collective knowledge by supporting dedicated KM systems and processes.

Review

1 Which type of cloud computing deployment model will be suitable for your organization? Provide justification for your answer and why other implementations are less suitable.
2 What are some of the underlying technologies of cloud computing implementation?

3 How do cloud-computing technologies enable KM systems and processes?
4 What are some of the limitations of cloud computing on KMS?
5 What are some of the benefits of cloud computing to organizations?

Application Exercises

1 Select one cloud service (IaaS, PaaS, SaaS) and explain the types of computing resources provided by the service you selected. How do clients use the service?
2 Identify a specific cloud service that you think can help your organization improve its KM systems and processes.
3 Explain how and why the services you selected can help KM systems and processes in your organizations.
4 How do shared cloud storage services, such as Google Drive, One Drive, and Dropbox enable and support KM systems and processes?
5 Do you think it is strategically wise for your organization to use cloud storage to store all organizational data and information? What are the benefits and risks?

References

Anshari, M., Alas, Y., and Guan, L.S. 2016. Developing online learning resources: Big data, social networks, and cloud computing to support pervasive knowledge. *Education and Information Technologies*, 21, 1663–1677.

Arpaci, I. 2017. Antecedents and consequences of cloud computing adoption in education to achieve knowledge management. *Computers in Human Behaviour*, 70, 382–390.

Beltre, A.M., Saha, P., Govindaraju, M., Younge, A., and Grant, R.E. 2019. Enabling HPC workloads on cloud infrastructure using Kubernetes container orchestration mechanisms. In *2019 IEEE/ACM International Workshop on Containers and New Orchestration Paradigms for Isolated Environments in HPC (CANOPIE-HPC)*, November 2019, 11–20. IEEE.

Boamah, F.A., Zhang, J., Wen, D., Sherani, M., Hayat, A., and Horbanenko, O. 2022. Enablers of knowledge management: practical research-based in the construction industry. *International Journal of Innovation Science*, 14(1), 121–137.

Comfort, J., Dolph, B., Robinson, S., Kesterson-Townes, L., and Marshall, A. 2020. IBM research insights: The hybrid cloud platform advantage. https://www.ibm.com/downloads/cas/QMRQEROB (accessed May 16, 2023).

Dropbox. n.d. Subscription plans. https://www.dropbox.com/plans.

Forrester Research. 2022. The total economic impact of Dropbox: Cost savings and business benefits enabled by Dropbox (October). https://assets.dropbox.com/dmep/en-us/assets/pdfs/TEI_of_Dropbox_2022_10_12_Final.pdf.

Google Mail. n.d. Secure, smart, and easy to use email. https://www.google.com/gmail/about/ (accessed July 23, 2023).

Gunadham, T. 2015. Potential of cloud storage application as knowledge management system. *International Journal of Innovation, Management, and Technology*, 6(2), 153.

Gupta, C., Fernandez-Crehuet, J.M., and Gupta, V. 2022. Measuring impact of cloud computing and knowledge management in software development and innovation. *Systems*, 10(5), 151.

IBM Market Development & Insights. 2020. Container in the enterprise; Rapid enterprise adoption continues. https://www.ibm.com/downloads/cas/VG8KRPRM (accessed May 20, 2023).

Microsoft Azure. n.d. AT&T develops a new way to work with cloud-first approach in Azure. https://customers.microsoft.com/en-us/story/1637199155802401650-att-telecommunications-azure (accessed May 15, 2023).

Pahl, C., and Lee, B. 2015. Containers and clusters for edge cloud architectures—A technology review. In *2015 3rd International Conference on Future Internet of Things and Cloud*, August 2015, 379–386. IEEE.

Salesforce. n.d.-a Digital engagement. https://www.salesforce.com/editions-pricing/service-cloud/digital-engagement/ (accessed May 15, 2023).

Salesforce. n.d.-b Fisher & Paykel builds human-centric experiences with Salesforce. https://www.salesforce.com/customer-success-stories/fisher-and-paykel/ (accessed May 15, 2023).

Saratchandra, M., and Shrestha, A. 2022. The role of cloud computing in knowledge management for small and medium enterprises: a systematic literature review. *Journal of Knowledge Management*.

Shehzad, M.U., Zhang, J., Dost, M., Ahmad, M.S., and Alam, S. 2022. Knowledge management enablers and knowledge management processes: a direct and configurational approach to stimulate green innovation. *European Journal of Innovation Management*, June 4.

Sultan, N. 2013. Knowledge management in the age of cloud computing and Web 2.0: Experiencing the power of disruptive innovations. *International Journal of Information Management*, 33(1), 160–165.

Wise, J. 2023. Gmail users: How many people use Gmail in 2023. https://earthweb.com/how-many-people-use-gmail/ (accessed May 25, 2023).

Younas, M., Noor, A.S.M., and Arshad, M. 2022. Cloud-based knowledge management framework for decision making in higher education institutions. *Intelligent Automation & Soft Computing*, 31(1), 83–99.

13 Knowledge Management through Communities and Crowds

We started this section on emergent trends in knowledge management with Chapter 12, where we examined cloud computing and how it can help with knowledge management. In this chapter, we focus on digitally-enabled forms of organizations and examine how digital platforms for collaboration influence KM systems and processes.

Digitally-Enabled Communities

Digitally-enabled communities are platforms for knowledge flows and cost-effective mechanisms for capturing external and internal organizational knowledge. They organize people with shared interests to openly collaborate, exchange information, dialogue, seek advice, and solve problems. Thus, they bring people with diverse backgrounds, expertise, experiences, and competency together, and through conversation and dialogue, jointly share and create knowledge that adds value and promotes innovation.

Customers, partners, consumers, and experts are external sources of knowledge. Employees, especially subject matter experts, are internal sources of organizational knowledge. Knowledge is embedded in the experiences and minds of people, customers, consumers, prospects, employees, and experts. Digitally-enabled communities provide platforms for knowledge flows and the opportunity to capture internal and external knowledge embedded in the minds and experiences of people (Blohm et al. 2018).

The focus of this chapter is to explore how digitally-enabled platforms enable organizations to exploit external and internal knowledge to develop products, solutions, and services. As depicted in Figure 13.1, internal sources and repositories of knowledge include employees, contractors, consultants, and experts within the boundaries of organizations, and external sources of knowledge are customers, consumers, suppliers, prospects, and experts. Digitally-enabled community platforms, such as crowdsourcing communities and online communities, help organizations to capture knowledge embedded in people and groups and extend the value of that knowledge to develop solutions, products, and innovation. In this chapter, we focus on two distinct types of digitally-enabled communities: online communities and crowdsourcing communities (Liu 2021).

There are various types of online communities, including communities on brands, support communities, questions and answer forums, and interest driven communities. The shared interests and goals of online communities foster interpersonal interaction and information and knowledge sharing among members (Faraj et al. 2016). Commitment to shared goals and interest motivates members of these online communities to engage others in a dialogue and share information and knowledge. The knowledge

DOI: 10.4324/9781003364375-17

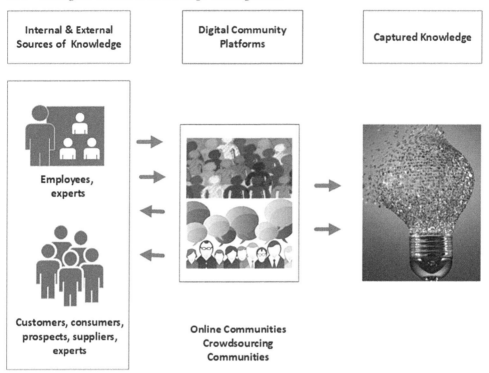

Figure 13.1 Knowledge Sources and Digital Communities

flows within these online communities combine and create new knowledge that creates value for organizations. The review of the Project Management Institute (PMI) online community in Box 13.1 demonstrates how knowledge created in online communities is captured and exploited by organizations. The case study on how Dropbox used Stack Overflow Teams to manage internal organizational knowledge is another example of how online communities facilitate knowledge sharing and creation.

Box 13.1 How the Project Management Institute Uses Online Communities to Support Members

The Project Management Institute (PMI) provides a digital community platform, or community of practice (CoP), where project management professionals meet to discuss and share information on the practice of project management. A community of practice consists of an interest-based digital community platform focused on a shared domain of specialization. Members of communities of practice share a passion and interest in a domain of practice and regularly collaborate with other members to learn and improve their competency in the domain of interest (Farnsworth et al. 2016).

Through a process of collective learning, members of the CoP share experiences, ask questions, seek answers to problems, and provide solutions relevant to the domain of interest. Communities of practice can be hosted by an employer via their Intranet, professional associations like PMI, or by third-party vendors. Membership may be restricted to only employees of an organization, members of the professional association, or open to the public, respectively.

The PMI community platform is hosted by the PMI organization on a purpose-built digital community platform with features for subscribing to a thread, rating comments, providing recognition via badges for contributors, and search capabilities. There are seven communities of practice on the PMI community platform. The domains of interest for the seven communities of practice are certification, citizen development, project management, process improvement, community, package selection, and disciplined agility. Members can join any of these communities on the platform and engage others in a dialogue (Project Management Institute n.d.). For example, the project management community has several discussions threads, such as how to create a project charter and stakeholder analysis tools. These discussion threads generate comments, opinions, experiences, lessons learned, and tricks related to the topic of discussion. Some of the knowledge and expertise on the practice of project management resides in the minds and experiences of geographically dispersed project management practitioners. These digitally-enabled communities allow participants to share their tacit knowledge with the community. Thus, through dialogues, conversations, and personal interaction, tacit knowledge is converted to explicit knowledge, which participants then combine with their existing knowledge to create new knowledge. Shared experiences and the documentation of cognitive shortcuts or tricks, and lessons learned become part of the knowledge base of the community, that members can reuse in their own practice.

The PMI community platform has search capabilities, so members can search the knowledge-base for answers to questions. The collective learning processes within the communities enable members to improve their skills and competency as project management practitioners. As members of the community engage in joint discussion and dialogue, and share information on the practice of project management, they learn and grow as project management practitioners.

Since project management is practiced in all disciplines, members of these communities are practitioners of project management from diverse disciplines and backgrounds. The PMI community platform helps to break down discipline silos in the practice of project management and integrates best practices across all disciplines. The knowledge and competency gained through communities of practice enhances the expertise of employees who in turn share that knowledge with others, and then becomes part of the collective knowledge. Thus, through communities of practice, organizations can leverage the value of external knowledge. For example, in the PMI communities, a member who practices project management in the field of technology can learn new skills from another practitioner in healthcare.

When employees participate in these communities of practice, they learn and acquire new knowledge that they share with other employees. Communities of practice are important mechanisms for organizations to internalize knowledge from external sources. Communities of practice are incubators for specialized knowledge in specific domains and can play a key role in the transfer of knowledge from external sources and repositories. To benefit from communities of practice, organizations should invest in the professional development of their employees and provide them with opportunities to engage with other professionals. The opportunities for employees to engage other professionals and participate in communities of practice can help organizations exploit the value in external sources of knowledge.

Sources: Compiled from Farnsworth et al. (2016); Project Management Institute (n.d.)

Unlike online communities, crowdsourcing communities are more project- and task-oriented. Open innovation strategies that solicit expert knowledge from external and internal sources use crowdsourcing communities to gather expert knowledge. Crowdsourcing digital communities elicit ideas from diverse perspectives and combine them to promote innovation. McDonald's, General Mills, Samsung, and Airbnb are some of the businesses that have used crowdsourcing for various purposes, including branding products, developing new products and flavors, and brand promotion (Greengard n.d.). The National Aeronautical and Space Agency (NASA) case study on the COVID-19 pandemic challenge demonstrates how NASA captured and extended the value of knowledge created in a digital community platform. The rest of this chapter examines how organizations can capture and extend the value of knowledge shared and created on crowdsourcing and online community platforms. Crowdsourcing community platforms, such as Kickstarter (www.kickstarter.com), Kaggle (www.kaggle.com), and IdeaScale (www.ideascale.com); and online communities, such as Quora (www.quora.com) and Reddit (www.reddit.com), are purpose-built platforms designed with Web 2.0 information and communication technologies.

Web 2.0 and the History of Digital Platforms

The term "Web 2.0" was coined by Darcy DiNucci in 1999 and made popular when the first Web 2.0 Conference was hosted in 2004 (Web 2.0 2023). Web 2.0 represents a collection of information and communication technologies that use multimedia to create interactive Web content. Web 2.0 technologies prompted a paradigm shift to an Internet with interactive Web content that promotes information sharing and interconnectedness.

Web 2.0 denotes a change to a more interactive Web using multimedia content to connect people to other people and content pages. JavaScript, AJAX, HTML5, Document Object Model (DOM), and Cascading Styles Sheets (CSS3) technologies enable the design of interactive content and webpages. Web 2.0 browsers can update webpages and send requests to Web servers asynchronously for seamless and continuous interaction with users. These technologies enable the design of webpages that mimic real-life experiences and connect people and content on the Internet. For example, you can use a dating site to plan and go on a date.

Web 2.0 technologies have promoted interactive content where users interact with Web pages and create content. Users are no longer passive consumers of static content, but active participants in the creation and consumption of Web content. Through Web 2.0 technologies, social media sites and online communities promote and support participatory culture. These interactive webpages empower users to actively participate in the Internet experience, publish articles, share their views, make comments, and dialogue with other participants and users.

Users create user accounts on digital platforms and profiles that enable personalization and customization of content, services, and products. These Web 2.0 technologies also promote equity, as users have access to all content and can also publish and post content. These technologies have made websites like Wikipedia (www.wikipedia.org), YouTube (www.youtube.com), Facebook (www.facebook.com), Reddit (www.reddit.com), Twitter (www.twitter.com), LinkedIn (www.linkedin.com), Instagram (www.instagram.com), Nextdoor (www.nextdoor.com), and Quora (www.quora.com) digital communities and platforms for social interaction, conversations, and knowledge sharing.

As the Internet becomes a platform for digital communities and social interaction, the challenges of real-life social interactions are reflected in these digital communities. Thus, these digital communities are not immune to online stalking, cyberbullying, misinformation, and criminal activities. To address these challenges, purpose-built online community platforms have features and policies in place to moderate interactions and monitor content to ensure safe and friendly digital communities. In the next sections, we focus on two types of digital communities, online communities and crowdsourcing communities, and examine how organizations capture the value of the knowledge shared and created in those digitally-enabled communities.

Digital Community Platforms and KM Processes

Digitally-enabled communities bring geographically dispersed people with a shared interest together to collaborate, share, and exchange information in support of a shared goal. There are various types of digitally enabled communities that bring people together in digital communities (Zablith et al. 2016). These digitally enabled communities share similarities and differences and provide a digital platform for organizing and coordinating innovation and knowledge creation.

As noted earlier, this chapter focuses on two distinct types of digital communities: crowdsourcing communities and online communities. We also examine how organizations capture and exploit the knowledge shared and created in these digitally enabled communities. Online communities and crowdsourcing communities are digitally enabled communities; however, they have different characteristics and member interactions and are driven by a different set of goals. Unlike online communities, crowdsourcing communities are task-oriented and transactional, and participants are motivated by rewards or may contribute freely with no expectations of rewards.

Online Communities

Online communities are digital platforms where members voluntarily collaborate and openly exchange and share information and knowledge to achieve a common goal. Members of these digital communities can post questions or ideas, reflect on responses, provide feedback, and share knowledge, primarily through the Internet (Ye and Jensen 2022). Although the primary mode of communication and interaction is through the Internet, members of digital communities may also engage in face-to-face activities. For example, members of digital platforms, such as Meetup (www.meetup.com) or Nextdoor (www.net door.com), can engage physically through face-to-face meetings and social events. Members of online communities create accounts and profiles for their online persona. Members log in to the online community digital platform to post content and participate in discussions with other members. Participation in online communities may be open to all, or only exclusively to members. Some digital communities may vet users before granting membership. Most online communities are hosted on purpose-built digital platforms with features, such as private messaging, moderation tools, multimedia capabilities, events, and polling. Examples of these online communities include Quora, Reddit, and Nextdoor.

Social media sites and messaging applications, such as Facebook, Instagram, WhatsApp (www.whatsapp.com), and Discord (www.discord.com) also provide digital platforms for online communities. Some of these online communities use chat rooms, forums, e-mail lists, and discussion boards to communicate, and share information and knowledge. For example, a Facebook group is an online community that brings members together around shared goals or interests. Online communities' members are driven by a common interest, such as hobbies, professional interests, support for each other, and social interests. These shared interests and goals motivate members of online communities to share information resources, seek advice from members, support members, and build social relationships.

These digital platforms provide safe environments for members to share ideas and discuss issues of interest. Digital communities give members equal opportunities to express themselves and dialogue on common challenges, find answers and share experiences. As members interact in these communities, they support each other and build rapport around shared interests and goals. Online communities provide a platform and environment for knowledge flows. As members share and exchange information through externalization, tacit knowledge is converted into explicit knowledge and then members can combine it with their existing knowledge to create new knowledge. Online community platforms also have rich search capabilities that enable users to search dialogues and conversations for relevant information.

Thus, conversations, views, opinions, feedback, and solutions become a searchable knowledge-base system. The knowledge shared and created is the value of the dialogues and conversations in online communities. The knowledge shared and created can enhance the competency or skills of participants, and members of the CoP can internalize and apply that knowledge. Figure 13.1 illustrates how digitally enabled CoP platforms facilitate knowledge flows and knowledge creation.

Online communities are different from social media sites because the interactions in online communities are more focused, and membership is goal-driven. Social media sites are geared toward social relationships and not goal-oriented. The collective goals of online communities drive member interaction and dialogue. On the other hand, social media sites connect people, and membership and participation are not driven by specific goals. Hence, conversations in online communities are more meaningful to members as they are driven by specific goals. These characteristics make online communities powerful tools for businesses and organizations to engage customers, prospects, and other stakeholders. Businesses and organizations recognize the power of online communities to capture and harness external and internal sources of knowledge. For example, Starbucks and Proctor and Gamble have used online communities to elicit consumer opinions on products (Vermicelli et al. 2021).

Online communities can be classified into several types based on their purpose, structure, and characteristics. There are four categories of online communities: interest-based, support-based, learning and education, and networking. Table 13.1 is a list of types of online communities, examples of these communities, and activities.

- **Interest-based communities:** These online communities are formed around shared interests, goals, or activities. Interest-based online communities provide a digital platform for people to connect, communicate, and collaborate with others who share similar passions or objectives. For example, fan-based communities, such as Fandom (www.fandom.com), bring like-minded people together around artists, entertainers, entertainment, books, movies, and computer games. Communities of practice are also interest-based communities that focus on professional interests. For example, the PMI online communities are examples of interest-based communities of practice.

Table 13.1 Types of Online Community Platforms

	Types	Examples	Activities
1	Interest-based	Facebook groups, Reddit communities, Quora, Fandom, PMI Communities, WhatsApp groups, CISCO communities, OpenSports	Discussion on shared interests and goals
2	Support-based	WebMD Support communities, Apple Support community, Microsoft Support Community, Stack Overflow Community	Provide support, advice, and knowledge
3	Learning and Education	ResearchGate, TeacherTube, Codecademy, edWeb Communities, TeachAde, Learn-Hub, Academia, wyzant	Learners and educators share information
4	Networking	LinkedIn, Nextdoor, Meetup, EventBrite, CitySocializer, Facebook, Instagram, DownToMeet, Get Together, Badoo, Match, MeetMe	Connect like-minded people

- **Support communities:** Provide a digital platform for members that seek advice, get support, share knowledge, seek answers to questions, and share solutions to problems. Examples of support-based online communities are Stack Overflow (www.stackoverflow.co), Apple support community, and WebMD (www.webmd.com) health communities.
- **Learning and education communities:** Members of these communities want to learn or teach. Digital platforms, such as ResearchGate (www.researchgate.net), Codecademy (www.codecademy.com) and TeacherTube (www.teachertube.com) are online communities for learners, educators, and researchers. Researchers, learners, and educators can share information and exchange ideas and knowledge with other people. Members engage in discussions on topics related to learning and teaching.
- **Networking communities:** Members join network online communities, such as LinkedIn, Nextdoor, and Meetup to network and connect with other people with similar backgrounds or interests. Members engage in conversations and dialogue to connect with other members. Nextdoor neighborhood communities bring neighbors together on a digital platform to discuss and dialogue on neighborhood related topics.

Online communities are complex and challenging to classify. Thus, not every online community fits into a specific classification, some fit in multiple classifications due to types of interactions and goals of the community. This taxonomy is only intended to simplify the categorization of online communities. Regardless of how an online community is classified, community members are both the sources and the repository of useful knowledge. Businesses and organizations use these digital communities to source external and internal knowledge. Figure 13.1 illustrates the relationship between digital community platforms and external and internal sources of knowledge. For example, members of Starbucks online community use this platform to share their views and opinions on various subjects with Starbucks employees (Starbucks Inc. 2023). Thus, this online community enables Starbucks to source knowledge shared by its customers with its employees.

Crowdsourcing Communities

The term *crowdsourcing* was coined in 2006 by Jeff Howe and Mark Robinson to describe how businesses use the Internet to outsource work to crowds. Crowdsourcing platforms use open calls to outsource tasks or problems to a diverse network of people (Greengard n.d.). Crowdsourcing digital platforms bring decentralized groups of people together to accomplish specific goals. Organizations may outsource a problem, challenge, competition, or idea generation to groups of people on a digital platform. Participants in these crowdsourcing communities are volunteers who may be paid for their services or may receive prizes.

The term crowdsourcing describes the process of using electronic groups and the Internet to solicit, initiate, nourish, and connect ideas. Crowdsourcing process starts with an open call to complete a task, project, or solve a problem. The open call specifies the requirements for the project and whether participation is voluntary, or participants are rewarded with prizes or payment. Participants submit solutions or completed tasks and get a chance to win a prize or payment. Interaction in crowdsourcing communities can be competitive, as participants are often motivated by the rewards and financial gain. The competitive goals may be inconsistent with the overall collective goals of the community; however, the competitive spirit in crowdsourcing platforms can spur innovation (Zhen et al. 2021).

As illustrated in Figure 13.1, businesses and organizations can tap into internal and external sources of knowledge through crowdsourcing platforms. For example, businesses can use the application Yelp (www.yelp.com) to solicit opinions and evaluations of products and services, in order to harness the views and opinions of customers and therefore deliver better services. Another example of an organization that takes advantage of crowdsourcing is Samuel Adams, an American brewery that crowdsourced the launch of a new beer project through an interactive application. The project invited participants to share their views and opinions on the body, malt, hops, color, clarity, and flavor of a beer (Vianna et al. 2019).

Crowdsourcing communities garner the collective intelligence and skills of groups of individuals to solve problems, generate ideas, or accomplish specific tasks. Members of crowdsourcing communities contribute their expertise, insights, or skills to achieve a common objective. The diverse perspectives, collective knowledge and creativity of participants make crowdsourcing effective mechanisms for exploiting external and internal sources of knowledge. It is more cost effective and efficient to use crowdsourcing platforms than hire expertise.

Boxes 13.2 and 13.3 provide early examples of crowdsourcing. Box 13.2 illustrates the use of crowdsourcing, which has also been labelled as collective intelligence (Bonbeau 2009). Box 13.3 describes the use of crowdsourcing for the purpose of raising funds, also known as crowdfunding.

Box 13.2 Open Innovation at InnoCentive

InnoCentive was founded in 2001, when pharmaceutical company Eli Lilly and Company funded its launch as a way to connect with people outside the company who could help in developing drugs and speeding them to market. InnoCentive is open to other firms eager to access the network's community of ad hoc experts. It connects public sector and nonprofit organizations, companies, and academic institutions all looking for breakthrough innovations, with a global network of over 160,000 creative thinkers (including engineers, scientists, inventors, and business people with expertise in life sciences, engineering, chemistry, math, computer science, and entrepreneurship) across the world. These creative thinkers, called "Solvers," join a community called "InnoCentive Solver" to address some of the world's toughest challenges posted by "Seeker" organizations, who offer registered Solvers considerable financial awards (anywhere from US$5,000 to US$100,000 per solution) for the best solutions. InnoCentive manages the entire process, while keeping the identities of Seekers and Solvers completely confidential and secure.

Companies like Boeing, DuPont, and Procter & Gamble also pay InnoCentive a fee to participate. They post their most tricky scientific problems on InnoCentive's website, and anyone in InnoCentive's Solver community can try solving them. The Solvers are quite diverse. Many of them are hobbyists, such as a University of Dallas undergraduate student who identified which chemical to use in an art restoration project, or a patent lawyer from Cary, North Carolina, who developed a creative way of mixing large batches of chemical compounds.

Dr. Karim R. Lakhani examined 166 problems posted by 26 research labs over four years on the InnoCentive site and found that an average of 240 people examined each problem, an average of ten people offered answers, and about 30 percent of the problems were solved (Wessell 2007). During its history, InnoCentive has paid out millions (in US$) in awards to hundreds of winning Solvers (Wazoku Crowd n.d.).

Sources: Compiled from the Howe (2006); Wazoku Crowd (n.d.); Wessell (2007)

Box 13.3 A New Way to Raise Capital: Crowdfunding

Crowdfunding refers to a collective effort to pool many small amounts of money together, via the Internet, to invest in a project or venture started by others. There are many crowdfunding platforms, including Kickstarter (www.kickstarter.com), Indiegogo (www.indiegogo.com), and RocketHub (www.rockethub.com) (Prive 2012). The idea is similar across all these platforms: project creators launch a profile and a short video that describes the project, the rewards per donation, and a convincing sales pitch that can raise money to fund their ideas.

Crowdfunding Web sites allow anyone to post their projects online and ask the online community to help fund it. Different from the traditional methods of raising capital, project sponsors don't necessarily expect equity in the project in return; and instead of traditional investors, crowdfunding campaigns are funded by the general public. The creator of the project can offer different incentives depending on the amount of money being donated, or sponsors can simply donate their money with the satisfaction of having contributed to the success of the project.

Projects are not limited to a certain category or scope and can vary anywhere from art, comics, dance, design, fashion, film and video, food, games, music, photography, publishing, technology, and theater among others. Also, crowdfunding is used to raise funds for philanthropic and disaster relief efforts, for instance Kiva (www.kiva.org), which provides support for Microcredit crowdfunding. After providing a detailed explanation of the project and pitching the idea (in the form of a video), the creator can then set a goal for the necessary funds as well as an end date for the fundraising campaign. Most campaigns last anywhere from 30 to 60 days. The campaign's progress is public and updated in real time so potential sponsors can see how much money is needed to successfully fund the project. If the goal is reached, the creator gets all of the moneys raised minus a small fee (about 5 percent) from the crowd-funding Web site. In the event that the project does not meet its goal, the creator does not receive any funds and the money is returned to the sponsors.

As an example, Pebble Technology, the discontinued maker of a digital watch compatible with Android and iPhone smartphones, had set out to raise US$100,000 on Kickstarter.com. It goes without saying that the more interesting and feasible the project, the more money it will receive. In their case, the projects exceeded the goal and their campaign ended up raising US$10.3 million, the largest funded project in Kickstarter history (Svensson 2012).

Sources: Compiled from Prive (2012); Svensson (2012).

The more recent example in Box 13.4 illustrates how InVitro Cell Research (ICR), a small company specialized in health and scientific research, used Kaggle crowdsourcing platform to tap into the collective intelligence of teams of scientists to gain access to external knowledge and expertise in data science and analytics. The example of Kaggle and ICR demonstrates how crowdsourcing community platforms can be a strategic tool in knowledge management processes.

Box 13.4 Kaggle Crowdsourcing and InVitro Cell Research

ICR is a privately funded company focused on regenerative and preventive personalized medicine. The company conducts research on how to diagnose and cure health issues affecting aging people, reverse biological aging, and prevent age-related diseases. The company operates labs fitted with up-to-date tools and equipment for scientists to conduct research. ICR is in the forefront of regenerative cell research and has valuable institutional knowledge but lacks expertise outside its core competency (InVitro Cell Research n.d.). Hence, ICR turned to Kaggle crowdsourcing community platform to elicit expert knowledge outside its core competency of scientific research. Kaggle is an online community of data scientists and machine learning practitioners and hosts a crowd-sourcing platform for data science competitions. Data science, machine learning, and analytics is not part of the core competency of ICR; however, the Kaggle crowdsourcing community platform enabled ICR to source the expertise of data scientists and machine learning practitioners. To gain access to the expertise of data scientist, ICR launched a competition on the Kaggle crowdsourcing platform (Kaggle 2023).

The competition consisted of soliciting ideas and expertise on using bioinformatics and analytics models to predict if a person will have any of three medical conditions. The competition started on May 11, 2023, and the final submission was due on August 10, 2023. There was a US$60,000 prize shared among six selected winners. The competition's data included fifty health characteristics related to three age-related conditions. The competition's goal was to develop a model that could predict whether an individual would be likely diagnosed with one of the three health conditions or not. Thus, it was a binary classification problem to determine, given certain health characteristics, what would be the likelihood that an individual would be diagnosed with any of three health-related conditions.

Figure 13.2 is a screenshot of the Kaggle platform and the ICR competition. Teams could join the platform and submit solutions. Two months after the competition was

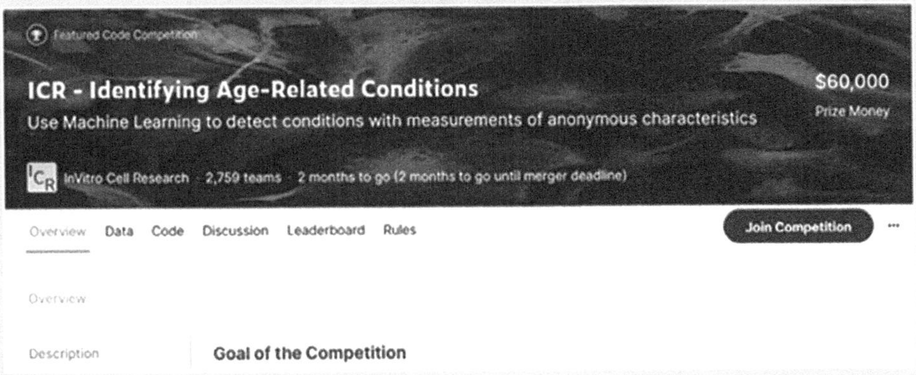

Figure 13.2 Kaggle and ICR Competition Screenshot

published there were 2,759 teams competing for the US$60,000 prize. As shown in Figure 13.2, the platform provided information about the competition and the data set for the competition. The platform had a leader board that informed teams of their standing in the competition. Additionally, there was a discussion forum where teams could ask and answer questions on the competition. The discussion forums enabled ICR and the teams of data scientists to engage in conversations and share information on the dataset and how the analysis and model should be developed to address the goals of the competition. The knowledge shared and created in those interactions informed the final solution, the development of a predictive model for three health-related conditions.

Through the competition, ICR was able to leverage knowledge and expertise it did not have internally. It would be more expensive and time-consuming to hire data scientists to perform the tasks required by the challenge. Through the crowdsourcing community platform, ICR had access to the expertise and knowledge of over two thousand teams of data scientists. In effect, this is analogous to paying for the expertise of over two thousand teams of data scientists to perform a task.

Sources: Compiled from InVitro Cell Research (n.d.); Kaggle (2023)

Wikipedia, Kaggle, and Kickstarter are examples of crowdsourcing communities that use open calls to solicit solutions, ideas, and knowledge from crowds. Participants in crowdsourcing communities generate ideas, provide feedback, solve problems, and assist with research and development. There are a variety of crowdsourcing communities, and they can be classified based on the structure and the goals of the community. There are four main types of crowdsourcing platforms based on the goals of the platform. The four types are content development platforms, tasks-oriented communities, crowdfunding platforms, and information exchange platforms (Oppenlaender et al. 2020). Below is a list of the types of crowdsourcing communities with some examples of communities and activities:

- **Content development crowdsourcing platforms** solicit content creators to create, update or edit content related to a specific topic. Usually, these tasks are voluntary with no expectations of financial reward. Participants in these crowdsourcing communities are engaged with the task because of their passion or commitment to the goals of the platform. For example, Appropedia (www.appropedia.org) is a crowdsourcing platform developed to share collaborative solutions in sustainability, poverty reduction, and international development. The platform enables participants to edit and add content. Another example of a content development crowdsourcing platform is TedTalk (www.tedtalk.com), a dedicated platform that uses short talks and presentations to share knowledge.
- **Task-oriented crowdsourcing platforms** focus on performing tasks, completing a project, developing solutions. Businesses and individuals can use these crowdsourcing platforms to outsource work to diverse groups of individuals. Amazon Mechanical Turk (www.mturk.com) is an example of task-oriented crowdsourcing platform where organizations and individuals can outsource tasks and projects to workers on the platform. Workers on the platform complete the task for monetary compensation. The platform brings diverse minds together that might not otherwise collaborate.
- **Crowdfunding platforms** link funding to projects. These platforms are used to launch fundraising campaigns for specific projects or interests. Participants contribute financially to the project, sometimes with the expectation of some return or rewards. Kickstarter (www.kickstarter.com) is a crowdsourcing platform where creators share their projects with communities that can fund them. According to the Kickstarter Web site the platform has funded 241,030 projects and secured about US$7 billion in funding (Kickstarter n.d.).
- **Information exchange crowdsourcing platforms** solicit opinions, evaluations, and reviews from participants. Usually, members participate voluntarily and are not rewarded for their participation. As illustrated in Figure 13.1, organizations use crowdsourcing communities to gather customer reviews and opinions. These information exchange crowdsourcing platforms can generate consumer reviews of products and services for restaurants, hotels, gyms, plumbers, physicians, and most kinds of businesses. Businesses and organizations can use crowdsourcing communities to solicit ideas, opinions, or votes for a new product or service. Some businesses use crowdsourcing to brainstorm ideas and develop new products. For example, in 2012 Proctor & Gamble used a crowdsourcing campaign to solicit ideas from customers about a new Lay's potato chip flavor, for a chance to win a US$1 million prize. Another example of an information exchange platform is Waze (www.waze.com). Waze uses drivers' knowledge to collect and share traffic information and aggregates that information with geographical positioning systems to provide real-time traffic updates to drivers.

Examples

In this section, we use the examples of the National Aeronautics and Space Administration (NASA) and Dropbox to demonstrate how organizations use digital community platforms, such as online communities and crowdsourcing platforms, to capture knowledge. Like ICR (Box 13.4), NASA (Box 13.5) uses crowdsourcing community platforms to solicit ideas and solutions to challenges and competitions, while Dropbox

(Box 13.6) relies on an online community platform to manage knowledge sharing and creation among technical support teams.

Box 13.5 illustrates how NASA has been using crowdsourcing technologies within the organization to find solutions to challenges related to space exploration and responding to the COVID-19 pandemic. This example describes how the NASA@work initiatives were instrumental in addressing challenges related to COVID-19 and demonstrates how crowdsourcing community platforms can facilitate knowledge sharing and creation outside normal workflows and operations. Using crowdsourcing community platforms, NASA was able to capture the knowledge of experts and extend the value of that knowledge to products and services, such as 3D-printed personal protective gear.

Box 13.5 NASA and Crowdsourcing

NASA is a U.S. government agency responsible for science and technology related to space exploration. The agency employs about 18,000 people in nine centers across the states in the U.S. (NASA 2020). Innovation and knowledge are key to NASA's mission of exploring space. NASA recognizes the value in the expertise, skills, and knowledge of employees and the need to exploit that value.

NASA had implemented several initiatives to solicit expert knowledge to support the mission of exploring space. Hence, since 2009, NASA had launched several crowdsourcing competitions and challenges. NASA@work is an internal crowdsourcing platform hosted by IdeaScale (www.ideascale.com), an innovation management platform that links organizations to people with ideas. IdeaScale innovation management software, services, and crowdsourcing platform enable organizations, like NASA, to innovate by capturing internal and external knowledge.

Through crowdsourcing community platforms, NASA taps into the wisdom of crowds to find solutions to problems. In the past NASA leveraged these crowdsourcing strategies to solve problems related to the mission of the agency. For example, the "Space Poop Challenge" addressed waste management issues in space. NASA@Work promotes collaboration and taps into the internal talent pool to solve problems. NASA crowdsourcing platform connects the talent pool and expertise within the NASA community to generate ideas and solutions to challenging problems (NASA 2023).

When the COVID-19 pandemic started in 2020, NASA was motivated to use the vast array of organizational expertise, skills, and knowledge to address some of the challenges posed by the pandemic. The pandemic was a challenge to healthcare systems across the world, international organizations, and national governments. Some of the challenges included sustainable sourcing of personal protective gear for healthcare providers and the public in general, development of vaccines for the virus, and tracking and monitoring the spread of the virus.

NASA saw the crisis as an opportunity to put the skills and expertise of its employees at NASA at work to address some of the challenges posed by the COVID-19 pandemic. In 2020 NASA launched a campaign on the IdeaScale crowdsourcing platform to solicit ideas and solutions from the NASA community to address the crisis and challenges of the COVID-19 pandemic. The NASA crowdsourcing challenge involved three focus areas: personal protective gear, tracking and tracing the spread of the virus, and ventilation systems. The first challenge solicited ideas for the development of self-sanitizing personal protective equipment and other novel approaches for sterilizing or repurposing personal protective equipment. This was an important challenge for the fight against COVID-19 because health care providers, and other essential and frontline workers, faced a shortage of personal protective gear needed to safely perform their duties.

The second focus area was for ideas on ventilations systems with simple interfaces that could be rapidly produced. During the pandemic, ventilation devices were in high demand and many healthcare providers did not have enough ventilation systems. The proposed ideas for this challenge included designs that allow for rapid prototyping, expedited regulatory approval, quick manufacturing, and rapid delivery of ventilation devices.

The third focus area was for ideas on innovative ways to use NASA data information products, data analytics, high performance computing, artificial intelligence, and/or other capabilities to predict the spread of COVID-19 and/or address the virus's environmental, economic, and societal impacts. This challenge required participants to develop models to forecast and track the spread of the virus (NASA 2020).

The NASA@Work crowdsourcing community consisted of two groups of participants, challenge owners and solvers. These crowdsourcing platform challenges were open to teams and individuals affiliated with NASA and challenge owners could select up to two winners. The winners earned a NASA@Work certificate or Digital Badge, an Innovator pin, and space memorabilia.

Once the challenge or competition was posted on the crowdsourcing platform, solvers joined the community and engaged the challenge owners through questions and answers to better understand and address any ambiguity on the challenge. Knowledge was shared as challenge owners and solvers exchanged information on the challenge. Challenge owners injected questions into the conversations and challenge solvers provided answers and explanations. Knowledge was shared and created as solvers conversed, dialogued, asked questions, and provided answers about the challenge. The dialogue that occurred on these platforms once a challenge was publicized could generate ideas and create new knowledge.

The COVID-19 challenges launched by NASA on the crowdsourcing platform generated several solutions and ideas that were implemented by NASA. Some of the ideas and responses generated on the personal protective gear challenge resulted in 3D-printed masks and other personal protective equipment. Some of the responses to COVID-19 challenges have spurred advanced research for treatments and a vaccine, as well as artificial intelligence expertise for data mining techniques to answer scientific questions related to COVID-19 (NASA 2020). The solutions included NASA-modified ventilators as well as sensors for COVID-19 virus detection, which were developed from the solutions and ideas generated from the challenge on the crowdsourcing platforms. The knowledge shared and created from these challenges enabled NASA to advance research for treatments and vaccine for the COVID-19 virus.

Sources: Compiled from NASA (2019, 2020, 2023)

The example in Box 13.6 illustrates how Dropbox utilized Stack Overflow to improve the capture and re-use of the corporate memory to better support its software development teams. Dropbox utilized an online community platform to support knowledge sharing, capture, and application, allowing software development teams to convert their tacit knowledge to explicit knowledge, and encouraging the re-use of historical knowledge via the corporate memory. Thus, online communities are KM systems that foster interpersonal interactions critical to knowledge sharing, capture, and application. Launching an online community is not enough to facilitate KM process, it is only when participants in the community are motivated to engage with others that the online community will serve as a vibrant platform for capturing, sharing, and applying knowledge.

Box 13.6 Dropbox and Stack Overflow

Dropbox was founded in 2007 and offers free and premium (also known as freemium) subscription cloud storage services to both individuals and enterprises. Several departments and technical teams are tasked with the support of the Dropbox cloud computing architecture. These teams primarily used Slack, a messaging application, and e-mail as the primary means of communication and workflow management. The workflows among the technical teams generated a considerable number of questions and answers in messages, documents within e-mail, and messages in Slack (Stack Overflow 2022).

At Dropbox, these communication and workflow tools were not centralized and did not have robust search capabilities. The decentralized architecture of the support tools hampered the technical support teams from effectively leveraging the corporate memory and historical knowledge embedded in messages, communication tools, and multiple document formats. This made it extremely difficult for the technical staff to exploit the tacit and explicit knowledge of team members, or search for answers to questions from the corporate memory. Hence, the technical staff spent time searching for answers to questions that had already been answered, and when answers were not found, the problems recurred. As an example, the Mobile Foundation team was overwhelmed with recurring problems and questions. Some of these questions were previously addressed, while others were not, but because the team did not have the capabilities to search for answers and re-use answers from the corporate memory, they spent time looking for answers and repeatedly sending links to recurring questions. The tools and documents that captured the corporate memory were not centralized or searchable, even when a technician had access to previous lessons learned, they were not able to locate the answers and re-use that prior knowledge. Furthermore, some subject matter experts (SMEs) with tacit knowledge did not have the means or mechanisms of capturing and sharing their knowledge with the technical team. These processes were further encumbered by the remote-work policy implemented with the start of the COVID-19 pandemic in 2020. Remote-work resulted in members of the technical team being geographically dispersed, and having to rely on Slack and e-mail to communicate and perform their duties (Stack Overflow 2022).

To address these challenges, the technical teams were looking for a system that would allow them to centralize their corporate memory and institutional knowledge and provide robust search capabilities. The technical team wanted a solution that kept track of historical knowledge in a corporate memory and could be used to provide answers to developers seeking answers. To address these challenges, the technical staff adopted the Stack Overflow for Teams platform and recruited SMEs and moderators to provide an initial set of questions and answers to get the conversation started and encourage knowledge sharing and creation. The Stack Overflow for Teams was first rolled out to the mobile development software team and then rolled out to the rest of the company.

Within the Stack Overflow for Teams online community platform, when a team member has questions, they search all the conversations generated through inter-personal interactions. If past dialogues and conversations provide an answer to the question, then the technical staff can re-use the answer, thus re-using and applying the corporate memory and historical knowledge. If the search does not provide an answer, then a question is posted to the group. This provides the opportunity for SMEs and others to share their tacit knowledge gained from experience and competency. The technical staff and experts engaged in dialogue and conversations convert their tacit knowledge to explicit knowledge, and then the explicit knowledge is combined with their existing knowledge to create new knowledge. The new knowledge is documented and captured in the corporate memory, and is searchable within the Stack Overflow for Teams community platform. The improved management of shared knowledge and knowledge creation resulted in fewer repeat questions and more knowledge re-use. Furthermore, the online community platforms fostered a culture of knowledge sharing, a critical component in any successful KM system implementation.

With a centralized online community platform and engaged team members, people are comfortable asking questions and sharing their knowledge to address questions. Furthermore, when new team members join the technical team, the online community makes their on-boarding easy. The corporate memory provides a trove of historical knowledge that new employees can rely on to execute their tasks. The Stack Overflow for Teams implementation at Dropbox is a community platform that provides business continuity and answers for the technical team in order to do their best work.

Source: Compiled from Stack Overflow (2022)

Summary

In this chapter we reviewed digital community platforms and discussed how they play a key role in accessing and exploiting external and internal sources and repositories of knowledge. Employees, customers, prospects, suppliers, experts, and partners are all sources of knowledge that can drive innovation. Crowdsourcing platforms and online communities are frequently used by organizations to capture the knowledge of people, internal or external to the organization. Through competitions and challenges, crowd-sourcing platforms use open calls to solicit solutions and outsource tasks to any inter-ested participant. In addition, online communities provide a platform for members with shared interests and goals to share information as they engage each other in con-versations and dialogues. Members ask questions, seek answers, offer advice, share experiences, and support each other. The knowledge shared and created from online community interactions is valuable to organizations.

Knowledge and expertise reside in employees, customers, consumers, experts, and partners. This knowledge is only valuable if organizations can capture, share, and apply that knowledge. Digital community platforms, such as crowdsourcing platforms, and online communities are some of the mechanisms that organizations use to capture external knowledge. Proctor and Gamble, Starbucks, Netflix, and NASA are some of the organizations that have successfully used digital community platforms to capture external and internal knowledge. It is cost effective and efficient to use digital community platforms to harness diverse knowledge sources. The case studies on NASA, ICR, and Dropbox demonstrate how organizations are leveraging digital community platforms. ICR and NASA used crowdsourcing platforms to harness knowledge from external and internal experts. On the other hand, Dropbox used an online community platform, Stack Overflow for Teams to manage internal software development teams to improve their productivity.

Review

1 What are the different types of digital community platforms that organization can use to capture external and internal knowledge?
2 What are the differences and similarities between online communities crowdsourcing community platforms?
3 How can your organization use online communities to improve knowledge sharing and creation?
4 Online communities can be sources of misinformation and disinformation. How do those issues impact knowledge sharing and creation?

Application Exercises

1 Select a community of practice of your choice and provide reasons why the community you selected is a community of practice and explain how the community you selected creates value for organizations.
2 What are the differences in the methods and means that online communities and crowdsourcing communities use to engage their members to share their knowledge and participate?
3 If you are advising your organization to implement a digital community platform strategy to access expert knowledge, which digital community platform would you recommend? Online communities or crowdsourcing communities?
4 When making purchasing decisions or seeking information on a product, do you rely on product reviews from online communities to make your decisions? Do you trust and believe in product reviews from online communities? Why?

References

Blohm, I., Zogaj, S., Bretschneider, U., and Leimeister, J.M. 2018. How to manage crowdsourcing platforms effectively? *California Management Review*, 60(2), 122–149.
Bonbeau, E. 2009. Decisions 2.0: The power of collective intelligence. *Sloan Management Review*, 50(2) (Winter), 45–52.
Faraj, S., von Krogh, G., Monteiro, E., and Lakhani, K.R. 2016. Special section introduction— Online community as space for knowledge flows. *Information Systems Research*, 27(4), 668–684.
Farnsworth, V., Kleanthous, I., and Wenger-Trayner, E. 2016. Communities of practice as a social theory of learning: A conversation with Etienne Wenger. *British Journal of Educational Studies*, 64(2), 139–160.
Greengard, S. n.d. Crowdsourcing. *Encyclopaedia Britannica*, https://www.britannica.com/topic/crowdsourcing (accessed June 14, 2023).
Howe, J. 2006. The rise of crowdsourcing. *Wired* (June). www.wired.com/wired/archive/14.06/crowds.html.

InVitro Cell Research. n.d. Our research. https://invitrocellresearch.com/our-research (accessed May 31, 2023).

Liu, H.K. 2021. Crowdsourcing: Citizens as coproducers of public services. *Policy & Internet*, 13 (2), 315–331.

Kaggle. 2023. Invitro cell research ICR—Identifying age-related conditions. https://www.kaggle.com/competitions/icr-identify-age-relatedconditions (accessed May 31, 2023).

Kickstarter. n.d. Bring a creative project to life. https://www.kickstarter.com/ (accessed June 14, 2023).

National Aeronautical and Space Agency (NASA). 2019. NASA@work. https://www.nasa.gov/sites/default/files/atoms/files/nasaatwork_slick_sheet_3.pdf (accessed May 31, 2023).

National Aeronautical and Space Agency (NASA). 2020. NASA taps workforce for innovative ideas for Coronavirus response efforts. https://www.nasa.gov/directorates/spacetech/nasa-taps-workforce-for-innovative-ideas-for-coronavirus-response-efforts (accessed May 31, 2023).

National Aeronautical and Space Agency (NASA). 2023. Welcome to NASA@work. https://www.nasa.gov/coeci/nasa-at-work (accessed May 31, 2023).

Oppenlaender, J., Milland, K., Visuri, A., Ipeirotis, P., and Hosio, S. 2020. Creativity on paid crowdsourcing platforms. In *Proceedings of the 2020 CHI Conference on Human Factors in Computing Systems*, April 2020, 1–14.

Prive, T. 2012. What is crowdfunding and how does it benefit the economy? *Forbes* (November). www.forbes.com/sites/tanyaprive/2012/11/27/what-is-crowdfunding-and-how-does-it-benefit-the-economy/.

Project Management Institute. n.d. Discussion forums. https://www.projectmanagement.com/discussions/ (accessed May 31, 2023).

Stack Overflow. 2022. How a searchable knowledge management system helped Dropbox reuse knowledge and work more effectively. https://resources.stackoverflow.co/topic/client-stories/dropbox-case-study/ (accessed May 31, 2023).

Starbucks Inc. 2023. https://stories.starbucks.com/search/customers+opinions/.

Svensson, P. 2012. Kickstarter projects generate millions of dollars. *Associated Press*, August 17. http://bigstory.ap.org/article/kickstarter-projects-generate-millions-dollars-0.

Vermicelli, S., Cricelli, L., and Grimaldi, M. 2021. How can crowdsourcing help tackle the COVID-19 pandemic? An explorative overview of innovative collaborative practices. *R&D Management*, 51(2), 183–194.

Vianna, F., Peinado, J., and Graeml, A.R. 2019. *Crowdsourcing platforms: objective, activities, and motivation*. Twenty-fifth Americas Conference on Information Systems, Cancun.

Wazoku Crowd. n.d. The story of InnoCentive. https://www.wazokucrowd.com/story-of-innocentive/.

Web 2.0. 2023. *Wikipedia*, June 10. https://en.wikipedia.org/w/index.php?title=Web_2.0&oldid=1159470312 (accessed June 14, 2023).

Wessel, D. 2007. Prizes for solutions to problems play valuable role in innovation. *Wall Street Journal*, January 25. http://online.wsj.com/news/articles/SB116968486074286927.

Ye, J., and Jensen, M. 2022. Effects of introducing an online community in a crowdsourcing contest platform. *Information Systems Journal*, 32(6), 1203–1230.

Zablith, F., Faraj, S., and Azad, B. 2016. Organizational knowledge generation: lessons from online communities. *Business Process Management Journal*.

Zhen, Y., Khan, A., Nazir, S., Huiqi, Z., Alharbi, A., and Khan, S. 2021. Crowdsourcing usage, task assignment methods, and crowdsourcing platforms: a systematic literature review. *Journal of Software: Evolution and Process*, 33(8), e2368.

14 Knowledge Management through Artificial Intelligence and other Emergent Technologies

In this chapter, we review artificial intelligence and explain how it facilitates knowledge management (KM) processes. As noted in Chapters 2 and 4, the collective knowledge of organizations resides in knowledge reservoirs and through the KM process this knowledge is discovered, captured, shared, and applied to improve operational efficiency and core competencies. Organizational knowledge is embedded in people, organizational artefacts, and organizational units. The focus of this chapter is to explain how AI enables KM processes to uncover hidden knowledge, and capture and transfer that knowledge for application.

History of Artificial Intelligence

Artificial Intelligence (AI) is an area of computer science that deals with the design and development of computer systems that exhibit human-like cognitive capabilities. There are various definitions of AI and most of these definitions include phrases such as: "systems that act like humans," "systems that think like humans," "systems that think rationally," and "systems that act rationally" (Campbell et al. 2020).

The idea of creating computers that mimic human intelligent abilities can be traced to the 1950s, when scientists predicted the development of such machines within a decade. Although those scientists may have underestimated the complexities of the human mind, AI research made significant strides. The term "artificial intelligence" was coined by John McCarthy during a workshop he organized at Dartmouth College in 1956, where he convened the four pioneers of the field: John McCarthy, Marvin Minsky, Allan Newell, and Herbert Simon. Since then, the idea of an intelligent computer system has fascinated researchers, academics, and practitioners.

In the 1950s, the Turing Test was considered an acceptable means of accessing the intelligence of computer systems (Turing 1950). The Turing Test evaluates the ability of computer systems to interact with humans and generate human-like responses. Computer systems that pass the Turing Test are considered intelligent since they understand humans and generate responses that are satisfactory to humans.

AI research first focused on games and natural language translation. In the area of gaming, scientists developed numerous chess programs including Greenblatt's "Mac Hack" and Slate and Atkin's "Chess 4.5" (Hsu et al. 1990). Back in 1997, an AI program called Big Blue defeated Boris Kasparov, the reigning world champion in chess, in a widely publicized match. However, early efforts in machine translation of natural languages were not as successful. Another seminal development in AI was the development of General Problem Solver (GPS) by Newell and Simon (1963). The importance of GPS was that it

DOI: 10.4324/9781003364375-18

demonstrated the computer's ability to solve some problems by searching for an answer in a solution space, which represented a new trend for AI.

Several decades later, IBM developed the IBM Watson, an AI system named after one of its founders. In 2011, IBM Watson played Jeopardy, a television quiz game with two human contestants. Jeopardy is an American quiz game show created by Merv Griffin where contestants use general knowledge clues in the form of answers and phrase each response in a question format. IBM Watson competed against two of the best Jeopardy winners, Ken Jennings and Brad Rutter, over three nights, and Watson won against the two champions. By defeating humans in Jeopardy on live national TV in front of millions of viewers, IBM Watson was proof that computers can pass the Turing Test, engage in tasks that require human intelligence, and can outperform humans.

Artificial and Human Intelligence

Typically, computers perform repetitive, logical tasks extremely well, such as complex arithmetic calculations, and database retrieval and storage. One common characteristic of these conventional computer tasks is their **algorithmic** nature, which means that they engage in precise and logically designed instructions and generate accurate output. Humans, by contrast, excel at solving problems using symbols with specific meaning, such as understanding the meaning of a poem. Text and speech are symbolic representation of human thoughts and perceptions. Artificial intelligence deals with the manipulation of these symbols. Therefore, we define AI as:

> The technology that provides computers with the ability to represent and manipulate symbols so they can be used to solve problems not easily solved through algorithmic models.

Modern AI systems are based on the understanding that intelligence and knowledge are tightly intertwined. Knowledge is associated with the cognitive symbols we manipulate, while human intelligence refers to our ability to learn and communicate to solve problems. People are born with a certain degree of intelligence, which they use to learn and thus acquire new knowledge. Thus, intelligence is the innate human abilities to manipulate and represent symbols in an environment. Furthermore, human intelligence enables the creation and acquisition of new knowledge. Much like KM and human intelligence, AI is associated with knowledge.

AI can also be viewed as the ability of computer systems to solve problems or make decisions that would usually require human intelligence. To understand AI, it is important to dissect human intelligence. Intelligence is the capacity to know, using reason, logic, and sound judgement to solve problems and make decisions. Some AI systems (also known as knowledge-based systems) try to imitate the problem-solving capabilities of skillful problem-solvers in a particular domain. In this chapter we explore how these intelligent technologies can facilitate KM processes.

AI technologies simulate human intelligence through the analysis of different types of data to identify patterns, trends, and relationships to address a problem or make decisions. Furthermore, using self-learning algorithms, machine learning (ML) and artificial intelligence (ML/AI) can mimic the human brain's neural network to uncover new patterns and generate new insights. A typically example is the AI-powered autocomplete that is widely used in text editors. The AI algorithms for these writing assistant tools can learn and evolve using experience, semantics, and lexicon to improve prediction accuracy. For example, Microsoft and Google use these AI-powered writing assistants in their e-mail editors to help users complete sentences when crafting e-mails, these tools can even remind users to add an attachment.

Advances in technology are making AI technologies affordable and accessible to both small and big businesses. These advances in technologies have expanded the capacity of AI algorithms to simulate visual, auditory, and tactile sensory to mimic human abilities to recognize images, understand speech, translate language, solve problems, and operate machinery. The general aim of AI technologies is to use algorithms to uncover patterns, trends, and relationships in data to solve problems and make decisions. AI technologies can perform a wide array of functions, such as improving productivity, language translation, visual perception, speech recognition and decision-making. In Box 14.1 we review a chatbot application to demonstrate the capabilities of intelligent systems to support the KM processes. Additionally, the three case studies and three application cases highlight how AI supports KM processes.

Box 14.1 OpenAI

Advances in technology and AI are making it more possible to develop computer systems that can mimic human intelligence, manipulate and convey information, and pass the Turing Test. Furthermore, these AI-driven systems are easily accessible to users and organizations. For example, Alexa and SIRI are AI-powered chatbots available on iOS and android mobile devices. To explain how intelligent systems support KM and knowledge creation, in this section we review ChatGPT (Generative Pre-Trained Transformer),[1] an AI-powered chatbot developed by OpenAI.

OpenAI, a San Francisco-based artificial intelligence company, released ChatGPT on November 30, 2022. ChatGPT is a Web-based chatbot available to individuals and organizations. ChatGPT can engage a user in specialized domains, such as writing code. ChatGPT is an AI-powered chatbot that interacts in a colloquial way, answers follow-up questions, acknowledges mistakes, challenges incorrect premises, and rejects inappropriate requests. Unlike most chatbots, ChatGPT remembers previous prompts in the same conversation and can intelligently answer follow-up questions. Figure 14.1 is a list of the specific domains available when you interact with ChatGPT. As shown in Figure 14.1, there are multiple domains for engaging ChatGPT, including generating code from requirements, grammar corrections, and SQL translation.

Supervised large language models (LLM) and reinforcement learning human feedback (RLHF) drive the ChatGPT chatbot system's ability to provide responses that are satisfactory to humans. Figure 14.2 is a screenshot of an interaction between the authors and ChatGPT,[2] where the authors ask the system "What is ChatGPT?" Besides the response there is the thumps up and thumbs down emoji that users can use to register their approval or disapproval of the answer generated.

LLM are supervised predictive models for language that can predict the next word in a sentence or phrase. ML algorithms train LLM with massive amounts of data to accurately predict what word comes next in a sentence. The GPT-3 ML programs initially trained the LLM to recognize and identify which words and sequences of words are more likely to occur in a collection of documents and text. For example, using deep learning algorithms, the GPT-3 trained with five hundred billion words. The iterative processes tweak these human-directed supervised models using semantics

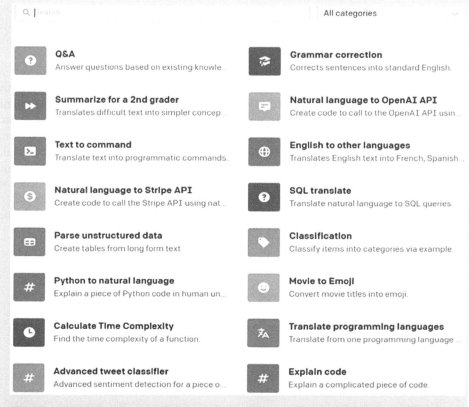

Figure 14.1 ChatGPT Web Interface

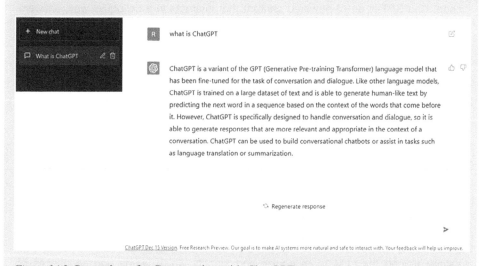

Figure 14.2 Screenshot of a Conversation with ChatGPT

and linguistics logic to improve the accuracy of prediction models. Eventually, these supervised LLM can predict the next word in a series of words, infill text, and complete sentences. The RLHF models use the pre-trained GPT-3 LLM to learn based on human feedback.

RLHF algorithms are an added layer that relies on human feedback to learn how humans follow directions and generate satisfactory responses. The initial models use feedback from humans to rank models and outcomes. As the method evaluates human feedback, it ranks the quality of responses by sampling several alternative responses to create a reward model. The RLHF uses proximal policy optimization to improve the reward model. These reward models enable the RLHF method to learn from human feedback and improve on outcomes or response. ChatGPT is publicly available, thus both individuals and business can leverage ChatGPT to make decisions and performs tasks. Chatbots, such as ChatGPT, can enhance our capacity to know, thus facilitating the knowledge creation processes. ChatGPT can integrate knowledge from multiple sources and convey that knowledge to a user. Thus, it facilitates knowledge creation and application in specific domains. ChatGPT is an example of AI-powered application that mimics human intelligence and can support the KM processes. Users can learn from the responses generated by ChatGPT. For example, Figure 14.2 is a screenshot of the response the authors got from ChatGPT, as they try to learn about ChatGPT.

Limitations: ChatGPT could write plausible sounding but incorrect or nonsensical answers because the model is unable to recognize all the nuances and dynamics of reasoning and intelligence. For example, ChatGPT may not be able to distinguish between truth and misleading logic. Learning is an on-going process for humans, it is no different from systems that simulate human intelligence, they must continuously learn through human supervision and interaction in order to be able to provide answers that are satisfactory to humans.

Notes:
1 OpenAI launched ChatGPT as a prototype on November 30, 2022. The company plans to charge for the AI services; however, the prototype is free to anyone. The authors accessed the site https://chat.openai.com/chat on December 27, 2022.
2 This interaction was captured on December 27, 2022.
Sources: Compiled from Graves (2023); OpenAI (n.d.)

AI and Knowledge Creation

Decreasing cost of data storage and the ubiquity of technology have spurred the storage of vast amounts of data. A significant portion of this data is semi-structured or unstructured and unprocessed. According to a Forrester Inc. report, enterprises do not use between 60 percent and 73 percent of their data for analytics (Gualtieri 2016). This implies that organizations are not fully exploiting their data to uncover hidden and useful knowledge. In Chapter 2, we noted that the collective knowledge of organizations resides in the people who make up the organization, organizational artefacts, and organizational units. In Chapter 4 we discussed how the KM processes discover and capture knowledge from these knowledge reservoirs and enable the application of the captured knowledge. The need to exploit the value in knowledge provides sufficient justification to leverage AI and ML technologies to discover new knowledge in unused and unprocessed data.

With advances in technology, computer systems can automatically filter and transform data into knowledge by automating the extraction of meaning and value from data. These automated processes enable the transformation and combination of knowledge. Organizations create knowledge as they transform data into information, add context and identify patterns and trends. Usually, organizations combine or reconfigure existing knowledge to create new knowledge. The discovery, capture, transfer, and application of knowledge enable organizations to learn and improve core competencies to sustain competitive advantage.

In this chapter, we explore how AI/ML influences the KM processes. Figure 14.3 illustrates the overarching goal of this chapter to explain how AI/ML influence the KM processes. Figure 14.3 shows that AI/ML technologies can support the discovery and capture of knowledge from multiple knowledge reservoirs and enable the transfer and application of that knowledge. The case studies and application cases provide practical examples of how AI/ML influence the KM processes.

Knowledge is embedded in organizational artifacts, such as processes, documents, and procedures, and people. Knowledge may also reside in other repositories that are

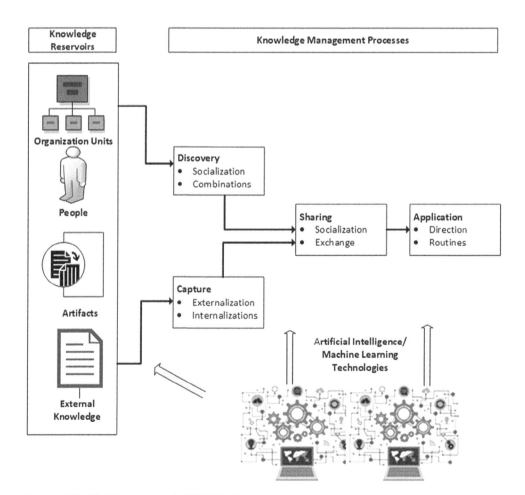

Figure 14.3 KM Processes and AI/ML Technologies

external to the organizations, such as best practices and customer feedback. AI and ML enable organizations to exploit these internal and external sources of knowledge. Some of the methods used in ML include data mining, text mining, and natural language processing (NLP). In addition to the illustration in Figure 14.3, the reviews of the case studies and the applications cases highlight the relationship between AI/ML and KM processes. The next section presents some of the ML methods and how they enable KM processes.

Machine Learning

AI/ML relies on multiple methods and techniques to analyze and transform data into information. Some of these techniques are more suitable for specific types of analysis or require data in a certain format. In this section, we review some of the ML methods and how they influence the KM processes. The case studies and the discussions of application cases are practical examples of how organizations use these artificial intelligence/machine learning (AI/ML) tools to support KM processes.

Data Mining

Data mining, also referred to as knowledge discovery in databases, is the foundation of AI/ML. AI relies on machine learning (ML) algorithms and methodologies to autonomously learn from experience and generate classifications and predictive models that help businesses make informed decisions. Data mining is the process of crawling through large amounts of data to identify attributes, patterns, and relationships between these attributes. Data mining is fundamental to ML; thus, ML algorithms analyze outputs from the data mining processes to create models and autonomously learn and adapt to improve the models.

In this section, we explain data mining processes and how they facilitate ML to support organizations, especially in their knowledge management processes and strategies. Data mining is the process of discovering and extracting knowledge from databases using data mining techniques. Data mining uses statistical and mathematical methods, and human directions to analyze data to discover relevant patterns between attributes. The data, information, knowledge, and wisdom (DIKW) pyramid advanced in the works of Ackoff (1989) and Zeleny (1987) constructs a knowledge hierarchy built on data. As depicted Figure 14.4, the DIKW hierarchy places wisdom at the top and data at the bottom of the pyramid. Statistical methods can transform data into information, and then to knowledge, which in turn facilitates wisdom.

Data mining processes transform raw data into information. Raw data is the symbolic representation of attributes that we perceive or observe. For example, in a retail operation the number of computers on the display shelves, the number of computers in inventory, and the weekly number of computers sold are numerical representations of raw and unprocessed data.

Data mining techniques can transform this raw data into information by identifying patterns and relationships linking the number of computers on the shelves, the inventory count of computers, and weekly number of computers sold. For example, statistical methods, such as average, median, outlier analysis, and correlations, can reveal patterns and relationships that are meaningful to decision makers. As illustrated in Figure 14.4, the data mining processes discard irrelevant data and transform data into

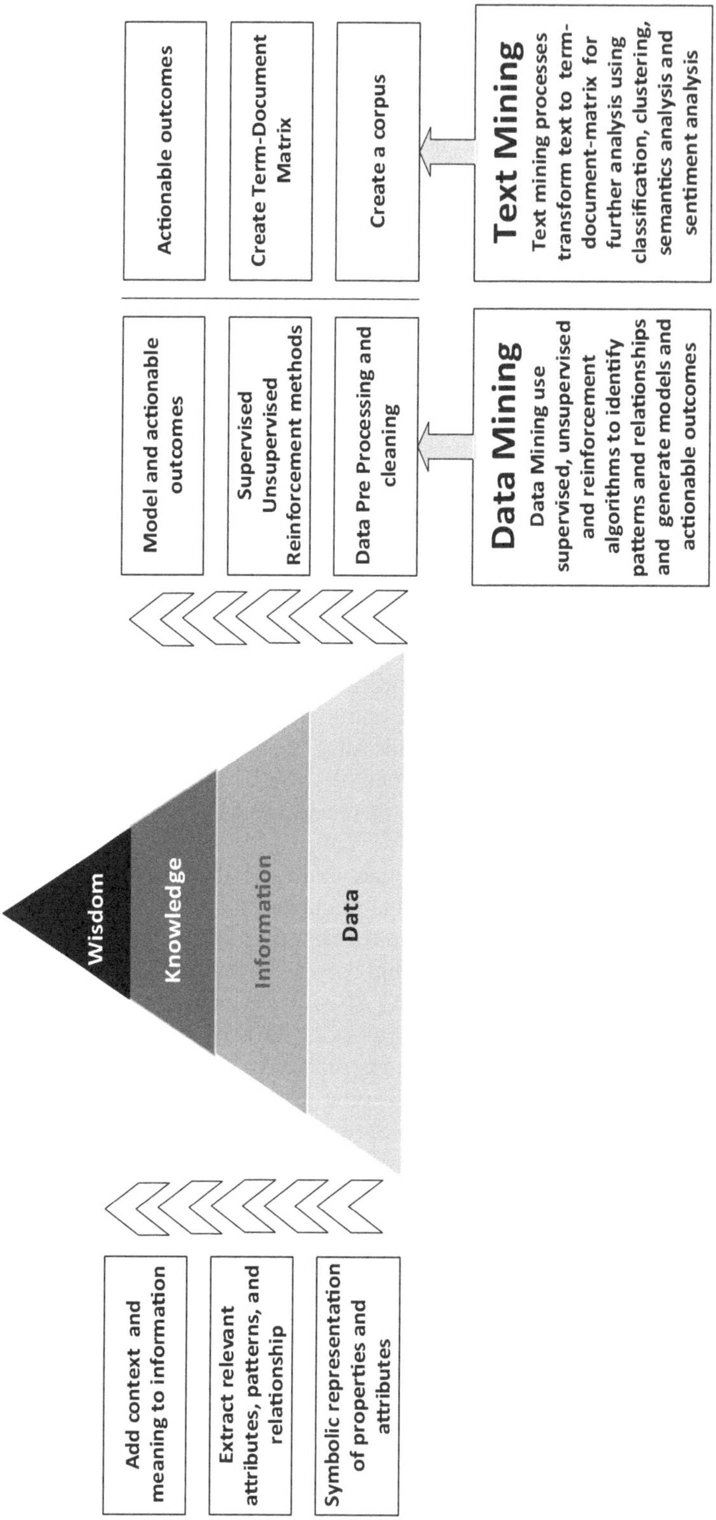

Figure 14.4 DIKW Pyramid and Data and Text Mining

information. Thus, information is refined data that informs knowledge. For example, knowing the relationship between the number of computers in inventory, and number of computers on the shelves, and the weekly number of computers purchased can inform decision makers on when to stock inventory and quantities to stock. This knowledge can help a retail outfit manage inventory. Figure 14.4 depicts how data mining transforms data into information, and then into knowledge.

Data mining processes are fundamental to AI and ML; thus, a sound methodology should guide the development and implementation of data mining projects to ensure a solid foundation for ML and AI projects. Several methodologies have been proposed to guide data mining processes; however, the Cross Industry Standard Process for Data Mining (CRISP-DM) remains one of the most widely accepted standardized processes for data mining. The CRISP-DM process was supported by the European Union and developed by a consortium made up of DaimlerChrysler, SPSS, Teradata, NCR Corporation, and OHRA, an insurance company (Azevedo and Santos 2008; Wirth and Hipp 2000).

Figure 14.5 depicts the CRISP-DM methodology showing how the six steps in the process are related. The first step in the process requires a good understanding of the business and knowledge requirements. In order words, what type of knowledge is the business seeking from the data mining project. For example, if the organization is seeking answers on customer behaviors, inventory, or product development, then the data mining project should generate outcomes that address those questions. An understanding of the

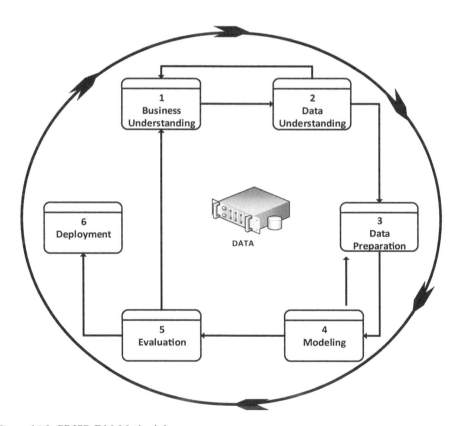

Figure 14.5 CRISP-DM Methodology

business and the problem the business is trying to address are important in guiding the subsequent phases in the process. The second phase of the CRISP-DM process is data understanding. In this phase, the process examines the sources of data, availability, variables, data types, and other characteristics of the data to gain a deeper insight into the data and identify relevant pieces of the data. The tasks in this step may include evaluating the quantity and quality of the data, and how the qualitative attributes are coded and stored. Insights into the data guides the next phase of the process, data preparation.

The data preparation phase filters relevant data and cleans the data by excluding errors, dealing with missing data, and formatting data. Usually, there are multiple sources of data that address a specific business question. The data preparation phase integrates data from multiple sources and ensures veracity and consistency. In step five the modeling process develops and tests multiple models. Through iterative processes, the model phase selects a modelling technique, tests the design of the models, and builds the models. The models are evaluated against the dataset to ensure that there is a fit between the data and the models selected. This process may require a review of the data preparation step to optimize the data for the selected models. The evaluation step assesses multiple models and reviews the models to ascertain how well they address the business question or requirements. ML programs use multiple metrics to ascertain if the outcomes of the models are rational, logical, and address the business question in step one of the data mining processes. If the outcome of the evaluation indicates that the model does not address the business question, then the process reviews the business understanding phase to ensure that there is an alignment between the business requirement and the model.

Figure 14.5 shows the CRISP-DM's iterative process of evaluating the business goals and objectives against the model. The last step in the process uses a validated model, whose outcome should be organized and presented in a format that enables decision makers to use the model. The actionable outcomes from the model can inform decision makers at all levels of an organization. For example, if the model outcome suggests that consumers buy certain combination of products when extreme weather conditions are imminent, then decision makers can use that information to manage product inventory.

ML relies on output from data mining to develop self-learning models that improve with experience. In the next section, we review machine learning and how it facilitates KM strategies. In summary, we have described how data mining, sometimes referred to as KDD, facilitates the transformation of data into information and then into knowledge using statistics, mathematics, and intelligent computational techniques. One of the challenges of data mining is analyzing and processing unstructured and semi-structured data. Recent advances in technology are enhancing the capability of data mining processes to use NoSQL databases which are more flexible in how they implement data storage and retrieval. Other methods such as NLP and text mining are more appropriate for unstructured and semi-structured data.

Machine Learning Algorithms

ML algorithms enable machines to build models for specific tasks, and independently learn from their experiences to improve on the models over time. These self-learning algorithms are the engines of AI. In this section we review ML and discuss some of the methodologies employed by ML to develop models. As we review these technologies, our focus is on how they facilitate KM processes. Thus, we discuss how ML methods support KM strategies in organizations. Samuel (1959) defines machine learning as "Field of study that gives computers the ability to learn without being explicitly programmed."[1] Thus, ML refers to autonomous systems that are initially programmed with specific algorithms and can learn and adapt on their own. Thus, ML algorithms analyze data sets and generate models that are capable of learning and adapting.

These ML algorithms enable the discovery and capturing of new knowledge through the KM process of Combination. Machine learning algorithms can combine existing knowledge with newfound patterns in the data to reveal hidden knowledge. There are three main types of methodologies that ML uses to develop models and learn from experience. These three methods are supervised, unsupervised, and reinforcement. Table 14.1 is tabular listing of the ML methods, computational techniques, application, and how they support KM processes.

Supervised methods: Supervised learning methods use labelled data that define the input data and target variable. Specified learning algorithms, for example regression, build predictive models based on the input and target variables. As listed in Table 14.1,

Table 14.1 Machine Learning (ML) Methods, Techniques, and Applications

ML Models	ML Methods	Learning Algorithms	Outcomes and Applications	KM Processes Supported
Supervised	Regression	Linear regression, neural networks	Predictive analysis, visual recognition, sentiment analysis, customer churn	Knowledge from the predictive models can help plan or explore different outcomes. Support knowledge creation and KM mechanism
	Classification	Naïve Bayes, logistic regression, decision tree, k-nearest neighbor, random forest		
Unsupervised	Association	Market-basket, link analysis, sequence analysis	Visual perception, recommendations engines, anomaly detection, fraud detection	Knowledge discovered through combination with other knowledge. For example, customer segmentation can inform cross-selling strategies. Support knowledge creation and KM mechanism processes
	Segmentation	Clustering, outlier analysis		
	Dimension reduction	Principal component analysis, singular value decomposition		
Reinforcement	Positive reinforcement learning	Q-Learning, Monte Carlo	Robotic navigation, computer games, robotic manufacturing, logistic optimization	Facilitates the creation of new explicit knowledge through combination. In the field of robotics engineering, reinforcement algorithms can provide new insights on how robots pursue goals and respond to feedback

supervised learning methods use several computational techniques, including neural networks, naïve Bayes, linear regression, logistic regression, and random forest. Box 14.2 provides a brief overview of artificial neural networks and how they work. In supervised methods, the ML algorithms use a training data set to iteratively build classification or predictive models. The outcomes of these models can inform business decisions. For example, if the outcome of a predictive model is that consumers who buy product A also buy product B, then decision makers can use that insight to guide their actions on those products.

Unsupervised methods: In unsupervised learning, the learning algorithms are not dependent on data labels. There are no input or target variables, the self-learning algorithm discovers structures and patterns to group and categorize the dataset. These algorithms are suitable for exploratory analysis due to their abilities to discover patterns of similarities and differences. Solutions from these ML algorithms can address business questions related to cross-selling strategies, market segmentation, and visual recognition. Some of the computation techniques include association, K-means clustering, outlier analysis, and market-basket analysis.

Reinforcement methods: Reinforcement learning algorithms are dynamic goal driven methodologies that train models to interact and learn from a changing environment. Unlike the data-driven supervised and unsupervised methods, reinforcement algorithms are goal-driven. Thus, with no existing or historical data, reinforcement algorithms learn by evaluating feedback on whether it achieved a goal or not. Thus, these algorithms rely on immediate and continuous feedback mechanisms to learn and improve. Hence, a reinforcement model can use feedback on its actions to revise strategies on how to achieve a goal.

Box 14.2 Artificial Neural Networks and KM Processes

Artificial neural networks (ANN) are computer models programmed to simulate the neural networks in human brains. ANN are made of layers of interconnected nodes, called neurons, which behave and learn just like human brains. Each node is connected to other adjacent nodes in a layered structure comprising layers of input nodes, hidden nodes, and output nodes. Figure 14.6 is a neural network consisting of interconnected nodes organized into layers. Input neurons receive external input in the form of information and data through multiple input channels and then process the input into outputs which may trigger other neurons in the hidden layer. At the other end of the network are the output neurons that generate results or outcomes.

The links between the neurons are conduits for signals. The links between neurons facilitate information flows through the network as output from one neuron becomes input to other neurons. In Figure 14.6, the links and connections between the nodes or neurons are weighted. The weights determine the strengths, importance, and influence of the links between neurons.

ANN can solve complex problems, such as image and speech recognition, quality control, and fraud detection. For example, in fraud detection, financial institutions can use ANN to evaluate credit card transactions and identify potentially fraudulent transactions and trigger warnings. Online automatic language translators can also use ANN to instantly translate texts, audio, and documents into other languages.

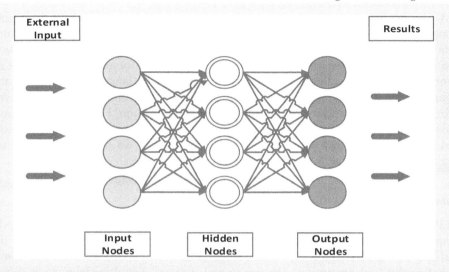

Figure 14.6 Artificial Neural Networks

The capacity of ANN to analyze large amounts of data and information makes it a useful tool in KM systems and processes. ANN creates opportunities to organize, extract, combine, and create new knowledge, and can automate and speed some of the KM processes. For example, ANN can analyze and process large amounts of data and information and identify patterns, relationships, and trends that are valuable to KM systems and processes.

Figure 14.6 shows input nodes linked to hidden nodes which in turn connect to output nodes. As information flows through the network, the self-learning algorithms train ANN models to learn by examples. ANN models learn through feed-forward and backpropagation mechanisms. In the feedforward mechanism, information or input is fed into the input nodes and then processed using the weights of the links. If the outcome from the processes in the input node meets certain conditions, it triggers other connected nodes in the hidden layer and the output becomes inputs for those hidden nodes. The output from the nodes in the hidden layer are transmitted through the weighted links to the output nodes which generate predicted outcomes for the model.

Backpropagation is a feedback mechanism that evaluates the difference between predicted and actual outcomes and adjusts the weights of the links between nodes to increase model accuracy. The process of adjusting the weights starts from the nodes in the output layers through the hidden layer nodes to the nodes in the input layer. The learning algorithms adjust the weights of the connection to minimize the difference between the predicted outcome and the actual outcome and improve model accuracy. This iterative process continues until predicted outcomes are consistent with actual outcomes. ANN supports KM systems and processes because it facilitates the transformation of information into knowledge and can automate some of the KM processes. Furthermore, the output from ANN models can inform decision-makers.

Source: Compiled from Woodford (2023)

A significant amount of organization data is unstructured, in the form of documents, e-mails, consumer reviews, meeting minutes, and contracts. Most of the unstructured data are stored in text format and are repositories for some of the collective knowledge of an organization. Data mining techniques are not suitable for analyzing text. Text is a symbolic and visual representation of speech and natural language; thus, it requires algorithms that use linguistics and semantics. Theses algorithms can extract relevant information that can add to the knowledge of an organization. For example, customer reviews of a product or experience with a product are replete with consumer opinions, sentiments, and usability experience. In the next section we discuss NLP and text mining and explain how they support ML and KM processes.

Natural Language Processing (NLP) and Text Mining

NLP is branch of AI that focuses on computer and human language interactions. NLP focuses on programming computer systems to process and analyze large amounts of natural language data. Humans use natural language in speech to communicate and convey their thoughts and perceptions. We use several types of digital medium, such as text, images, documents, and audio to store natural language. NLP algorithms can process and analyze large amounts of documents, text, and digital audio using qualitative and quantitative methods to extract relevant content, including context and nuances. Content extracted through NLP can be classified and organized in ways that are more meaningful. While NLP enables computer systems to process, recognize, and manipulate natural language, text mining extracts meaning from text using quantitative and qualitative analysis. Nonetheless, both text mining and NLP techniques can analyze semi-structured and unstructured data and automate the extraction of useful information from text.

An often-cited conjecture is that 80 percent of organization data is unstructured in the form of text, which is often unprocessed because of the challenges associated with extracting information from unstructured data (Shacklett 2017; White 2018). Text mining and analytics use computational linguistics and algorithms to overcome those challenges of analyzing and extracting data from text. Text mining is a subset of methodologies used in text analytics to extract relevant content and knowledge.

Text mining is knowledge discovery in textual databases. Text mining and NLP can extract relevant information and aggregate that information into knowledge. In the next section we describe the text mining process and how it supports KM processes.

Advances in technology are rapidly increasing the creation and storage of human-generated data in the form of text, audio, and video. The computational methods for analyzing these types of data include sentiment analysis, information extraction, NLP, classification, concept linking, and topical analysis. For example, sentiment analysis uses ML and NLP to analyze text and identify sentiments in the content, and word classification methods use part-of-speech tagging of words (such as nouns, verbs, adjectives, and adverbs) to extract relevant patterns and word associations. These computational methods can generate actionable insights from text; for example, location and place information extracted from consumer reviews and feedback can inform location-based marketing decisions and sales and marketing strategies. As illustrated in Figure 14.4, the text mining processes enable the transformation of data into information and then into knowledge. To provide further insights into how text mining processes influence and support the knowledge KM processes, we review the steps in the text mining process. As illustrated in Figure 14.7, there are three main steps in the text mining process. The steps are discussed below:

1 **Create a corpus:** The first step in an iterative process of transforming text into a structured or semi-structured format to enable computational analysis. The first step transforms the text into records, consisting of plain text documents with no formatting. Thus, each plain text document has a unique identifier to facilitate processing. At the end of this step, the process transforms the text into a collection of plain text documents, excluding formatting and any metadata.

2 **Create a term-document matrix:** As shown in Figure 14.7, the next step in the process creates a term-document matrix from the collection of plain text documents. This step involves decomposing each document into terms or words, excluding redundant words, stemming words, removing punctuations, and decoding emojis to create a term-document matrix (TDM). This step adds more structure to the original text. Thus, the TDM is a structured matrix of all the plain text documents created in the corpus and the frequency of occurrence of each word or term. Since the TDM is structured, it is suitable for analysis by supervised and unsupervised methods, such as clustering and classification.

3 **Extract relevant content:** In the last step, the process extracts knowledge by identifying interesting and relevant word patterns using methods such as semantic analysis, part-of-speech-tagging, clustering, classification, and n-gram analysis. The classification, clustering, association, and visualization methods can reveal new and relevant patterns and trends. For example, using sentiment analysis to classify relevant words as neutral, positive, or negative sentiments and measure the frequency of occurrence in customer reviews are actionable outcomes that can inform marketing and sales strategies.

As shown in Figure 14.7, text mining is an iterative process that evaluates the output of each step before proceeding to the next step or revising actions in the previous steps. For example, if the word classification in the last step included redundant words or punctuations that are meaningless to the analysis, then the process revises the term-document matrix in step 2 to exclude those words. The text mining processes facilitate knowledge creation and KM processes. For example, customers and employees may document their tacit knowledge in e-mails, customer reviews, social media postings, and solution documents. Text mining methods can uncover these nuggets of knowledge, some of which are not fully codified into explicit knowledge, and combine them with other knowledge to create new knowledge.

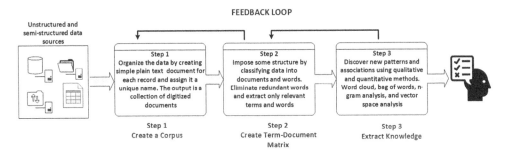

Figure 14.7 Text Mining Process

Case Studies

In this section, we review three case studies to demonstrate how AI/ML technologies enable KM processes. The first case study describes how a bank in Brazil used a virtual assistant to improve customer services. The cases studies on Amazon Comprehend intelligent document processing system and digital platforms for professional tennis are practical examples of how AI/ML can support KM processes.

Virtual Assistant and Customer Service

Virtual assistants are variations of chatbots that assist in the execution of a specific task. Businesses and organizations usually deploy chatbot technologies to assist support staff and guide customers. It is common to see virtual assistants when you visit some corporate and e-commerce websites, such as AT&T or Bank of America. These virtual assistants are trained by powerful computer programs to respond to commands or questions in natural language and perform specific tasks. Virtual assistants can record conversations and answer questions using a human-like voice. In this case study we review how Bradesco, a Brazilian bank, used IBM Watson virtual assistant to improve customer support and experience, and performance of support staff. Bradesco is one of the largest banks in Brazil with 5,200 branches across the country and offers over sixty products and services with various options. The collective knowledge of the bank was scattered across operational documents and processes across the branches, employees, and head office. When the branch offices needed product or service information or when customers needed answers to questions, the head office was unable to provide timely answers. Usually, it would take days for the support staff to respond to customer inquiries since the head office was unable to respond to questions from the branches in a timely manner. As a result, customers were unsatisfied, and the support staff were overworked.

As competition from other financial institutions intensified, Bradesco was concerned that its ineffective customer service would drive away customers to the competition. Hence, Bradesco started looking for ways to increase the speed of service and improve the level of personalization for each customer. Bradesco implemented the IBM Watson Assistant solution to address the prior poor customer services provided by the bank. The IBM Watson virtual assistant uses deep learning, ML/NLP models to interpret questions, search for the best answers, and complete the user's intended action through conversational dialogue. Figure 14.8 is a screen shot of an interaction with Watson Assistant. As shown in the dialogue, the system can generate satisfactory answers even when questions contain spelling errors.

Watson Assistant AI uses text analytics and NLP to break through data silos and retrieve speech answers to your questions, convert written text into natural-sounding audio in a variety of languages. Watson Assistant can learn from customer conversations, and develop capabilities to resolve issues the first time, and improve the customer and support staff experiences. Deep learning and NLP methods were used to train the Watson Assistant to understand any language and adapt to any business domain based on the training data.

Figure 14.9 is a diagram of the Watson Assistant architecture showing how the system processes and routes user utterances and generates responses. Powerful entity detection mechanisms can be used to identify synonyms, dates, times, and numbers,

Figure 14.8 Screenshot of Watson Assistant Dialogue

and to recognize plain-language utterances from users. There are numerous user inter-faces, including a Web interface and a customized user interface that can integrate with other third-party applications, including Internet of things applications. The Watson Assistant ML algorithms can ask follow-up questions to better understand customers and pass them off to a human agent when needed.

As illustrated in Figure 14.9, the Watson Assistant architecture routes user requests in the form of utterances to the Dialogue Skill engine. The Dialogue Skill uses NLP,

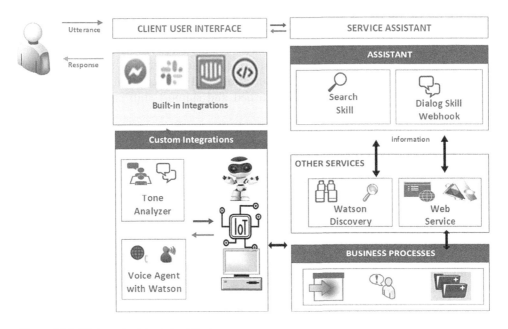

Figure 14.9 Watson Assistant Architecture

natural language generation (NLG), and ML to process the input and respond if the algorithm finds a satisfactory answer to the request. If the Dialogue Skill engine is unable to find a satisfactory answer, then it routes the request to the Search Skill engine. The Search Skill engine uses Watson Discovery services to search for satisfactory answers from knowledge bases and returns the most satisfactory answer.

Bradesco implemented the IBM Watson Assistant virtual assistant to improve customer service and personal support. Since Portuguese is the official language of Brazil, Watson Assistant must learn to speak and understand Portuguese. Although Watson Assistant can learn, the training process should be supervised, structured, and planned by humans. Thus, the ML and NLP algorithms learn the Portuguese language including the regional variations in accent, colloquial, formal, and plain-spoken Portuguese.

Watson Assistant trained the ML algorithms with ten thousand customer questions on products and services. As the machine learning algorithm answered the questions and got human feedback, it adapted and learned. The Watson Assistant AI learning algorithm used large volumes of data to learn how to imitate human-like interactions in Portuguese, recognizing speech and text inputs and translating their meanings in Portuguese. The learning models also integrated aspects of Brazil's culture, regional accents, and the way each region asks a question into the learning models.

During implementation and testing, Watson Assistant was able to understand 100 percent of written questions and 83 percent of spoken questions after five months of training, and after ten months the system was answering 96 percent of all questions. When the project was finally implemented, Watson was trained on 62 product and answers 283,000 questions a month with a 95 percent accuracy rate, with just 5 percent requiring calls for further assistance. In some cases, response times have been reduced from ten minutes to just seconds. More importantly, the responses generated by Watson Assistant are timely, accurate, and consistent.

Watson Assistant uses intent classification and entity recognition to better understand customers' context and transfer them to a human agent when needed. The AI-powered assistant understands customer requests the first time—and then automates answers and actions with seamless integration with backend systems and processes. Using AI technology to transform customer voice into usable, searchable text in real time enables seamless conversation, call transcription, and speedy live agent call resolution. Customers are satisfied and support staff can give customers the attention they deserve.

This case is another demonstration of how AI/ML can facilitate KM processes. Bradesco used AI/ML to integrate knowledge from multiple knowledge reservoirs and made it easily searchable so that the collective knowledge of the bank is accessible to customers, support staff, and management. Watson Assistant enabled Bradesco to integrate information from multiple sources and extract relevant content to create a knowledge base for customers and support staff.

AI and Sports Athletics

AI and analytics are becoming popular and powerful tools in sports athletics, especially for players, fans, coaches, owners, and trainers. The interest in analytics and AI in sports athletics began in 2001 when the Oakland Athletics baseball team used in-game activity statistics to select and recruit players. At the time, most baseball teams used the intuition and knowledge of coaches and scouting staff to recruit players. The decision by the Oakland Athletics baseball team to use game statistics to make player recruiting decisions ushered in a new era of analytics in sports and athletics.

Two decades after the Oakland Athletics baseball decision, advances in intelligent technologies are making it easier to integrate AI with sports and athletics. Now smart AI technologies are used in almost every sport, including football, soccer, baseball, basketball, hockey, and volleyball. Sport is a competitive endeavor, and the focus of most sports activities is to gain advantage over other competitors. AI, with improved algorithms, can help players and coaches gain competitive advantage over other contenders. Furthermore, management of sports franchises can use AI models to improve marketing of events, services, and products. The following case focuses on how professional tennis has leveraged AI to enhance multiple aspects of **professional tennis**.

During the 2021 French Open tennis tournament, Roland-Garros, and the 2022 Wimbledon championship, fans, players, coaches, and organizers were able to experience the benefits of AI in professional tennis (Moorhead 2021). The Infosys Tennis Platform powered the 2021 French Open Tennis tournament and IBM Watson supported the 2022 Wimbledon championship.

Tennis matches have many layers and players have several shot options, including the serve, backhand shots, forehand shots, volleys, overhead, and dropshot. These complexities make it extremely difficult for humans to absorb all the nuances of the game and use that information to predict which player should win a match. Powerful computers can store match and game data, such as the number of shots in a rally and classify rallies as short, medium, or long using the number of shots. Identifying patterns specific to rally length, by grouping rallies in short rallies, long rallies, or medium rallies, can inform coaches and players. These insights change how coaches view the game and players train for matches.

The 2021 French Open tennis tournament enabled fans, players, coaches, journalist, and organizers to download and install the Roland-Garros Players Application, an AI powered mobile application with NLP capabilities. Using natural language, players, coaches, and fans could use the app to search for player or match information, ask questions about a player, a match, or a point. With the aid of NLP and NLG, players and fans were able to use voice commands to search content and retrieve content relevant to their search.

During the 2021 French Open matches were played by 128 players on 18 different courts. The Infosys Tennis Platform used the Amazon Web Services (AWS) Cloud Watch and AWS X-Ray to capture all the action in each match on each court. These technologies provided uninterrupted digital service to players, coaches, journalists, broadcasters, and to millions of fans across the world. Figure 14.10 shows the interface where users could search for podcasts on the French Open tournament. Due to tournament play happening on multiple courts by several players, it was impossible for fans to experience every match in real-time. Thus, this interface enabled fans to get an audio summary of highlights of events at the tournament.

The Infosys Tennis Platform architecture included six immersive products, five focused on fans and one focused on players and coaches. The MatchBeats and MatchBeats ++ were used to decode the quality of a play and a set-by-set view of the matches. The MatchBeats software was trained to spot game activity that would be difficult for a human to perceive in real-time, such as unforced errors or the speed and trajectory of a serve. CourtVision and Hawkeye data offered a bird's eye view of the court, showing where each point was won or lost, trajectory of balls, and player

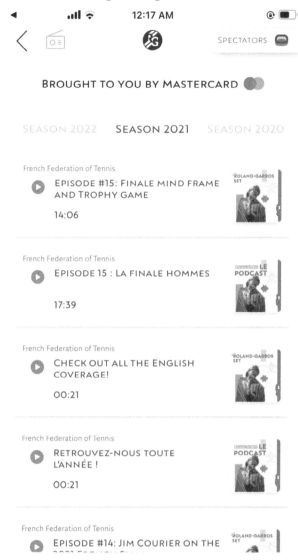

Figure 14.10 Podcast Search Screen Shot on the French Open 2021 App

position. The Infosys tennis platform used AWS Elemental MediaConvert to encode and process live real-time video streams from all the courts, including player emotion, crowd noise and match-context.

AI/ML models were used to process the videos generated by the AWS Elemental MediaConvert in order to identify highlights and shots of the day based on fan reactions. AI/ML methods used these videos and NLG-based match summary to develop intelligent narratives for broadcasters, media reports, and articles accurately and timely.

Figure 14.11 is a screen shot of a real-time display of score between the third and eighteenth seeds, with A. Zverev, the third seed, serving. As shown on the screen, users could also check upcoming matches and check scores for completed matches. NLG

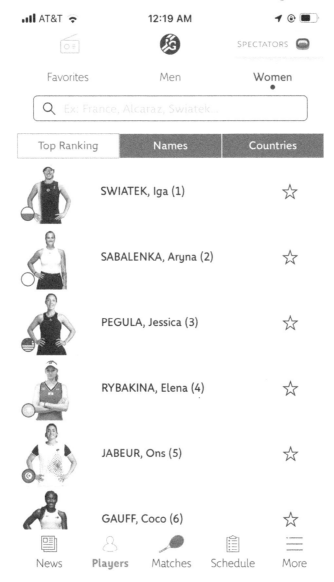

Figure 14.11 Screen Shot French Open 2021 App

algorithms analyzed what would be interesting or important to transmit to a certain audience, then translated that intelligent insight into content that is full of audience-relevant information and written in conversational language.

Professional tennis is increasingly using analytics and AI to broaden the appeal of the sport. The Wimbledon 2022 digital platform developed predictive models for players using uncertain quantification to improve prediction accuracy. The AI-powered IBM Power Index (IPI) and Match Insights enabled fans and players to get precise and accurate information on games (Baughman et al. 2022).

The IPI uses 52 weeks of historical data, recent history, reports, and player momentum to recommend compelling match ups. The on-court actions at Wimbledon generated player statistics that were particularly useful when previewing an upcoming matchup because they could indicate the relative strengths and tendencies of each player. AI algorithms were used to analyze shot trends, number of shots in a rally, errors, speed of serves, double faults, and to uncover the areas in which each player stands out.

The Match Insight algorithms used AI/ML to mine the most recent player statistics and media commentary for insight and construct a natural language summary of key performance metrics. The platform used the Watson Discovery, IBM Natural Language Understanding, IBM Natural Language Processing core, and NLG techniques to create understandable context. Match Insights was used to generate comparative analysis for fans, players, and coaches in natural language.

The Wimbledon 2022 Match Insight used historical data on player performance to make predictions on tennis matches. Figure 14.12 is the mobile app interface used to compare player's skills and generate a probability model of a player's chance of winning. Users can use the information to decide on which matches are appealing to them and could influence their ticket purchases.

In summary, the implication from using AI in tennis is that coaches can use a variety of shot metrics, such as spin, speed, placement, and the position of players, to make an

Figure 14.12 Mobile App Interface Wimbledon 2022

improved decision. AI can extract video clips of every player's winning tactic for visual analysis to help coaches develop counter-strategies. AI is also changing the way sports journalism records and disseminates sports events. AI-generated content using NLG produces summaries of the significant events of the day and journalists can access NLG-based match synopses and collate them into media reports. Coaches also have access to relevant and new information that can inform them on how to coach their players. Furthermore, players have more reliable and efficient means of evaluating their opponents and developing winning strategies.

The above case demonstrates how AI and analytics can facilitate the extraction of knowledge from experience, in this case professional tennis matches, and use that knowledge to inform decisions regarding training, coaching, counter-strategies, marketing, and fan experience. Advances in technology enable the capturing of vast amounts of data on sport events and using AI to transform that data into information and knowledge can enhance multiple aspects of any sports athletics.

Intelligent Document Processing: Amazon Comprehend

Digitization strategies have increased the amount of data captured and stored by organizations. A significant amount of this organizational data is stored in semi-structured and unstructured format. Some of these data are stored in documents, text, PDFs, and e-mails. Due to the challenges of processing these types of data, a significant amount of unstructured and semi-structured data are unprocessed. Many organizations use intelligent document processing (IDP) technologies to confront these challenges.

IDP technologies scans, reads, extracts, categorizes, and organizes meaningful information into accessible formats from large streams of data. These technologies can process many different types of documents, text, PDFs, Word docs, spreadsheets, and a multitude of other formats. The primary goal of IDP is to extract valuable information in large sets of data without human input. Intelligent document processing solutions are capable of automating data processing of structured, unstructured, and semi-structured data.

Amazon Comprehend is a popular IDP solution. Apart from Amazon Comprehend, there are several open-source frameworks for processing natural language including Natural Language processing Toolkit (NLTK) and Core NLP, which can process unstructured data, specifically text, but may not have all the capabilities of IDP.

Organizations often have so much data that it is difficult to extract valuable information quickly and accurately. Some of these unstructured and semi-structured data may be contracts, patents, research findings, e-mails, social media posting, customer reviews, posting on online communities etc. Some of these contents may include emojis and images, audio, and videos.

Many organizations recognize the value hidden in their vast amounts of semi-structured and unstructured data. However, mining vast amounts of data for actionable insights can be costly and time-consuming. IDP can address this problem and eliminate the need for manual data entry, reducing processing cost, and human error. IDP extracts relevant and valuable information from different data sources automatically.

IDP uses complex deep-learning AI/ML technology to scan documents and classify them. Machine learning algorithms are trained using large collections of documents and the models learn to process new data inputs and make decisions without human intervention. IDP relies on ML-driven technologies, such as computer vision, which utilizes deep neural networks for image recognition. It identifies patterns in visual data and classifies images accordingly. IDP uses language elements such as sentences, phrases, words, and symbols in documents, interprets them, and performs a linguistic-based document summary. Once the data is classified, intelligent document automation software extracts valuable insights from the documents. Extraction is accomplished through cognitive AI technologies that identify specific pieces of data from collections of documents. IDP then organizes the relevant data and presents it in an easily accessible format.

The image in Figure 14.13 illustrates the Amazon Comprehend architecture (Amazon n.d.). As illustrated in the image, the system processes images, PDFs, word documents, plain text, communication from e-mail, chats, social media, and phone and converts them into text which is then stored on Amazon Data Lakes. Data lakes are centralized repositories for storing structured and unstructured data. Data lakes can store raw data and enable a variety of analytics and data manipulation, such as big data processing, real-time analytics, and machine learning. The Amazon Comprehend ML algorithm in Figure 14.13 has built-in training data that can classify documents by identifying classes and entities. Custom data sets can also be used to train the model to identify custom entities. The Amazon Comprehend platform can also perform real-time analysis of social media posts or customer product reviews to gauge what customers are saying.

Next, Amazon Comprehend engine processes the text in documents to extract key phrases, sentiments, and entities. The Amazon Comprehend engine then generates various insights including entities that are references to the names of people, places, items, and locations contained in a document. If for example you want to identify location information in a document, you might look for entities that reference places. Key phrase insights retrieve relevant information related to a topic, for example if you are evaluating political parties in a document, keywords such as the GOP or the DNC may be relevant to your analysis. The Amazon Comprehend ML algorithms can also identify the dominant sentiment in a document, which can be positive, neutral, negative, or mixed. The Amazon Comprehend enables custom classification; for example, the algorithms can categorize the content of customer support requests and automatically route the request to the proper support team or classify customer e-mails to provide appropriate and efficient support. One of the intelligent features of the Amazon

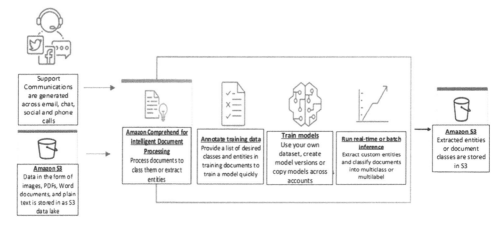

Figure 14.13 Amazon Comprehend Architecture

Comprehend engine is the ability to identify personally identifiable information (PII). When these AI/ML processes detect PII, they take appropriate steps to comply with privacy and confidentiality rules.

These intelligent document processing applications can be used to classify and extract critical information from medical bills and claim forms, such as policies and medical codes, to provide accurate insights for completing claims processing. Sometimes context, temporal, and geospatial information are necessary to fully process the hidden meaning of terms and vocabulary in a document. Sometimes it is difficult to fully unravel the context and other nuances to conversation recorded in text. However, these models have the capabilities to learn, after the initial training. Thus, over time these models can classify, categorize, and extract relevant value from documents using accurate predictive models that adapt to linguistics, semantics, and syntax changes. Colloquial use of language in social media can also pose some challenges; however, these challenges can be overcome as these models are trained to learn and adapt.

AI/ML and Knowledge Application Cases

In this section, we review three application cases of AI/ML and discuss implications on KM processes. The application cases focus on autonomous driving vehicles, fraud detection, and symptom diagnosis in healthcare. In all these application cases, we focus on how AI/ML and other intelligent technologies enable the transformation of data into information, and then into knowledge. The actionable outcomes from AI/ML algorithms and models enable data-driven and evidence-based decisions in symptom diagnosis, designing autonomous driving vehicles, and managing fraud detection.

Autonomous Vehicles and Driver Assistants

Automobile manufacturers have gradually integrated AI technologies into automobiles to enhance the driving experience. Late model vehicles from manufacturers such as Mercedes, KIA, Nissan, Audi, and Ford have integrated driving assistant features into their vehicles. These driving assistant features enable some level of automation in the operation and control of vehicles.

There are levels of application of AI and levels of autonomy in controlling vehicles. SAE International,[2] a global professional association of automotive engineers created levels of autonomy for automobile manufacturers. Level 0 are automobiles with no automation and Level 2 increases automation to starting, steering, and braking, but requires full control by the driver. Level 3 extends automations to all functions with the supervision of the driver. Level 4 is a more advanced version of level 3; the automobile performs all tasks while the driver's supervision is minimal. Regardless of the level of autonomy, all these self-driving vehicle technologies rely on AI and ML to analyze data and information from sensors, radars, and cameras. These automated driving tasks rely on AI/ML programs to collect data on the surroundings of the vehicle and process that data with powerful computer ML algorithms that can use voice commands to alert drivers on lane control and provide weather and traffic alerts (Stilgoe 2018).

These self-driving and driving assistant technologies must have the capabilities to perceive their surroundings, process their perceptions about surroundings, and use appropriate controls to navigate a vehicle based on surroundings. This is analogous to how humans drive; we use our eyes and ears to collect information about the driving environment and send the information to be cognitively evaluated and processed and then, based on the outcome, we use appropriate controls. Figure 14.14 depicts the driving process for human-driving cars and self-driving cars. For example, when drivers perceive an object in the middle of the road while driving, they cognitively process that object and use their judgment to decide how to use their feet and hands to navigate around the object. As illustrated in Figure 14.14, self-driving cars use cameras, Light Detection and Ranging (LiDAR), and radars to collect vehicle surrounding information, and AI-powered computer programs process the information and determine which electronic controls to use to navigate the vehicle (Menke 2017).

The main technologies that self-driving cars use for perception are cameras, LiDAR, and radars. Cameras are installed on the roof and other parts of the car to provide a comprehensive view of the surroundings of the vehicle. Cameras can capture shapes, colors, objects, and motion, but are unable to evaluate distance. The LiDAR devices use rotating laser beams that send invisible light pulses to calculate distances by measuring the travel time of these beams to objects around the vehicle. The rotating laser beams also identify the shapes and location of objects. The driving environment is dynamic with other moving and standing objects that can obstruct the path of a vehicle. The radar sensors mounted on several parts of the vehicle detect moving objects around the vehicle. The AI/ML algorithms combine global positioning system (GPS) data and information from cameras, LiDAR, and radars to generate actionable outcomes on what controls to use to navigate the vehicle. Deep learning algorithms combine all the information to improve decisions on what controls to use to navigate a vehicle.

As illustrated in Figure 14.14, the driving processes is cyclic: as you drive and interact with the road, other drivers, and vehicles you are constantly processing new data and discarding obsolete data. Many of the technologies that automate driving implement these processes.

Many new model vehicles integrate some form of automation in the form of driving assistance which may include features that assist a driver in controlling and navigating a vehicle. Ford Motor Company has integrated the Ford Co-Pilot360 Technology driving assist into several late model vehicles, including the F150 truck. The Ford Co-Pilot360 Technology driving assist features include the Adaptive Cruise Control, Speed Sign Recognition, Rear View Camera, and Pre-collision Assist (Ford Motor Company 2022).

The Adaptive Cruise Control uses intelligent adaptive cruise control with stop-and-go lane centering. The system enables drivers to set cruise speed and distance from the

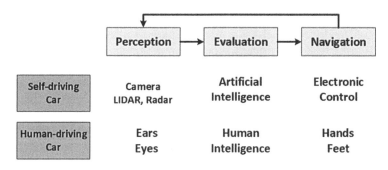

Figure 14.14 Car Driving Process
Source: Adapted from Menke (2017).

vehicle ahead, so that cruise speed automatically adjusts and adapts to the flow of traffic. The Speed Sign recognition enables drivers to monitor hands-free operation of a vehicle to ensure that the vehicle complies with posted speed limit. The Pre-collision Assist with automatic emergency braking can scan the road using high cameras, LiDAR, and radars, and alert to potential a crash. When a collision is imminent and drivers do not take corrective action, the system will apply the brakes to prevent a collision.

Figure 14.15 is a screenshot of the user interface for the parking assistant in some Ford vehicles that drivers can use to interact with their vehicles and activate some of the Ford Co-Pilot360 driving assistant features. When drivers activate the parking assist, they have options to choose from three types of parking scenarios, as shown in the image in Figure 14.16. The vehicle relies on surrounding information generated by the cameras, LiDAR, and radars. Using information from the cameras, LiDAR, and radars, if there is a stationary object in the path of the vehicle, the algorithm reviews the object and uses past behaviors to learn how to safely maneuver around the object and park a car with minimal driver supervision.

These hands-free driving options are enabled by intelligent technologies and devices that collect data on the surroundings of a vehicle and use powerful computers with AI/ML algorithms to transform the data into information, and then into knowledge that drives decisions on what controls to activate to navigate a vehicle. Fully autonomous driving cars require comprehensive GPS information on all roads and algorithms that are more precise and not prone to errors. Errors or mistakes by self-driving cars can be

Figure 14.15 User Interface for Hands-Free Driving
Source: Adapted from Ford Motor Company (2022).

Figure 14.16 User Interface for Hands-Free Driving
Source: Adapted from Ford Motor Company (2022).

fatal; thus, until the algorithms and supporting intelligent technologies mature, fully autonomous vehicles are still a thing of the future.

Fraud Detection

Digital transformation has increased payment channels and options for financial transactions, especially in e-commerce and mobile platforms. Alternative payments methods continue to grow globally, especially in the US and Canada. Consumers and users are taking advantage of these flexibility options and using these platforms to make payments and other financial transactions. For example, changes in consumer perceptions and habits are encouraging a shift to online banking and financial services. As these forms of payment increase among consumers, criminals are also exploiting new fraudulent ways to steal from banks, businesses, and consumers.

As mobile transaction volume grows, fraudsters are increasingly targeting this channel to scam businesses and consumers. In 2021, the cost of fraud for U.S. merchants increased by 19.8 percent since 2019, and mobile channels are driving the increase in fraud attacks. The threats of fraud to banks, organizations, and individuals have increased with the new ways of accessing, buying, and exchanging money online. In the U.S., the number of monthly fraud attacks on banks earning more than US$10 million in annual revenue increased from 1,977 in 2020 to 2,320 by 2021 (Varga 2022; LexisNexis 2022).

According to the Association of Certified Fraud Examiners (ACFE 2020), fraud costs organizations an average of about 5 percent of annual revenue. These fraudulent attacks may include account takeovers, fake accounts, chargebacks, money laundering, and promotional abuse. Fraud has become more complex, as criminals use a combination of digital and physical methods to scam consumers and business. These types of financial fraud require layers of different solutions to address unique risks from different channels, payment methods, and products.

The FICO Falcon Fraud Manger (FFFM) is a fraud detection tool that relies on several technologies, including AI/ML to monitor and detect fraud in real-time (FICO 2021). FFFM integrates information and collective knowledge on all payment channels and their risks. This information is analyzed and fed into ML algorithms that model fraud risk profiles. The FFFM also provides real-time solutions as it operates unnoticeably in the background and evaluates every transaction in every channel and can initiate a two-way customer interaction through virtual communication agents. Thus, FFFM can detect and stop fraudulent transactions in real-time and engage the customer in the process. After all, it is significantly more important to monitor and prevent fraudulent transactions than just monitoring without prevention. FFFM uses the Falcon Intelligent Network architecture in Figure 14.17 to monitor and prevent fraud using a variety of intelligent agents. The network uses a real-time analytics engine with ML/AI models that can generate multiple types of fraud profiles using rules and historical cases.

The analytics engine analyzes and processes all transactions across all channels to identify patterns and trends. The analytics engine uses ML/AI to develop profiles and fraud risk. The machine learning models in the analytics engine use fraud data contributed by a consortium of 9,000 global institutions. There were two billion anonymized payment transactions tagged as good or bad behavior in the consortium data set (FICO 2021). Unsupervised and supervised outlier models used the two billion transactions records to train models to profile the behaviors of individuals, accounts,

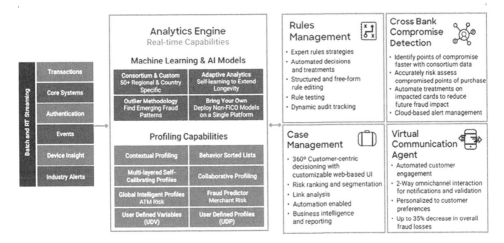

Figure 14.17 Falcon Intelligent Network

and devices. FFFM is a learning and adaptable platform, thus it tweaks the profiling algorithm as new fraud vectors, payment types, or channels emerge.

As shown in Figure 14.17, the analytics engine has multiple profiling capabilities. For example, profiles can be based on patterns of behaviors, context, or merchant risk. The behavior profiling mechanisms use powerful multi-dimensional behavioral profiling to examine behavior patterns in real-time, uncovering even the subtlest indication of fraud or deviation from peer group behavior. The behavior profile capabilities use frequently used entities, such as payer accounts, payee accounts, foreign account countries, and favorite merchant locations to develop a profile. The profiling capabilities also retrieve past cases from the case management system and use business rules to further improve the profiling capabilities of the analytics engine. This combination of technologies enhances the capabilities of FFFM to detect new types of fraud risks and develop appropriate profiles for preventing new fraudulent activities.

This case demonstrates that when it comes to fraud detection, the complexity of factors makes it very challenging for manual methods, or human-driven methods, to monitor and detect frauds. These layers of complexity require some automation in the process. In the field of fraud detection, AI/ML technologies can crawl through billions of transactions, extracting relevant knowledge, and leveraging that knowledge to develop transactions profiles. The patterns and relationships identified in transaction data and the profiles created with that knowledge underscore the combination of explicit knowledge to create new knowledge that increases operational efficiency and core competency for financial institutions and banks.

AI in Healthcare and Medicine

In the field of medicine, AI can assist healthcare professionals in diagnosing symptoms and recommending appropriate treatments. In medicine, some of the tasks of physicians are laborious and time consuming, while others are complex. The speed and consistency of AI technologies can automate those time-consuming and laborious tasks, and physicians can focus on the complex tasks. For example, recording and capturing symptoms of a patient and comparing symptom with similar cases are tasks that AI systems can perform more consistently with speed and accuracy than humans. AI algorithms can analyze vast datasets of past and real-time medical information with greater speed and consistency than a physician (He et al. 2019). For example, virtual nurse assistants can record symptoms and update electronic medical records, and AI algorithms can compare symptoms to thousands of similar symptoms to help the physician make a diagnosis and recommend treatment. With improved computing power and artificial intelligence, researchers can create "virtual patients," i.e., computer simulations using real patient data. Medical devices that can learn and adapt to the needs of a specific patient can help providers create more tailored individualized care for patients.

This application area reviews how AI/ML technologies can detect age-related macular degeneration (AMD), one of the leading causes of vision loss in the U.S. The macula is the central area of the retina, the location of central vison where AMD can deteriorate the macular leading to blurry vision that can drastically worsen over time. Researchers at New York Eye and Ear Infirmary of Mount Sinai (NYEE) developed a diagnosis system that trained AI/ML models to accurately diagnose AMD grade and stage from retinal photographs (Smith 2020). This enables patients and doctors to initiate timely preventive treatments.

The system uses inexpensive cameras that take retinal images and screens the images for AMD. The AI/ML algorithm generates instant results, so patients get immediate diagnosis and can pursue follow-up care with an ophthalmologist if necessary. This is an important and cost-effective tool for patients who may not have direct or frequent access to eye screening, as early detection is critical to preventing AMD.

The AMD diagnosis system uses deep-learning AI to screen retinal images and generate prediction models. A large data set from a 15-year study of AMD patients sponsored by the National Institutes of Health trained the machine learning models and algorithms. The study included patients between the ages 55 and 80 years, grouped into categories of normal, early, intermediate, and advanced or late AMD. The AI algorithm trained models with a data set of 116,875 color fundus photos (images that capture the interior surface of the eye) from 4,139 participants. The model trained the algorithm to classify the images of the interior surface of the eye into "no," "early," "intermediate," or "advanced" AMD along a 12-level severity scale to match the findings of human experts. Furthermore, the developers validated the predictive model with 923 participants who had AMD progression within two years, 901 patients who had progression within one year, and 2,840 patients who did not progress within two years. The developers further tweaked the AI models to include the risk of progression to late AMD.

The subsequent predictive models took the severity scores and combined them with the patients' sociodemographic clinical data (including age, gender, and medical history, such as cardiac illness or diabetes, diet, and tobacco use) and other imaging data to predict AMD progression, specifically risk for progression to late AMD within one or two years. Thus, physicians can use that information to predict the exact type of progression of late AMD within one or two years. Overall, the algorithm achieved 98 percent accuracy when matching decisions of experts.

The system can improve the operations of primary care clinics, with early detection of AMD and recommend referral for specialty care. The system can also identify at-risk patients with intermediate and advanced AMD for referral to an ophthalmologist and help eye doctors manage these patients by predicting if they will develop late AMD in one to two years.

AI/ML will not replace doctors or nurses soon, but these technologies can support healthcare by processing large amounts of data to find relevant patterns and relationships in electronic healthcare records. These patterns and relationships across several millions of patients' health records can offer insights and that should be useful to patients and care givers. Thus, AI-based analytics can support the decision-making process in the provision of healthcare.

Limitations and Future Directions

AI technologies are appropriate for explicit knowledge stored in structured and unstructured data. Tacit knowledge is know-how that resides in the memory of individuals. This knowledge is acquired through years of learning and experience and can be transferred through socialization processes, such as on-the-job training, or apprenticeship. While AI technologies can facilitate these processes, human intervention is necessary for the transfer of tacit knowledge. AI-powered virtual assistants can interact with experts to capture their tacit knowledge and store that knowledge. Tacit knowledge embedded in intuition and experience are not easily articulated and documented.

Summary

In this chapter, we reviewed AI and provided a brief background and history of AI. The chapter also describes some of the ML methods, techniques, and intelligent technologies that support AI. Throughout this chapter, we underscored how these AI/ML technologies support KM processes. We discussed supervised and unsupervised ML methods and how these methods generate models with actionable insights that facilitate decision-making. Many of these AI/ML techniques involve combining data from multiple sources and using a variety of techniques and methods to process the data, extract relevant data, and identify patterns and associations that generate classification or predictive models. These AI/ML processes also help organizations discover new knowledge by combining existing knowledge in novel ways. Thus, by programming computer systems to be intelligent, we are empowering computers with the capabilities to create knowledge and enable KM processes.

Review

1   Describe the six steps in the CRISP-DM methodology.
2   What is the difference between supervised, unsupervised, and reinforcement machine learning methods?
3   How do the supervised, unsupervised, and reinforcement machine learning methods facilitate KM processes?
4   NLP, NLU, NLG are all tools that facilitate AI. Explain the role of these technologies in AI.
5   Describe and explain the text mining process and how it facilitates the transformation of data to information, and then knowledge.

Application Exercises

1   We all use devices and software that use some type of AI software. List one example of AI-powered software or device that you use frequently. What are the

supporting AI technologies? How do these technologies assist you in your task? What are some of the shortcomings, if any?

2   Given what you know about AI, do you feel that self-driving cars are safer than human-driving cars? What are the risks of self-driving cars? Why are self-driving cars not everywhere if they are safe?

3   In your organization, what are some of the processes or tasks that you think could potentially benefit from AI/ML technologies? Why are some processes and tasks more suitable for AI/ML technologies that others?

4   Voice assistants, such as SIRI and Alexa, are becoming popular. What are some of the intelligent technologies driving these voice assistant applications? How much confidence and trust do you have in the answers generated by voice assistants, such as SIRI and Alexa? Would you use answers from a voice assistant to help you perform tasks on your job?

5   There several and numerous areas of AI/ML applications; in your opinion what area or field can benefit most from the implementation of AI/ML? What makes this field suitable for AI/ML technologies?

Notes

1   Arthur Samuel was a computer gaming and AI pioneer who worked at IBM.
2   Society of Automotive Engineers is an international association of engineers that develops and publishes consensus automotive, aerospace, and commercial standards on safety and testing procedures.

References

Ackoff, R.L. 1989. From data to wisdom. *Journal of Applied Systems Analysis*, 16, 3–9.

Amazon. n.d. Amazon Comprehend. https://aws.amazon.com/comprehend/ (accessed July 25, 2023).

Association of Certified Fraud Examiners. 2020. ACFE report to the nations: The average fraud costs companies more than $1.5 million. https://www.acfe.com/about-the-acfe/newsroom-for-media/press-releases/press-release-detail?s=report-to-the-nations-2020#:~:text=According%20to%20a%20new%20report%20from%20the%20Association,5%25%20of%20their%20revenues%20each%20year%20to%20fraud (accessed December 26, 2022).

Azevedo, A., and Santos, M.F. 2008. KDD, SEMMA and CRISP-DM: a parallel overview. *IADS-DM*.

Baughman, A., Perelman, S., Calhoun, E., and Wilkin, N. 2022. Trusted AI-generated content at the 2022 Championships. *IBM Developer*.

Campbell, C., Sands, S., Ferraro, C., Tsao, H.Y.J., and Mavrommatis, A. 2020. From data to action: How marketers can leverage AI. *Business Horizons*, 63(2), 227–243.

FICO Falcon Fraud Manager. 2021. Fraud protection and compliance enterprise payments fraud. https://www.fico.com/en/products/fico-falcon-fraud-manager (accessed December 26, 2022).

Ford Motor Company. 2022. What is Ford Co-Pilot360?https://www.ford.com/support/how-tos/ford-technology/driver-assist-features/what-is-co-pilot360/ (accessed December 26, 2022).

Graves, C. 2023. Generative AI can help you tailor messaging to specific audiences. *Harvard Business Review*, 1–9.

Gualtieri, M. 2016. Hadoop is data's darling for a reason. *Forrester*. https://go.forrester.com/blogs/hadoop-is-datas-darling-for-a-reason/ (accessed December 20, 2022).

He, J., Baxter, S.L., Xu, J., Xu, J., Zhou, X., and Zhang, K. 2019. The practical implementation of artificial intelligence technologies in medicine. *Nature Medicine*, 25(1), 30–36.

Hsu, F., Anantharaman, T., Campbell, M., and Nowatzyk, A. 1990. A grandmaster chess machine. *Scientific American*, 263(4) (October), 44–50.

LexisNexis. 2022. Thirteenth annual True Cost of Fraud™ study for ecommerce and retail U.S. & Canada edition. https://risk.lexisnexis.com/insights-resources/research/us-ca-true-cost-of-fraud-study.

Menke, T. 2017. Self-driving cars: The technology, risks and possibilities. *Harvard University Graduate School of Arts and Sciences.* https://sitn.hms.harvard.edu/flash/2017/self-driving-cars-technology-risks-possibilities/ (accessed December 26, 2022).

Moorhead, P. 2021. Tennis is now on the cloud and powered by applied AI and this is how Roland-Garros did it. https://www.infosys.com/navigate-your-next/tales-of-transformation/documents/now-serving-virtual-tennis.pdf#:~:text=TENNIS%20IS%20NOW%20ON%20THE%20CLOUD%20AND%20POWERED,a%20new%20set%20of%20immersive%20and%20intelligent%20tools (accessed December 25, 2022).

Newell, A., and Simon, H.A. 1963. GPS, a program that simulates human thought. In *Computers and thought*, ed. E.A. Fiegenbaum and J. Feldman, 279–296. New York: McGraw-Hill.

OpenAI. n.d. About. https://openai.com/about (accessed July 26, 2023).

Samuel, A.L. 1959, Some studies in machine learning using game of checkers. *IBM Journal of Research and Development*, 3, 211–229.

Shacklett, M. 2017. Unstructured data: Cheat sheet. *TechRepublic.* https://www.techrepublic.com/article/unstructured-data-the-smart-persons-guide/ (accessed December 24, 2022).

Smith, R.T. 2020. Artificial intelligence algorithm can rapidly detect severity of common blinding eye disease. Press Release Mount Sinai Health System. https://www.mountsinai.org/about/newsroom/2020/artificial-intelligence-algorithm-can-rapidly-detect-severity-of-common-blinding-eye-disease-pr (accessed December 26, 2022).

Stilgoe, J. 2018. Machine learning, social learning and the governance of self-driving cars. *Social Studies of Science*, 48(1), 25–56.

Turing, A. 1950. Computing machinery and intelligence. *Mind*, 49(236), 433–460.

Varga, G. 2022. Global banking fraud index: The cost of fraud to banks & organizations. https://seon.io/resources/global-banking-fraud-index/ (accessed December 28, 2022).

White, M. 2018. 80% of corporate information is unstructured. Really? *IntranetFocus.* http://intranetfocus.com/80-of-corporate-information-is-unstructured-really/#:~:text=Along%20with%20the%20time%20that%20knowledge%20workers%20spend,rarely%20are%20the%20implications%20discussed%20in%20any%20detail (accessed December 24, 2022).

Wirth, R., and Hipp, J. 2000. CRISP-DM: Towards a standard process model for data mining. In *Proceedings of the 4th international conference on the practical applications of knowledge discovery and data mining*, vol. 1, 29–39.

Woodford, C. 2023. Neural networks. https://www.explainthatstuff.com/introduction-to-neural-networks.html (accessed July 26, 2023).

Zeleny, M., 1987. Management support systems: Towards integrated knowledge management. *Human Systems Management*, 7(1) 59–57.

15 Knowledge Management during Global Crises

Thus far, we have examined knowledge management under normal circumstances. In the light of the recent COVID-19 crisis, and before concluding the book in the next chapter on the future of KM, it is appropriate to examine KM during crises. Therefore, in this chapter, we review the role of KM systems and processes in crisis management. More specifically, we discuss crisis management concepts and use case studies to demonstrate how KM systems and processes support crisis management in organizations.

Crises and Knowledge Management

A crisis is an unexpected disruptive event that requires significant resources to mitigate and contain. A crisis event disrupts normal operations and can potentially collapse an organization, country, or even the world. Due to an increasingly inter-connected global economy, local crisis events can reverberate across the world. Hence, crisis events tend to have global implications; for example, extreme weather conditions in United Kingdom can disrupt air travel in Europe and impact air travel across the world because the operations of international airports and airlines are intertwined. The Ebola infectious disease crisis in 2015, severe acute respiratory syndrome (SARS) in 2003, 9/11 terror attack in New York City, 2005 Hurricane Katrina in the Gulf Coast, and the COVID-19 pandemic are examples of crises that resonated across the world.

Crises can happen anytime, and most often organizations do not have the expertise to effectively manage every type of crisis. KM systems and processes that are used to capture, share, and apply knowledge about a crisis can enable timely and accurate decision-making. In this chapter, we review the role of KM systems and processes in crisis management. Effective KM systems and processes can provide timely and accurate information to decision-makers during a crisis. In Box 15.1, we review how Lincoln College collapsed due to a ransomware attack and the COVID-19 crisis, which underscores the importance of KM systems and processes in managing crises. Decisions made under stressful conditions are prone to human error and bad judgement. The case studies presented in Boxes 15.2 and 15.3 illustrate how human errors and lack of adequate KM in decision-making could be disastrous.

DOI: 10.4324/9781003364375-19

**Box 15.1 How the COVID-19 Pandemic and a Cybersecurity Attack
Caused the Closure of Lincoln College**

Lincoln College was, in 2019, a small, private, and predominantly black college with an enrollment of about 1000 students. The college was in the small town of Lincoln and it played a prominent role in the community, fielding sports teams, operating a student-run radio, and TV outlets (Nietzel 2022). The College had been struggling to sustain enrollment, and the leadership was determined to increase enrolment, maintain operations, and raise funds for the College. As part of that drive, Lincoln College invested in technologies and software to track and recruit students, promote enrollment, manage admissions, and raise funds for the college. These efforts paid off and in 2019 Lincoln College saw an increase in enrollment and residence halls and dormitories were all filled. Unfortunately, the College did not invest any resources in developing a crisis management plan. Hence, the College failed to develop capabilities to manage crisis situations.

Lincoln College has faced numerous crises in its 157 years of existence, including a major fire in 1912, the Spanish Flu in 1918, economic hardships, the Great Depression, and World War II, but unfortunately it failed to learn from those experiences to develop a crisis management strategy, in particular in cybersecurity measures to protect its systems from cyberattacks. When the pandemic hit in 2020, it disrupted the growth trajectory of the college. Like for most colleges around the Nation, the pandemic disrupted sports activities, hindered fundraising campaigns, campus activities, and restricted living conditions in dormitories and halls of residence. As the pandemic raged, Lincoln College was relatively in a better financial position due to successful fundraising, so it invested in technologies to accommodate the changes in the learning environment caused by the COVID-19 pandemic. Many students left the campus and continued their programs through online classes and Lincoln College invested resources to offer academic programs virtually. Just as the college was investing significant resources into technologies and infrastructure to support virtual and online learning, enrollment numbers dipped again due to the COVID-19 pandemic.

Then in December 2021, a ransomware attack struck and disabled access to all the electronic data of the institution (Chappell 2022; Vigliarolo 2022). The college could not use the systems to manage and project admissions or pursue any fundraising activities necessary to sustain the institution (Chappell 2022). The attack disabled access to institutional data and hindered admission activities. All systems related to recruitment, retention, and fundraising were rendered inoperable by the ransomware attack. With no crisis response management plan, the College did not have any means of regaining access to its data and information. Sadly, the College had no other choice but to pay the attackers a ransom of US$100,000 to restore its systems.

When the College regained systems access in March, the projection for the Fall 2022 was about 630 full time students, a number that could not sustain the college operations. Efforts to raise the necessary funds to save the college were unsuccessful. The case of Lincoln College demonstrates the importance of KM systems and processes. Lincoln College did not have a culture of capturing and applying institutional knowledge to guide decision-making during a crisis. On May 12, 2021, Lincoln College announced that it was closing its doors after 157 years of providing education.

Sources: Compiled from Chappell (2022); Nietzel (2022); Vigliarolo (2022)

Box 15.2 The Electric Reliability Council of Texas (ERCOT) and the Uri Winter Storm

Texas is the largest energy producer and consumer in the U.S. Electricity Reliability Council of Texas (ERCOT) and the Public Utility Commission of Texas (PUCT) oversees the regulation and policing of the Texas energy ecosystem to ensure the provision of affordable energy to Texas residents. The Railroad Commission of Texas (RCT) regulates the natural gas industry. The Federal Energy Regulatory Commission (FERC) is responsible for electricity reliability across the U.S. including the power systems in ERCOT. The North American Electric Reliability Corporation (NERC) oversees the enforcement and compliance with reliability standards set by the FERC. These regulatory agencies oversee and police the Texas energy ecosystem to ensure reliability.

After the 2011 Groundhog Day blizzard and experiences in the industry influenced many of the pre-crisis management plans and strategies prior to the 2021 Uri Winter Storm, NERC recommended to weatherize systems. After the 2011 Groundhog Day blizzard crisis, the FERC also recommended winterization of energy production systems to prevent reoccurrence in the future. Due to cost concerns, the industry did not heed the recommendations to winterize systems.

In February 2021, the Uri Winter Storm struck Texas and other neighboring states, which led to massive power failures and consequent disruption of the operations of several lifeline services, such as water, food, and heat. Freezing temperatures paralyzed several parts of the energy infrastructure. Power plants were inoperative due to the equipment freezing, natural gas wellheads froze, and the ensuing power outages crippled the water supply and disrupted supply chains for food. The Texas energy ecosystem lacked reliability, especially in extreme wintry weather.

Hence, the crisis response management plans were inadequate to manage the extreme wintry weather during the Uri Winter Storm in February 2021. The cold temperatures froze pipelines for transporting gas to power plants. Also, frozen instruments shut down coal plants and nuclear reactors and wind turbines, and snow and ice downed transmission lines. The Uri Winter Storm froze the power plants and the natural gas infrastructure that fed plants and heated homes. Most of the plant outages were due to natural gas supply challenges. Because the Texas energy ecosystem was unprepared for extreme wintery weather conditions, the storm knocked out nuclear facilities, coal and gas power stations, and wind turbines. Consumers were cut off through a blackout roll out to avoid the complete failure of the power system grid. Critical infrastructures, such as hospitals, were excluded from the rolling outages. About 4.5 million residents did not have power, mostly customers served by the ERCOT system. The ensuing crisis lasted for about four days. The temperatures in Dallas dipped to -2 degrees Fahrenheit and temperatures in Austin remained below freezing point (Giberson 2021).

In Texas, natural gas facilities provide 66 percent of the state's winter power and heat (Ivanova 2021). Some of the natural facilities were down for maintenance in preparation for the higher anticipated demand during the summer and others were not weatherized for the extremely wintry weather. About 9,000 MW of generation capacity capable of serving 1.8 million households was offline due to the lack of natural gas.

Although there are multiple sources to generate power in Texas, the mutual dependency of the natural gas and power generating plants hastened the crisis as natural gas generating power plants did not have fuel to generate electricity. Furthermore, rolling outages frequently cut power supplies to natural gas pipelines since many of the natural gas companies did not request exemption for the rolling outages.

As the storm surged on with extreme wintry weather, demand for electric power and gas increased beyond ERCOT estimated demand projections. Knowledge and experience from previous crises were used to estimate projected demand and capacity, but the context and the extreme weather rendered those estimates inaccurate. Due to shortages, the wholesale price of electricity shot up from US$30 megawatt-hour (MWh) to US$9,000 MWh and stayed at that price for four days. Consumers paying flat fees for wholesale prices saw their utility bills skyrocketing to hundreds of dollars. Thus, product failures and high demand created a crisis within the Texas energy ecosystem. It was clear that the agencies responsible for overseeing the energy production and distribution had not adequately implemented policies to bolster energy crisis or emergency response capabilities of the Texas energy ecosystem.

The post-crisis assessment recommended that power generation plant owners protect cold-sensitive equipment, retrofit existing and future units, do annual winterization training, develop an action plan for freeze-related outages and account for climate changes. These recommendations are evidence that regulatory agencies, ERCOT and PUCT, are using lessons learned from the crisis and knowledge from other energy-producing states that weathered the storm, in order to develop strategies to plan and manage future crisis events of this nature.

In the lessons learned discussions, PUCT noted the messy coordination in identifying that the natural gas infrastructure depends on electricity to operate, depriving this critical infrastructure of power, and limiting the capacity of the ecosystem to meet the demand for energy. Leveraging knowledge from the crisis and learning from the event, ERCOT is requiring winterization of power plants in Texas. This requires power plants to winterize plants and submit to ERCOT inspections to confirm winterization of plants. According to ERCOT, it will inspect over 300 generating units from 21 owners, and 54 transmission service providers (Postelwait 2022). PUCT has also increased penalties for violating winterization policies to one million dollars per day per incident. Thus, learning from the crisis response experience, the regulatory agencies are putting controls in place to compel power plants to mitigate and minimize the impact of an energy crisis from winter storms. Thus, knowledge from the crisis response and experience is influencing decisions on how to better mitigate the effects of an energy crisis. There is now an awareness that power plants in Texas should winterize their operation to withstand extreme wintry weather. Thus, the experiences and historical data are shaping new knowledge on how crisis management plans should address climate change.

Sources: Compiled from Giberson (2021); Ivanova (2021); Postelwait (2022)

Box 15.3 Costa Concordia Cruise Ship Disaster

The Costa Concordia was an Italian luxury cruise ship owned by Costa Crociere, a subsidiary of Carnival Corporation. The luxurious Costa Concordia was launched in 2005 and was Italy's largest cruise ship with a passenger capacity of 3,780 (Tikkanen 2012).

In January 2012, the Costa Concordia left Civitavecchia for a seven-day cruise to Savona, Italy, with 3,206 passengers and 1,023 crew members. As the Costa

Concordia approached Giglio Island, it deviated from the planned route and regular course and sailed closer to the coast for a maritime salute, a common cruise ship practice, except this was not planned and it was at night. The captain of the ship, Capt. Francesco Schettino, who was later convicted for mishandling the Costa Concordia disaster, ordered a change in course, but his orders were misunderstood by Indonesian helmsman, Jacob Rusli Bin, and the stern of Costa Concordia collided with rock outcrops.

The collision resulted a 53-meter tear on the port side of the Costa Concordia and the engine room was flooded, causing a blackout and disabling the rudder and engines, and making it impossible to steer the ship (Tikkanen 2012). The flood caused the ship to list on the starboard side and eventually the Costa Concordia ran aground. As water flooded the several compartments of the ship, there were fears that the ship would sink with passengers still onboard. Schettino, the captain of the ship, requested a tugboat from the Italian Coast Guard, but he was not forthright on the condition of the vessel and did not share the exact cause of the accident when contacted by the Italian Coast Guard.

The commotion aboard the ship left passengers scrambling and scuttering with no direction and instructions from the crew. Some of the crew, who knew the cause of the problem, started launching lifeboats to evacuate the vessel without the authority of the captain and before the captain ordered the ship to be abandoned. At the same time while some crew members were instructing passengers to evacuate the ships, others were informing passengers that everything was under control and passengers should return to their cabins. Because the vessel was listing, it was difficult to launch lifeboats to evacuate passengers. Some passengers used ladders to get to lifeboats or jumped into the sea and swam ashore. Rescue vessels arrived at the accident scene and started evacuating some passengers and crew to safety.

Against all standard procedures for captains of cruise ships, Schettino abandoned and left the ship in a lifeboat leaving several passengers and crew with no leadership and direction. Schettino refused the orders of the Italian Coast Guard to return to the ship and direct the evacuations to assist the rescue operation. With no direction and leadership and miscommunication among the crew, when the last crew left the bridge, there were about three hundred passengers still on the ailing vessel.

The rescue and operation involved 25 patrol boats, 14 merchant vessels, and helicopters, and 4,194 people were evacuated and 32 people died from the disaster (Pianigiani 2022). The recovery of the damaged vessel started after the evacuation of all passengers and crew. The recovery was critical as there were fears that the fuel and other pollutants from the ship could destroy the delicate marine ecosystem along the coast of Giglio Island. Salvage workers successfully removed 2,000 tons of fuel and after a delicate and painstaking process the wrecked vessel was tugged away from the coast of Giglio Island.

In the cruise ship industry, safety and security are important for passengers and crew, thus knowledge from best practices and experiences are frequently used to develop training manuals and exercises for crew. Additionally, there are local, national, and international maritime laws that regulate cruise ships depending on national registration. The International Convention for Safety of Life at Sea (SOLAS) regulates crew competency, fire protection, lifesaving equipment, navigation safety, vessel integrity, and safety management.

The crew of the Costa Concordia had all undergone the mandatory training required by maritime laws. These training programs teach crew members safety procedures and provide training manuals detailing maritime laws and regulation, and specific protocols that Costa Concordia crew members should follow before and during an incident. The training manuals contain lessons-learned and accumulated prior experience from maritime experts on evacuation in the event of an accident, safety procedures, and survival at sea.

Leadership teams on cruise ships also get additional training on crisis management, so that they can lead and direct crisis response initiatives. Crisis management knowledge is transferred to crew members through the mandated training programs and exercises. Costa Concordia had a crisis management plan and processes to follow in the case of an accident (Little 2021). Roberto Ferrarini was the crisis manager for Costa Crociere, owners of Costa Concordia, and responsible for executing the crisis management plan.

Crisis management plans are informed by the collective knowledge and experiences of an organization. Past experiences and historical data are captured in the collective knowledge and then guide decisions on creating crisis management plans. The crew of the Costa Concordia underwent weekly mandatory drills to test their abilities to follow processes and procedures during a crisis. This underscores the importance of knowledge management in preparation and processes prior to a crisis when the goal is to develop plans to minimize the impact of a crisis. The transfer of knowledge on safety and how to manage a crisis equips crewmembers with skills to meet their responsibilities in the case of a crisis event.

Despite the training, the captain of the ship made decisions that were not guided by the accumulated knowledge from experience and knowledge in the training guides. Records indicate that Captain Schettino contacted the Costa Crociere's crisis coordinator, Roberto Ferrarini, to seek advice on relaying information on the accident to the media. All the while, Schettino was covering up his negligence with an excuse that the accident was caused by a blackout on the vessel. Schettino did not inform the Italian Search Rescue Authority until 15 minutes after the collision and did not accurately communicate the cause of the accident but tried to cover up his actions. Furthermore, the crisis coordinator, Roberto Ferrarini, did not follow procedures to execute the crisis response, and failed to contact and inform the appropriate Italian authorities of the crisis.

Five crew members and the crisis coordinator were convicted for their role in the grounding of the Costa Concordia. The disaster was caused by a series of failures in decision-making because decisions were not guided by prior knowledge. An investigation of the Costa Concordia disaster focused on the actions and inactions of the captain of the vessel and how other officers of the crew acted during the emergency, and their failure to prioritize the safety of the crew and passengers.

Italy's Institute for Environmental Protection and Research (ISPRA), an agency of the Ministry of the Environment, monitored the wreck for environmental risks, and Smit Internationale and NERI SpA removed the vessel's 2,380 tons of fuel oil. After the defueling of the vessel, it was salvaged by Titan, a Florida-based salvage company, and Micoperi, an Italian undersea engineering company (Little 2021).

The eventual trial and legal suites after the crisis revealed some of shortcomings of the leadership of the crew. Evidence from this investigation indicates that training manuals and mandatory training failed to provide the leadership of the crew with the knowledge and skills to act in an emergency. The decisions of the leadership were not based on the knowledge captured in the corporate memory and the mandatory training programs. Although Costa Crociere was not implicated in the court case, it should use the crisis as a learning experience to understand how to improve training and other knowledge sharing processes so that crew members will make decisions guided by prior knowledge and best practices focused on passenger safety in case of a crisis. The capsizing of the Costa Concordia in 2012 and the ensuing disaster illustrate the importance of effective KM systems and processes in managing crisis.

Sources: Compiled from Little (2021); Tikkanen (2012)

KM Systems and Processes during Crisis

The use of KM systems and processes during a crisis can minimize human errors and poor judgements. KM systems and processes can facilitate the discovery, capture, sharing, and application of crisis-related knowledge that can help decision-makers make timely and accurate decisions (Buhagiar and Anand 2021). For example, in Box 15.4 we will discuss the case study on how Swedish Health Services leveraged institutional knowledge to deal with the COVID-19 pandemic crisis.

Box 15.4 Swedish Health Services and How to Effectively Deal with the COVID-19 Pandemic Crisis

The COVID-19 pandemic was a global crisis that disrupted the operations of local and national governments, non-government agencies, and businesses across the world. A new set of capabilities were required at the local, national, and international levels to address the effects of the COVID-19 pandemic. Effective KM systems and processes can bolster an organization's capability to prepare for a crisis, manage a crisis, and recover from a crisis. The Swedish Health Service's (SHS) pre-crisis capabilities and how it managed the COVID-19 crisis demonstrates how a culture for sharing valuable knowledge can make an organization agile and resilient in the face of crises.

SHS operates five acute care hospitals, two ambulatory care centers and a network of 202 primary and specialty care locations throughout the greater Puget Sound area in the state of Washington, U.S. (Swedish Health Services 2023). In January 2020, before the first case of COVID-19 was admitted in the U.S., SHS was treating an increasing number of COVID-19 patients in distress from a nursing home and began collecting data and tracking the illness. Using data and information on the symptoms and care, SHS developed models that suggested that the region's healthcare system could be overwhelmed if the trend continued. At the time, the world and SHS did not know enough about the pandemic and the virus that caused COVID-19.

During all that, nearly 7,800 caregivers at SHS embarked on a three-day strike that disrupted the operations of the hospital system (Dale et al. 2020). When the strike began, the administrators activated the Hospital Incident Command System (HICS) a crisis response management team used to coordinate with representatives from all the five hospitals and other facilities. Collective knowledge captured in the SHS, and an effective crisis response plan, ensured that services to patients were not compromised during the strike. Furthermore, because of an effective and coordinated response to the disruption caused by the strike, SHS learned and developed new knowledge that assisted decision-makers during the COVID-19 crisis a few weeks later.

After the strike, SHS analyzed and captured its response and experiences and used that knowledge to immediately improve practices and daily operations. Effective communication and delegation of authority were the key learning experience from the strike. Due to a workplace culture that values knowledge and learning, the leadership viewed the response to the strike as a learning experience that enhanced the collective knowledge of SHS to prepare for future crises. Prior to the COVID-19 crisis, the strike was an opportunity for SHS to develop the capacity and ability of the HICS to manage through a crisis and test its crisis response management plan. The experiences from the response to the strike translated into better crisis response practices during the COVID-19 pandemic.

The SHS leadership discovered through practice that focusing on people and sustainability is key to effective crisis management in health services delivery. Thus, three key factors, effective communication, delegation of authority, and a focus on people and sustainability were critical to the capabilities of SHS to manage crisis and sustain operations. The combination of adequate KM systems and processes as well as a culture of valuing knowledge were instrumental in sustaining those three key factors.

When the COVID-19 crisis started to stress the operations of healthcare services, SHS was determined to use effective communications, delegation of authority, and a focus on people to manage the response to the crisis. The fears, uncertainty, and anxiety created by the pandemic spurred rumors, misinformation, and conspiracy theories that demoralized and distracted caregivers. SHS leadership created an intranet page to inform caregivers and share knowledge relevant to care givers, such as information on personal protective equipment (PPE) and protocols for clinical treatment. This ensured that caregivers at SHS were exposed to the same knowledge and could leverage that knowledge in the daily practices and operations. This shared information and knowledge were augmented with consistent and repeated communication to staff through e-mails at all levels of the organization to reinforce the message and content communicated.

SHS also engaged the staff and caregivers and leadership through an online discussion forum and virtual town halls that gave caregivers the opportunity to ask questions in real-time and interact with leadership. These forums encouraged discussion of the challenges and problems of caregivers and frontline staff with the leadership. The leadership was able to use information from caregivers and frontline workers to allocate and reassign resources to maximize patient care. These mechanisms for sharing information provided opportunities for capturing, sharing, and combining existing knowledge to create new knowledge that influence leadership decisions at SHS.

The organizational complexity and structures hampered the agility and resilience of SHS. Siloed functional units undermined the ability to make and implement timely decisions. To overcome these challenges, especially during a crisis, leadership delegated decision to those closest to operations and service delivery. SHS used the RACI (Responsible, Accountable, Consulted, and Informed) approach to delegate and facilitate information flow between the leadership teams and frontline workers, enabling SHS to capture and share innovative practices across the organization.

To illustrate how RACI facilitated knowledge sharing and application during the pandemic, patients who tested positive for the COVID-19 virus had been typically isolated, and monitoring intravenous pumps required caregivers to repeatedly wear and remove the PPE, increasing their risk of infection. Through the experience and knowledge of frontline workers, SHS realized that it is more prudent and safer to keep these intravenous pumps in the hallways outside of the isolation rooms. This practice was implemented across SHS to improve the monitoring of intravenous pumps and the safety of caregivers and patients.

The culture of valuing knowledge enabled SHS to capture knowledge from practices in an operational unit and apply that knowledge across the organization. The focus on people and sustainability was another key in the strategy used by SHS to manage the crisis. Expressing gratitude by acknowledging the efforts and deeds of staff and providing mutual support was also important in building trust and motivating staff to engage in efforts to manage a crisis. For example, running a backup childcare program at SHS was a good example of the organization's focus on people. Feedback loops that enabled frontline workers to share their concerns and challenges with leadership and obtain a swift response from leadership encouraged knowledge sharing and application.

SHS management of the COVID-19 pandemic is an illustration of how KM systems and processes and a culture of valuing knowledge can be instrumental in improving the capabilities of an organization to manage and respond to a crisis. While a crisis is unexpected and happens suddenly, it requires effective and timely decision-making, and effective KM systems and processes can enhance the ability to prepare for a crisis and manage successfully through the crisis when it occurs. SHS is an example of an organizational culture that values knowledge and promotes the capture, sharing, and application of knowledge to improve organizational performance, even in a crisis.

Sources: Compiled from Dale et al. (2020); Swedish Health Services (2023)

The goal of a properly designed crisis management infrastructure is to mitigate, prevent, cope, respond, and recover from a crisis. Crisis management can be complex and unstructured because every crisis event is unique and requires context-specific tactics (Xia et al. 2011). The case study on the Uri Winter Storm crisis in Texas, discussed in Box 15.2, reflects the complexity of managing a crisis. Crisis management teams and stakeholders need timely, accurate information and knowledge during the crisis. Knowledge sharing processes are particularly important because access to accurate information is critical in a crisis. During a crisis, people need to have the ability to share prior knowledge relevant to the crisis at hand as well as current information about the crisis with those who need that information to make decisions to manage through the crisis. Thus, mechanisms to capture and share knowledge about the crisis can help with timely and accurate decisions.

Types of Crises

A crisis is an unexpected event that threatens the survival of an organization. These events could be man-made or natural events. Advances in technology and globalization have linked the world economies together. Through financial networks, logistics, trade, technology, climate change, and nature, the world is a complex interconnected sophisticated global ecosystem. The interconnected global ecosystem is vulnerable and susceptible to natural and man-made events that can disrupt the normal operations of components within the system. Fires, terror attacks, bombings, cyber-attacks, financial crisis, and power outages are man-made disruptive events that can trigger a crisis. The 9/11 terror attack in New York City is an example of a man-made crisis event with global implications that changed how airlines and airports operate and how passengers travel today.

Natural crisis events are caused by changes in the surface or atmosphere of the earth that are beyond human control. Natural events like rain may be controlled, but floods, hurricanes, and earthquakes are difficult to control. Advances in technology enable meteorologists and climatologists to develop predictive models that provide advance warnings for weather related events, such as hurricanes, tornadoes, floods, rains, and storms, which are disruptive and can develop into a crisis.

Other natural events such as earthquakes are difficult to predict. Although seismic models use existing faults and locations of previous earthquakes to develop seismic hazard models, these models are not able to predict earthquakes. Other natural events such as fires may be caused by a combination of both man-made and natural causes. Some parts of the world, such as Australia, are susceptible to wildfires. Fire experts are not able to predict when a fire will start, but once the fire starts, experts can build models that can predict the path of the fire. Epidemics, such as COVID-19 or SARS, are natural events that can spin out of control and develop into a global crisis.

Crisis Management Plans and Models

Managing a crisis is important in many disciplines and the mechanisms and processes to manage a crisis are influenced by a variety of diverse views and perspectives (Bhaduri 2019). For example, the focus of a cybersecurity expert in a crisis is to secure information systems' infrastructure, and a facility manager will focus on protecting facilities from a crisis. Regardless of the focus, the goals of crisis management are the same. Experts in a variety of disciplines have advanced several crisis management models.

Fink's (1986) crisis management model recommends processes and procedures for proactively monitoring in order to limit and mitigate a crisis, activating a crisis plan to manage a crisis, and assessing the impact of a crisis. Mitroff's crisis management model (Pearson and Mitroff 1993) advances a four-stage crisis management model with processes for detection, prevention, containment, recovery, and lessons learned. Another crisis management model by Burnett (1998) provides management plans for three broad stages of a crisis: identification, confrontation, and reconfiguration.

The crisis management model advanced by Jaques (2007) elaborates on how to create systems for crisis preparedness, prevention, management, and post-crisis assessment. A common theme in all the crisis management models is a prescription for an organizational plan and strategy prior to a crisis, during a crisis, and after the crisis (Bundy et al. 2017). Hence, regardless of the approach and perspective, common to all the crisis management models are processes for pre-crisis management, crisis response management, and post-crisis management. A three-stage approach to crisis management that broadly defines and recommends leadership roles, actions, procedures, and processes to mitigate, respond, and recover from a crisis can integrate concepts from multiple crisis management models advanced by scholars from multiple disciplines.

The three phases of the crisis management model advanced in Figure 15.1 are pre-crisis, crisis response, and post-crisis response. The flow and exchange of organizational knowledge and information are important to managing a crisis, and KM systems and processes facilitate information and knowledge flows. Through the case studies, we demonstrate how KM systems and processes are instrumental in crisis management, especially in processes related to capturing, combining, and sharing knowledge.

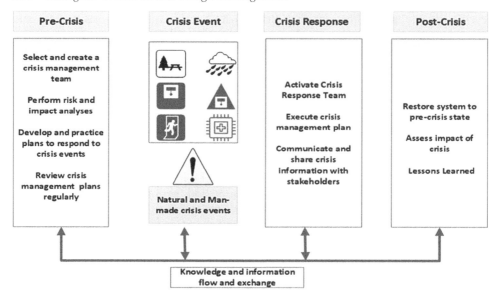

Figure 15.1 Crisis Response Systems

As illustrated in Figure 15.1, in this chapter we divide crisis management into three stages: pre-crisis management, crisis response management, and post-crisis management. KM systems and processes are critical to each of the three phases of the crisis management process. Decision makers in all of the three phases of the crisis management process require different sets of information, data, and knowledge to perform their duties. Figure 15.1 illustrates the knowledge and information flows between the crisis management phases. The pre-crisis phase relies on knowledge and information on previous crisis events, response, and assessment to develop a crisis management plan and prepare for a future crisis. During a crisis, the crisis response team shares information and knowledge about the current crisis with stakeholders, including the crisis management team. Codified knowledge in the form of lessons learned from prior post-crisis assessments are an important part of the organizational memory that can guide pre-crisis management strategies. Crisis management is an evolving and dynamic process with each phase influencing decisions and actions in other phases, and the capacity to capture and share knowledge is important through all the phases of the crisis management processes.

Pre-Crisis Management

Crises are inevitable, yet it is difficult to predict their occurrence. This paradox makes planning for an eventual crisis difficult. However, with a deliberate and structured methodology, organizations can devise plans and management strategies to prepare for a crisis and minimize the eventual impact of future crisis. One of the first steps in the pre-crisis management plan is to select a crisis management team.

The composition of the crisis management team should be representative of the core functional units within the organization and other stakeholders, such as senior management and public relations officers. The team should meet periodically to ensure that all members are active and understand their duties, roles, and responsibilities in the event of a crisis. A diverse team composition is useful to cultivate cognitively diverse ideas and the knowledge necessary for managing a crisis. Expertise and know-how from a variety of perspectives will ensure that plans and actions to mitigate the effects of a crisis are comprehensive and thorough (Gudi et al. 2018).

Organizational preparedness is the first step in dealing with a crisis. When an organization is prepared, it has the capacity to manage unexpected disruptive events. The leadership of the organization should be mindful of their internal and external environment to understand vulnerabilities, risks, and potential threats to normal operations. Crisis management plans rely on impact and risk analyses to identify vulnerabilities, potential threats, probability of occurrence, frequency, and impact of a potential risk.

Crisis management plans should include a monitoring mechanism that can signal early warning signs of impending crisis. Early warning systems can take a variety of forms depending on the context and identified risks. Some early warning systems might be mechanical or electronic. For instance, hurricane forecasts use satellite imagery and computer models to develop and create hazard information and provide early warnings for evacuation in the case of a hurricane. Other early warning systems may consist of financial metrics. For example, an organization might be able to anticipate a substantial drop in revenue by monitoring stock prices of competitors in the market. Situational awareness requires information flows and exchange within the organization and with external sources of knowledge.

The crisis management team develops a crisis response plan using the results from the impact and risk analyses. This plan should include simple but comprehensive instructions specifying duties, roles, and responsibilities of the crisis response team. Furthermore, the plan should be tested periodically to ensure that when a crisis happens, the plan can be executed, and members of the crisis management team know their roles and responsibilities. Organized training sessions, and regular reviews and updated knowledge on roles and responsibilities, are important to reinforce crisis management skills.

A crisis management plan is only good if it can be executed by the crisis management team when a crisis occurs. Personnel and staff should be trained to understand their roles and responsibilities in a crisis. The training should prepare staff and employees to respond to a crisis. With proper training and knowledge sharing, once an event becomes a crisis, staff and employees should know what to do immediately and how to act in crisis situations. Knowledge on what to do during a crisis should be shared with all employees and reinforced periodically through practice and drills.

The pre-crisis management plan should list the names of people to contact in case of a crisis. Some of these contacts will be internal and others will be external. For example, if there is fire, which may require assistance from outside the organization, the instructions should include a list of contacts who can help with fire outbreaks. An example of a checklist for a fire outbreak would be: first to activate the building alarm systems, second to call 911 and verify alarm notification, third to evacuate the building in an orderly manner, and finally, to activate the crisis response management plan.

A pre-crisis management plan should include an activation protocol that specifies when an event turns into a crisis and when to activate the crisis management team. The activation protocol will clearly specify the threshold of disruption, or potential level of threats that warrants the activation of the crisis management team. The criterion for activating the crisis management team should clearly define the conditions that dictate the activation of the crisis management plan. Once the impact or effects of a crisis event reaches that threshold level, then the crisis management team is ready to execute the plan and strategies for managing a crisis.

External and internal sources of knowledge are important ingredients in the pre-crisis management plan. The crisis team should have access to institutional knowledge to evaluate vulnerabilities and risk, to develop the capacity to detect or sense impending crisis. Some of this knowledge is scattered across the organization and some is tacit, thus KM systems and processes that facilitate the discovery, capture, sharing, and application of knowledge are important for developing a pre-crisis management plan.

Knowing who to share knowledge with and what knowledge is appropriate is important in the pre-crisis phase of crisis management. Teams directly dealing with the crisis will need relevant knowledge to execute their duties. Those not directly involved with managing the crisis should also know what to do in a crisis. Thus, KM systems and processes can empower those managing the crisis with the necessary know-how to execute their duties. Those affected by the crisis and other stakeholders should have access to relevant information and knowledge on the crisis to act appropriately in order to mitigate the effects of the crisis. Therefore, it's important to capture knowledge relevant to the crisis management team in a central repository and make the repository available to those who will need to access to this knowledge during the crisis.

Crisis response teams can be better prepared to handle a crisis if they are trained via scenario planning (Nikolai et al. 2009) in how to execute crisis response plans and manage the crisis a priori. Knowledge acquisition and transfer on how to respond to a crisis are critical to providing the required skills. This knowledge should be codified and simplified to facilitate timely decision-making under stress.

Crisis Response Management

When an organization is prepared for a crisis, it avoids an emotional reaction. When a crisis occurs and the crisis plan is activated, the crisis team manager is responsible for directing the team to respond to the crisis based on the plans and procedures created in the pre-crisis phase of the planning. Making decisions under stress and with limited time is challenging, but with the right guidelines and knowledge of what to do, the crisis response team can execute and minimize the impact of the crisis.

Crisis managers initiate a communication plan to disseminate information and knowledge about the crisis to team members, employees, and other stakeholders. Sourcing and sharing knowledge are important processes during a crisis. Alternate channels of communication may be exploited to reach all stakeholders and employees. Most often the communication will include information on the status of the crisis and what steps the organization is taking to ameliorate the effect of the crisis and return to business continuity state of operations. Effective, efficient, and timely and accurate decision-making is essential during a crisis, and organizations can manage crisis better if they have KM systems and processes that foster information flows and exchange (Buhagiar and Anand 2021).

Rules-based and case-based KMS help in making decisions during a crisis. These types of knowledge systems use rules, heuristics, rules of thumb, routines, and historical cases to capture knowledge to facilitate prompt, timely, and accurate decisions. During the crisis it is important that an organization communicate and share information both internally and externally, so that employees and stakeholders are informed and know what is expected of them. Simple and comprehensive instructions are necessary for staff involved with the management of the crisis. Instructions are often framed in a checklist format to simplify the actions of those responsible for managing the crisis. Crisis response management plans should incorporate those processes that typically run on autopilot and are devised to simplify decision-making. Routines, rules of thumb, and heuristics can simplify decision-making during a crisis.

Knowledge acquisition and sharing is critical as the crisis unfolds and communicating that knowledge to stakeholders, employees, and management is also important for effective response to a crisis. Effective communication of the shared knowledge of the crisis and actions can allay fears and anxiety during a crisis. Crisis response plans should explore multiple channels of communication, such as e-mail, social media, and messaging apps to reach a wide range of stakeholders. Timely situational information to stakeholders and others involved with the crisis is important to address the crisis and mitigating the undesirable effects of the crisis. Through information flows and exchanges, all stakeholders should have a shared knowledge of the evolving crisis.

The crisis management team should assess the impact of the crisis, sometimes they may not have firsthand information, but rely on first responders or others who have real-time information on the crisis. KM systems and processes that facilitate knowledge flows and exchange can facilitate knowledge capture and transfer of relevant knowledge to the crisis response team (Nyoni and Kaushal 2022). When the crisis team arrives on the scene, they should have the means to communicate and collaborate with other teams.

Sometimes, efforts are directed toward coping with the crisis and minimizing the negative effects of the crisis. Timely and accurate decision-making depends on how effectively and efficiently prior relevant knowledge is acquired and utilized. The quality of the decision made during the crisis depends on how prior knowledge relevant to the crisis is captured and shared within the organization and among stakeholders. During a crisis, members of the organizations involved must be able to make swift decisions, and effective KM systems and processes can ensure the availability and accessibility of accurate and reliable information and prior knowledge relevant to the crisis. As the crisis unfolds new knowledge is discovered, captured, and shared using appropriate channels of communication. Dealing with a crisis requires diverse sources of knowledge. Cognitive diversity among team members will ensure that the crisis response team is not hampered by biases.

Post-Crisis Management

The post-crisis assessment occurs after the crisis response, and the main goal after the crisis is to assess the damage and impact of the crisis and explore means of returning to normalcy and business continuity. The knowledge and information captured during the post-crisis will serve to inform future pre-crisis management plans, thus KM systems and process that facilitate the capture and sharing of knowledge are important to crisis management. KM processes ensure that the three phases of crisis management are aligned and work collectively to mitigate, respond, and recover from a crisis.

Post crisis management plans, for example using After-Action Reports, should review the crisis response to determine if the crisis response activation was timely, how effective were the crisis communication practices, reflect on other coordination structures, and evaluate the effectiveness of policies, plans, and procedures followed during the response to the crisis. In a culture that values knowledge and learning, crisis response challenges are learning experiences. After a crisis, the crisis management team can reflect, contemplate, think critically, and explore alternative assumptions to learn from the crisis and prepare for the next crisis with more skills and know-how.

After a crisis, historical data and experience becomes part of the collective knowledge of the organization. Maintaining and updating organizational knowledge is important to sustaining the value of knowledge. During the post-crisis assessment and recovery, the crisis response team evaluates what actions and communication strategies worked and were effective during the crisis. The organizational memory of the crisis embedded in documents, procedures, data, information, and knowledge is synthesized to develop new knowledge on how to prepare for a crisis and respond to a future crisis as it unfolds.

Closed-loop learning and effective KM systems and processes enable the crisis response team to leverage organizational knowledge to prepare and respond to a crisis. Learning from experience enhances the capacity and abilities of the crisis management team to prepare for future crises. Thus, crisis management teams can combine knowledge from preventing and managing a crisis to create new knowledge to enhance the capacity of the crisis team and the organization, in order to better prepare for the next crisis event.

Case Studies

The case studies illustrate how KM systems and processes are critical to planning and managing a crisis, regardless of the cause of the crisis. If an organization fails to plan for a crisis, then it is planning to fail during a crisis. Man-made or natural events can disrupt the operations of organizations. Crisis events are unexpected because, in most cases, it is impossible to predict when, where, and how the crisis will happen and unfold. This makes it difficult to devise plans to manage a crisis. Organizations that develop capabilities to mitigate, respond, and recover from a crisis are likely to minimize the adverse effects of a crisis.

- The case study in Box 15.2 above describes how the Electricity Reliability Council of Texas (ERCOT), which coordinates all the natural gas and electric power generating plants in Texas, were unable to deal with the extreme winter during the Uri Winter Storm. This case underscores the complexity of managing crisis in a tightly-coupled interdependent ecosystem.
- The case study in Box 15.3 is about how Swedish Health Services, an organization with a culture that values knowledge, effectively implemented KM systems to capture and share knowledge that played an instrumental role in crisis mitigation, response, and recovery.
- Human error and bad judgement were the cause of the Costa Concordia disaster in Italy described in Box 15.4.

While it is impossible to eliminate human error and poor judgement, training programs, knowledge transfer from experts, and controls can limit errors and bad judgements. Regardless of the causes of the crises, all three case studies below reflect the challenges of managing crises and how KM systems and processes can support crisis management.

Summary

In this chapter we reviewed the role of KM systems and processes in the management of crisis. Crisis can be caused by man-made or natural events. These man-made and natural events are considered a crisis because of the significant disruption they cause to normal operations. A major challenge for many organizations is the unexpected nature of crisis events and the sudden occurrence of these events.

Digitization and globalization have interconnected national and local economies and made it difficult to isolate or localize the effects and impact of crisis events. Climate changes and an integrated supply chain spanning many countries make natural and man-made disasters a global phenomenon. Efforts to mitigate, cope with, and recover from any crisis require a three-phased approach of developing a pre-crisis management plan to prepare and mitigate the impact of a crisis. Additionally, a crisis response management plan is necessary to cope with a crisis as it unfolds. Finally, assessment and recovery plans are essential to dealing with the aftermath of a crisis. It is important to note that a robust crisis management plan is dynamic and should be responsive to changes in vulnerabilities, potential threats, and risks. For example, relocating a business to an area prone to floods changes the risks and vulnerability of the business to floods and those changes should be factored into a revised crisis management plan.

KM systems and processes that encourage prior crisis knowledge capture, sharing, and application are especially important to crisis management plans. Expert knowledge on crisis management and the collective knowledge of the organization should guide decisions on devising crisis management plans. Prevention and mitigation plans can benefit from internal and external sources of knowledge to develop comprehensive plans. Organizations should learn from their experiences of dealing with crisis events and capture those experiences as part of the collective knowledge of the organizations. These experiences become part of the collective intelligence of the organizations. It is only when organizations have structures and systems in place to manage knowledge and promote a culture that values knowledge that they can leverage the collective knowledge to manage crises.

The case studies on the Uri Winter Storm in Texas, the Costa Concordia, and the Swedish Health Services' management of the strike and COVID-19 crisis demonstrate how KM systems and processes can be helpful in managing through a crisis. On the other hand, the example in Box 15.1 on Lincoln College is an example of how a crisis can cause the collapse of an institution when it does not prioritize crisis management. Crises will occur, but we do not know when. However, if we devise a crisis management plan guided by prior knowledge and experience, then we will be ready to respond and minimize the impact of crisis events when they occur.

Review

1   What are the main causes of global crises? Why are crises becoming global in nature?
2   Pre-crisis preventive and mitigations plans prepare an organization for a crisis. How should organizations prepare and plan to anticipate the unexpected?
3   How do post-crisis recovery and assessment influence pre-crisis management plans?
4   How do KM systems and processes influence the three phases of crisis management?

Application Exercises

1   Do you think that your organization's management of the COVID-19 pandemic crisis demonstrated a proactive strategy rather than reactive one? Why?
2   Cyberattacks can disrupt organizational operations; what pre-crisis prevention and mitigation strategies is your organization pursuing to reduce the risk of a cyberattack?
3   How have KM systems and processes influenced how your organization prepares for a crisis? Do you know your roles and responsibilities in case of a crisis? How does your organization transfer crisis response knowledge to the staff and management?
4   How would you go about developing a crisis management plan for your organization that will mitigate crisis, respond to a crisis, and recover from a crisis?

References

Bhaduri, R.M. 2019. Leveraging culture and leadership in crisis management. *European Journal of Training and Development*, 43(5/6), 554–569.

Buhagiar, K., and Anand, A. 2021. Synergistic triad of crisis management: Leadership, knowledge management and organizational learning. *International Journal of Organizational Analysis*, 31 (2), 412–429.

Bundy, J., Pfarrer, M.D., Short, C.E., and Coombs, W.T. 2017. Crises and crisis management: Integration, interpretation, and research development. *Journal of Management*, 43(6), 1661–1692.

Burnett, J.J. 1998. A strategic approach to managing crises. *Public Relations Review*, 24(4), 475–488.

Chappell, B. 2022, Lincoln College closes after 157 years, blaming COVID-19 and cyberattack disruptions. *NPR*. https://www.npr.org/2022/05/10/1097855295/lincoln-college-closes-157-years-covid-cyberattack (accessed June 21, 2023).

Dale, C., Welling, L., and Clearfield, C. 2020. How one Seattle health system is managing the COVID-19 crisis. *Harvard Business Review*.

Fink, S., and American Management Association. 1986. *Crisis management: Planning for the inevitable*. Amacom.

Giberson, M. 2021. Texas power failures: What happened in February 2021 and what can be done. Reason Foundation Policy Brief. https://reason.org/policy-brief/the-2021-texas-power-crisis/ (accessed June 21, 2023).

Gudi, A., Xia, W., and Becerra-Fernandez, I. 2018. When things go right in disasters: The moderating effect of specific knowledge on task performance. *International Journal of Information Systems for Crisis Response and Management (IJISCRAM)*, 10(2), 1–27.

Ivanova, I. 2021. Texas' frozen power grid is a preview of climate change disasters to come 2021 CBS Interactive Inc. https://www.cbsnews.com/news/texas-power-outage-storm-climate-change/ (accessed June 21, 2023).

Little, B. 2021. The Costa Concordia disaster: How human error made it worse. *A&E Television Networks*. https://www.history.com/news/costa-concordia-cruise-ship-disaster-sinking-captain (accessed June 21, 2023).

Jaques, T. 2007. Issue management and crisis management: An integrated, non-linear, relational construct. *Public Relations Review*, 33(2), 147–157.

Nietzel, M. 2022. Lincoln College in Illinois to close after 157 years. *Forbes*. https://www.forbes.com/sites/michaeltnietzel/2022/04/01/lincoln-college-in-illinois-to-close-after-157-years/?sh=77cd40403fa3 (accessed June 21, 2023).

Nikolai, C., Prietula, M., Becerra-Fernandez, I., and Madey, G. 2009. Project Ensayo: Designing a virtual emergency operations center. In *2009 IEEE International Conference on Systems, Man and Cybernetics*, 3934–3939.

Nyoni, A.M., and Kaushal, S. 2022. Sustainable knowledge management during crisis: Focus on Covid-19 pandemic. *Business Information Review*, 39(4), 136–146.

Pearson, C.M., and Mitroff, I.I. 1993. From crisis prone to crisis prepared: A framework for crisis management. *Academy of Management Perspectives*, 7(1), 48–59.

Pianigiani, G. 2022. How the wreck of a cruise liner changed an Italian island. *New York Times*. https://www.nytimes.com/2022/01/14/world/europe/giglio-costa-concordia-italy.html   (accessed June 21, 2023).

Postelwait, J. 2022. Texas' big freeze: The 2021 power crisis and the lessons learned one year later. *T&D World*. https://www.tdworld.com/disaster-response/article/21213032/texas-big-freeze-the-2021-power-crisis-and-the-lessons-learned-one-year-later (accessed June 20, 2023).

Swedish Health Services. 2023. Facts and figures. https://www.swedish.org/about/facts-and-figures (accessed June 21, 2023).

Tikkanen, A. 2012. Costa Concordia disaster. *Encyclopedia Britannica*. https://www.britannica.com/event/Costa-Concordia-disaster (accessed June 21, 2023).

Vigliarolo, B. 2022. Ransomware the final nail in coffin for small university. *The Register*. https://www.theregister.com/2022/05/12/ransomware_dangerous_enough_to_close/ (accessed June 21, 2023).

Xia, W., Becerra-Fernandez, I., Gudi, A., and Rocha, J. 2011. Emergency management task complexity and knowledge-sharing strategies. *Cutter IT Journal*, 24(1), 20.

16 The Future of Knowledge Management

As we have seen throughout this book, the goals of knowledge management are for the members of an organization to discover, capture, share, and apply knowledge. However, the nature of KM is undergoing a dramatic change primarily because of emerging technologies, such as social media, augmented reality, generative artificial intelligence, and cloud computing. In Chapters 12 to 14, we discussed some of the roles of emerging technologies in knowledge management practices and methods. In this concluding chapter, we identify and discuss five critical issues for the future of KM. These issues are discussed in the next five sections, followed by some concluding remarks.

Using Knowledge Management as a Decision-Making Paradigm to Address Wicked Problems

The development of management information systems, decision support systems, and KM systems has been influenced by the works of five influential philosophers, namely Leibniz, Locke, Kant, Hegel, and Singer (Churchman, 1971). Based on Churchman's definition of *inquiring organizations* (they have also been called *learning organizations*), a new paradigm for decision-making in today's complex organizational contexts has been developed (Courtney, 2001).

In the conventional decision-making process, the emphasis is first on recognizing the problem, then on defining it in terms of a model. Alternative solutions are then analyzed, and the best solution is selected and implemented. Thus, KM systems have successfully supported solving semi-structured problems, those characterized by a limited number of factors and a certain future. Recent developments in KM have helped extend the reach of those involved in the solution. But the jury is still out on how well KM systems support problems that are characterized as wicked (Lönngren and van Poeck 2021; Rittel and Webber 1973). **Wicked problems** are unique and difficult to formulate. Their solutions are good or bad (rather than true or false) and generate waves of consequences over time. Solutions to wicked problems are accomplished in one-shot occurrences, and so there is no opportunity to learn from prior mistakes and solutions cannot be undone. Moreover, solutions to wicked problems are not a numerable set of solutions, and many may have no solutions.

For example, a project plan for an **enterprise resource planning (ERP) system** implementation is a wicked problem. ERP systems' implementations are one-shot occurrences, in the sense that organizations will typically only implement them once. Therefore, there's no opportunity to learn over time how to successfully implement these systems. Usually organizations only find out if their implementation was

DOI: 10.4324/9781003364375-20

"good" or "bad" on the deployment or "go-live" date, and at this point "bad" implementations result in disastrous economic consequences for the organization.

As globalization expands, the number of stakeholders affected by the organization increases, each one affected by different customs, laws, behaviors, and environmental concerns. Globalization also leads to wicked planning problems for organizations, and methods to help make decisions in such situations are greatly needed. The new paradigm for KM support, suggested by Courtney (2001), defines the decision-making process as starting with the recognition that the problem exists, but then rather than proceeding immediately into analysis the process consists of developing multiple perspectives. These multiple perspectives consider the following:

1 *Technical perspective*: The alternatives to the selected option should be analyzed and considered for implementation. This is the primary perspective used in existing decision-support and KM systems.
2 *Personal and individual perspective*: Complex problems involve a multiplicity of actors. Each sees the problem differently and generates a different perspective based on individual experiences, intuition, personality, and attitudes about risk.
3 *Organizational and social perspective*: Complex problems involve various organizations. Organizations also each view the problem in a different fashion, and thus generate a different perspective. Organizations may also consist of diverse members with different interests.
4 *Ethics and aesthetics perspective*: Complex problems involve business ethics and aesthetic issues that are so high that they require the involvement of key stakeholders since there are no simple solutions. Perhaps the utilitarian emphasis of the Industrial Age neglected the spirituality of the "rational man" and contributed to the demise of ethics and aesthetics in decision-making today (Courtney 2001).

The new paradigm for decision-making bases decisions on the use of the above perspectives. The prior view of decision-making environments minimizes the importance of relationships, collaboration, and trust in the organization. Personal relationships define organizational boundaries to a large extent. The future calls for the development of KM systems that support the human aspects of decisions: the personal, organizational, ethical, and aesthetic perspective. Thus, KM systems should help decision makers make more *humane* decisions and enable them to deal with wicked problems.

Further work is needed on how KM can be used to address problems that are not only wicked but also critical to humanity. Some of the biggest threats currently being encountered are climate change, sustainability, and global crisis events. Could emerging technologies, such as Web 3.0 technologies, generative artificial intelligence, blockchain, and cloud computing, play a role in generating ideas and taking actions needed to address such wicked and crucial problems?

Promoting Knowledge Sharing while Protecting Intellectual Property

Knowledge sharing could also bring forth certain risks, namely that the knowledge falls into the wrong hands either maliciously or accidentally. The same communication technologies that support the sharing of knowledge within an organization also enable the knowledge to leak outside the organization to competing firms. Given the value of the knowledge, and the reliance that an organization places on this knowledge, losing this knowledge could have severe negative consequences for the organization. It is therefore critical for organizations to manage knowledge such that knowledge sharing is enhanced but knowledge leakage is controlled. This is not an easy balance to achieve. Below we discuss some of the ways in which knowledge leakage can be controlled.

Intellectual property (IP) can be defined as any result of a human intellectual process that has inherent value to the individual or organization that sponsored the process. It includes inventions, designs, processes, organizational structures, strategic plans, marketing plans, computer programs, algorithms, literary works, music scores, and works of art, among many other things. KM enables the effective use of IP, but it could also lead to loss of IP, which can damage the organization just as much as losing real capital property. In fact, in many cases IP is an organization's most valuable asset. One of the earliest KM initiatives actively pursued by The Dow Chemical Company was harvesting little-used patents and intellectual assets (Davenport and Prusak 1998).

As discussed in the earlier chapters, organizations often capture knowledge from documents stored in Web-based repositories. The more codifiable this knowledge is and the more it is documented and distributed, the greater the risk of losing this knowledge. IP losses can happen in many ways including the following:

1   Employee turnover. The employee may leave the organization to be hired by a competitor. The employee may deliberately or accidentally share her knowledge with her new employer.
2   Physical theft of sensitive proprietary documents, either by outsiders or by insiders.
3   Inadvertent disclosure to third parties without a nondisclosure agreement.
4   Reverse engineering or close examination of a company's products.
5   The Web repository security is breached, and unauthorized access to the proprietary documents takes place.
6   Unauthorized parties intercept electronic mail, fax, telephone conversation, or other communications for the purpose of illicitly acquiring knowledge.
7   Attempts by insiders or outsiders to corrupt documents or databases with false data, information, or knowledge. This could be done directly via hacking into a database and effecting unauthorized modifications or indirectly via a virus. This is a variation of the electronic breach of data problem in item 5, but it is somewhat different in that the actions can destroy the system in question. There are significant criminal implications with this act.

Note that the first four types of IP loss are not related to technology, while the last three are. Also, some of the intellectual capital losses are related to legal practices used to acquire sensitive competitive intelligence (items 1, 3, and 4), while the law prosecutes others (items 2, 5, 6, and 7). Clearly the losses related to technology are easier to prove and therefore easier to prosecute. Companies can take a number of steps to protect their organization against IP losses as follows.

1 Nondisclosure Agreements

A nondisclosure agreement is a contract between an organization that owns the IP and outside individuals to whom the organization's sensitive and proprietary information is disclosed on the condition that they maintain it as confidential. Divulging this knowledge to a third party constitutes a breach of confidentiality, and the offending party can be sued for damages. Employees of the organization owning the IP are, by definition, expected to maintain confidentiality not only while they are actively employed by that organization, but also after they terminate their association for whatever reason. Nondisclosure agreements can serve to protect against loss of knowledge via employee turnover as well as via covered disclosure to outsiders.

2 Patents

Patents are the oldest and most traditional means of protecting inventions. They grew out of the need to encourage exceptionally bright people to invent products and processes that benefit humankind. Patents do this by giving exclusive rights (a monopoly) to any product containing the patented works to the inventor, with all rights therewith. This means that an inventor, for a fixed period of either 16 or 20 years from patent issuance, can control the duplication of the patented works or process. Patent law can be quite complex in what can and cannot be patented, at what time, and for how long. However, as long as a patent is not overturned, it provides the most secure of protections. Unfortunately, this protection is only exercised through court action taken by the patent holder against the individual or organization allegedly infringing the patent. In some cases, small inventors holding valid patents cannot successfully sue large corporate entities with large legal staffs. Patents are excellent vehicles for protecting knowledge about technical innovations and products. They can protect against reverse engineering of a product as well as unauthorized acquisition of any design or other documents that detail the nature of the invention. In fact, loss of such documents is considered immaterial since the design of the patented invention is already part of the public record by virtue of its patented nature.

3 Copyrights

While patents protect the ideas behind the invention (the so-called claims), copyrights protect the expression of the work. They have been traditionally used to protect literary works, works of art, architecture, and music. However, they can also be used to protect computer programs, albeit weakly. The advantage is that while patents require a rather rigorous process to be granted, a copyright can be done by merely stating on a copy of the body of the work that it is copyrighted. Registration of the copyrighted work with the government in the United States is not required, although it's highly advisable. Other countries require registration. This is done using the symbol ©. Copyrights typically last for the life of the creator plus up to 70 more years, depending on the country of filing. A copyright holder maintains the rights to publish, broadcast, reproduce, or copy the work. She has the exclusive right to translate it into another language, either wholly or in part. Copyrights can protect stolen or illicitly obtained IP only if it is valuable in its expression. For example, computer programs may fall into that category.

4 Trade Secrets

An organization may choose not to patent an invention but instead keep it as a trade secret. This invention may not fulfil all the criteria for patentability. Alternatively, the organization may want to avoid the legal process required to protect IP. Stealing trade secrets is illegal and punishable by law if the damaged organization takes legal action.

However, said organization must make a strong effort to maintain confidentiality to maintain its legal rights. Organizations may accomplish this by instituting reasonable safeguards of its IP. Lacking that, a court may decide that it was not a very important trade secret to begin with.

We have discussed some legal avenues of IP protection. However, once the organization resorts to legal remedies, the damage has already been done and it most likely can only aspire to damage recovery. An effective KM initiative must include institutionalizing policies and safeguards that will prevent the loss of IP in the first place. Installing **firewalls** in computer systems, access controls, and protecting all the sensitive information through **encryption** can go a long way toward this. Furthermore, organizations should clearly educate their employees about their responsibility for confidentiality and the consequences they could suffer if they violate this confidentiality whether accidentally or purposely.

As mentioned earlier, these avenues for IP protection should be used with some caution. Although they do help in preventing knowledge leakage, they may also inhibit the ability of the organization's own employees to seek knowledge from individuals outside the organization who may be able to provide them with helpful advice.

Exploiting Internal and External Knowledge Sources

Two interrelated and emerging aspects of knowledge management focus on involving collaborations of a large numbers of individuals: (a) from across various levels within the organization; and (b) from outside the organization to share and create knowledge.

The Value of Grassroots Contributions

As discussed in Chapter 13, the democratization of knowledge refers to providing every employee within an organization with the ability to make grassroots contributions that stand the chance to influence the company's direction. This ability is becoming increasingly valuable because people at the lowest levels of the organization are the ones who most commonly interact with customers and are often the ones involved to the least extent in important decisions. Web 2.0 technologies enable widespread participation in decision-making, or at least the consideration of ideas from across the organization, by drastically reducing the time that it takes for such ideas to be communicated and aggregated. This could be done through virtual communities, blogs or wikis, for example, as they allow individuals across the organization to contribute to content and for individuals across the organization to access that content. Advances in AI technologies make it possible for content in blogs, wikis, and online communities to be processed and analyzed to identify trends and patterns. Box 16.1 illustrates some of the human-like intelligence associated with AI technologies.

Box 16.1 Automation, Augmentation, and Avoiding the Turing Trap

One foundational element of the field of AI is the Turing test, which evaluates a technology's capacity to display intelligent behavior similar to or indistinguishable from a human's. Passing the Turing test, powerful AI systems now match humans in tasks like image and speech recognition, impacting fields like autonomous vehicles, medical diagnosis, and product recommendations. Robotics advancements rely on improved mechanical capabilities and increasingly human-like artificial intelligence (HLAI).

Replicating human capabilities with AI has dual benefits: reducing reliance on human labor and building adaptable intelligence. HLAI excels in handling unexpected and complex situations, and offers numerous benefits: increased productivity, more leisure time, and a deeper understanding of our minds.

But many powerful AI systems differ greatly from humans. Solely fixating on HLAI is problematic. Overemphasizing HLAI can lead to issues as it replaces human labor, diminishing workers' bargaining power and dependence on technology controllers. Automation replaces human labor, eroding workers' influence. Entrepreneurs and executives may opt for machines that replicate human capabilities, leading to workforce displacement. Automation enhances productivity, especially in dangerous or monotonous tasks. In theory, a fully automated economy could distribute benefits broadly, even to those not directly involved in value creation. However, weak bargaining power could lead to wealth and power concentration. HLAI offers tremendous potential for wealth, leisure, and self-understanding, but also risks if it leads to labor automation. Brynjolfsson (2022) calls this situation the Turing Trap.

By contrast, augmenting humans with AI, instead of imitating them, allows people to retain influence and claim value. Augmentation leads to complementarity, where humans remain essential for value creation and retain bargaining power. Augmentation creates new capabilities, products, and services, generating more value than HLAI alone. Thus, HLAI's impact on society depends on whether it augments or automates human labor.

Both automation and augmentation boost productivity and wealth. However, an imbalance currently favors automation over augmentation, and an unregulated market may prioritize automating human labor over human augmentation due to excessive incentives. The Turing Trap risks are driven by misaligned incentives among technologists, businesspeople, and policymakers, who all find automation appealing due to different reasons.

In 1988, Hans Moravec observed that computers can excel in intelligence tests but struggle with one-year-olds' perception and mobility skills. However, Moravec's ambition might have been limited. Machines can often surpass humans in new domains more easily than matching their regular tasks. Therefore, augmenting humans with technology unlocks vast new abilities and opportunities. The range of tasks achievable by humans and machines *together* surpasses those that either AI or humans can do alone. Machines perceive the imperceptible, perform unique actions, and even comprehend the incomprehensible to the human brain.

Slowing down technology is not the answer; instead, we should eliminate excessive incentives for automation over augmentation. Introducing practical benchmarks beyond the Turing Test can spur progress toward AI systems surpassing human capabilities. Strengthening political and economic institutions against automation through AI is vital. Redirecting efforts toward augmentation can evade the Turing Trap and foster a prosperous, inclusive society for all.

Sources: Compiled from Brynjolfsson (2022); Turing Test (2023)

Information Technologies and KM

Recent industry trends reveal that organizations are increasingly adopting cloud computing to manage their IT resources. In Chapter 12, we discussed how cloud computing supports and facilitates KM practices. Cloud computing refers to the ability to access software and/or hardware resources from remote locations using browsers or thin-client application interfaces.

The main benefits of using Cloud computing relate to optimizing the utilization of hardware and software infrastructure while minimizing the upfront investment, and customers can take advantage of established IT infrastructure in the Cloud and focus their efforts on the business and innovation. Cloud computing supports the growth of big data in organizations, which in turn creates new opportunities for smart analytics and improved customer service, but this can only happen if the IT and business units work together. Big data refers to collecting large data sets in organizations, a phenomenon of increasing concern to IT leaders.

Generative AI and other smart technologies that use large language models (LLM) can leverage machine learning algorithms to generate new insights from existing content. Organizations can use their internal documents, processes, procedures, and electronic content to train generative AI models and change how organizational knowledge is discovered and captured. AI and LLM technologies can speed the knowledge creation and capture processes and make organizations more agile. Thus, organizations will continue to explore ways to leverage AI and LLM to support and promote KM practices and improve decision-making.

Controlling knowledge leakage and protecting proprietary and sensitive information, trade secrets, and IP are critical elements of managing organizational knowledge. In addition to non-disclosure clauses and agreements, cryptographic technologies, such as blockchain, can protect organizational knowledge. Blockchain technologies enable the exchange and storage of information using cryptography and decentralized computing systems. Blockchain is typically used to record financial transactions in a tamper-resistant and irrevocable format on decentralized computer systems. Blockchain protocols for the exchange and storage of encrypted information can be extended into KM practices. Trade secrets, IP, and other confidential content can be shared, tracked, and stored using blockchain technologies. The storage of encrypted information along with the history of changes and contributors can be useful in KM practices, especially in acknowledging knowledge contributors and identifying expertise. Although generative AI and blockchain technologies have the potential to influence KM practices and methods, it is also important to note that KM practices are more than information technologies.

In 2021, Deloitte's Global Human Capital Trends study noted that technology, by itself, is not enough to leverage the value of knowledge, unless it is supported by a knowledge-sharing culture (Sikora 2021). Information technologies cannot eliminate all the barriers to effective KM; however, Web 2.0 technologies can serve as IT infrastructure to promote and support a knowledge-sharing culture, which is critical to KM practices.

What makes Web 2.0 technologies critical to the future of KM is the capacity of these technologies to engage and bring people together within and outside the organization. People are repositories of tacit and explicit knowledge, thus technologies that enable interpersonal interaction, collaboration, and information exchange and sharing should play a key role in the future of KM practices. Web 2.0 technologies make it easy to create and consume electronic content; thus, these technologies inject some level of fairness and equity into the transfer and sharing of knowledge. Hence, KM practices will continue to rely on applications that enable people to share and exchange ideas, such as crowdsourcing platforms, blogs, virtual communities, messaging and communication applications, and collaborative and productivity software.

Addressing Barriers to Knowledge Sharing and Creation

Although it is important to involve internal and external knowledge creators, and Web 2.0 technologies provide some interesting ways of doing so, it may not be easy to accomplish this. Three main problems constrain individuals' contributions to KM: (a) privacy concerns; (b) concerns related to "knowledge as power"; and (c) senior executives' reluctance to adapt. Each of these barriers is discussed next.

Privacy Concerns

Perceived threats to privacy may inhibit individuals from contributing knowledge both within the organization as well as across organizational boundaries. An individual may be less forthcoming with honest opinions if she believes that the recommendations she is providing for a decision would be compiled and potentially viewed in the future in the light of all other comments she makes over time, either within the organization or over the Internet, all the decisions she makes, and her demographic and other personal information. This is especially true when the individual perceives that the comments might not be liked by a powerful individual within the organization. This applies to comments sent via e-mail as well as posted on blogs (DePree and Jude 2006).

People expect a certain level of privacy even beyond traditional organizational boundaries, such as in social networking sites, and are likely to react strongly to threats to privacy (McCreary 2008; Pottie 2004). Box 16.2 provides one illustrative example.

Box 16.2 Privacy Concerns at Facebook

Facebook is a social networking website that provides free access to people who can join networks organized by interest, region, city, place of work, or academic institution, and connect and interact with others. Users can also add friends and communicate with them and update personal profiles to inform friends about themselves. Facebook's (one of the applications that support Meta, www.meta.com) mission is "to give people the power to build community and bring the world closer together" (Facebook 2023). Operated and privately held by parent company Meta, it had over 2 billion users worldwide, i.e., 36.7 percent of the world's total population, as of July 2023 (Facebook 2023).

In 2007, Facebook encountered problems with the default settings that provide advertisers the product preferences that its users share with their friends. Users reacted negatively to this "privacy intrusion," and Facebook management had to change the default settings from "yes" to "no" (i.e., Facebook would not be able share these product preferences) (McCreary 2008).

Following this incident, Facebook decided to change its policy on user-generated content, such that it would have a "perpetual" license to use any material uploaded by users for advertising or other venues, even if the user had subsequently deleted the content or even cancelled the account. However, Facebook rescinded the decision upon learning that the Electronic Privacy Information Center (EPIC), an advocacy group based in Washington, DC, was planning to file a formal complaint with the Federal Trade Commission over the changed license agreement.

Credited for this protest against Facebook was a grassroots effort by Julius Harper Jr., a 25-year-old who formed the "People Against the Terms of Service" Facebook group, with over 80,000 members. This group started as a simple protest, and then submitted its major concerns to the service's legal team. The most significant concerns included why the revised terms of service appeared to give Facebook the right to use members' photos if the company had no intention of utilizing them, and what would occur if Facebook were to be acquired by another corporation in the future and the new owner wanted to utilize the user-generated content in ways the current Facebook leaders were not considering.

In 2013, Cambridge academic Aleksandr Kogan created the "This Is Your Digital Life" app, which mined data from 300,000 users and their friends through a psychological questionnaire. This data access gave Kogan's employer, Global Science Research, information from 87 million Facebook users. In 2018, the FTC launched investigations into allegations that Cambridge Analytica harvested and utilized Facebook users' data to create psychographic profiles of American voters. The Senate questioned Facebook CEO Zuckerberg. In July 2019, the U.S. Federal Trade Commission (FTC) approved a settlement of approximately US$5 billion with Facebook for its handling of users' data. Cambridge Analytica and its parent company faced their downfall due to the scandal.

In addition to the data privacy scandal, Facebook also faced allegations of misinformation on its platform. There were public demands for the government to compel Facebook to sell Instagram and WhatsApp, acquired by the company in 2012 and 2014, respectively. The scandal led to prominent figures like Steve Wozniak, co-founder of Apple, urging people to find a way to quit Facebook.

In April 2021, Facebook faced another data scandal, compromising the personal data of half a billion users, including birthdates, phone numbers, email addresses, and full names. Despite previous fines and promises to tackle data scraping, the breach raised doubts about Facebook's credibility and user trust. This scandal highlights the significant failure of all accountability systems, both past and present.

Overall, data breaches have become all too common recently. Tech giants like Facebook, eBay, LinkedIn, and Adobe have also fallen victim to hackers. Users trust these reputable companies to keep their data secure and not misuse it. Discovering that personal data has been leaked and used for malicious purposes is a significant breach of trust and privacy. Social media platforms should proactively notify users about breaches, enabling them to stay vigilant against phishing scams that exploit their compromised data.

Sources: Compiled from Confessore (2018); Facebook (2014); Facebook (2023); McCreary (2008); Raphael (2009); TechRepublic (2020)

The privacy concerns have increased due to growth in both structured and unstructured data, as discussed below.

Growth of Structured Data: As companies invest heavily in enterprise resource planning systems, customer relationship management systems, radio-frequency identification tags, and other technologies, the amount of data collected per transaction is multiplying. For example, companies collect data on inventory levels, transportation movements, and financial transactions, enabling them to communicate more accurately with customers, accelerate supply chains, manage risks, and identify business opportunities. Increased structured data can be a double-edged sword: increased granularity creates opportunities for analytics that could lead to improved business processes and customer service, but duplicated and conflicting data can undermine service delivery, resulting in conflicts over whose data is more accurate. A large percentage of stored data serves no useful purpose in practice because management has not specified how it will be used or who will make what decisions on the provided data.

Explosion of Unstructured Data: Documents, images, videos, and e-mail make up a significant percentage of the data stored in most organizations. This growth is the result of many factors such as increased regulatory requirements. Some organizations are finding that unstructured data collected through social media enabled greater sharing of information and knowledge. However, realizing business value from this unstructured data typically requires indexing and reorganizing of some information. Box 16.3 discusses the capabilities of Web 3.0 to promote interactive and engaging Web sites that generate unstructured data.

Box 16.3 The Promise of Web 3.0

Background: The Web, short for the World Wide Web, is the internet's fundamental information retrieval system. In the past, WWW initials were typed into web browsers to access specific online resources. Tim Berners-Lee, an internet pioneer, coined the term World Wide Web to describe the interconnected global network of information and resources through hypertext links. Web 1.0 started with the introduction of web browsers such as Netscape Navigator, and static webpages retrieved from servers. It was based on the three fundamental technologies written by Berners-Lee (who also wrote the first webpage editor/browser—WorldWideWeb.app): HyperText Markup Language (HTML), the markup or formatting language of the web, Uniform Resource Locator (URL) a unique address used to identify each resource on the web, and HyperText Transfer Protocol (HTTP), which enables the retrieval of linked resources from across the web.

Current Web 2.0: During the first two decades of the 21st century, Web 2.0 revolutionized the internet, replacing static pages with interactive, socially connected platforms, and user-generated content. This shift, fueled by innovations like mobile Internet and social networks, led to explosive growth and dominance of apps like Facebook, Instagram, X (formerly Twitter), and YouTube. These tech giants, along with others like Apple, Amazon, Google, Meta (formerly Facebook), and Netflix (FAANG), became some of the world's largest companies. Web 2.0 also fueled the gig economy, offering income opportunities through ride-sharing, home rentals, and online sales. However, traditional sectors like retail, entertainment, media, and advertising struggled to adapt, facing existential threats from this digital transformation. Web 2.0 is the version of the Internet with which all of us are familiar.

Web 3.0: Web 3.0 is the third generation of the World Wide Web (WWW). With a vision of a decentralized and open Web with greater value to users, it is currently a work in progress. Web 3.0 signifies the next evolutionary phase of the Internet, and its potential impact could be as disruptive and transformative as the shift to Web 2.0. Web 3.0 is built upon the core concepts of decentralization, openness, and greater user utility.

Defining Features of Web 3.0: Though there is as yet no standard definition of Web 3.0, it does have a few defining features:

Decentralization: Unlike Web 2.0, where information is located on specific servers accessed via unique web addresses, Web 3.0 finds data based on content, allowing for simultaneous storage in multiple locations. This shift breaks down the massive databases held by internet giants like Meta and Google, giving users greater control.

With Web 3.0, users can sell the data generated by various computing resources through decentralized networks, ensuring ownership control remains in their hands.

Trustless and Permissionless: Web 3.0 relies on open-source software, making it trustless and permissionless. Participants can interact directly without intermediaries, and anyone can join without authorization. Web 3.0 apps, also known as dApps, run on blockchains or decentralized peer-to-peer networks.

Artificial Intelligence (AI) and Machine Learning: Web 3.0 enables computers to grasp information like humans, using Semantic Web concepts and natural language processing. It incorporates machine learning, an AI branch that improves accuracy by imitating human learning from data and algorithms. This empowers computers to deliver faster and more relevant results in areas like drug development and new materials, moving beyond the current focus on targeted advertising.

Connectivity and Ubiquity: Web 3.0 fosters greater connectivity and ubiquity of information and content across multiple applications, with numerous everyday devices being connected to the Web. The Internet of Things (IoT) is a prime example of this integration.

Potential and Pitfalls of Web 3.0: Web 3.0 promises greater utility beyond Web 2.0's social media and online shopping. With its core features like Semantic Web, AI, and machine learning, it can expand into new areas and enhance user interaction. Additionally, Web 3.0's decentralization and permissionless systems give users more control over their data, reducing data extraction and exploitative practices. However, this decentralization poses legal and regulatory challenges, making it difficult to police cybercrime, hate speech, and misinformation without central control. Determining jurisdiction for websites hosted in multiple nations would also be complex in a decentralized Web.

A Simple Example of How Web 3.0 Will Improve Knowledge Access: Web 3.0 will simplify vacation planning on a budget. Intelligent search engines or bots will gather flight, accommodation, and car rental options, generating personalized recommendations based on your profile and preferences. This advanced ability to access information and provide actionable knowledge in a simple form would save hours of manual searching across multiple websites.

Sources: Compiled from Essex et al. 2023; Investopedia 2022

At the tactical level, IT units can take the lead in ensuring safe, reliable, cost-effective data storage and access, but that will not necessarily lead to business success. In order to achieve the maximum value from data, senior management must commit to three practices (Beath et al. 2012):

- Identify the "sacred data": Information about customers, sales orders, inventory items, employees, and so forth constitute most of the data. This information can provide different opportunities for different segments of the business. By scoping the "sacred data," management can clarify how the business will set the parameters for the organization's enterprise architecture on which IT can build.
- Define the workflows that will use unstructured data: To derive business value from the unstructured data, management needs to define the workflows that create, retrieve, change, and reuse documents, messages, images, and other unstructured data. In particular manual or automated processes need to be defined for adding the "metadata"—tags that categorize unstructured data.

- Use data to refine business processes: Deriving benefits from the information available is an iterative process. Improving business processes and service can lead to richer data allowing innovation and efficiencies.

Advances in technologies and AI capabilities to analyze unstructured data with human-like intelligence comes with other challenges. Box 16.4 discusses some of these challenges.

Box 16.4 Think for Yourself Amidst all the Technologies

Our reliance on experts, protocols, and technology seems to have led us to outsource much of our thinking, becoming overly reliant on experts, protocols, and technology. Technology's algorithms can shape our focus, leading to potential biases. Outsourcing decisions may lead to losing control over framing key choices. Following them blindly can lead to mistakes, like GPS leading to deserted parking lots, or health protocol oversights. Integrating information sources effectively is crucial to maintaining informed decision-making without losing our ability to think independently.

An overreliance on technology has thus diminished our autonomy. We must find a balance between expertise and critical thinking to regain autonomy. Education should focus on developing critical thinking capabilities to assess default assumptions and not prioritize short-term skills-based training. We should be aware of our own focus and the influence of those we rely on. In an era of experts and AI, it is necessary to balance depth of expertise with broad perspective. Liberal general education is vital, and should not be overshadowed by short-term skills-based training. We should be mindful of our focus and those we rely on for thinking. We should acknowledge technology's subtle impact on our focus through algorithms and AI in order to avoid losing control over crucial decisions.

Consider the difference between traditional in-person book shopping and today's online experience. Online searching is convenient, with algorithms suggesting books you may like. However, browsing bookshelves can lead to unexpected discoveries, fostering diverse thinking. Online algorithms cater to your immediate preferences, while physical browsing allows for chance findings. Neither approach is inherently superior, but being aware of online search's limitations can prevent overlooking opportunities. We conclude with the following insightful remarks:

> Because of the algorithms used, companies like Google, Facebook, and Amazon are de facto able to influence your decisions in ways that may not be obvious. They manage your focus and do your filtering. They set your decision frames. … We are at a serious inflection point. In an age of experts and artificial intelligence, critical thinking skills and the expression of moral judgements are more important than ever. Thinking for ourselves can inoculate us from many ills and may even help us defend against big tech's attempts to rob us of our autonomy.
>
> (Mansharamani 2020, p. 248)

> Dots are everywhere. The real sustainable know-how we must all develop is the ability to connect them. To lift our heads up and notice the context. And to constantly question the underlying assumptions that we retain as "true," thinking for ourselves independently and not relying on the opinion of others. … The future, it seems, belongs to those who think for themselves.
>
> (Mansharamani 2020, p. 249)Source: Compiled from Mansharamani (2020)

Concerns Related to "Knowledge as Power"

KM mechanisms and technologies that help capture and store employee's knowledge reduce knowledge loss when expert employees leave the organization. However, this may lead to employees, who are not nearing retirement and are concerned about job security at the organization, being concerned about sharing their knowledge with others in the organization. The perception that "knowledge is power" could lead to the belief that by sharing one's privately held knowledge, one might become dispensable or lose some influence within the organization. Uniqueness is widely considered to be an important determinant of power within the organization (Hickson et al. 1971), and by sharing private knowledge individuals risk losing their unique contribution to the organization (Gray 2001).

When job security is low due to adverse economic conditions and frequent layoffs, workers have an even stronger motivation to attach greater utility to, and consequently withhold, their private knowledge (Davenport and Prusak 1998). By contrast, when the level of trust or care among employees in an organization is high, they may perceive a lower psychological cost of knowledge sharing due to greater concern about how they contribute to solving organizational problems and are useful to others (Constant et al. 1996).

A similar perception may inhibit knowledge sharing across departments. Therefore, managers need to be sensitive to issues related to power and control (Gray 2001). Incentives might help to some extent and only in some situations. Despite the progress in IT and in the field of KM, motivating employees to share private knowledge remains a critical issue.

Senior Executives' Reluctance to Adapt

As discussed above, individuals possessing the knowledge might be reluctant to share it due to concerns about privacy and perceived loss of power. In order to convince employees to share their knowledge and contribute to the creation of new organizational knowledge, senior executives need to play an important role. Senior executives should make considerable changes in organizational forums as well as in their own attitudes. Some of the important changes are:

1   The creation of a flatter organizational structure, because "most companies have hierarchical structures, and differences in status among people impede the exchange of ideas" (Amabile and Khaire 2008, p. 102).
2   The incorporation of diverse and multiple, and often starkly conflicting, perspectives to facilitate knowledge creation (Yoo 2008).
3   The willingness to allow redundancy and slack resources needed for the incorporation of these diverse and multiple perspectives.
4   The willingness to let go of their power, much more so than the traditional notion of "empowerment" might imply, as is needed for a true knowledge democracy.

Unfortunately, a number of senior executives are unwilling to recognize the importance of the above changes. A knowledge democracy in an organization cannot be achieved unless senior executives truly believe that people across the organization, including at the very lowest levels where interactions with customers most often occur, might have truly valuable ideas that would influence the organizational strategy, or product road-map. For example, according to Amabile and Khaire (2008, p. 101), Scott Cook, the cofounder of Intuit Inc., wondered whether management is "a net positive or a net negative for creativity." He further asked: "If there is a bottleneck in organizational creativity, might it be at the top of the bottle?"

Concluding Remarks

The benefits from knowledge management are considerable, and progress in information technology as well as the experience gained within the field of knowledge management implies that there are also some valuable ways of managing knowledge so as to increase efficiency, effectiveness, and innovation for both organizations and individuals. However, KM is not easy, and encounters numerous challenges related to the adoption of technologies, motivation of individuals within and outside the organization, and the integration of people and technologies within the KM processes. In this book, we have tried to provide the reader with a comprehensive overview of the foundations of KM, the opportunities and challenges, as well as some of the important emerging and future directions.

In conclusion, the future of KM is one where people and advanced technology will continue to work together, enabling knowledge integration across diverse domains and with potentially high payoffs. However, the new opportunities and greater benefits will require careful management of people and technologies, synthesis of multiple perspectives, and effectively dealing with a variety of trade-offs. Although interesting challenges lie ahead for knowledge managers, the future of KM is clearly exciting because of the opportunities it promises for generations to come.

Review

1   Identify the one issue you consider most important for the future of knowledge management. Why?
2   How do you see organizations changing in the future, especially in terms of knowledge management, but also in terms of their structure, as a result of Web 2.0 technologies?
3   Based on both Chapters 3 and 16, what role do you see top management playing in knowledge management in organizations in the future?
4   How might privacy concerns affect knowledge management in the future, both within organizations as well as in social networks?
5   Briefly identify any three ways in which you see employees changing their behavior related to knowledge management in the future.

Application Exercises

1   Select any three topics on Wikipedia (http://cn.wikipedia.org/) and track the identified pages for a week (visiting each page twice a day) to see how the knowledge changes on these pages. What lessons do you learn from this experience?
2   Select any one organization that utilizes crowdsourcing, and find out more information about whose knowledge is being managed at this organization through crowdsourcing. Then summarize the lessons you learn from this organization about the relationship between crowdsourcing and knowledge management.

3   Visit a local area firm to study how knowledge is being managed there at present, examine whether Web 2.0 technologies and AI are being used, and talk to some of its people regarding how knowledge management might change in the future.
4   Visit a small local area firm and a large local organization, and talk to two individuals at each organization to examine whether concerns related to privacy and "knowledge is power" affect knowledge management at this organization.
5   Identify one wicked problem that seems really important to you. Investigate ways in which knowledge management, including knowledge management through crowdsourcing or collective intelligence, might help address this wicked problem.

References

Amabile, T.M., and Khaire, M. 2008. Creativity and the role of the leader. *Harvard Business Review* (October), 100–109.

Beath, C., Becerra-Fernandez, I., Ross, J., and Short, J. 2012. Finding value in the information explosion. *MIT Sloan Management Review*, 53(4), 18.

Brynjolfsson, E., 2022. The Turing Trap: The promise & peril of human-like artificial intelligence. *Daedalus*, 15(2), 272–287. https://digitaleconomy.stanford.edu/news/the-turing-trap-the-promise-peril-of-human-like-artificial-intelligence/.

Churchman, C. 1971. *The design of inquiring systems: Basic concepts of systems and organization.* New York: Basic Books.

Confessore, N. 2018. Cambridge Analytica and Facebook: The scandal and the fallout so far. *New York Times*, April 4. https://www.nytimes.com/2018/04/04/us/politics/cambridge-analytica-scandal-fallout.html (accessed July 25, 2023).

Constant, D., Sproull, L., and Kiesler, S. 1996. The kindness of strangers: The usefulness of electronic weak ties for technical advice. *Organization Science*, 7(2), 119–135.

Courtney, J. 2001. Decision making and knowledge management in inquiring organizations: Toward a new decision-making paradigm for DSS. *Decision Support Systems*, 31, 17–38.

Davenport, T., and Prusak, L. 1998. *Working knowledge: How organizations manage what they know.* Boston: Harvard Business School Press.

DePree., C.M. Jr., and Jude, R.K. 2006. Who's reading your office e-mail? Is that legal? *Strategic Finance*, 87(10).

Essex, D., Kerner, S.M., and Gillis, A.S. 2023. What is Web 3.0 (Web3)? Definition, guide and history. *TechTarget*. https://www.techtarget.com/whatis/definition/Web-30 (accessed July 25, 2023).

Facebook. 2014. *Wikipedia*. http://en.wikipedia.org/wiki/Facebook.

Facebook. 2023. Company info. https://about.meta.com/company-info/ (accessed July 23, 2023).

Gray, P. 2001. The impact of knowledge repositories on power and control in the workplace. *Information Technology and People*, 14(4), 368–384.

Hickson, D.J., Hinings, C.R., Lee, C.A., Schneck, R.E., and Pennings, J.M. 1971. A strategic contingencies theory of intra-organizational power. *Administrative Science Quarterly*, 16, 216–229.

Investopedia. 2022. Web 3.0 explained, plus the history of Web 1.0 and 2.0. *Investopedia*, October 23. https://www.investopedia.com/web-20-web-30-5208698 (accessed July 25, 2023).

Lönngren, J., and Van Poeck, K. 2021. Wicked problems: A mapping review of the literature. *International Journal of Sustainable Development & World Ecology*, 28(6), 481–502.

Mansharamani, V. 2020. *Think for yourself: Restoring common sense in an age of experts and artificial intelligence.* Harvard Business Review Press.

McCreary, L. 2008. What was privacy? *Harvard Business Review* (October), 123–131.

Pottie, G.J. 2004. Privacy in the global e-village. *Communication of the ACM*, 47(2) (February), 21–23.

Raphael, J.R. 2009. Facebook's privacy flap: What really went down, and what's next. *PC World*, February 18. www.pcworld.com/article/159743/facebook.html.

Rittel, H., and Webber, M. 1973. Dilemmas in a general theory of planning. *Policy Sciences*, 4, 155–169.

Sikora, S. 2021. The New Knowledge Management. The Human Factor Activates the Collective Intelligence. *Deloitte Insights*. https://www2.deloitte.com/content/dam/insights/articles/emea 103993_the-new-knowledge-management/DI_The-new-knowledge-management.pdf (accessed June 20, 2023).

TechRepublic. 2020. Facebook data privacy scandal: A cheat sheet. *TechRepublic*, July 30. https://www.techrepublic.com/article/facebook-data-privacy-scandal-a-cheat-sheet/ (accessed July 25, 2023).

Turing Test. 2023. *Wikipedia*. https://en.wikipedia.org/wiki/Turing_test (accessed July 27, 2023).

Yoo, Y. 2008. Mobilizing knowledge in a Yu-Gi-Oh! world. In *Knowledge management: An evolutionary view, vol. 12, Advances in Management Information Systems*, ed. I. Becerra-Fernandez and D. Leidner, 127–144. Armonk, NY: M.E. Sharpe.

Index